The Circus Is in Town

The Circus Is in Town

SPORT, CELEBRITY, AND SPECTACLE

Edited by Lisa Doris Alexander
and Joel Nathan Rosen

UNIVERSITY PRESS OF MISSISSIPPI · JACKSON

The University Press of Mississippi is the scholarly publishing agency of
the Mississippi Institutions of Higher Learning: Alcorn State University,
Delta State University, Jackson State University, Mississippi State University,
Mississippi University for Women, Mississippi Valley State University,
University of Mississippi, and University of Southern Mississippi.

www.upress.state.ms.us

The University Press of Mississippi is a member of
the Association of University Presses.

First printing 2021
∞

Library of Congress Control Number: 2021042889

Hardback ISBN 978-1-4968-3650-2
Trade paperback ISBN 978-1-4968-3655-7
Epub single ISBN 978-1-4968-3651-9
Epub institutional ISBN 978-1-4968-3652-6
PDF single ISBN 978-1-4968-3653-3
PDF institutional ISBN 978-1-4968-3654-0

British Library Cataloging-in-Publication Data available

For All the Editors, Contributors, and the Many Other Selfless People Who Helped Make This Project Possible

CONTENTS

ACKNOWLEDGMENTS

This project in the collective sense has been a labor of love for everyone involved since 2005's "mini-muffin heard 'round the world" moment[1] when Drs. Ogden and Rosen first contemplated turning abstract thought into actual scholarship. From then on, it has born witness to some fifty direct contributors with indirect contributions from at least another fifty or so in various capacities. As one reader commented, this is the sort of series that can help set the terms for the discussion of sport for a generation to come, which if true has made it all worthwhile.

In terms of this particular effort, the final of five volumes on celebrity athletes and the nature of reputation, we have once again traveled the highways and byways of phrasing, deadlines, and the maintenance of a critical mass. But once again, we have prevailed, and, as a result, we have yet another quite remarkable collaborative effort to show for it.

To be sure, we have enjoyed the input and well-wishes of scores of individuals and groups throughout this process, and we would like to acknowledge their assistance. First and foremost, we are, as always, indebted to our conscientious and sublimely talented contributors. You are the backbone of this collective effort, and your words and thoughts within are a testament to your dedication above and beyond any of our expectations.

This is particularly true in the case of the inimitable Jack Lule, who has been with us now for all five volumes of this project. But even beyond Dr. Lule's remarkable patience and endurance was that we were able to coax David C. Ogden himself out of retirement to join us for this last push. In a word, having their voices to open and close these proceedings was just . . . right!

Special thanks go to Maureen M. Smith of California State University, Sacramento, for assuming the role of co-lead editor for the fourth volume of this series, and to C. Richard King, Roy F. Fox, Roberta J. Newman, and Roberta J. Park for their inspiring forewords that adorn the early stages of the previous four books.

As for our publisher, the University Press of Mississippi, who, like Dr. Lule, has stood by us for all five books, we once again thank you for everything each of you has done on our behalf. This list includes, among others, Katie Keene, Emily Bandy, Carlton McGrone, and Shane Gong. This is especially true in the case of erstwhile editor in chief–turned–director Craig W. Gill, whose prints lie on all of these pages. Craig: you always saw what we saw, and you never stopped urging us to exceed our grasp. For these reasons and many more, you are to be fêted.

To those of you who have read portions of this manuscript in various forms and offered substantive and perceptive commentary, namely Earl Smith, Ryan Morse, and copy editor extraordinaire Norman Ware, we thank you each for opening our eyes to possibilities that had for one reason or another alluded us up 'til then.

Of course, to our friends, families, colleagues, and the like who throughout have offered inestimable support, yours may have been a more silent presence, but we never failed to hear you twice the first time. And we remain grateful for all the love and encouragement that drip from these pages.

And finally, to Mark S. Gutentag, who has also continued to watch over us throughout our entire run here, we certainly could not have done any of it without you either.

Lisa Doris Alexander and Joel Nathan Rosen

NOTE

1. This reference is best explained in the preface to the first book in the series, David C. Ogden and Joel Nathan Rosen, eds., *Reconstructing Fame: Sport, Race, and Evolving Reputations* (Jackson: University Press of Mississippi, 2008), xi–xii.

FOREWORD

Looking inside the Cave . . . and Out

—DAVID C. OGDEN

INTRODUCTION

As a former broadcast journalist and journalism professor, I appreciate the value and role of newspaper, TV, and radio reporters as secondary sources in historical and cultural research. I use them often for such research, as do the contributing authors in this volume and the four volumes in the series that preceded it.

As I read through the chapters of this collection, I realized how much they capture elements of certain theories regarding mass communication. In fact, they would serve as excellent citations for research on the effects of mass-mediated news on its audiences, or in simpler terms, the work of reporters and news pundits.

The essays here also serve as a reminder of how important that work is. For scholars and chroniclers alike, newspapers and their online versions still serve as the public record of a community. But, once again, they are *secondary* sources. That means, journalists interpret for their readers or viewers the language, behavior, and actions of the individuals (the primary sources) about whom they are writing. Readers or mass media consumers then use that information to construct or reconstruct their perceptions of the individuals. That is the very exercise the authors in this volume do in synthesizing the "take" on sports celebrities by numerous and varied sports reporters, columnists, and authors. With those reporters and authors in mind, as well as the interpretations by this volume's contributors, I suggest that a better understanding of the fragility of fame and celebrity can be gained by understanding the influence of media, both online and traditional, in serving as the stage on which public personalities are configured and reconfigured. The chapters in this anthology, if not most of the chapters in the preceding four volumes of this series, demonstrate that mass communication, as an agent in the social construction of reputation, helps to propel public opinion while leaving a timeline in the evolution of how history judges a public figure's career and/or character.

INSIDE PLATO'S CAVE

The extent to which journalists, columnists, and other pundits drive public opinion, rather than reflect public opinion, has garnered considerable scrutiny. The impact of mass media bears consideration when reading these essays to grasp more fully what the authors are suggesting. So my purpose here is to examine that impact and give you, the readers, some perspective, or perhaps a set of "lenses," through which to see the material in this book.

To understand the evolving scholarship on mass media and its effects, I begin by examining briefly some of the early, but seminal, research and concepts in the effects of mass media, in particular news media, on public sentiment. One of the better and oft-cited analogies regarding the early research is Plato's "Allegory of the Cave," a work that media analyst and blogger Anne Manera sums up quite well.[1] In that allegory, Plato describes prisoners who have been in a cave all their existence and are shackled and oriented in such a way that they can only see the cave wall in front of them and not the objects or people behind them, whose shadows appear on the wall. Thus, the prisoners only see the shadows and base their reality strictly on those shadows.

Like the prisoners in Plato's cave, media consumers must accept the images, sounds, and messages presented to them via print, TV, online platforms, and film as "real" or as the essence of what's being described. Like the cave where the prisoners can't see the figures casting the shadows, mass media present readers or viewers with images, or "shadows," derived from the actual figures or objects. To take Plato's allegory a step further, if consumers accept those mediated images as "truth," then they would be unaware of any distortions, just like the prisoners would think that any warping of the shadows because of irregularities in the cave wall reflects the shape of the object itself. When media consumers have no direct access to the object (or person), they have no choice but to accept the reflections of personalities as the personalities themselves while not knowing exactly how the press and media filter those reflections.

Plato's allegory feeds into the concept of the "omnipresence" of mass media in carving out public perception of celebrities and public figures. As mentioned earlier, media scholars and scribes have long debated the effects of mass media on public opinion, and the debate can become contentious when considering the ever-burgeoning online and digital platforms. Dating back to the 1940s, some of the earlier debates created a wave of research that examined the influence of mass media. Some of that research debunked what was called *the* "magic bullet" or "inoculation" theory arguing that mass media directly affects public perceptions and *imbues* people with ideas. That theory gave way to the findings of researchers like Paul Lazarsfeld, who introduced the two-step flow theory.[2] In it, he and his colleagues contend that people depend on other people they consider as "opinion leaders" more than they do mass media in deciding which presidential candidate they favor. More than a decade later, Elihu Katz elaborated on the work of Lazarsfeld in *Public Opinion Quarterly*, proposing a multistep flow and arguing that other social connections, such as family and peer groups, and not just opinion leaders, influence personal sentiments on a topic as much as the media does.[3] Lazarsfeld's and Katz's research, as well as that of others exploring the impact of personal communication, came to be known as the "limited effects" paradigm.

In 1960, Joseph Klapper summed up the "limited effects" theory's portrayal of the interplay between mass media and other influences on public opinion, including one-on-one communication, in his seminal work *The Effects of Mass Communication*. Mass media, he wrote, does not shape public opinion but instead "functions among and through a nexus of mediating factors and influences."[4] But other theories concerning the effects of mass media emerged, stirring further the debate on media's influence. In 1972, Maxwell McCombs and Donald Shaw published their research on the "agenda-setting" function of the news media, crediting the media with being a powerful force in driving what the public perceived as the most important issues in the 1968 presidential campaign.[5]

Now some communication scholars say that such theories on mass media are losing their relevance. The burgeoning digital world and all its online avenues of interpersonal and mass communication, with some serving both purposes, have caused those scholars to step back and reexamine communication theories. Some feel that online platforms are obliterating traditional avenues of mass communication. But the late communication scholar Steven Chaffee and Miriam Metzger argue that any theory dealing with the "selective exposure" of media content to audiences is likely to be "reinvigorated in the new media environment."[6]

I bring up limited effects and agenda setting because those were the prominent theories that came to mind as I read through this volume. But yet another concept also came to mind—one that lies in the realm of sports sociology and adds another layer of theory to analyzing some of the chapters in this volume: internalization.

This is indeed an important concept when discussing the media images, reflections, and portrayals of sports stars and, if in team sports, the organizations for whom they play. Perhaps more so than other public personalities and celebrities, internationally known athletes become internalized by their fans. Sports stars become elements of fans' self-image and self-esteem. They become conduits through which fans can "bask in reflected glory," or BIRG.[7] They occupy the leisure time and discretionary capital of millions of sports followers around the world. Thus, media narratives about sports figures can be used to leverage positive aspects of the athletes' sporting life and personal life, or at least play a role in buffing the athlete's or team's image, or rebuffing their fans and followers. Like Plato's prisoners, media consumers must judge the object by its shadows. That's for the vast majority who have never met their favorite sports figures and must re-create their favorite's identity through those shadows, which in this case are media narratives.

UNDER SPORT'S BIG TENT

One of the best examples of the interplay of media, the athletes they cover, and public perception is the case of the late Kirby Puckett, who played center field for the Minnesota Twins. In the second volume of this series, *Fame to Infamy: Race, Sport, and the Fall from Grace*, Sherrie Wilson notes how the media narrative about Puckett's weight problems shifted when press coverage of allegations of sexual assault and domestic problems marred the Hall of Famer's post-baseball career. During the height of Puckett's baseball career, *Sports Illustrated* described him as "adorable" and "chubby."[8] Another reporter wrote that Puckett's "girth made him huggable."[9] But during his sexual assault trial, the *Minneapolis Star Tribune*'s Jay Weiner reported that witnesses called Puckett "a big fat black guy" and that Puckett wore a size 52 suit.[10] When Puckett died in 2006 from complications of a stroke, reporters lamented the downward spiral of a great ballplayer, while the *Star Tribune* described the two stages of his legacy—baseball and after baseball—and how one stage seemed contrary to the other.[11]

The *Star Tribune*'s posthumous comments speak to the duality of sports celebrities' public lives—one being on the playing field or surface and the other involving actions away from the playing surface. Puckett's case illustrates the constant tension between the two and how an athlete's sporting life and his or her personal life can seem at odds for the sport consumer, but many other examples chronicled in this volume do likewise. Tiger Woods's rise and palpably messianic role in professional golf have echoed well beyond the world of sports, as have the tawdry details of his disastrous domestic side. As Henry Yu notes in his chapter on the golfing icon, the "hydra" of Woods's extramarital activities fit the emerging hyper news cycle by providing a continuous stream of salacious fodder.

David Beckham was branded as both being maritally unfaithful and being a cuckold, the latter label directly interfering with his sporting life. The British press criticized Beckham in 2000 for missing a training session with his team, Manchester United, so he could stay at home with his sick son. The press intensified its ire when it was discovered that Beckham was staying home to accommodate his wife's shopping trip to London. A few years later, the press revealed Beckham's extramarital affair, perhaps initiating a wave of negative news about his personal life that became amalgamated with his sporting life. Mass media were among the actors in the public staging of both Woods's and Beckham's careers. So were social expectations of marital behavior, loyalty to sport, and gender roles. That is one of the strengths of this volume—pointing out other reputation-shaping forces that constitute that "nexus of factors" to which Klapper alluded and through which mass media work.

For NBA player Jason Collins and NFL prospect Michael Sam, the sexual hegemony of men's major professional team sports and circumstantial influence on behavioral expectations not only played out in the media but were factors on their own in how Sam and Collins were cast in the public light. And in his chapter on the phenomenon of players kneeling during the pregame singing of the "Star-Spangled Banner," Brian Carroll discusses nationalism and militaristic ritual as factors that spurred the public reaction to NFL players' silent protests during the national anthem. Carroll does so partly by analyzing how they helped to shape media coverage and were expressed through that coverage.

This collection of essays teases out such factors—some subtle and some not—beyond mass media. The essays also demonstrate how mass media help to shape those factors while at times being shaped by them. But the contributors in this volume also go a step further. They provide theoretical and conceptual foundations that illuminate how these factors work together in stirring public opinion, as it has to do with fame, reputation, celebrity, and the issues that surround them. Carroll, for example, takes a deeper dive when he explains the public reaction to and media coverage of the "Take a

Knee" campaign through the lenses of Jean Baudrillard's and Guy Debord's expositions on public spectacle.

The extent to which *The Circus Is in Town* provides evidence to support the limited effects and agenda-setting theories calls into question the dependability of reputation formation. But at face value and framed by the work of Katz and Klapper, the essays collectively offer numerous examples of the dynamics between social and cultural expectations and mass media content. Implicit is the understanding that individual situations constrict the extent to which the theories function. Circumstances keep the relationship between mass media and other social factors in flux.

The Circus Is in Town provides a richer understanding of that flux and the relational flow between celebrity, the press, and the public. In doing so, it provides a look inside the cave where the shadows appear and how they're being cast; but just as importantly, this collection of essays suggests that the prisoners might be able to turn and see more than the wall itself.

NOTES

1. Anne Manera, "The 'Allegory of the Cave's Influence on 21st Century Media," Digital BrushStrokes, 2007, http://digitalbrushstrokes.blogspot.com/2011/05/allegory-of-caves-influence-on-21st.html.

2. Paul Lazarsfeld, Bernard Berelson, and Hazel Gaudet, *The People's Choice: How the Voter Makes Up His Mind in a Presidential Campaign* (New York: Columbia University Press, 1948).

3. Elihu Katz, "The Two-Step Flow of Communication: An Up-to-Date Report on an Hypothesis," *Public Opinion Quarterly* 21, no. 1 (Spring 1957): 61–78.

4. Joseph T. Klapper, *The Effects of Mass Communication* (New York: Free Press, 1960), 48.

5. Maxwell E. McCombs and Donald L. Shaw, "The Agenda-Setting Function of Mass Media," *Public Opinion Quarterly* 36, no. 2 (Summer 1972): 176–87.

6. Steven H. Chaffee and Miriam J. Metzger, "The End of Mass Communication?," *Mass Communication and Society* 4, no. 4 (2001): 365–79, quotation on 378.

7. Two papers, among numerous others, are: Robert Cialdini, Robert J. Borden, Richard Thorne, Avril Walker, Marcus Freeman, Stephen Sloan, and Lloyd Reynolds, "Basking in Reflected Glory: Three (Football) Field Studies," *Journal of Personality and Social Psychology* 34, no. 3 (September 1976): 366–75; and Martin J. Lee, "Self-Esteem and Social Identity in Basketball Fans: A Closer Look at Basking in Reflected Glory," *Journal of Sport Behavior* 8, no. 4 (December 1, 1985): 210–23.

8. Sherrie Wilson, "Kirby Puckett: A Middle American Tragedy," in *Fame to Infamy: Race, Sport, and the Fall from Grace*, ed. David C. Ogden and Joel Nathan Rosen (Jackson: University Press of Mississippi, 2010), 30–44, quotation on 32.

9. Wilson, "Kirby Puckett," 33.

10. Wilson, "Kirby Puckett," 37.

11. Wilson, "Kirby Puckett," 40.

INTRODUCTION

Notes from under the Big Top

LISA DORIS ALEXANDER AND JOEL NATHAN ROSEN

In societies where modern conditions of production prevail, life is presented as an immense accumulation of spectacles. Everything that was directly
lived has receded into a representation.
GUY DEBORD, *SOCIETY OF THE SPECTACLE*

The Nike/Jordan alliance discloses the extent to which contemporary society is constituted by image and spectacle and mediated by the institutions
of consumer culture. We are thus undergoing an increasing commercialization and spectacle-ization of the world of which Michael Jordan and Nike
are a significant and highly revealing part.
DOUGLAS KELLNER, "THE SPORTS SPECTACLE, MICHAEL JORDAN, AND NIKE"

INTRODUCTION

In a September 2019 interview with *WSJ. Magazine*'s J. R. Moehringer,
National Basketball Association (NBA) superstar Kevin Durant remarked,
with nary a hint of irony: "Some days I hate the circus of the NBA."[1] Durant
then went on to explain to Moehringer—again with nary a hint of irony
nor perhaps even a splash of self-awareness—how much the business and
politics inherent to the NBA distracts players from the game itself. And yet,
if anyone could understand the sort of three rings of excessiveness that often
emerges from the NBA, it would certainly be Durant, whose entire sojourn in
the spotlight thus far has come with everything but the proverbial elephants
and cotton candy.

No less a *divo* than anyone else this side of Enrico Caruso, Durant has
watched his personal-professional narrative ebb and flow repeatedly, starting

with his 2007 debut as a member of the now defunct Seattle Supersonics followed by that once storied franchise's improbable move to Oklahoma City, followed by his contentious decision to bolt the Cinderella City for the glamour of the already formidable Golden State Warriors shortly after they eliminated his scrappy Thunder squad from the 2016 playoffs. Once he was in San Francisco, and as the Warriors continued to pile up one championship after another, reports of recurring locker room spats with teammates were thought to have led directly to Durant's decision to bolt once again, choosing to rehab the Achilles tendon that he tore in the 2018–2019 championship series the next season as a member of the upstart Brooklyn Nets.

To be sure, Durant's travelogue would give the most agile wanderer a pretty sizable limp, but through it all, Durant has also demonstrated a remarkable ability to switch off the noise once the ball tips, which says as much about him as an athlete as it does about the power of recognizing where his interests truly lie. In other words, celebrity may feed this once and former University of Texas Longhorn, but his brand begins and ends on the hardwood. And in this regard, Durant, like so many of those profiled herein, has shown himself to be one of those rare luminaries who has successfully mastered the ability to turn the volume up or down as the situation dictates.

CONTEXTUALIZING THE SPECTACULAR

Throughout this work, we liken the distinctive noise that emanates from high-profile sport to a sort of circus with all the clamor and tumult that such an atmosphere suggests. This final volume of a project that now spans the first three decades of this century will once again look to add clarity to questions regarding how it is that the reputations of celebrity athletes are forged, maintained, transformed, repurposed, and at times even rehabilitated. But in this particular case, we will be doing so against the backdrop of spectacle, which in sport is typically expressed through enviable physical displays alongside a show business–like flair for the dramatic in ways ranging from the ridiculous to the sublime.

The subjects that grace this collection have all exhibited across their reputational arcs that they have been driven by this notion of the spectacle in ways that offer interesting and at times entertaining fodder for such inquiry. Through their compelling narratives, we can observe a range of situations emerging from within this cultural entity—sport—which also continues to exhibit extraordinary resilience as an industry that for the most part manages to keep its consumers locked in and eager for more despite any perceived excesses or moral failings. But as it has evolved, we have also witnessed a dramatic change in the way that sport presents itself, especially at the level of entertainment, bringing to mind that in terms of American sport's most pervasive public face, the first letter of the ESPN family of networks does indeed stand for "entertainment."

In this now prosperous environment where the dollar amounts often seem surreal, the average fan who once clamored for little more than scores, up-to-date standings, playoff seedings, and even betting lines are also typically barraged by accounts ranging from the number of zeros on National Football League (NFL) running back Ezekiel Elliott's new contract, or why it is that erstwhile baseball phenom turned journeyman Yasiel Puig's temper tantrums make for great copy and equally compelling video footage. And seemingly everyone is in on this game as sports talk radio, the original chat room for the industry's fandom, has advanced beyond its original formula as a platform for discussing, for instance, who was the best center fielder in New York during the city's dominant decades-long run atop Major League Baseball[2] into one that is just as likely to consider such noncompetitive topics as the family dynamics of famed NFL quarterback Tom Brady or the marital status of Women's National Basketball Association (WNBA) star Brittney Griner.

In today's climate, such matters, well, matter, especially as the entertainment side of sport more than at any other time in American or even world sport broadly conceived has effectively trumped all else, which, among other matters still, forces us to reconsider the nature of contemporary sport while reconciling it to once and former postulates concerning the commodification of people and culture. As Guy Debord, author of the enduring critique *Society of the Spectacle*, contends in Thesis 42 of his vaunted work: "The spectacle is the moment when the commodity has attained the total occupation of social life."[3]

Indeed, while various scholars offer invaluable explanations for our conceptual renderings herein, it is Debord's 1967 work that delivers a most useful framework for this particular analysis. As he observes in the tenth thesis of this enduring appraisal:

> The concept of "the spectacle" interrelates and explains a wide range of seemingly unconnected phenomena. The apparent diversities and contrasts of these phenomena stem from the social organization of appearances, whose essential nature must itself be recognized. Considered in its own terms, the spectacle is an affirmation of appearances and an identification of all human social life with appearances. But a critique that grasps the spectacle's essential character reveals it to be a visible negation of life—a negation that has taken on a visible form.[4]

Here Debord, the best known of the French situationists observing the ebb and flow of the contentious post–World War II years that would culminate in the Parisian student revolts of the late 1960s, lays a foundation for reinterpreting just about any social interaction within his purview. And, although his work must be regarded as historically specific, his knack for presaging many of the developments characteristic of the early twenty-first century helps tie nuances of his social landscape to ours. While he certainly had no way of divining, for example, the course of modern politics, the sway of social media, or the merging of the private and public spheres, his locating of postwar perspectives helps paint a most intriguing evolutionary road map, in particular how such manifestations wedded to the notion of the spectacular serve to diminish even more a communal spirit deflated by nearly a century of warfare and economic dislocation.

Throughout, Debord accepts that the increasingly modern obsession with appearance above substance is part and parcel of this decline, one that ultimately challenges any lingering impulses toward halting a momentum that situationists contend fly in the face of individual freedom or collective civic engagement. He argues that a continued embrace of the spectacle redrafts the realm of appearance into a condition whereby all reality emerges from a simplified, monosyllabic representation of social discourse. Referring to celebrity as a sort of shorthand commodified into behavioral motifs fit for consumption and profiteering, he perceives an evolving order fashioned around the comings and goings of a select few seemingly always within the public's gaze.

Debord furthers this point by asserting that this clustering of celebrity demonstrates a proclivity for burying historical memory by substituting it with striking yet ultimately inconsequential moments that nevertheless sear themselves into public consciousness. In Thesis 11, for example, he observes:

> In order to describe the spectacle, its formation, its functions, and the forces that work against it, it is necessary to make some artificial distinctions. In analyzing the spectacle we are obliged to a certain extent to use the spectacle's own language, in the sense that we have to operate on the methodological terrain of the society that expresses itself in the spectacle. For the spectacle is both the meaning and the agenda of our particular socio-economic formation. It is the historical moment in which we are caught.[5]

In this respect, Debord concedes that the spectacle stands poised to subsume the moment—any and perhaps all moments—reducing it (or them) to a sort of facade that threatens to reduce actors to objects, which in sporting terms is reflected in the notion and rise of the spectator.[6] Moreover, he laments that what he concedes is a metaphorical loss of the public space in the most Greek ideal (i.e., the agora) is even further decontextualized by a near-constant crush of modern media, a condition that he typically expresses in his critiques of art and the impulse to seek relief through political subversion in such a conservative-seeming climate. As he recounts in Thesis 186:

> Once society has lost its myth-based community, it loses all the reference points of truly common language until such time as the divisions within the inactive community can be overcome by the inauguration of a real historical community. When art, which was the common language of social inaction, develops into independent art in the modern sense, emerging from its original religious universe and becoming individual production of separate works, it too becomes subject to the movement governing the history of all separate culture. Its declaration of independence is the beginning of its end.[7]

Committed as he was to revitalizing an exhausted populace, Debord anticipates that the spectacle hollows out any subversive qualities to be found in human activity by substituting purely aesthetic features where once existed substance, meaning, and context. In this regard, he contends that the spectacle blinds us to the possibility of uncovering truly big ideas that demonstrate a capacity, if not an enthusiasm, for fostering genuine, lasting change, harking back to his Marxist roots insomuch as it echoes the ubiquitous refrain from Marx's introduction to his critique of Hegel's embrace of religion: that spectacle, similar to religion, serves as the "opium of the people."[8] Or, as he chides in Thesis 62:

> The false choices offered by spectacular abundance—choices based on the juxtaposition of competing yet mutually reinforcing spectacles and of distinct yet interconnected roles (signified and embodied primarily by objects)—develop into struggles between illusory qualities designed to generate fervent allegiance to quantitative trivialities. Fallacious archaic oppositions are revived—regionalisms and racisms which serve to endow mundane rankings in the hierarchies of consumption with a magical ontological superiority—and subplayful enthusiasms are aroused by an endless succession of farcical competitions, from sports to elections.[9]

ALONG THE SPOTLIGHT'S EDGES

The explosion of popular media, and of late the spread of social media in the public sphere, is what allows Debord's often dated critique to carve out a place among similar assessments of the new century. Once again, Debord is not speaking directly to contemporary matters here, though he is remarkably effective in terms of helping to draw lines that might connect human development then to where it exists today. For him, thus, the continued engagement with spectacle serves merely to underscore the significance of the growing divide between substance and triviality.

In the American experience, the roots of such displays trace back to the 1871 merging of the Ringling Brothers and Barnum & Bailey Circus, the former "Greatest Show on Earth." Although it closed for good (and to surprisingly little fanfare) in 2017, its ubiquitousness as a cultural base remains virtually unmatched. To be sure, even those who never attended a circus can still describe its giant tents filled with exotic animals, entertainers in suggestive costumes routinely defying death, and clowns crammed ten or more at a time into vehicles in such a way as to both delight and scare the daylights out of myriad spectators.

Until contemporary fears of animal cruelty, which plagued the many franchises that emerged from the original model, ostensibly led to their collective demise, circuses successfully marketed themselves as bastions of wholesome entertainment that offered, in the parlance of long-standing advertising campaigns, "fun for the entire family"—a sort of vaudevillian experience that could offer danger and a hint of prurience for young and old. But behind the scenes, that was never the entire story.

While a bemused public often lionized "carneys," as they came to be known, if only because they did what most could not or would not, the performers themselves lived their lives on the margins, knowing that each performance in whatever nameless or faceless locale they found themselves could be their last. In this regard, they were a most novel form of human chattel insomuch as they could be beloved and admired but also reviled as antiestablishment aberrations. In an industry where only the most heralded celebrities enjoyed anything close to what we today can identify as corporate protection, most worked without nets by every literal or figurative definition of the phrase.

To be sure, the abilities that acrobats, animal trainers, high-wire artists, and even human oddities would display on a nightly basis under the big top is the closest analogy we have to contemporary athletes. But while today's competitors are overseen by a village's worth of personal chefs and trainers, psychologists, business managers, agents, publicists, and social media administrators, the functional equivalent of a celebrity entourage for carneys was often little more than a cadre of clowns and a handful of maintenance workers. Still, like the athletes, they were the show. As Jay-Z points out in the remix to Kayne West's "Diamonds of Sierra Leone," "I'm not a business man; I'm a business, man."[10]

Picking up on this theme, in his book *Media Spectacle*, Douglas Kellner offers rather trenchant commentary on such developments as they pertain to the prevailing world of sport. He argues that while today's celebrity athletes launch and ultimately preserve their brands with the aid of a twenty-four-hour news cycle that features an aggressive paparazzi and a mass engagement with social media, someone as heralded as, say, Michael Jordan, the very symbol of sports media spectacle, had to push his way into the forum in a manner that by contemporary standards seems remarkably quaint and old-fashioned.[11] Harnessing more contemporary concerns, Kellner asserts that the sport milieu "articulates spectacles of race and nationalism, celebrity and star power, and transgression and scandal, elevating its icons to godlike status, and then sometimes bringing them down into the depths of scandal and disgrace." He then goes on to suggest that deep within the fixation on sports is an equally debasing preoccupation with spectacle that sits precariously at the center of "an almost religious fetishism in which sports become a surrogate religion and its stars demigods."[12]

Given the stakes—financial, cultural, and the like—one might conclude that keeping such an explosive atmosphere at arm's length could be construed as a form of self-preservation. As many of those chronicled within have discovered, one wrong spin through the modern news cycle can stymie a celebrity's reputation and lead to millions of dollars in lost revenue. On the other hand, history is replete with instances whereby the once salacious would morph into the truly celebrated, culminating time and again in an end result that reminds us that there may indeed be no such thing as bad publicity.

But at what cost? In an age in which celebrities become famous by virtue of their having established some sort of public profile (e.g., the Kardashians, the cast members of *Jersey Shore*, and countless niche-based internet stars), it really should not come as a shock that Michael Jordan could come to resent his celebrity if only because he found himself trapped by it,[13] bringing to mind the plight of John, Paul, George, and Ringo running from ravenous teenage mobs in *A Hard Day's Night*[14] or Julia Roberts's portrayal of Anna Scott in the comedy *Notting Hill* lamenting to her would-be lover, played by Hugh Grant, that the price of her fame was that even her romantic failures became fodder for the celebrity-driven press.[15] And while it is certainly difficult to show a great deal of sympathy for those so acclaimed by their public who then turn around and complain about the adulation, it would be similarly callous to refuse to recognize the challenge of having to meet expectations day in and day out simply to survive. Such is the plight of those ensconced in the machinery that Debord describes in this spectacle-driven age: that it is the display itself that renders the human element virtually irrelevant.

THE HAND OF GOD

International football's Diego Maradona, who passed away in late November 2020, offers intriguing grist for this particular mill. A remarkably gifted athlete who on the pitch managed to live up to the assertion that he was no less than the second coming of the great Pelé himself, Maradona grew to be one of the most heralded yet polarizing athletes of the twentieth century. Despite the accolades his play generated, Maradona's time in the spotlight is also marked by a series of swift and certainly ignominious falls.

Maradona was the quintessential sport celebrity with a larger-than-life persona and a genuinely compelling narrative insomuch as he came from nothing and through hard work and determination managed to achieve everything. And as might be expected, given his circumstances, once he arrived at the top, he availed himself of every opportunity before him, only to have it all wrested away through brazen self-promotion, a taste for self-indulgence, and a string of bad fortune that ultimately shredded his once inviolable image. As his trainer Fernando Signorini would explain, Maradona, like so many others in his position, developed strategies for coping with such challenges, strategies that he would come to find had limits of their own:

> I learned that there was a Diego, and there was a Maradona. Diego was a kid who had insecurities—a wonderful boy. Maradona was the character he had to come up with in order to face the demands of the football business and the media. Maradona couldn't show any weakness. One day I told him that with Diego, I would go to the end of the world. But with Maradona, I wouldn't take a step. And he said "Yes, but if it wasn't for Maradona, I'd still be in Villa Fiorito."[16]

To his credit, Maradona never shied away or hid from his propensity to err in full view of his public. Nevertheless, after his 2002 retirement, Maradona was more often than not portrayed as a tragic figure—an otherwise unwitting victim of his own excesses and demons and the general pathos that often underscores celebrity. Like Kevin Durant, discussed above, Maradona grew to be quite adept at switching off the noise when the ball was in play, but unlike Durant, many of Maradona's contemporaries, and others who have since emerged from his enormous shadow, he was never able to successfully manage his environment after the final whistle, which might account for why, in a sense, he became the sort of cautionary tale that typically eclipses most if not all of his athletic exploits.

To this day, however, there remains nothing close to a consensus when it comes to what the Maradona story actually tells us. As an example of this, in a poignant yet often sentimentalized reflection of the man he refers to as his childhood idol, *New Yorker* contributor Daniel Alarcón portrays Maradona's fall as a situation whereby enjoying too much too soon left him ill equipped to manage his fame. But Alarcón then goes on to chide Maradona's fans and detractors alike by suggesting that the public's inability to rein in its own excesses is as much a causal factor in Maradona's fall as his own failings.[17] Alarcón concedes that while Maradona is ultimately responsible for his many shortcomings, he also maintains that the public's disposition toward indulging in what he calls a "transactional relationship" with their hero left Maradona a dried-up husk of the young and energetic Argentinian who first burst onto the international scene with the Barcelona club in 1983. Citing contemporary fandom's tendency to demand all from its champions while rarely forgiving or forgetting their transgressions, Alarcón reconfigures the Maradona narrative into something akin to a modern form of original sin for which we are all responsible. He admonishes supporters and detractors alike for having essentially ignored Maradona's inevitable breakdown while encouraging us all to be more perceptive when it comes to the challenges and fragility of fame, a clash of competing images that he claims is on full display in a 2019 documentary titled, simply, *Diego Maradona*. As Alarcón avows:

> In a sense, we *all* missed it: not what happened on the field but Maradona's decline, which took place away from the fans. Now, with this film, it's all there, right before our eyes. As the fame wears on him, he puts on a little weight. We see him with a local Mafioso, going out for the night. He describes his routine: after the weekly game, on Sunday, he parties until Wednesday, with cocaine provided by his Mafia friends; he takes a few days to dry out; he plays again; he repeats. It all seems so joyless.[18]

But indeed, such are the vagaries of fame.

Our aforementioned carneys certainly knew little about such circumstances. Under the big top, as it were, once the evening came to a close, their audiences would simply leave the spectacle behind. They cared not at all where the trapeze artists took their meals or to which political party the clowns belonged or where and with whom the lion tamer slept. In sharp contrast is Maradona's world whereby his every move was scrutinized by a twenty-four-hour news cycle driven by the rhetoric of a public's right to know undergirded by the elevation of the trivial into a commodified if not weaponized depiction of what is important. As noted Argentinian football critic Daniel Arcucci would observe of the wake of Maradona's fame and legacy, "all that survived was the myth."[19]

WHAT FOLLOWS

Like Maradona, the subjects chronicled throughout this volume have all proven themselves to exist somewhere on the spectacular spectrum, as it were—so much so that the spotlight seemed for one reason or another to gravitate toward them. All have displayed phenomenal feats of athletic prowess and artistry, and all have faced a controversy or been thrust into a situation that grew from Debord's notion of the spectacle. Some handled the hoopla like the champions they are/were, while others struggled and even faded amid the hustle and flow of their mounting celebrity.

For example, in his consideration of the multifaceted and often compli-cated career of Michael Jordan's successor, basketball's LeBron James, Curtis M. Harris traces a life informed by a circus-like atmosphere that began while the young phenom was still in high school. As Harris demonstrates, despite the noise, James would grow to become one of those exceedingly rare figures who has managed to live up to the hype. Using Curtis Mayfield's discography as a backdrop, Harris chronicles the love, the hate, and the overall dysfunction in James's relationship with northeastern Ohio while asking what, if anything, fans and athletes owe each other.

In a markedly similar vein, Carlton Brick reconsiders the many personas of world football's David Beckham. Among the many features of Beckham's life both on and off the pitch, Brick addresses the increasingly challenging ques-tion of how fans imbue celebrities with various meanings to fill their needs.

Coming on the heels of that inquiry, if ever there were an athlete whose time in the spotlight has been marked by range and near constant evolution, it is Eldrick "Tiger" Woods. As Henry Yu outlines, from the beginning of his professional career to the public sex scandals and injuries to his triumphant redemption and rebirth, golf's preeminent *Panthera tigris* has stood in the crosshairs of spectacle while managing to reemerge from the abyss.[20]

Before the maelstrom that would mark Woods's complicated public narrative was 1994's unprecedented—if not flat-out bizarre—Kerrigan-Harding affair, which for various reasons has remained in the public sector all these years since. As Kevin A. Stein, Matthew H. Barton, and Arthur T. Challis illustrate, Tonya Harding's latest attempt to resurrect her public persona through an admixture of image repair through deflection evolved over time. And yet, despite this strategic apologia, she has been unable to escape the scandal surrounding her role in the attack on Nancy Kerrigan.

Whereas Harding's troubles came from something she did, Brian Carroll highlights the curious chain of circumstances that befell quarterback Colin Kaepernick based solely on what he would not do: stand idly by—at least on someone else's terms. Carroll reveals how Kaepernick's time in the glare shows him to be the rarest of breeds whose troubles erupted not from an active disregard of rules and standards but, rather, from a relatively benign display of political activism. And unlike other high-profile sport-related exiles (e.g., Curt Flood, "Shoeless" Joe Jackson, and Pete Rose), Kaepernick's "unofficial" banishment from professional football stems from his decision to simply and unobtrusively kneel rather than stand during the pregame playing of the American national anthem.

While Kaepernick remains beloved by certain segments of the population and remains a hot topic both within and without sporting circles, erstwhile tennis phenom Maria Sharapova has known little more than scorn throughout her career. As Rory Magrath reminds us, Sharapova, who in 2016 was slapped with a temporary ban from professional tennis due to a failed drug test, was always marketable but never truly beloved, which helps explain why few of her colleagues came to her defense in the wake of her fall from grace.

Having the support of one's colleagues can certainly make a huge difference when the circus decides to stampede upon one's career, which is why NBA journeyman Jason Collins's experience as an openly gay man shortly before his official retirement from the game appeared to be a much more manageable state of affairs when compared to the loneliness that Michael Sam endured during his brief postdeclaration dalliance with professional football. Andrew C. Billings, Leigh M. Moscowitz, and Melvin Lewis analyze the multiple differences between these two coming-out narratives, surmising, among other things, that these experiences can someday serve as a guide for other closeted LGBTQ athletes most assuredly to follow.

In a sort of clashing of Western cultural imperatives, Andrew McIntosh discusses the first decade of the career of a man whom his own agent once referred to as "the convergence of sport and entertainment,"[21] basketball center Shaquille O'Neal. Among the many matters that the larger-than-life

O'Neal brings to bear, McIntosh delves nimbly into Shaq's hip-hop career and how it intersected with the extraordinary marketability of one of the NBA's most affable big men.

Along similar lines, Roxane Coche elicits aid from the characters who adorn *The Lion King* franchise as a means to discuss the life and legacy of the US Women's National Soccer Team's first modern star, Michelle Akers. Coche explains how this maned queen of the American pitch managed to do what few imagined possible: make Americans care about women's football.

On the polar opposite end of the parental advisory scale is Ted M. Butryn, Matthew A. Masucci, and jay johnson's analysis of 2017's so-called money fight between Conor McGregor and Floyd Mayweather and the toxicity that the prefight spectacles unleashed. As the authors chronicle, it would be stage-managed displays of machismo buttressed by near constant barrages of racial and ethnic animus that managed to generate interest in what proved to be something of a mismatch for the ages.

And, finally, the book and the series both come to a conclusion with a long-overdue discussion of Major League Baseball star Fernando Valenzuela, and how a momentary embrace of Mexican culture led to one of the more intriguing chapters in the history of American sport, Fernandomania. As Jorge Moraga shows, Fernandomania created its own circus environment that, in its own way, countered anti-immigrant hostility in the United States and inspired Latinx communities. In the legacy of this most unlikely of Hollywood leading men, Moraga helps bolster prior claims that Valenzuela's emergence on the public stage offered a broadly conceived array of Latin American cultures a renewed outlook on their collective place in a burgeoning American immigration narrative.

Certainly, there were dozens of other subjects who for what can best be described as logistical reasons were left off this roster. We regret that there are limits to a project such as this while encouraging others in this field to take up the mantle. Stories such as those found in the legacies of Ervin "Magic" Johnson, Dennis Rodman, Zinedine Zidane, and Caster Semenya, to name but a few, are compelling in their own right and certainly warrant inclusion in future endeavors such as this, in particular Semenya's narrative, which in every way imaginable cuts to the heart of contemporary discussions of what it means to be a man and a woman even beyond the competitive arena. If spectacle is emblematic of the epoch, then hers is a story emblematic of today.

NOTES

1. J. R. Moehringer, "Kevin Durant's New Headspace," *WSJ. Magazine*, September 10, 2019.

2. See, for example, Joel Nathan Rosen, "All-Sports Radio: The Development of an Industry Niche," *Media History Monographs* 5, no. 1 (2001–2002), https://blogs.elon.edu/mhm/2017/03/15/volume-5-2001-2002/.

3. Guy Debord, *Society of the Spectacle*, trans. Ken Knabb (Berkeley, CA: Bureau of Public Secrets, 2014), 16.

4. Debord, *Society of the Spectacle*, 4.

5. Debord, *Society of the Spectacle*, 4.

6. See also Douglas Kellner, "The Sports Spectacle, Michael Jordan, and Nike," in *Sport and the Color Line: Black Athletes and Race Relations in Twentieth-Century America*, ed. Patrick B. Miller and David K. Wiggins (New York: Routledge, 2004), 305–26, posted online at https://pages.gseis.ucla.edu/faculty/kellner/papers/MJNIKE.htm.

7. Debord, *Society of the Spectacle*, 100.

8. Karl Marx, *Critique of Hegel's "Philosophy of Right,"* trans. Annette Jolin and Joseph O'Malley (1843; Cambridge: Cambridge University Press, 1970), 1.

9. Debord, *Society of the Spectacle*, 25.

10. Kanye West and Jay-Z, "Diamonds from Sierra Leone (Remix)," *Late Registration*, Def Jam Recordings and Roc-A-Fella Records, 2005.

11. Douglas Kellner, *Media Spectacle* (New York: Routledge, 2003), 65.

12. Kellner, *Media Spectacle*, 69.

13. Jordan's legacy is addressed in the second volume of this series. See Jeffrey Lane, "Mortgaging Michael Jordan's Future," in *Fame to Infamy: Race, Sport, and the Fall from Grace*, ed. David C. Ogden and Joel Nathan Rosen (Jackson: University Press of Mississippi, 2010), 122–45.

14. Richard Lester, dir., *A Hard Day's Night*, United Artists, 1964.

15. Roger Michell, dir., *Notting Hill*, Universal Pictures, 1999.

16. Asif Kapadia, dir., *Diego Maradona*, Altitude Film Distribution, 2019. Villa Fiorito, Argentina, is Maradona's hometown.

17. Daniel Alarcón, "The Tragedy of Diego Maradona, One of Soccer's Greatest Stars," *New Yorker*, October 13, 2019, https://www.newyorker.com/culture/culture-desk/the-tragedy-of-diego-maradona-one-of-soccers-greatest-stars?verso=true.

18. Alarcón, "The Tragedy of Diego Maradona."

19. Kapadia, *Diego Maradona*.

20. News of Woods's horrific car accident in February 2021 broke just as this manuscript was going to press.

21. Quoted in Kellner, "The Sports Spectacle."

The Circus Is in Town

"YOU MUST BELIEVE ME"

Northeast Ohio and the Promise(s) of LeBron James

CURTIS M. HARRIS

INTRODUCTION

The often-mercurial nature of human emotion finds paradoxical expression in the word "promise," which carries both a certainty and an elusiveness. One can "keep a promise," or one can "hold promise." The former is an absolute edict of dedication. The latter evokes the amorphous possibilities of what can be. And when it comes to promises, they can be merely broken or cruelly unfulfilled.

Few popular artists of the twentieth century balanced the dualistic nature of "promise" and other human experiences like Curtis Mayfield. A master wordsmith, Mayfield wrote songs that seized upon the gospel underpinnings of soul music and identified the human condition in a way that transfers to the emotional world of sport. Tunes such as "People Get Ready," "You Must Believe Me," and "I'm So Proud," among the many others, capture sentiments such as hope and despair, rejection and faith, celebration and dismay.

Given Mayfield's aural mastery, it is unsurprising that an October 2018 Nike advertisement for LeBron James titled "I Believe" featured the musician's handicraft. The spot opened with footage of an eighteen-year-old LeBron James speaking to assembled reporters in his hometown of Akron, Ohio. The teenage James declared that he was a leader who would do his best to deliver championships. The statement drew upon the dual meaning of "promise." James was a prodigy with promising talent, yet he refused to promise a championship. All he could guarantee was tireless effort toward the goal.

James's statements in the commercial floated upon Aretha Franklin's angelic rendition of the Mayfield-penned "People Get Ready." Written in 1965

3

at the height of the civil rights movement, the song was first recorded by the Impressions, for whom Mayfield sang lead vocals. Although soothing in its promise of ultimate freedom, Mayfield's musical masterpiece acknowledged that humanity could not hurry final deliverance. This certainty of God's power coincided with the elusiveness of when it would take effect, again demonstrating the anxiety of promise.[1]

James's stardom does not rise to the level of religious fervor, although his "Chosen One" and "King James" nicknames tempt the feeling. But his relationship with sports fans certainly brought to life the human conditions that Mayfield wrote and sang about half a century ago. But James's stardom and the fandom of Northeast Ohio also reveal a tension dovetailing from promises and belief touched upon in "People Get Ready." With James hailing from nearby Akron, sports fans in Cleveland automatically assumed that James would be their deliverer—or at the very least struggle heroically to make good on their quest for glory—rightfully making the region proud of their homegrown son. James seemed the good athletic soldier as he led Cleveland's Cavaliers to their first-ever NBA Finals appearance in 2007. And nearly a decade later, in 2016, belief in the superstar was fully rewarded with championship glory, eliciting a celebratory pride found in Mayfield's "We're a Winner."

Infamously, however, there was an interregnum when James left Cleveland wholly unfulfilled. Northeast Ohio's sports fans disowned him in vicious fashion. The superstar's decision to join the Miami Heat in the summer of 2010—billed as "the Decision" on a primetime ESPN special—was viewed by many in Cleveland's fandom as an insulting shirk of responsibility; a promise broken in flagrant fashion. The biting Mayfield paean to bitter love in "I Loved and I Lost" comes to mind. Fortunately, tempers cooled, time passed, and a series of overtures by James and Cavaliers' owner Dan Gilbert eased the acrimony. Returning to Cleveland, James's athletic promise finally bore full fruit for Northeast Ohio with that 2016 NBA title. And when James left the Cavaliers a second time in the summer of 2018, there was certainly disappointment, but no vitriol like there had been in 2010. The sports fans of Northeast Ohio seemingly took stock of the situation and concluded that "It's Alright."

The stardom-fandom relationship of James and Northeast Ohio involved aspects found in most such relationships. These include the agency of athletes to negotiate their salary and play where they want. In addition, advertisers and sports leagues prime fan attachment to the success and loyalty of the superstar in order to popularize their sports products and programs. Fascinatingly, the James-Ohio relationship also showcases how these generalized features can become further complicated by a fandom's unique history in and beyond sport as well as by the biography of the superstar.

Cleveland and Northeast Ohio for decades have felt a particular sense of abandonment and suffering when it comes to athletics alongside the overall economic and social struggles that befell the industrial Midwest starting in the mid-twentieth century. But while James is from *Northeast Ohio*, he is not from *Cleveland*. He very publicly left *Cleveland* in 2010, but it can be argued compellingly that James never left his hometown of *Akron*, keeping a promise he made to his hometown that had nothing to do with sports whatsoever. The intonations of Mayfield's "You Must Believe Me" come to mind when considering James's repeated statements to always aid Akron, no matter his place in sports. Indeed, even during his title-winning stay in Florida, James maintained a home in Akron and created a large philanthropic presence in the city. As James left Cleveland a second time in 2018 for the Los Angeles Lakers, he opened a public school in Akron dedicated to educating low-income children.

Clearly, there is more to this story than what happened on the hardwood. To piece it together, I have primarily depended upon newspaper coverage of James, James's 2007 memoir *Shooting Stars*, Nike advertisements, and academic scholarship on sports fandom and the Midwest's struggles through deindustrialization. The two dominant newspapers I have consulted are Cleveland's *Plain Dealer* and the *Akron Beacon Journal*. However, national newspapers and websites such as the *New York Times* and ESPN also make significant contributions.

Upon analyzing these sources, this chapter argues that understanding the interplay between the stardom of LeBron James and the fandom of Northeast Ohio requires holistic consideration of athleticism, philanthropy, pride, tensions between free will and obligation, expectations of deliverance and the specter of failure, the thrill of uplift, and the sorrow of abandonment. Altogether, these interlocking emotions and actions created a relationship that at various moments delivered immense hope, disappointment, redemption, and glory structured around stated and assumed promises that were broken and kept, fulfilled and unrealized.

"PEOPLE GET READY"

The Northeast Ohio upon which LeBron James entered on December 30, 1984, had long suffered from afflictions ailing many industrial areas across the Midwest. Collapsing public infrastructure and tax bases, relocation of jobs from the urban core to suburbs, and depopulation to the Sun Belt were among the many issues that cities like Cleveland and Akron battled during the latter part of the twentieth century. The loss of jobs and investment left a myriad of social crises in many cities, which desperately combated those issues with mixed or fleeting success.[2] Athletic achievement did not solve these problems, but talented sports teams could salvage civic pride to an extent.[3] From Oakland to Jacksonville to Milwaukee, civic leaders across the country hailed professional sports as a sign that their city was "big league" and a major player on the national stage.[4] Unfortunately for Cleveland, sports were just as brutal as the economic and demographic situation. This vortex of dismay ratcheted up the eventual hype and hope for James when he made his professional basketball debut with the Cavaliers in 2003.

During the first half of the twentieth century, Cleveland was a city on the rise. Thanks to immigration from Europe and the internal migration of African Americans from the South during the Great Migration, Cleveland's population climbed from just under 382,000 people in 1900 to nearly 915,000 people in 1950.[5] However, seven decades later, Cleveland's population had nearly returned to its 1900 level, with approximately 385,000 people in 2017.[6] This population decline of the city occurred thanks to suburbanization siphoning residents to outer areas of the metro region as well as the wider population stagnation of Ohio and the Midwest. Nearby Akron mirrored the urban core depopulation and regional suburbanization that occurred in Cleveland. Growing to a peak of 290,000 people in 1960, Akron has since declined to a population of 198,000 in 2017.[7]

These demographic shifts and the attempt at "managing decline" have been masterfully studied by J. Mark Souther and Daniel R. Kerr. Souther argues that Cleveland "is not the textbook example of failure or success—or reinvention." Cleveland did not "endure a collapse as thorough" as what occurred in Detroit, but it also did not have the benefit of Chicago's largesse and international connections to weather the deindustrialization storm.[8] Cleveland, Souther argues, was a story of resilience that demonstrated the tension between civic booster campaigns designed to keep local spirits high by trumpeting short-lived and often illusory economic progress. Meanwhile, poverty, racial segregation, and unemployment continued to haunt the city despite slogans such as "The Best Location in the Nation," "Believe in Cleveland," and "The Best Things in Life Are Here."[9]

Kerr comes to a similar conclusion, although he frames his analysis around revitalization projects proposed by city elites that adversely influenced the lives of the poor and homeless. Impoverished Clevelanders resisted top-down economic and social impositions via urban rebellions, anti-eviction struggles, rent strikes, and other methods. If these efforts by the poor were often unsuccessful in ending exploitation, Kerr believes that the elite failed in their objectives as well. "Their efforts to contain and control those below," he concludes, "have repeatedly opened up new avenues for opposition and rebellion."[10]

As Cleveland was economically "managing decline" with decidedly mixed results, it was definitively in the midst of extended athletic misery. In the National Basketball Association (NBA), the Cleveland Cavaliers began play in the 1970–1971 season. Over the next seventeen years, the Cavaliers were so horrible that their one playoffs series victory was dubbed "the Miracle of Richfield" after the suburban town where the Cavaliers played. The miracle was fleeting. Ted Stepien, who owned the franchise in the early 1980s, gained lasting infamy for his atrocious management, which the *New York Times* in 1982 characterized as athletic malpractice:

> [The Cavaliers have] become perhaps the worst club and most poorly
> run franchise in professional basketball, only because they have seemed
> to have worked so hard and resourcefully to achieve these lows.[11]

Gordon Gund purchased the Cavaliers from Stepien in 1983, and the franchise finally gained some measure of stability. After a rebuilding phase, the Cavaliers became regular playoff participants and boasted a winning record nine times over eleven seasons from 1988 to 1998. During this same period, midwestern cities dominated the NBA, winning eight of eleven titles. But in typical fashion, Cleveland was out of that championship mix. The Detroit Pistons won the championship in 1989 and 1990, while the Chicago Bulls captured six titles (1991–1993 and 1996–1998). The true insult, however, came from the Bulls breaking Cleveland's heart time and time again. From 1988 to 1994, the Bulls eliminated the Cavaliers in the playoffs on five different occasions. The most infamous defeat came via Michael Jordan's "the Shot." This buzzer-beating jump shot cruelly bounced the favored Cavaliers from the 1989 playoffs.[12]

The scene was not much prettier in Major League Baseball (MLB) or in the National Football League (NFL). The Cleveland Indians won MLB's World Series in 1948. In 1954, the Indians again appeared in the World Series with an MLB record for wins in a season, but they were swept by the New York Giants in part thanks to "the Catch" by Willie Mays, which denied Cleveland a game-changing RBI in the eighth inning of Game 1. Thereafter, the Indians would not appear again in MLB's playoffs until 1995. In that year and again in 1997, the Indians reached the World Series but failed to win the championship. The 1997 World Series was emblematic of Cleveland fandom's heartbreak. Holding a 2–0 lead in the seventh inning of Game 7, the Indians proceeded to lose the game 3–2 in extra innings after allowing the upstart Florida Marlins to tie the game in the ninth inning with one out.[13]

Perhaps most psychologically disastrous were the Cleveland Browns. The once-proud NFL franchise delivered a championship to Cleveland in 1964, while also appearing in the title game in 1965. The Browns, although they've never since appeared in the NFL's title game (renamed the Super Bowl in 1967), were regular participants in the playoffs and drew enormous crowds. Still, misery followed the Browns like it did their baseball and basketball brethren. On the field, the Browns were victims of "the Drive," which saw the Denver Broncos drive ninety-eight yards down the field for a touchdown in the closing minute of the fourth quarter to tie a 1987 playoff game. Winning that contest in overtime, the Broncos kept Cleveland from reaching the Super Bowl in 1988 and 1990 as well. But the lasting disaster came off the field when Browns' owner Art Modell moved the beloved team to Baltimore after the 1995 season. The shocking departure, locally known as "the Move," was a tremendous insult to long-suffering injury. Although granted an expansion franchise that began play in the 1999 season, the nouveau Browns have only appeared in the playoffs once and endured a 2016–2017 winless season.[14]

LeBron James was aware of the stigma attached to Northeast Ohio, which the Cleveland metro area anchored. In *Shooting Stars*, James described his childhood and teenage years as well as the dire outlook of Akron:

> I rode my bike all over Akron when I was small, going here, going there, just trying to stay out of trouble. . . . If you went up on North Hill in the 1980s, you could tell that life was not like it once was: the obsolete smokestacks in the distance, the downtown that felt so tired and weary. I won't deny it—there was something painful about all of that. It got to me, this place in northeastern Ohio that had once been so mighty (at one point it was the fastest-growing city in the country) but was mighty no more.

Despite Akron "struggling to be something again," James was proud that it "was still my hometown."[15] The violence and drugs that could be found in Akron certainly bothered James, but he was also upset that Akron was never on a map of the United States. "There was Cleveland, of course, because everybody knew Cleveland," James opined. He noted that some maps might also include Columbus and Cincinnati, but never Akron. "That always got to me," James admitted. He promised that "one day I was going to put Akron on the map." He was going to make sure that people knew Akron existed, and where it was.[16]

In James's admiration for Akron, one can see a distinction that he drew between Cleveland and his hometown. Despite all its troubles, Cleveland *was* on the map, unlike Akron. When describing gangs, James noted that the inner city of Akron was "maybe not as bad as Cleveland or Chicago or Philadelphia." Furthermore, he looked at the city's modest population as symbolic of its heart: "There was something wholesome about it, the best of the Midwest, *Cleveland without the 'hoods* where you could go in and never come back out."[17] Furthermore, James noted that "going to Cleveland was a long trip" for him, while recalling an even longer journey to Florida during his adolescence for an Amateur Athletic Union (AAU) tournament.[18] Although both cities were nestled in Northeast Ohio, the forty miles separating them held significance.

The AAU tournament in Florida began the rise of James and his childhood friends Dru Joyce, Sian Cotton, and Willie McGee as stars who would capture multiple Ohio state basketball championships for St. Vincent–St. Mary High School. The collective decision by James, Joyce, Cotton, and McGee to play for St. Vincent–St. Mary caused quite a stir in Akron, which perhaps presaged the backlash James received a decade later when he left the Cleveland Cavaliers for the Miami Heat. Akron may have been "the best of the Midwest," but the city was not immune to racial politics. As talented Black athletes, these teenagers were expected to attend the predominantly Black Buchtel High School. With their choice to attend the predominantly white St. Vincent–St. Mary, James recalled that many in Akron's Black community were upset with them.

Nonetheless, the teenagers expressed a level of mature agency and had committed to a fraternal pact with each other. Wherever one would go, they all would go. Joyce led the break for "St. V," since he had a close relationship Keith Dambrot, the head basketball coach, which he reasoned gave him a better chance of making the varsity team. McGee suspected he would be placed on junior varsity at Buchtel and therefore agreed that St. Vincent–St. Mary was a better option as well. Cotton had an older brother attending Buchtel and did not appreciate the way his brother was treated there, so he, too, was willing to give St. V a chance. The final hurdle were lingering questions over Coach Dambrot's firing from Central Michigan University for using a racial slur. After poring through the legal fallout and asking Dambrot about it face-to-face, the players and their families were satisfied that he had made a careless mistake and had not acted out of any true racial animus.[19]

Although James insisted that the players had made this choice on their own volition, Dru Joyce's father joining the teenagers as an assistant coach at St. V aroused suspicion and criticism of the boys' decision to bypass Buchtel. One man accused the elder Joyce of "pimping for St. V" and steering the boys to the white school. Cotton's father, who also got an assistant coaching job at St. Vincent–St. Mary, was asked racially loaded questions such as, "When you coming home?" Spectators at an AAU game heckled the younger Cotton that he and the rest of the gang were "fucking traitors, and your coach is a pedophile." Clearly, there were hard feelings over their decision in Akron.[20]

Throughout the verbal abuse from some in the community, the adjustment to the private Catholic school, and the incorporation of Romeo Travis as part of their brotherhood, James and his teammates nonetheless attracted plenty of attention via their on-court success. By the end of their senior year in 2003, ESPN had broadcast two of their games on national television, and *Sports Illustrated* had featured James as their cover athlete on February 18, 2002.[21] But negative attention also came via the Ohio High School Athletic Association's attempt to sideline James for allegedly violating amateur rules involving two basketball jerseys and a GMC Hummer sport utility vehicle. The Hummer incident showcased James's latent financial wealth, since his mother was able to secure a loan to buy the vehicle based on his impending income playing pro basketball.[22] With the obvious ability to garner millions of dollars immediately in the NBA, James officially declared for that league's draft in late April 2003.[23]

Meanwhile, the hapless Cavaliers had once again slid into mediocrity after their decade of relative success in the late 1980s and 1990s. By the early 2000s, the franchise was outright awful just as the messianic James was ascending.[24] After a miserable 17–65 record for the 2002–2003 season, the Cavaliers secured the right to pick number one overall in the 2003 NBA draft.[25] There were no doubts whom the Cavaliers would choose to rescue the franchise. The *Plain Dealer* published a full-page "Think LeBron" advertisement. Featuring a photoshopped James sporting a Cavaliers jersey, the ad urged Clevelanders to cut out the image and put the decades of misery behind them:

Forget Cleveland's sports history. Forget the heartbreaks, the blown chances, the injuries, the mistakes and the horrible endings. Our luck changes tonight. But only if we THINK LeBRON. . . . Fill your heart with the certainty of the Cavs finally getting what they deserve—THE BEST PLAYER EVER. The power of positive thinking has cured countless human ailments, and it CAN HEAL THE CAVALIERS.[26]

The very next month, the Cavaliers officially selected LeBron James in the NBA draft. This perfect storm of misery and greatness meant that Cleveland's long-awaited sports deliverance would arrive in the form of the kid from nearby Akron. Hopefully, after decades of economic, social, and athletic disappointment, King James would swiftly make Cleveland and Northeast Ohio "major league" once more and help wash away the stigmas the region had acquired.

"I'M SO PROUD"

Newspapers in Ohio wasted no time in heralding the arrival of James and celebrating him as a hometown hero. "Coronation complete" and "LeBron crowned a Cavalier" blared the *Akron Beacon Journal*'s front page. Tellingly, the paper acknowledged that this momentous occasion belonged not only to James but as well "to Akron and Cleveland and really all of Northeastern Ohio."[27] More ominously, surveillance was already underway scrutinizing signs of (dis)loyalty from James. The Cleveland Indians ushered in James as the ceremonial pitcher for an opening toss versus the in-state rival Cincinnati Reds. Prior to the pitch, James met another athletic prodigy: Reds outfielder Ken Griffey Jr. A representative for Nike, which had James and Griffey signed to endorsement deals, led the basketball star to the Reds' dugout, presenting him with "a Cincinnati jersey with James' name emblazoned on the back." Approvingly, in the eyes of an Akron journalist, James "refused to wear it" and instead wore an Indians shirt.[28] As for the teenage James, the hoopla of the NBA draft appeared to have somewhat worn on him. Following a postdraft press conference, he eagerly took to a basketball court. "I haven't played a game in three and a half months; it's killing me," he stated. "The only games I've been playing are on PlayStation."[29]

Luckily for James, the desperate Cavaliers gave him all the playing time he could ever want for years to come. The Cavs opened the 2003–2004 season with a game in Sacramento versus the Kings. Naturally, ESPN nationally televised the game, and the eighteen-year-old played forty-two minutes, more than any other player in the contest. The teenage star also led all players in points (twenty-five) and assists (nine) that night. So, even though the Cavs lost 106–92, the Associated Press declared, "Expectations for James more than met," in the after-action report. Kings center Vlade Divac was made a believer: "It was the first I've seen of him, and I was real impressed. He's the real deal." James even scored his first NBA points in spectacular fashion with a thunderous fast-break dunk, leading one inattentive Kings employee to lament, "That steal and dunk, I can't believe I had my head down and missed it."³⁰

From that opening night in 2003–2004 through the 2009–2010 season, the Cavaliers leaned heavily on their prodigious forward. Combining the statistical output of those seasons, James led all NBA players in total minutes played and total points scored. More importantly for desperate Ohio basketball fans, the Cavaliers won eight playoff series in this seven-year stretch, which was twice as many playoff series victories as in their previous thirty-three years combined. Twice James was voted by basketball media as the NBA's Most Valuable Player (MVP), and he led the Cavaliers to their first NBA Finals appearance in 2007.

James's star power was irrepressible as fans voted him an All-Star Game starter six consecutive times and corporations like Nike signed him up as a product endorser. Indeed, after his first NBA game back in October 2003, James eagerly chatted with journalists about the impending release of his first signature shoe. "They look good," said James, who had signed a pact with Nike in May 2003 worth $90 million.³¹ That original agreement lasted seven years and was altered in 2010 to pay James an estimated $30 million a year. In 2015, James and Nike cemented their alliance in perpetuity with a lifetime deal.³² This sports marketing nexus forged into civic grandiosity when Nike unveiled a gigantic, twelve-story mural of James in 2005 just off Public Square in the heart of downtown Cleveland that featured James with outstretched arms with the words "We Are All Witnesses." And even teammate Zydrunas Ilgauskas, the senior-most member of the team, voiced his hope that LeBron James would stay in Cleveland for his entire career. His praise of the superstar ended with a holy observation: "[James] loves being here, he's a hometown kid, people treat him like a god."³³

This physical manifestation of LeBron's grace was furthered by Nike in television commercials, and the Cavaliers were all aboard, linking LeBron's success to civic salvation. In a press release celebrating Nike's "Witnesses" campaign, the Cavaliers alerted fans to all the possible ways to essentially become followers of the movement and to not miss the debut of a thirty-second television ad on ESPN. Leaving no doubt as to how fans should emotionally feel, Nike chose a cover version of Bob Dylan's "I Shall Be Released" as musical accompaniment to the commercial. The athletic company even went so far as to set up a website where fans could submit testimonials and bear witness to James's greatness. "[N]otable testimonials" would be selected daily, and a chosen fan would be designated as "Witness of the Day."³⁴

Although the Cavaliers failed to win the NBA title in their 2007 Finals appearance, having been swept by the San Antonio Spurs, James in 2009 and

2010 led the franchise to the NBA's best regular-season record both years. The Cavaliers routinely sold out home games and drew enormous crowds on the road. Nike set up James as the marketing heir apparent to Los Angeles Lakers star Kobe Bryant in its bizarre "MVPuppets" campaign. Simply put, James put Cleveland on the sports map in a way it had not enjoyed in decades, if ever, when considering the combination of winning and star-studded glamour.

In hindsight, this deliberate entanglement of one man to civic pride, athletic success, and marketing pumped Cleveland's fandom full of combustible emotion. That energy could spew forth in catharsis should Cleveland win a title. However, it could also resentfully stew, if expectations were never met. Indeed, rumblings brewed that James might not stay in Cleveland forever. He could enflame the misery and embody the depopulation of Northeast Ohio by leaving for another city. Some feared that the city's downtown economy would dip following any departure of "King James." Rough estimations by economists interviewed by the *Plain Dealer* in 2010 concluded that $150 million in spending would be lost annually should James leave Cleveland. More concretely, the Cavaliers franchise itself would considerably depreciate should its most valuable asset go elsewhere.[35] Whether the economic forecasts were correct, losing LeBron in free agency would prove a social disaster for Northeast Ohio, if pro sports were indeed that important to the region's sense of self.

By 2010, LeBron had certainly succeeded in making Cleveland more prominent. Somewhat lost amid this sea of marketing and basketball was James's adolescent promise to put Akron on the map. The multimillionaire had not forgotten his pledge and had already begun marshaling his wealth via the LeBron James Family Foundation to uplift Akron.[36] But aiding Akron through charity did not necessitate playing basketball for the Cleveland Cavaliers. A multi-million-dollar contract from Los Angeles, New York, or Miami could just as easily fund his foundation as a contract with the Cavaliers. Therein lay the rub as James contemplated whether to soldier on as a Cavalier or strike out for a better chance at championship success elsewhere.

"[THEY] LOVED AND [THEY] LOST"

On July 8, 2010, LeBron James delivered "the Decision," another in the city's long line of sports travesties. Although James characterized his choice to join the Miami Heat as "very tough," fans in Cleveland were not in the mood for nuance and took to the streets in rage-fueled disgust. The lasting image of their displeasure was the widespread burnings of James jerseys. The vitriol was certainly not enacted solely by people on the streets. Condemnation poured in from the media on James's televised spectacle during which he first announced his decision to relocate. Addressing the financial value of the ESPN telecast, one *Plain Dealer* writer asked, "What's the actual market value of 30 pieces of silver today?"[37] Alluding to the betrayal of Jesus by Judas certainly upped the stakes of criticizing James.

Most vengeful was the hastily written online letter from Cavaliers owner Dan Gilbert. Simply known as "the Letter," Gilbert's assessment of James's departure was nothing less than a venomous call to arms that Northeast Ohio's fandom should never forgive the fallen king: "As you now know, our former hero, who grew up in the very region that he deserted this evening, is no longer a Cleveland Cavalier." The rhetoric escalated thereafter describing James and his decision as a "cowardly betrayal," a "shocking act of disloyalty," and a "heartless and callous action." Once upon a time, the Cavaliers had been gung ho in priming fans to witness James's greatness. Now, "witnessed" was mockingly placed in scare quotes by Gilbert as he assiduously razed any positive feelings that may have accrued over the previous seven years between James and Cavs fans. Promising a championship in Cleveland before James would ever win one in Miami, Gilbert comically declared that the "so-called 'curse' on Cleveland, Ohio," would depart with "[t]he self-declared former 'King' [who] will be taking the 'curse' with him down south." Lastly, Gilbert decreed that until he apologized and atoned for his treatment of Cleveland, "James (and the town where he plays) will unfortunately own this dreaded spell and bad karma."[38]

The sight of an NBA owner stirring up such negative passion embarrassed the league, and Gilbert was fined $100,000 by commissioner David Stern for his actions.[39] Backlash to Gilbert and the spiteful fans could also be found in other quarters. Particularly, Black journalists and activists noted the racist undertones of the whole situation. Dan Gilbert owned the Cleveland Cavaliers, *not* LeBron James or any other person. Gilbert and the team's fans may have disagreed with James's decision—and how he executed it—but it was not their place to lay claim to another human's services in perpetuity.[40] The national consensus eventually settled on the idea that LeBron had the right to leave Cleveland, and may have been justified in doing so, but the way he left was embarrassing and disrespectful.

The national consensus also settled on a desire to see the Miami Heat fail. James joined the team along with Chris Bosh, another coveted free agent, to form a triumvirate with returning Heat star Dwyane Wade. Unveiling "the Big Three," the Heat were not averse to vanity. A rally resembling a professional wrestling extravaganza was produced for the Big Three's introduction, and James proclaimed that their goal was to win as many championships as possible. Not just one, "[n]ot two, not three, not four, not five, not six, not seven."[41] The celebration was widely lambasted and further ratcheted up disdain for the Heat, which James later admitted sapped some of the joy he had in playing basketball. He was used to being liked and respected rather than being booed vociferously wherever he played.[42]

The collision between betrayed fandom and a superstar's perceived arrogance was due to arrive on December 2, 2010, when the Heat visited Cleveland. Given the talent and expectations going into the 2010–2011 season, Miami began in somewhat of a funk, sporting an 11–8 record as the star trio of James, Wade, and Bosh awkwardly adjusted to one another.[43] Meanwhile, given their underwhelming roster, the Cavaliers began the season respectably with a 7–10 record. When the two clubs finally met in early December, Northeast Ohio and all the sports world wondered what the game would bring.

The front page of the *Akron Beacon Journal* declared, "James' return escalates from game into event" and "Shunning LeBron simply not enough." The newspaper noted that James's "supporters in Akron" often had their voices "drowned out by the chants from the angry mob 40 miles north" in Cleveland. One Akron-area barber, Terry Walker, admitted he was disappointed that James had left the Cavaliers but sharply rebuked the mob-like atmosphere that overtook Cleveland in July 2010. In the end, Walker thought that James was "a role model and a good man." He had the "right to do whatever he wants. He's from here. I support him in whatever he's doing and congratulate him on whatever he accomplishes." Another Northeast Ohioan, Eric Maroun, did not support the jersey burnings either but acknowledged that the incendiary displays were expressions by fans who "felt betrayed and want to take out their anger." *Beacon Journal* columnist Bob Dyer urged fans to keep their vitriol within reason: "[LeBron James] didn't kill anyone. His major offense is lousy manners." Any unruly display such as "[t]hrowing objects or running onto the court" would portray Northeast Ohio as a region "populated by immature idiots." Then came a sharp turn that backhandedly insulted James: "One immature idiot on the floor is plenty."[44]

Meanwhile, in Cleveland, some attempted to tamp down what felt like an impending riot. Reporter Mary Schmitt Boyer urged introspection from Clevelanders. Yes, "LeBron James snubbed us on national television." Yes, "he took out a farewell ad in the *Akron Beacon Journal*," but not in the *Plain Dealer*. And yes, he "granted a magazine interview in which he explained that he and other kids grew up in Akron hating Cleveland." However, "[w]hat should *we* do?" Schmitt Boyer asked as she reminded readers that "our national reputation [is] at stake" and that international media was flocking to

Cleveland expecting "[u]ncontrolled fury" from the fans.[45] One columnist even urged Gilbert to publicly call off the proverbial hounds and spare the fans, the city, and the NBA an embarrassing spectacle.[46]

Well, no blood was shed, but the vitriol certainly flowed forth that December night. Leading the charge was Gilbert, who was not in a conciliatory mood. Instead of calling off the hounds, and five months after "the Decision," the Cavaliers announced the day before the big game that they were initiating a tampering investigation into the Miami Heat's recruitment of James.[47] Fans in the arena held signs showing "Quitness," "Witnessed No Championship," and "I Hate LeBron." Lusty, deafening boos rained down on the court whenever James touched the basketball during the game. Particularly galling from the Cleveland crowd were chants of "Akron hates you." Veteran sports journalist Howard Beck summed up the prevailing view of those in attendance who had no rooting interest in hating LeBron:

In my 21 years of covering the NBA and covering how many hundreds of games, I've never seen anything like that night, and I hope I never see anything like that night again. . . . There were chants that invoked LeBron's parents. I thought the chants involving his parents were way below the belt and over the line.[48]

The next day, Bill Lubinger of the *Plain Dealer* chalked up the ominous atmosphere to a spiritual cleansing. "For one night, the Cleveland sports fan unleashed what at times sounded like decades of pent-up frustration every time James handled the ball," he wrote, "not just for James' flippant departure for Miami, but decades of losing, championship near-misses and all-stars bailing on them."[49] Terry Pluto, the dean of Northeast Ohio sports reporters, dismissed the scariness as just horseplay. Where others in attendance or watching at home saw a frightening scene, Pluto declared that the "crowd supplied mostly laughs with its signs and chants." Defensively, Pluto seemed determined to not give in to "the national media" and its expectation for another embarrassing night for Cleveland. "After all, we are supposed to be the land of the Great Unwashed, where people still live in caves, killing dinosaurs for dinner," Pluto sarcastically wrote. "Beer Night, Bottlegate and general ugliness is supposed to rule in this cultural wasteland." After chiding the Cavaliers players for their lackadaisical performance in the game, Pluto tipped his hat to the fans of Cleveland: "They were at their best when so many people expected the worst."[50]

The bitterness that accompanied that December 2010 game was an outlet not only for the immediate betrayal of "the Decision" but also for a long-simmering feeling among Clevelanders that LeBron James was insufficiently loyal. There was uproar in 2007 when James wore a New York Yankees cap during a playoff game between the Yankees and Indians. A Cleveland fan grumbled, "The guy is the face of Cleveland sports and he's not even rooting for a team that's 100 feet from the building he plays in."[51] All throughout the 2009–2010 season, other NBA teams were obviously aligning their finances to have a shot at signing James. Even national media members were pitching their cities as the best location for LeBron, should he leave Cleveland.[52] During the actual free agency period, James held meetings with six different teams who continued the temptation of James.[53]

Most ominous and infuriating for Cleveland fans, however, was the performance James had versus the Boston Celtics in the 2010 playoffs. Cavaliers' owner Gilbert accused James of quitting during that series. That accusation from Gilbert was belatedly leveled only after James had left Cleveland for Miami.[54] However, during the series, fans and journalists noticed that James played in an aloof manner, particularly in Game 5. While pondering James's underwhelming statistical performance after the thirty-two-point loss to the Celtics in that contest, journalist Brian Windhorst pointed to trouble far beyond the box score:

> Those numbers are not why James' performances have been shocking. Is it his nonchalant attitude that mixes with tentative play when he is trying to make something happen? That is what will be remembered for years, and what has thrown so many of his supporters off balance.[55]

Returning to the December 2010 spectacle of James's first game back in Cleveland, whether one thought the fans were borderline riotous or comedic relief, the on-court result was not in dispute. LeBron James finished with thirty-eight points in Miami's 118–90 victory over the Cavaliers. The Heat would go on to finish the 2010–2011 season with fifty-eight wins, while Cleveland floundered with just nineteen victories on the season. The Heat wound up making the NBA Finals but lost in an upset to the Dallas Mavericks. The fandom in Northeast Ohio took delight in maligning their erstwhile superstar's demise. In a proclamation made by Ohio governor John Kasich, the Mavericks were made honorary Ohioans for their defeat of James. In particular, longtime Mavericks star Dirk Nowitzki was praised for his fidelity to Dallas in an obvious swipe at James. Kasich's proclamation read in part:

> Whereas, NBA Finals Most Valuable Player Dirk Nowitzki chose to re-sign with the Dallas Mavericks in the summer of 2010, forgoing free

agency and keeping his talents in Dallas, thus remaining loyal to the team, city and fans for whom he played his entire career.[56]

That LeBron James's departure from a sports team could elicit political commentary from a governor showcased just how fraught the dynamic was between Cleveland and LeBron James. However, Reggie McKenzie of Akron, interviewed by the *Beacon Journal*, bluntly stated that "[i]f Akron had a professional basketball team, he never would have left." Terry Walker, the barber from West Akron, perhaps put his finger on the crux of all the angst that swirled around James's decision and tension with Cleveland. "They tried to take LeBron from us," Walker stated. Bolstering his hometown pride, Walker continued:

They act like [Cleveland is] his hometown. That's not his hometown. He's from here and that's the whole reason why he feels like he doesn't owe anybody anything. They tried to adopt him like he ran around those streets and he didn't. He was around here and he still comes back here and he's more than welcome.[57]

Cleveland's catharsis seeing James fail was short-lived. In the 2011–2012 and 2012–2013 seasons, the Miami Heat won the NBA title, and James was named the regular season and Finals MVP both times. Achieving the pinnacle of success in the sport validated James's decision to venture to South Florida. Meanwhile, the Cavaliers managed to win the NBA's draft lottery three times (2011, 2013, and 2014) while James was away. This perverse form of winning accurately showcased the Cavaliers' success in this period. They failed to make the playoffs each season, and their best win total of this era was just thirty-three games.

Despite the success in Miami, not all was rosy there. Statistically speaking, the Heat maintained a fairly stable reliance on James, but in the 2014 season, thirty-two-year-old Dwyane Wade endured a noticeable slip in his production as he battled knee problems. He missed significant time during the regular season and had a subpar outing in those playoffs, which concluded with the San Antonio Spurs drubbing the Heat four games to one in the Finals.

Given the strain beginning to show in Miami, and their own rut of mediocrity, Cleveland fans began to cautiously, but noticeably, broach the idea of LeBron James returning to Cleveland, as his contract with Miami concluded after the 2013–2014 season. As speculation grew that LeBron might athletically return to Northeast Ohio, it should not be forgotten that he had never abandoned Akron, as barber Terry Walker attested. In fact, as he delivered

titles to Florida, James was deepening his impact on Akron through philanthropic efforts. Furthermore, the NBA superstar began to exercise his clout
beyond basketball and Akron, wading into the waters of racial and social
issues. The man who would eventually return to Cleveland would be much
different from the one who left in 2010.

"WE'RE A WINNER"

At an event for LeBron James's Wheels for Education initiative in August
2012, Akron mayor Don Plusquellic declared: "For my money, [James is]
the greatest Akronite because he cares about Akron." The mayor also announced that nine signs would be placed at prominent roadways entering
the city announcing that Akron was the home of LeBron James.[58] Earlier
that summer, James flew six Akron schoolchildren to Miami for the public
ceremony celebrating his selection as the NBA's MVP that year. During the
service, James noted: "Where I come from, Akron, Ohio, they automatically
think you're going to be a statistic." Elaborating, he stated, "You're either going
to fall in the streets or you'll end up in prison."[59]

   James expanded his collaboration with Akron public schools over the
years while also deepening his rhetorical connection to the idea of "promise."
The children who attended his MVP ceremony wore black wristbands with
"promise" written on them, similar to a wristband James himself wore during
the 2012 NBA playoffs. James determined that he would not disappoint any
Akron children "as a professional athlete and as a role model," declaring that
they were his "biggest inspiration in the last two years."[60] At a 2013 Wheels
for Education event, a grandmother of the one of the participating students
lauded James: "I think it's wonderful that he's giving back to the community;
he hasn't forgot us." Children recited the promises that would hopefully
tether them to success: "I promise to always do my homework," "I promise
to always do my best," "I promise to go to college," and "I promise to read."[61]

   The philanthropic expansion coincided with James's resolve to express
himself socially and politically. In March 2012, James and his Miami Heat
teammates wore hoodies protesting the killing of unarmed Black teenager
Trayvon Martin.[62] In December 2014, James was part of a mass movement
of NBA players wearing "I Can't Breathe" shirts protesting another killing of
an unarmed Black person, Eric Garner.[63] In the summer of 2016, James spoke
out against gun violence at ESPN's ESPY Awards show[64] and campaigned
for Hillary Clinton in that year's presidential election.[65] In September 2017,
James even came to the defense of his on-court rivals, the Golden State

Warriors, after US president Donald Trump withdrew an invitation for the Warriors to visit the White House. James called Trump a "bum" while noting that "[g]oing to the White House was a great honor until you showed up!"[66] James's outspoken stances led one commentator to insist he just "shut up and dribble." James sardonically used that phrase as the title of a documentary he produced on athlete activism.[67] None of these political moves by James elicited much, if any, noticeable blowback from sports fans.

As time and philanthropy wore on, an acknowledgment seemed to permeate the air that the jilted reaction James received for leaving Cleveland had been melodramatic. As one op-ed contributor to the *Beacon Journal* put it, "You would have thought that by exercising his free-agent option and taking his talents to South Beach, LeBron not only left the Cavaliers, but joined the Taliban."[68] After a March 2014 game in Cleveland, James was asked whether he was considering a return to Ohio. James demurred, "As of right now, it's too hard for me to think about."[69] At the conclusion of the 2014 NBA season, James again became a free agent. Rumors had percolated for some time that he was strongly considering a return to the Cavaliers following four years in Florida.[70] And indeed, on July 11, 2014, the basketball world received the stunning news that James would return to Cleveland.

Ever the showman, James made the announcement of his return to the Cavaliers in public fashion. However, lessons had been learned from "the Decision." Instead of a cable television production, the older and wiser James reached out to *Sports Illustrated*. With the help of writer Lee Jenkins, James authored a letter explaining his return to the Cavaliers.[71]

In this open letter, James immediately emphasized a connection with *Northeast* Ohio, not just Akron, thus broadening his horizons. He explained that Northeast Ohio was where he experienced a variety of mundane yet important moments of humanity: walking, running, crying, and bleeding. Acknowledging that the passions of the region "can be overwhelming," James nonetheless starkly laid down an unequivocal stance: "My relationship with Northeast Ohio is bigger than basketball. I didn't realize that four years ago. I do now."[72]

Even though the relationship was declared bigger than sports, LeBron was still keen on making Cleveland a title town: "My goal is still to win as many titles as possible, no question. But what's most important for me is bringing one trophy back to Northeast Ohio." To this point, it would be remiss to not acknowledge that the Cavaliers in 2014 offered a more amenable path to long-term championship glory than the Miami Heat could. Cleveland featured twenty-two-year-old guard Kyrie Irving, who was the NBA's 2012 Rookie of the Year. The Cavaliers were also in the process of trading for twenty-five-year-old forward Kevin Love, a three-time All-Star. In contrast, the Heat's core was thirty-year-old Chris Bosh and thirty-two-year-old Dwyane Wade. The twenty-eight-year-old James was exchanging Wade for Irving, who was ten years younger, and Bosh for Love, who was seven years younger.

Key in the rapprochement of the superstar and the fandom was Dan Gilbert. The Cavaliers owner met face-to-face with James and apologized for the letter that had sanctioned so much of the vitriol in 2010. "I told him how sorry I was, expressed regret for how that night went and how I let all the emotion and passion for the situation carry me away," Gilbert contritely expressed in an interview. "I told him I wish I had never done it, that I wish I could take it back."[73] James, too, expressed embarrassment at how "the Decision" had unfolded. In his open letter, James assumed the role of a young Ohioan and walked through "the Decision" from that young person's standpoint: "What if I were a kid who looked up to an athlete, and that athlete made me want to do better in my own life, and then he left? How would I react? I've met with Dan, face-to-face, man-to-man. We've talked it out. Everybody makes mistakes. I've made mistakes as well. Who am I to hold a grudge?"[74]

James ended his letter on the larger theme of building community in Northeast Ohio. In the last full paragraph, James finally and explicitly mentioned Akron: "I want kids in Northeast Ohio, like the hundreds of Akron third-graders I sponsor through my foundation, to realize that there's no better place to grow up." Implicitly, James acknowledged the decades-long struggle the region had endured in maintaining economic and social vibrancy. "Maybe some of [the kids] will come home after college and start a family or open a business. That would make me smile. Our community, which has struggled so much, needs all the talent it can get."[75]

In typical James fashion, his return to Cleveland featured a strong marketing campaign to augment heartfelt sentiments. A black-and-white Nike commercial showcased James and his Cavaliers teammates huddled during pregame introductions. As James gives a speech to his fellow Cavaliers, fans in the arena begin to stream down from the stands onto the court, enlarging the huddle. As the advertisement continues, Clevelanders throughout the arena concourse and eventually throughout the city engage in a massive huddle as James continues intoning to teammates: "Every single night, every single practice, every single game, we gotta give it all we got." After insisting that the team "grind" its way to success for Cleveland, James leads chants of "hard work" and "together" before the commercial ends with everyone raising clenched fists. This emphasis on midwestern grittiness contrasts starkly with the glossy sheen that marked James's Miami Heat welcome rally in 2010.[76]

The marketing campaign may have been somewhat heavy-handed, but James certainly led the Cavaliers to glory. A title in 2016 broke over half a century of sports futility for the city of Cleveland and for all fans of Northeast Ohio sports. The victory was all the sweeter since the Cavaliers defeated the Golden State Warriors, whose owner had declared that team to be "light years ahead" of the competition.[77] Based in the San Francisco Bay area, the Warriors surprisingly became the NBA's powerhouse in 2015, making the first of five consecutive NBA Finals. Additionally, their proximity to Silicon Valley wealth juxtaposed harshly with the Rust Belt Cavaliers. In perhaps the greatest comeback in NBA history, the Cavaliers fought back from a three-games-to-one deficit to force a Game 7 in the 2016 Finals. In that decisive game, the Cavaliers flipped the script on Cleveland's sports misery. Tied at 89 points with two minutes left in the game, the Cavs secured the championship on a trio of plays: "the Block," "the Shot," and "the Stop." First, James made an improbable block on the fast break to prevent Golden State from taking the lead. Next, Kyrie Irving hit a step-back three-point shot that put Cleveland ahead 92–89 with fifty-three seconds left. Finally, Kevin Love, a player not noted for his defensive acumen, managed to stop sharpshooting Stephen Curry's attempt to get off an open three-pointer that would have tied the game and forced overtime. As the final buzzer sounded, James crumpled to the floor, weeping at the astonishing accomplishment.

The emotional James was interviewed on the court immediately following the game. "I set out a goal two years [ago] when I came back to bring a championship to this city. I gave everything that I had. I poured my heart, my blood, my sweat, my tears to this game," James stated. Noting the Herculean task of downing the Warriors, who that year had set an NBA record of seventy-three regular-season wins, James yelled, "CLEVELAND, THIS IS FOR YOU!" Days after the championship, Clevelanders turned out in record-setting numbers to celebrate. The title parade was estimated to include at least one million people.[78] Cleveland was finally a championship city again, and James had delivered on his athletic promise.

Reaching that celebratory moment was filled with the customary basketball drama that follows James. The same summer Cleveland retrieved LeBron, they hired David Blatt as head coach. James and Blatt did not get along, and the Cavaliers got off to a languid 19–20 start in the 2014–2015 season. Fences were mended well enough for Cleveland to reach the 2015 NBA Finals, where they lost to the Warriors in six games. The next season, Blatt coached Cleveland to an impressive 30–11 start, but the friction with James was insurmountable. Blatt was fired and assistant coach Tyronn Lue elevated to the lead position. Although Lue's record was not appreciably

Percentage of Total Cleveland Cavaliers Statistics Produced by LeBron James, 2015–2018						
Season	Minutes	Points	Assists	Rebounds	Steals	Blocks
2014–2015	12.6%	20.6%	28.2%	11.8%	18.1%	14.4%
2015–2016	13.6%	22.4%	27.6%	15.5%	18.9%	15.5%
2016–2017	14.1%	21.6%	34.8%	17.8%	17.1%	13.5%
2017–2018	15.3%	24.8%	39.0%	20.5%	19.9%	22.8%
Statistics derived from Basketball Reference, at https://www.basketball-reference.com/.						

different from Blatt's, the King was satisfied, and the Cavs pulled off their epic Finals upset of the Warriors.

In 2017, the Cavaliers and Warriors met for a third consecutive season in the NBA Finals. Thanks to signing superstar Kevin Durant, the Warriors regained the upper hand in the rivalry, winning the series four games to one. The offseason drama in Cleveland reached a fever pitch when it became known that Irving was unhappy and demanded a trade from the Cavaliers. The guard was eventually shipped to the Boston Celtics in August 2017, setting up a chaotic finale to James's time as a Cavalier. The roster turnover in 2018 was unlike any season since James's return, resulting in a less reliable core of players.[79] This upheaval set the stage for the team's increasing dependence on an aging James, who wanted to make the most of his final years of basketball as well as set up life afterward.

Subtly, LeBron James's *Sports Illustrated* letter announcing his return contained a double-edged sword: "My relationship with Northeast Ohio is bigger than basketball." Being "bigger than basketball" meant a love that might, and did, bring James back to lift the spirits of the region via athletics, but it also meant from his viewpoint that leaving the region's NBA team would not (or at least should not) harmfully affect the relationship. Indeed, the ever-growing presence of James's philanthropy in Akron deepened a real presence in the area. Combined with the near-mythic accomplishment of winning the 2016 NBA title, James perhaps had created a bond that no future free agency move could ever break. And that talk was rampant as the Cavaliers trudged through the 2017–2018 season, which ended with yet another Finals defeat to Golden State. In all, the four consecutive finals appearances were an unprecedented feat in Cleveland's sports history and one rarely accomplished by any team in any sport.[80]

Maturation and appreciation prevailed when James left for the Los Angeles Lakers in the summer of 2018. Fans did not riot in the streets or set jerseys ablaze. To his credit, James also conducted his second departure much more quietly than "the Decision" of 2010, sparing Ohioans the primetime national embarrassment. James simply distributed a press release via his sports agency announcing that he would join the Lakers.[81] In retrospect, Northeast Ohio investing itself so deeply in a twenty-five-year-old man in 2010 was foolhardy. LeBron James's athletic and entertainment prowess could soothe and temporarily make one forget hard economic times or provide a sense of pride, dousing the usually unflattering national image of Cleveland. However, one athlete cannot erase decades of sports misery, let alone social ills. The complex fault lines of athletics, economics, civic pride, and regional rivalry fueled the emotional outbursts of 2010. However, James's temporary rejection of Cleveland on the basketball court did not loosen by any means his ties to Akron, and indeed he felt a need to return home—a home he eventually extended to include Cleveland. In return, it appears that Northeast Ohio, and Clevelanders in particular, have realized that commitment to the region by an exceptional athlete could be accomplished beyond the realm of sport.

"IT'S ALRIGHT"

"A 6-foot-8 forward from St. Vincent–St. Mary High School," bellowed the Quicken Loans Arena announcer. "Welcome home! Number 23, LeBron James." That's the reception James received when the Lakers played in Cleveland on November 21, 2018. A thunderous applause followed during the player introductions, and a video tribute was played that acknowledged the 2016 NBA title. Instructively, though, the video spent more time focusing on James's I Promise School in Akron than it did on basketball in Cleveland. Eight years after "the Decision," the relationship between James and Northeast Ohio had truly evolved into this phrase used in the video: "Thank you for what you did on the court, but we all know it's bigger than basketball."[82]

The opening of that school is thus far the pinnacle of James's philanthropic work and should anchor his continued involvement in the region.[83] Notably, I Promise is not a charter school. Operating within the Akron public school district under public scrutiny, James's project is enhancing a public good rather than displacing it. As a sign of his commitment, James has promised $2 million yearly to help operate the school, which is estimated to have an annual operating budget of $8 million once it is fully operational.[84] The I Promise School augments a commitment James made in 2015. In conjunction with the University of Akron, the tuition of students who have attended James's foundation and graduated from Akron public high schools would be completely covered at the university.[85] These good deeds nonetheless drew the ire of President Trump, who insulted James's intelligence shortly after the I Promise School's opening. The *Plain Dealer*'s editorial board roundly denounced the president, with most calling his statement racist or bigoted.[86] And, perhaps the surest sign of how the winds were now blowing, Ohio governor John Kasich, who once upon a time celebrated LeBron James's defeat in the 2011 NBA Finals, defended James against the president.[87] It is amazing that a professional athlete engendered that reaction when directly confronting the president of the United States, but James had created that level of support due to his athletic and societal success on behalf of Ohio. Thus, after nearly two decades of push-and-tug, acrimony, personal agency, and regional angst, James and Northeast Ohio seem to have at last arrived at an answer for what this particular star athlete means and owes to the region. Ever since his time as a teenage prodigy, James had valued the ability to make decisions for himself. Closely linked to his sense of self were his close friends and family, as well as the city of Akron. Early on, he had shown a willingness to defy expectations when his band of "Shooting Stars" chose St. Vincent–St. Mary as their high school. This decision, keyed on friendship and winning, foreshadowed his later move in 2010 to play with Dwyane Wade and Chris Bosh in Miami.[88] Each of those decisions, at least in James's mind, were not rejections of other institutions or cities but, rather, an embrace of certain persons and opportunities amid his ability to enhance his stardom and influence. And these decisions to better himself did not necessarily harm others. After all, as a teenager, he still played in the city of Akron when he went to St. Vincent–St. Mary. As an adult in the NBA, he continued living in and doing philanthropic work for Akron even though he played for the Miami Heat.

Cleveland, and other parts of Northeast Ohio, including sections of Akron, understandably perceived James's choices as rejections. Choosing the predominantly white Catholic school over the Black public school in Akron was a rejection. "The Decision" was a rejection. Wearing a Yankees baseball cap was a rejection. Whether intended by James as rejections, they were perceived as such by enough people in Ohio to cause acrimony. Calculating degrees of wrong is hard to do in these circumstances, but, given time, both sides came to realize that they had acted at times without proper consideration. LeBron James apologized for the spectacle of "the Decision." The fandom of Northeast Ohio realized that the jersey burnings and venomous reception of James thereafter were wildly disproportionate responses to the perceived effrontery by James. Cavaliers owner Dan Gilbert repudiated the letter he wrote castigating James as a traitor to Ohio.

So, apologies aside, what do athletes and fans owe each other? It is hard to deliver a one-size-fits-all answer, but chronicling the relationship between LeBron James and Northeast Ohio leads to the conclusion that a combination of thoughtfulness and time is the only path to some semblance of harmony. Given the stress and demand for winning in sports, that is not easy to achieve. Players feel pressure to succeed on and off the court, while fans can grow weary waiting for promised results. Layer onto the James-Cleveland scenario the overwhelming sense of embarrassment and rejection, whether it dovetails from deindustrialization, depopulation, or sports-induced anxiety, and what is left is the typical fandom powder keg, which is particularly explosive. That same layering, however, is what made the rapprochement and championship more satisfying for James and Ohio. It is truly one of the wildest story lines in the history of American sports and is unlikely to be duplicated. James's philanthropic commitment to the region just further enhances and solidifies the mark he has made there.

The sage Curtis Mayfield grasped the curative lesson of time and thought in his easygoing, sauntering "It's Alright." Acknowledging that real struggles exist in the world—"When you wake up early in the morning / feelin' sad like so many of us do"—Mayfield and his Impressions nonetheless insisted that, at the end of the day, enough goes right in life "that you got to say it's alright." As Northeast Ohio continues NBA life without LeBron James, the wildest dreams that the promises of James held may not have been completely fulfilled. Yet, who would believe that, as wild as the course may have been, the decades-long sports misery was indeed ended by the kid from Akron.

CODA: "I PLAN TO STAY A BELIEVER"

Since signing with the Los Angeles Lakers, LeBron James has only increased his athletic and cultural footprint. However, his initial season with the Lakers in 2018–2019 was a relative bust. For the first time since 2006, he did not appear in the NBA playoffs, and for the first time since 2007 he was not named to the All-NBA first team. But the 2019–2020 season was a marked return to form for Akron's *Chosen One*. Unsurprisingly, he helped secure a star teammate when the Lakers traded for erstwhile New Orleans Pelicans forward Anthony Davis in the summer of 2019. Together, the pair led the Lakers to the NBA championship in 2020. For the fourth time in his career, James was named Most Valuable Player of the NBA Finals.

That 2019–2020 NBA season was unlike any other in league history, and predictably James was at the center of activity. During the preseason, then Houston Rockets executive Daryl Morey criticized the Chinese government's repression of democratic protests in Hong Kong. James and the Lakers happened to be in China during that tempest and were promptly sidelined as

China demanded that the NBA punish Morey for his comments. Although the NBA did not bow to that pressure, James caused a stir when he chided Morey for endangering the money that the league and players made from the Chinese marketplace. That maelstrom proved minor compared to the onset of the COVID-19 pandemic, which interrupted the NBA season in March 2020.

While waiting for the season's restart, the league and its players were then consumed by uprisings against racism and police brutality after a series of Black people were killed at the hands of police officers in the late winter and spring of 2020, punctuated by the murder of George Floyd in May. When the NBA finally resumed play in a "bubble" designed to limit the spread of COVID-19, James and other players demanded that the league prominently center messaging around the Black Lives Matter movement and the importance of voting in the impending presidential election that fall. To the latter point, James threw his support behind Joe Biden's ultimately successful bid to unseat President Trump by creating the "More Than a Vote" campaign to register voters and recruit poll workers.

As for the 2020–2021 season, James started the season in fine form and was thought to be the early leader in a crowded race for MVP. But a high ankle sprain suffered in late March against the Atlanta Hawks sidelined him for a significant part of the spring. With both James and Anthony Davis, also injured, out of the lineup, and with no timetable set for either man's return, there is really no telling how the rest of the season will play out for James or the Lakers franchise.

NOTES

1. Nike, "I Believe," YouTube, 2018, https://www.youtube.com/watch?v=XMggxvn-6QU, accessed October 20, 2018. Nike has subsequently removed the video from YouTube, but it maintains a webpage from the video's launch: Nike News, "Watch 18-Year-Old LeBron James Predict His Future Success," https://news.nike.com/featured_video/lebron-james-just-do-it -film, accessed June 3, 2019. Searching for the phrase "LeBron James I Believe" on YouTube yields third-party copies of the commercial.

2. Jefferson Cowie and Joseph Heathcott, eds., *Beyond the Ruins: The Meanings of Deindustrialization* (Ithaca, NY: Cornell University Press, 2003).

3. Mark S. Rosentraub, *Major League Losers: The Real Cost of Sports and Who's Paying for It* (New York: Basic Books, 1997). Rosentraub's chapter 7, "Sports and Downtown Development II: Cleveland, the Mistake by the Lake, and the Burning of the Cuyahoga," aptly showcases the desperate lengths Cleveland civic leaders went to maintaining or building state-of-the-art athletic facilities. However, professional sports teams, in this case the Cleveland Indians

and Cleveland Cavaliers, often leverage stadium deals to continuously up the ante on what "state-of-the-art" is as well as to lobby for more favorable public financing deals.

4. Michael N. Danielson, *Home Team: Professional Sports and the American Metropolis* (Princeton, NJ: Princeton University Press, 1997), 102–3.

5. Carol Poh Miller and Robert Wheeler, *Cleveland: A Concise History, 1796–1900* (Bloomington: Indiana University Press, 1990), 170.

6. "U.S. Census Bureau QuickFacts: Cleveland city, Ohio," US Census Bureau, https://www.census.gov/quickfacts/fact/table/clevelandcityohio/, accessed June 3, 2019.

7. "U.S. Census Bureau QuickFacts: Akron city, Ohio," US Census Bureau, https://www.census.gov/quickfacts/akroncityohio, accessed June 3, 2019.

8. Aaron Cowan, *A Nice Place to Visit: Tourism and Revitalization in the Postwar Rustbelt* (Philadelphia: Temple University Press, 2016). Cowan explores this idea thoughtfully, particularly on pages 125–26, where he explicitly contrasts Cleveland's reputation with that of Pittsburgh, another city undergoing economic stress but that was nonetheless hailed as a city of sports champions: "Still, as one scholar has argued, the perpetual failure of Cleveland's professional sports teams in the era of deindustrialization deeply affected the city's standing in the national discourse about American cities. The teams and the city simultaneously developed an image as losers and became the butt of late-night talk show jokes; hence, both the city and Cleveland Municipal Stadium became known as the Mistake by the Lake during the 1970s. Pittsburgh fared little better than its rival in retaining industry and population during the same decade, and yet it was labeled the City of Champions and perpetually drew the national television spotlight to its remade downtown."

9. J. Mark Souther, *Believing in Cleveland: Managing Decline in "The Best Location in the Nation"* (Philadelphia: Temple University Press, 2017), 3–11, 200–204.

10. Daniel R. Kerr, *Derelict Paradise: Homelessness and Urban Development in Cleveland, Ohio* (Amherst: University of Massachusetts Press, 2011), 246–50.

11. Ira Berkow, "Everything Changes on the Cavaliers but the Face of Failure," *New York Times*, December 6, 1982, https://www.nytimes.com/1982/12/06/sports/everything-changes-on-the-cavaliers-but-the-face-of-failure.html, accessed June 3, 2019.

12. "Cleveland Cavaliers Franchise Index," Basketball Reference, https://www.basketball-reference.com/teams/CLE/, accessed June 3, 2019.

13. "Cleveland Indians Team History and Encyclopedia," Baseball Reference, https://www.baseball-reference.com/teams/CLE/, accessed June 3, 2019.

14. "Cleveland Browns Franchise Encyclopedia," Pro Football Reference, https://www.pro-football-reference.com/teams/cle/, accessed June 3, 2019.

15. LeBron James and Buzz Bissinger, *Shooting Stars* (New York: Penguin, 2007), 5.

16. James and Bissinger, *Shooting Stars*, 7–9.

17. James and Bissinger, *Shooting Stars*, 7, emphasis added.

18. James and Bissinger, *Shooting Stars*, 30.

19. James and Bissinger, *Shooting Stars*, 65–69.

20. James and Bissinger, *Shooting Stars*, 70–74.

21. Grant Wahl, "Ahead of His Class," *Sports Illustrated*, February 18, 2002, https://www.si.com/vault/2002/02/18/318739/ahead-of-his-class-ohio-high-school-junior-lebron-james

-is-so-good-that-hes-already-being-mentioned-as-the-heir-to-air-jordan, accessed June 3, 2019.

22. Frank Litsky, "LeBron James's S.U.V. Prompts an Investigation," *New York Times*, January 14, 2003, https://www.nytimes.com/2003/01/14/sports/basketball-lebron-james-s -suv-prompts-an-investigation.html, accessed June 3, 2019. See also Tatiana Morales, "LeBron James: Nothing I Regret More," CBS News, February 3, 2003, https://www.cbsnews.com/ news/lebron-james-nothing-i-regret-more/, accessed June 3, 2019.

23. Brian Lavrich, "LeBron James Officially Declares for NBA Draft," *News Herald* (Port Clinton, OH), April 26, 2003, https://www.newspapers.com/image/294032306/, accessed June 3, 2019.

24. After making the NBA playoffs in 1998 with a win percentage of .573, the Cavaliers' win percentage decreased every single season from 1998 to 2003, finally resting at an underwhelming .207 mark in 2003.

25. Tom Canavan, Associated Press, "Cavaliers Get Lucky, Get Top Pick," *News Herald* (Port Clinton, OH), May 23, 2003, https://www.newspapers.com/image/294043460/, accessed June 3, 2019.

26. Rich Exner, "Think LeBron James—Cleveland; Flashback to 2003," *Plain Dealer* (Cleveland), July 11, 2014, originally published May 22, 2003, https://www.cleveland.com/ cavs/index.ssf/2014/07/think_lebron_james_-_cleveland.html, accessed June 3, 2019.

27. Tom Reed, "Coronation Complete," *Akron Beacon Journal*, June 27, 2003, https://www .newspapers.com/image/170243857/, accessed June 3, 2019.

28. Sheldon Ocker, "James Hits Right Target with Loyalty," *Akron Beacon Journal*, June 28, 2003, https://www.newspapers.com/image/170257132/, accessed June 26, 2019.

29. Brian Windhorst, "Coming Out to Play," *Akron Beacon Journal*, June 28, 2003, https:// www.newspapers.com/image/170257132/, accessed June 26, 2019.

30. Associated Press, "Expectations for James More Than Met," ESPN, October 30, 2003, http://www.espn.com/nba/recap?gameId=231029023, accessed June 26, 2019.

31. Associated Press, "LeBron's Zoomin'," *Cincinnati Enquirer*, October 30, 2003, https:// www.newspapers.com/image/103985565/, accessed June 26, 2019.

32. Kurt Badenhausen, "LeBron James Is NBA's Top Shoe Salesman, Keeping Nike Firmly in Lead," *Forbes*, April 30, 2018, https://www.forbes.com/sites/kurtbadenhausen/2018/04/30/ nikes-lebron-james-is-the-nbas-best-selling-shoe-salesman/#3d02203c5313, accessed June 26, 2019.

33. Liz Robbins, "In Cleveland, It's Good to Be the King," *New York Times*, April 30, 2006, https://www.nytimes.com/2006/04/30/sports/basketball/in-cleveland-its-good-to-be-the -king.html, accessed June 26, 2019.

34. "Nike Reminds Fans 'We Are All Witnesses,'" Cleveland Cavaliers, NBA.com, June 5, 2007, https://www.nba.com/cavaliers/news/witnesses_070606.html, accessed June 26, 2019.

35. Robert Schoenberger and Teresa Dixon Murray, "How Much Is LeBron James Worth to Northeast Ohio?," *Plain Dealer* (Cleveland), June 28, 2010, https://www.cleveland.com/ business/index.ssf/2010/06/how_much_is_lebron_james_worth.html, accessed June 26, 2019; and Chris Good, "What Cleveland Lost When It Lost LeBron," *Atlantic*, July 9, 2010, https://www.theatlantic.com/national/archive/2010/07/what-cleveland-lost-when-it-lost -lebron/59480/, accessed June 26, 2019.

36. "The LeBron James Family Foundation," ProPublica, Nonprofit Explorer, https://projects.propublica.org/nonprofits/organizations/20716277, accessed June 26, 2019; and "The LeBron James Family Foundation," GuideStar, https://www.guidestar.org/profile/02-0716277, accessed June 26, 2019.

37. Starting Blocks, "LeBron James' 'Decision' Generated $6 Million in Ad Revenue," *Plain Dealer* (Cleveland), July 12, 2010, https://www.cleveland.com/ohio-sports-blog/index.ssf/2010/07/lebron_james_decision_generate.html, accessed June 26, 2019.

38. Dan Gilbert, "Letter from Cavs Owner Dan Gilbert," ESPN, December 13, 2010, http://www.espn.com/nba/news/story?id=5365704, accessed June 26, 2019. The letter was originally posted on the Cavaliers' website on July 8, 2010, but was subsequently removed.

39. Brian Windhorst, "NBA's David Stern Fines Dan Gilbert $100,000 for Outburst, Criticizes LeBron James' TV 'Decision,'" *Plain Dealer* (Cleveland), July 12, 2010, https://www.cleveland.com/cavs/index.ssf/2010/07/nba_commissioner_david_stern_f_1.html, accessed June 26, 2019.

40. Associated Press, "Jesse Jackson Rips Cavaliers Owner for 'Slave Master Mentality' for Criticisms of LeBron James," *Plain Dealer* (Cleveland), July 11, 2010, https://www.cleveland.com/cavs/index.ssf/2010/07/jesse_jackson_rips_cavaliers_0.html, accessed June 26, 2019.

41. "On Stage Interview with Wade, Bosh and James," Miami Heat, NBA.com, July 10, 2010, https://www.nba.com/heat/news/onstageinterviewwadeboshjames20100710html, accessed June 26, 2019.

42. Brian Windhorst, "LeBron James: No More Mr. Bad Guy," ESPN, December 7, 2011, http://www.espn.com/nba/truehoop/miamiheat/story/_/id/7322299/lebron-james-miami-heat-says-done-villain-role, accessed June 26, 2019.

43. The disappointing Heat record delighted fans across the NBA as the team became a notorious yet popular road attraction. Fans turned out across the nation to express their displeasure of the Heat's star-studded experiment. Brian Windhorst, "'The Chosen One' LeBron James Now Singled Out across League for Fans' Vitriol," *Plain Dealer* (Cleveland), December 2, 2010, https://www.cleveland.com/cavs/index.ssf/2010/12/the_chosen_one_lebron_james_no.html, accessed June 26, 2019.

44. Bob Dyer, "Shunning LeBron Simply Not Enough," *Akron Beacon Journal*, December 2, 2010, https://www.newspapers.com/image/170417027/, accessed June 26, 2019; and Jason Lloyd, "James' Return Escalates from Game into Event," *Akron Beacon Journal*, December 2, 2010, https://www.newspapers.com/image/170417027/, accessed June 26, 2019.

45. Mary Schmitt Boyer, "LeBron James Returns, and Cleveland Cavaliers Fans Face Their Own Decision," *Plain Dealer* (Cleveland), December 2, 2010, https://www.cleveland.com/cavs/index.ssf/2010/12/lebron_james_returns_and_cleve.html, accessed June 26, 2019.

46. Bud Shaw, "He Needs to Be Bigger Than That Tonight on Behalf of the City and the NBA," *Plain Dealer* (Cleveland), December 2, 2010, https://www.cleveland.com/budshaw/index.ssf/2010/12/post_24.html, accessed June 26, 2019.

47. Starting Blocks, "Cleveland Cavaliers Hire Law Firm to Investigate LeBron James' Signing with Miami Heat," *Plain Dealer* (Cleveland), December 1, 2010, https://www.cleveland.com/ohio-sports-blog/index.ssf/2010/12/post_147.html, accessed June 26, 2019.

48. Jeff Zillgitt, "As LeBron James Returns to Cleveland Again, Memories of Vitriolic 2010 Heat Game Surface," *USA Today*, November 20, 2018, https://www.usatoday.com/story/

sports/nba/2018/11/20/lebron-james-returns-cleveland-lakers-heat/1994560002/, accessed June 26, 2019.

49. Bill Lubinger, "Cavaliers Fans Don't Get Win, but Plenty of Catharsis toward LeBron James in Their Jeers," *Plain Dealer* (Cleveland), December 2, 2010, https://www.cleveland.com/cavs/index.ssf/2010/12/cavaliers_fans_dont_get_a_win.html, accessed June 26, 2019.

50. Terry Pluto, "The Fans Made Their Point Known, but Weren't Rewarded by Cavaliers," *Plain Dealer* (Cleveland), December 2, 2010, https://www.cleveland.com/pluto/blog/index.ssf/2010/12/the_fans_made_their_point_know.html, accessed June 26, 2019.

51. Associated Press, "LeBron's Yankees Cap Causes Uproar in Cleveland," ESPN, October 5, 2007, http://www.espn.com/mlb/playoffs2007/news/story?id=3050742, accessed June 26, 2019.

52. Ian O'Connor, "Only One Choice for LeBron's Kingdom," ESPN, April 2, 2010, www.espn.com/new-york/nba/columns/story?columnist=oconnor_ian&page=oconnor/lebron-james/100402, accessed June 26, 2019.

53. Ric Bucher and Associated Press, "Cavs, Bulls Cap LeBron's Meetings," ESPN, July 4, 2010, http://www.espn.com/nba/news/story?id=5351794, accessed May 14, 2021.

54. Associated Press, "Dan Gilbert Says LeBron James 'Quit' during the Playoffs," *Plain Dealer* (Cleveland), July 9, 2010, https://www.cleveland.com/cavs/2010/07/dan_gilbert_says_lebron_james.html, accessed June 26, 2019.

55. Brian Windhorst, "LeBron Has Different Look This Series," ESPN, May 12, 2010, http://www.espn.com/nba/playoffs/2010/columns/story?page=lebrongame5-100512, accessed June 26, 2019.

56. Reginald Fields, "Gov. John Kasich Takes Swipe at LeBron, Makes Mavericks Honorary Ohioans for a Day," *Plain Dealer* (Cleveland), June 13, 2011, https://www.cleveland.com/open/index.ssf/2011/06/gov_kasich_takes_swipe_at_lebr.html, accessed June 26, 2019.

57. Jason Lloyd, "James' Return Escalates from Game into Event," *Akron Beacon Journal*, December 2, 2010, https://www.newspapers.com/image/170417027/, accessed June 26, 2019.

58. Carol Biliczky, "LeBron Returns to Akron to Encourage Kids to Stay in School," *Akron Beacon Journal*, August 20, 2012, https://www.ohio.com/akron/news/lebron-returns-to-akron-to-encourage-kids-to-stay-in-school, accessed June 26, 2019.

59. John Higgins, "Akron Students Take 'Field Trip' to Miami to See LeBron Named MVP," *Akron Beacon Journal*, May 16, 2012, https://www.ohio.com/akron/sports/akron-students-take-field-trip-to-miami-to-see-lebron-named-mvp, accessed June 26, 2019.

60. Higgins, "Akron Students Take 'Field Trip.'"

61. Marla Ridenour, "LeBron James Has Promises to Keep for Akron Students' Education," *Akron Beacon Journal*, August 10, 2013, https://www.ohio.com/akron/news/top-stories-news/lebron-james-has-promises-to-keep-for-akron-students-education, accessed June 26, 2019.

62. "Heat Don Hoodies after Teen's Death," ESPN, March 24, 2012, http://www.espn.com/nba/truehoop/miamiheat/story/_/id/7728618/miami-heat-don-hoodies-response-death-teen-trayvon-martin, accessed June 26, 2019.

63. Joe Vardon, "LeBron James, Kyrie Irving Join 'I Can't Breathe' Protest," *Plain Dealer* (Cleveland), December 8, 2014, https://www.cleveland.com/cavs/2014/12/lebron_james_kyrie_irving_i_ca.html, accessed June 26, 2019.

64. Maya A. Jones, "NBA Stars Explain How ESPYs Awards Speech Came About," The Undefeated, July 18, 2016, https://theundefeated.com/features/nba-stars-explain-how-espys-awards-speech-came-about/, accessed June 26, 2019.

65. Associated Press, "LeBron James Campaigns with Hillary Clinton in Cleveland," NBA.com, November 6, 2016, https://www.nba.com/article/2016/11/06/lebron-james-campaigns-hillary-clinton, accessed June 26, 2019.

66. LeBron James (@KingJames), "U bum @StephenCurry30 already said he ain't going!," Twitter, September 23, 2017, 10:17 p.m., https://twitter.com/kingjames/status/91161045587702 1697?lang=en, accessed June 26, 2019.

67. Jeff Zillgitt, "'Shut Up and Dribble': LeBron James–Produced Documentary Looks at Alternate History of NBA," *USA Today*, November 2, 2018, https://www.usatoday.com/story/sports/nba/2018/11/02/lebron-james-shut-up-and-dribble-documentary/1857312002/, accessed June 26, 2019.

68. Melba Tolliver, "Life Lessons from LeBron James," *Akron Beacon Journal*, June 22, 2013, https://www.ohio.com/akron/editorial/melba-tolliver-life-lessons-from-lebron, accessed June 26, 2019.

69. Associated Press, "LeBron James Scores 43 to Power Heat past Cavaliers," ESPN, March 19, 2014, http://www.espn.com/nba/recap?gameId=400489876, accessed June 26, 2019. For more on the de-escalation of tensions, see Marla Ridenour, "Cavs Fans Might Be Warming to LeBron James, but His Haters Still Winning," *Akron Beacon Journal*, November 28, 2013, https://www.ohio.com/akron/sports/marla-ridenour-cavs-fans-might-be-warming-to-lebron-james-but-his-haters-still-winning, accessed June 26, 2019; and Jason Lloyd, "It's Time to Forgive, or at Least Forget, LeBron James," *Akron Beacon Journal*, June 12, 2012, https://www.ohio.com/akron/news/top-stories-news/jason-lloyd-it-s-time-to-forgive-or-at-least-forget-lebron-james, accessed June 26, 2019.

70. Chris Fedor, "The Decision Part Two: Top 5 Destinations for LeBron James in Free Agency," *Plain Dealer* (Cleveland), June 30, 2014, https://www.cleveland.com/cavs/2014/06/2014_nba_free_agency_top_5_des.html, accessed June 26, 2019; and Ben Golliver, "Heat's LeBron James Sidesteps Questions about Future after Third Finals Loss," *Sports Illustrated*, June 16, 2014, https://www.si.com/nba/point-forward/2014/06/16/lebron-james-free-agency-rumors-finals-heat-spurs, accessed June 26, 2019.

71. LeBron James as told to Lee Jenkins, "LeBron: I'm Coming Back to Cleveland," *Sports Illustrated*, July 11, 2014, https://www.si.com/nba/2014/07/11/lebron-james-cleveland-cavaliers, accessed June 26, 2019.

72. James as told to Jenkins, "LeBron: I'm Coming Back to Cleveland."

73. Adrian Wojnarowski, "How LeBron James Forgave Cavs Owner Dan Gilbert and Returned to Cleveland," Yahoo! Sports, July 11, 2014, https://sports.yahoo.com/news/how-lebron-james-forgave-cavs-owner-dan-gilbert-and-returned-to-cleveland-191445831.html, accessed June 26, 2019.

74. James as told to Jenkins, "LeBron: I'm Coming Back to Cleveland."

75. James as told to Jenkins, "LeBron: I'm Coming Back to Cleveland."

76. Nike, "Together," YouTube, 2014. Nike has since removed the video from its YouTube channel, but it remains available via third-party YouTube users, such as pennyccw, October 30, 2014, https://www.youtube.com/watch?v=-8yOG3qYko8, accessed June 26, 2019.

77. Bruce Schoenfeld, "What Happened When Venture Capitalists Took Over the Golden State Warriors," *New York Times*, March 30, 2016, https://www.nytimes.com/2016/04/03/magazine/what-happened-when-venture-capitalists-took-over-the-golden-state-warriors.html, accessed June 26, 2019.

78. Paula Schleis, "Cavs Million-Person Parade Crowd Is One for the Record Books: Sixth Largest Sports Celebration—Ever," *Akron Beacon Journal*, June 23, 2016, https://www.ohio.com/akron/news/top-stories-news/cavs-million-person-parade-crowd-is-one-for-the-record-books-sixth-largest-sports-celebration-ever, accessed June 26, 2019.

79. Using the website Basketball Reference's roster data, the 2016 Cleveland Cavaliers were the most stable iteration of the Cavs during James's second stint. Sixteen players appeared in at least 10 percent of games, while seven appeared in 80 percent or more of games. By 2018, twenty-one players appeared in at least 10 percent of games, while only four were able to muster an appearance in 80 percent or more of the games.

80. To boot, Cleveland hosted the Republican National Convention in the summer of 2016, helping further burnish the city's unflattering national image. However, these achievements have helped spur anew the cycle of premature exuberance at economic turnarounds that Souther's *Believing in Cleveland* identifies. See Leila Atassi, "'Mistake on the Lake' No More: World Sees Cleveland through New Eyes after RNC Week," *Plain Dealer* (Cleveland), July 22, 2016, https://www.cleveland.com/rnc-2016/2016/07/mistake_on_the_lake_no_more_wo.html, accessed June 26, 2019.

81. Klutch Sports Group's announcement on Twitter read, verbatim, "LeBron James, four time NBA MVP, three time NBA finals MVP, fourteen time NBA All Star, and two time Olympic gold medalist has agreed to a four year, $154 million contract with the Los Angeles Lakers." Klutch Sports Group (@KlutchSports), Twitter, July 1, 2018, https://twitter.com/KlutchSports/status/1013574315411849216, accessed June 26, 2019.

82. Chris Fedor, "LeBron James Receives a Hero's Welcome in Return to Cleveland," *Plain Dealer* (Cleveland), November 21, 2018, https://www.cleveland.com/cavs/2018/11/cleveland_cavaliers_fans_give_1.html, accessed June 26, 2019.

83. Brent Larkin, "LeBron James' Big Gamble on a Big Idea for Kids in Akron," *Plain Dealer* (Cleveland), August 10, 2018, https://www.cleveland.com/opinion/2018/08/lebron_james_big_gamble_on_a_b.html, accessed June 26, 2019.

84. Patrick O'Donnell, "Who's Paying for LeBron James' New I Promise School? LeBron or Akron Public Schools?," *Plain Dealer* (Cleveland), August 5, 2018, https://www.cleveland.com/metro/2018/08/whos_paying_for_lebron_james_n_1.html, accessed June 26, 2019.

85. Joe Vardon, "LeBron James, University of Akron Pave Way for College Scholarships for Inner-City Children," *Plain Dealer* (Cleveland), August, 13, 2015, https://www.cleveland.com/cavs/2015/08/lebron_james_university_of_akr.html, accessed June 26, 2019.

86. Editorial Board, "The President's LeBron James Tweet: Editorial Board Roundtable," *Plain Dealer* (Cleveland), August 8, 2018, https://www.cleveland.com/opinion/2018/08/the_presidents_lebron_james_tw.html, accessed June 26, 2019.

87. Joe Vardon, "President Donald Trump Questions LeBron James' Intelligence in Tweet on Eve of Ohio Campaign Appearance," *Plain Dealer* (Cleveland), August 4, 2018, https://www.cleveland.com/cavs/2018/08/president_donald_trump_questio.html, accessed June 26, 2019.

88. Unsubstantiated reports have surfaced since "the Decision" suggesting that the third spot in the Heat triumvirate was intended for James's friend and fellow "Banana Boat" rider Carmelo Anthony, who instead chose to sign a "max-contract" with the New York Knicks, which is why the Heat turned to Toronto's Chris Bosh.

I DESIRE HIM SO MUCH
HE REPULSES ME

The Transcendentally Disappointing Fantasy of David Beckham (Or Why There Is Only One David Beckham)

CARLTON BRICK

Beckham's inclusive popularity should be seen as a positive step in terms
of the masculine norms which he clearly transcends[,] and the subversive
trends and behaviour he explicitly displays . . . could stimulate change in
terms of the way in which masculine norms and expectations are configured both inside and outside of sporting locales in the years to come.
—ELLIS CASHMORE AND ANDREW PARKER, "ONE DAVID BECKHAM?"

These days you are more likely to see Beckham in commercials than on
the football pitch. He has been incredibly promiscuous with his endorsement. There is a price, though. He had made his reputation as an honest
footballer and man, but how can he be trusted when he is prepared to flog
anything and everything?
—SIMON HATTENSTONE, *IRISH TIMES*

INTRODUCTION

Since around the year 2000, there has been pronounced interest in David
Beckham as a symbolic point of reference for academic study. This interest
has been shaped by wider social, political, and economic trends that have
elevated sporting celebrities to the status of spectacular cultural intermediar-
ies. But just who is David Beckham, and why does he matter so?

In the years that span the two above quotations, David Beckham, then
the England national football team captain, Real Madrid *galáctico*, and the

highest earner in world football at £16.9 million annually including salary, commercial endorsements, and image rights,[1] occupied two contradictory positions on the symbolic register: multicultural masculine role model and crude, venal celebrity. As Ellis Cashmore and Andrew Parker suggest, while football fans may chant "One David Beckham. There's only one David Beckham,"[2] there are many meanings to David Beckham, and in turn many David Beckhams that coexist quite happily, but not without contradiction within the new postmodern political economy of signs.[3] However, despite (or maybe because of) the excessive production of meanings within the postmodern sign economy, contemporary culture seems increasingly troubled by its inability to navigate and attach significance to signs themselves. Fredric Jameson has described this as a state of cultural "depthlessness," a condition whereby meaning is decoupled from structure and subjected to pronounced intellectual suspicion, adopting a flat *Schein*-like appearance.[4]

This chapter is concerned with the processes by which meaning is attributed to and invested in contemporary celebrity culture. Through an exploration of the "many David Beckhams," I suggest that celebrity culture is indicative of the logical consequence of the politics of identity and the result of increasingly fragmented and relativistic frameworks of understanding and social engagement. In a culture where signs are so abundant yet so fragmented and unstable, the ability to ascribe meaning becomes fragmented and partial. As Slavoj Žižek might suggest, the subject's attempt to interpret and assign meaning is experienced as an acute burden, and is expressed as a form of subjugation, paranoia, and narcissism.[5] It is my contention that the contemporary discussion on celebrity brings to the fore both the "depthless" nature of social relations and the fragmented, partial, and narcissistic nature of the postmodern subject. Taking as its subject the semiotic narratives that surround a particular period in David Beckham's career that includes the aftermath of the 1998 World Cup, his transfer to Real Madrid from Manchester United in 2003, and his alleged 2004 adulterous affair with his then personal assistant, Rebecca Loos, I outline an apparent contradiction that dogs the contemporary symbolic realm. While we are quite willing to accept the idea that David Beckham is constituted by a system of signs that are constantly in a state of flux and fragmentation, we are nevertheless compelled to "know him" and to get "behind" the "facade" to the real David Beckham. However, this desire to give order and shape to the symbolic structures that orient our social lives is doomed to failure, as the "depthless" nature of contemporary culture seemingly invalidates any attempt to fix meaning. Using a case study of David Beckham, I hope to shed some light upon the structures by which our relationship with celebrity is shaped by and in turn shapes the paradoxical need to ascribe meaning but simultaneously estrange ourselves from meaning.

ONE DAVID BECKHAM: THE TRANSCENDENTAL OBJECT

Citing in particular the research of Garry Whannel, Canadian sociologist Mohmin Rahman suggests that David Beckham's celebrity has two distinct characteristics that make him unique among his sporting contemporaries. Rahman argues that as Beckham is "one of the few footballers in the UK to achieve full celebrity status," he also demonstrates a proclivity for dodging "the discipline and work ethic associated with sporting bodies, indulging himself through conspicuous and narcissistic consumption."[6] Beckham's emergence as footballer occurred during the development of a UK men's style press in Britain in the mid- to late 1980s, which became associated with the emergence of new forms of masculinity.[7]

David Beckham retired from professional football in 2013 at the age of thirty-eight, following a successful twenty-year career in which he played for Manchester United, Real Madrid, A.C. Milan, LA Galaxy, Paris Saint-Germain, and the England national football team, making him the nation's third-most capped player in international play after Peter Shilton and Wayne Rooney. Beckham made his first-team debut for Manchester United in 1992 at age seventeen, but it was in the 1996–1997 season that he was to become an integral part of United's dominance of English football. In July 2007, following four seasons at the Spanish giant Real Madrid, Beckham signed a five-year contract with the Major League Soccer (MLS) club LA Galaxy. In 2014, Beckham exercised the option included in his Galaxy contract to buy the $25 million franchise for an MLS club in Miami following the folding of Miami Fusion in 2001. The new franchise, Inter Miami CF, joined the MLS and began play in 2020.

Beckham was both lionized and demonized by the British media and cultural commentators in equal measure, leaving his career and subsequent celebrity to be extrinsically bound up in the increasingly symbiotic relationship with global commerce, sport, and media as forms of selfhood are reworked and reconstituted within new regimes of representation. On the opening day of the 1996–1997 English season, Beckham announced himself to the world by scoring a particularly spectacular goal in a 2–0 victory away at Wimbledon, lobbing the opposition goalkeeper from the halfway line. During the 1998 World Cup, Beckham was infamously sent off during the last sixteen clash with Argentina, a match that England would go on to lose following a penalty shootout, for petulantly kicking out at the Argentinian midfielder Diego Simeone. The following year he married the pop star Victoria Adams, better known as Posh Spice of the all-girl group the Spice Girls. His relationship with Adams and his growing celebrity outside of football would propel him to global fame, much to the chagrin of his United manager, Sir Alex Ferguson, and many within the British football media.

Increasingly, Beckham's celebrity has become identified with marked social change and transcendental cultural significance. He is seen as a prime mover in the forging of a new, multicultural Britain and a key role model in the refashioning of gender and ethnic identity that began to emerge at the turn of the millennia. By most measures, he has grown to become one of Britain's most dominant male figures, whose influence is felt by both young and old.[8]

Sarah Gee suggests that Beckham's celebrity has been increasingly constructed through a reformulation of masculinity.[9] She suggests that Beckham embodies a form of "flexible masculinity" that offers "alternative versions of masculinity while simultaneously negotiating the borders of masculine identity."[10] Significantly, Gee suggests that Beckham's reformulation of the masculine ideal has transcendental qualities, noting:

> The broad scope of Beckham's appeal, in his ability to traverse the traditional means to which Western society is socially organized (i.e., class, ethnicity, gender, race, sexuality), converts the currency of his increasing magnetism and the interest generated by his universal image into economical dividends.[11]

In her analysis of the intersection between Beckham's celebrity and reformulated notions of gender, Gee concludes that the apparent "transcendental nature of Beckham's celebrity" has two notable features or effects that are of interest here. The first is that the consumption of Beckham's "flexible masculinity" is a private, internalized experience.[12] Second, she points to the palpable sense of frustration and disappointment that dogs "the often highly idealized, stylized, exaggerated examples of both dominant male stereotypes and alternative versions of masculinity that may be difficult or even impossible to attain."[13]

TWENTY-FIRST-CENTURY PHENOM: A NEW SORT OF CELEBRITY

While the focus of this chapter is not David Beckham's masculinity per se, I do address the themes of traversal, impossibility, and privatization. My principle argument is that David Beckham's celebrity offers a salient case study of the role, effect, and process of forms of desire within contemporary cultural contexts that are increasingly dominated by the decoupling of notions of social change from collectivized forms of intervention, which are then relocated within increasingly privatized and therapeutic forms of authority.

The 2003 Channel 4 documentary *Black Like Beckham* claimed that Beckham had played a pivotal role in promoting multiculturalism by breaking down barriers between ethnicities through his penchant for so-called Black style.[14] The evidence presented to justify this claim is predicated entirely upon the particular and personal nature of his lifestyle and consumerist choices. For example, his Rottweiler dogs, named Snoop and Puff, are clearly named after famous American rappers. Likewise, some claim that his son Romeo is named for a member of the British rap/soul band So Solid Crew.[15] According to Michael Eboda, then editor of the *New Nation*, Beckham epitomizes the notion that "Britain is a multicultural country." Further, Eboda adds, Beckham "has absorbed aspects of black culture in the way he dresses, the people with whom he associates, and his personal cultural tastes."[16] But given such a burden, such a weight of expectation, it is perhaps not surprising that at times the halo slips. And indeed, within a year of Eboda's claims, the initial emotional investment in Beckham turned to disappointment. Crass commercialism and stories of extramarital affairs gave rise to a growing sense of disillusionment with the England captain.

Once the story of the alleged affair with his personal assistant, Rebecca Loos, broke, the contours of Beckham's coverage changed rapidly. For instance, *Guardian* columnist Sarfraz Manzoor lamented the "fall of the last good man," noting that revelations of adultery had robbed Beckham of his iconic status, reducing him to the risible position of "just another celebrity to argue about, no longer an icon to believe in."[17] His alleged off-field behavior, Manzoor concludes, "diminishes us all," leading the *Guardian* to pose the question, "Has Beckham's pulling power pushed off?," which refers to a specifically Beckham-focused academic conference planned to be held at University College Winchester that was ultimately canceled due to lack of interest.[18] Indeed, it is the premise of this chapter that the dynamic that characterizes readings of David Beckham is shaped by a synthesis between extreme attraction and revulsion, which I have analyzed via an attempt to map the cultural and intellectual signifying structure within which he is located.[19] As Cashmore and Parker suggest, while Beckham "affords all the hallmarks of celebrity status, his identity remains both fluid and negotiable in accordance with the role and audience he seeks to address and the ends he seeks to achieve."[20]

Through global commodification, then, Beckham is transformed into a sign that Whannel defines as a "floating signifier."[21] By this, Beckham's meaning emerges not from his substantive materiality but via his "place in the real order of needs and objects, . . . from [his] position within codes of meaning and semiotic processes."[22]

As a "floating signifier" or "sign," Beckham embodies a moment whereby the material and social divisions of contemporary capitalism are transcended symbolically, if only partially. Beckham traverses the "traditional" markers of identity such as class, ethnicity, gender, and sexuality and recasts them anew. However, this growing sense of Beckham's transcendentalism is itself inscribed within a system of meaning akin to Jacques Lacan's understanding of the function of fantasy as a form of protection from the traumatic.[23] The trauma in question is that Beckham the icon, the celebrity, and the sign is not the arbiter of cultural transformation and change[24] but rather a product of pronounced social and cultural fragmentation. In essence, then, Beckham embodies what sociologist Frank Furedi has characterized as the rejection of the social as the sphere of transformation and a turn to the individuated and inwardly orientated sphere of the self, the personal, and the cult of the therapeutic.[25]

Cultural critic Andrew Calcutt suggests that the rise of contemporary celebrity culture is concomitant with a diminishing of "the role of modern politics in mediating social contradiction."[26] Calcutt argues that there is nothing intrinsic in celebrity itself strong enough to hold our gaze but for a moment. There is nothing substantive within the cult of celebrity that can sustain it as a phenomenon or cultural institution in its own right. It is, he suggests, an altogether too tangential, temporary, and solipsistic thing to have anything but the briefest allure. He maintains that the obsession with celebrity "is not explicable in terms of individual celebrities." Rather, he contends that this cult "represent[s] the amplification of one aspect of the interpretation and understanding of human experience to the exclusion of its cognitive counterpart. In short, the phenomenon of celebrity is the triumph of the concrete (subjective and individuated particularity) over the abstract (the attempt to locate human experience within objective social processes)."[27] Calcutt continues:

> Disregard, if you will, the personal characteristics of individual celebrities, and consider what is being celebrated in the forward march of celebrity. If we are momentarily indifferent to the differences between individual celebrities, what's left is preoccupation with the personal, the individual, the tangible—the particular in the concrete form of individual human beings, to the exclusion of ideas or notions that

entail the general. This—the retreat from abstraction to the single plane of the concrete—is key to what constitutes celebrity today. Or, what celebrity celebrates is the turn from abstraction, the subtraction of anything but the particular in the now generally expected mode of interpreting human experience.[28]

As far back as the 1970s, American cultural theorist Christopher Lasch began to detect this notion of the victim being endowed with a curious moral authority in Western societies,[29] a matter that Furedi maintains has become the dominant expression, as well as the principle organizing concept, of contemporary culture.[30] Furedi charts how social institutions have reorientated themselves to reflect and cultivate the beatified subjectivity of the victim and its protracted sense of individual alienation, inauthenticity, and disconnectedness.[31]

Both Lasch's and Furedi's critiques speak to the ideology of diminished subjectivity, defined as the postmodern death of the subject and its subsequent patronage in the spheres of cultural enquiry.[32] Furedi suggests that the contemporary expression of the victim is most prevalent in the formulation of a new culturally dominant therapeutic ethos, the principle characteristic of which is an overt "psychologization" of life experience that transforms both the nature of social authority and the subject's relationship to it. Couching this phenomenon in language more typically used to describe the relationship between a therapist and a patient, James Nolan suggests that the increasing authority invested in counseling resides precisely in its perceived "ability to give meaning to experience in a world strongly wedded to a therapeutic ethos."[33] Within this therapeutic colonization of the self is a tendency to stigmatize the subject as lacking or emotionally deficient.[34] This therapeutic narrative replaces the interpretive framework of ideological grand narratives, as viewed through the prism of Calcutt's realm of the abstract, and substitutes them with the fragmentary and debilitating discourse of the psychological, namely Calcutt's realm of the individuated, and the particular, of which celebrity culture seems a telling contemporary example.[35]

As narrative, this therapeutic ethos provides a means for a politicization of contemporary celebrity. Furedi goes on to argue that problems of political legitimacy currently experienced in Western liberal democracies are increasingly outsourced to the realm of celebrity.[36] In this sense, celebrity functions as an alternative source of normative social authority. Predicated upon increasingly individualistic and therapeutic forms of selfhood, contemporary celebrity culture becomes a fertile ground for the expression and promotion of the new victim/therapeutic sensibility. As Furedi suggests, this heightened concern with the self is "underpinned by anxiety and apprehension, rather than a positive vision of realising human potential."[37]

The contradiction of the simultaneous degradation of the self through its apparent elevation underpins the dynamic behind the veneration and subsequent disapproval of David Beckham as a postmodern role model. Via his veneration as sign of new inclusivity and source of self-esteem, Beckham emerged as both a solution to trauma and the trauma itself, a matter expressed through the profound disappointment that accompanies the failure to know the "real" him, the fear that he has let us down, and the lingering suspicion that he has duped us. Moreover, this contradiction is mirrored in a wider demand for authoritative meaning that coexists alongside a deeply held suspicion of claims to authoritative meaning. The investment in Beckham as a site of cultural change embodies this antagonism. Beckham's status as a mediator of social and cultural change is predicated upon little more than his temporally bound faddish behavior as a particularly skilled and playful consumer. This is exemplified by his fashion sense and his long, golden locks, rendered all the more visible once he shaved his head after he signed a sponsorship deal with men's grooming brand Brylcreem in 2000 for a reported sum of £4 million. Recalling Calcutt, attributing significance to Beckham's behavioral and aesthetic characteristics rejects the political and relocates meaning to the realm of consumption and "playful parody," marked as a rather theatrical subversion of signs characterized by Andreas Schedler as "aesthetic antipolitics."[38] The construction of David Beckham as transgressive "floating signifier" constitutes, thus, an overinvestment in the transformative capacity of consumption as a dynamic social motor. Put another way, Beckham is the logical excess of postmodern identity politics that renders him the embodiment of contemporary "aesthetic antipolitics."

JESUS CHRIST! JUST WHO DO WE THINK HE IS?

David Beckham has been called and compared to many things in his career. Respected media commentator William Rees-Mogg, writing of the player's possible departure from Manchester United following yet another of many confrontations with United manager Sir Alex Ferguson, drew upon the weight of English literature and history, labeling Beckham "England's young Hamlet" and the "handsome young prince to Ferguson's wicked uncle." Rees-Mogg continues:

[Beckham] comes into the rare category of the Beatles or Diana, Princess of Wales: not just a star, not just a superstar, but a global star of stars. . . . Apart from Princess Diana herself, there has been no greater celebrity in England since Charlie Chaplin was a young man, or before Chaplin since Nelson.[39]

As if that array of English notables wasn't enough, in 2004 Sarfraz Manzoor suggested that Beckham was "New Britain incarnate, like the Tony Blair we remember falling for seven years ago."[40] Manzoor goes on to find further parallels between Beckham and another working-class white boy, Elvis Presley, who Manzoor suggests was similarly "unashamedly pretty, was taunted for what was then considered an outrageous hairstyle and who was comfortable borrowing from black culture."[41] This likening of Beckham to such luminaries as Elvis, the Beatles, Charlie Chaplin, Admiral Nelson, Hamlet, Princess Diana, and Tony Blair begs the question, to whom might Beckham be compared next? Might it be Jesus Christ himself? Informally, one might be tempted to answer that query with a resounding "yes," as Beckham's career as the quintessential celebrity athlete has been dogged by an ersatz spirituality within which the Christian narratives of sacrifice, resurrection, redemption, and salvation are writ large. And, perhaps predictably, they have become consciously appropriated by the Beckham brand itself.

Garry Whannel has identified three discernible periods within Beckham's Manchester United career that define the broader media and cultural construction of his celebrity: punishment, redemption, and celebration.[42] For Whannel, the period of punishment is most discernible in the immediate aftermath of England's aforementioned defeat to Argentina in the quarterfinals of the 1998 World Cup in France. Following his sending off for an immature and petulant kick at the Argentinean captain, Diego Simeone, Beckham became the universal scapegoat for England's defeat among its football supporters and the media alike. Consistent with the pseudoreligious symbolism of Beckham's career, a Judas effigy, complete with sarong, hung outside a South London public house while the Mansfield Road Baptist Church in Shipley, West Yorkshire, offered prayers asking God to forgive the sinning number 7.

Redemption occurs and subsequently passes into full-blown celebration initially by an increasingly forgiving media and followed more generally by the public. Coinciding with Manchester United's historic treble of the Premiership title, an FA Cup, and a European Champions League title in 1999, Beckham grew to be associated with what previously would have been uncharacteristic maturity. From the ignominy of the previous year to the celebratory tenor of the next, he was praised for showing strength in the face of protracted abuse, although it is important to remember that such imagery was created by the same media that was largely responsible for his abusive scapegoating all along. That this turnabout occurred in parallel with his becoming a father for the first time leads his reputational arc away from the cynicism of his presumed irascibility toward a much more lofty portrayal of Beckham as a strong and caring family man poised to replace the popular conjecture that once imagined him as sophomoric and unreliable. Moreover, Whannel suggests that Beckham's redemption is part of a more conscious effort to offer a facelift to the Beckham brand. For example, in 1999 in the London listing magazine *Time Out*, Beckham appears on the front cover, barefoot and adorned in white.[43] Bathed in a translucent serenity by the lighting effects, Beckham stands hands outstretched in an unmistakably Christ-like pose with an accompanying cover headline that reads "Easter Exclusive: The Resurrection of David Beckham."[44]

Madame Tussauds, the waxworks museum and exhibition hall in London, created life-size models of Beckham and his wife Victoria, with his Buddhist script and crucified angel tattoos prominently displayed. Depicted as Joseph and the Virgin Mary, this image was further underscored by the Beckhams' decision to name their third son Cruz (Spanish for cross), though, perhaps ironically, when a reporter asked if they were eager to have his son christened, the Beckhams explained that they were unsure into which religion it might be! However confusing Beckham's use of spiritual symbolism might be, one cannot ignore that it is a significant axis upon which the celebrity and postmodern allure of Beckham turns. And yet, Beckham's appropriation of religious symbolism seems to pale in comparison to the ways in which he has at times been graced with messianic qualities by the British press.

THE METATARSAL OF THE MESSIAH?

In April 2002, during the sixteenth minute of Manchester United's European Champions League quarterfinal second-leg victory over the Spanish team Deportivo La Coruña, Beckham suffered a broken metatarsal bone in his left foot. Certainly Beckham was out for the rest of United's season, and it was feared that the injury would mean his having to miss England competing in that summer's World Cup in South Korea and Japan. Writing in the *Chicago Tribune*, Chris Vallance noticed a rather messianic significance attributed to the player's injury in the British press:

This was a race against time. Medical opinion suggested a healing period of at least 6 to 10 weeks for the broken bone. England will play an important warmup against Cameroon on May 26, seven weeks after the injury, and face its first real match against Sweden on June 2.[45]

Vallance continues:

Out of desperation, usually secular Brits sought spiritual assistance. Under the headline "Beck Us Pray," the tabloid newspaper the *Sun*, perhaps best known for the naked lady on Page 3 each day, had a religious turn and urged readers to touch a front page picture of his foot while beseeching the almighty to mend the metatarsal. Three bishops also offered prayers. There were even appeals to more occult forces. A white witch (the good sort, apparently) cast a healing spell as spoon bender Uri Geller attempted to enlist the nation's psychic powers in straightening out Beckham's foot on the popular ITV Network program "Good Morning Britain."[46]

Given the intensity of the symbolic transcendentalism afforded Beckham's celebrity, it is perhaps difficult to see him as anything other than a religious icon, albeit a postmodernly ironic one. Indeed, there are strong associations between sport and religion, be they historical, philosophical, or social. Johan Huizinga and Rudolph Brasch note the centrality of physical competition within the ritual and performance of primitive religious ceremony.[47] The historical origins and development of modern sport in Britain are strongly associated with an idealized Christian masculinity,[48] but this is by no means unique to Western religious ideals. John Nauright and Tara Magdalinski draw attention to the development of Muslim rugby in South Africa during the 1930s, promoting a "hardy Muslim masculinity" as something of a response on the part of the Muslim community to forms of sporting and social apartheid in South Africa during the interwar years.[49]

There is a considerable literature that draws parallels between the philosophical groundings of sport and religion. Both require and promote a disciplined observance of codes of sacrifice and pain as indicators of moral worth and achievement. According to Michael Novak, sports are a form of natural religion based as they are upon an "impulse for freedom, respect for ritual limits, a zest for symbolic meaning, and a longing for perfection."[50] But, as Magdalinski and Timothy Chandler note, "despite the most ritualistic nature of fandom, sport simply does not address the basic questions that religious communities try to answer."[51]

This goes to the heart of the issue. At a formal level, there is more than a passing similarity between sport and religion in both their emotional and cultural structures. Furthermore, it is possible to determine strong similarities between the promotion of David Beckham as a symbolic representation of social change and that of the religious impulse. Michael Mann notes that religion is defined in part by its "beliefs and actions related to ultimate concerns or symbols which formulate conceptions of a general order of existence."[52] As Ruphine S. Obare continues:

> Religion is thus seen in one such model where all the rules, norms, values, dogmas, truth, denomination, conviction, and principles come out with one common meaning, Beliefs, Creed, Doctrine, and Faith. ... [R]eligious beliefs ... provide ... psychological support in the face of uncertainty. Religions provide systems of meaning that can be used to make sense out of one's life.[53]

The investment in Beckham as a postmodern role model mirrors in many ways the religious pursuit of meaning and material transcendence. But while the religious pursuit of meaning is flawed and doomed to failure, in the Žižekian sense of the impossibility of desire, it is nonetheless predicated upon a universal totalizing desire. In contradistinction, however, the transcendental investment in Beckham is predicated, as Calcutt suggests, upon the particular and the ambiguous, a retreat from the universal rather than its embrace.[54] Faith in Beckham is conditional, unlike that of a Christian for Christ, or a Muslim for Mohammed. The belief in Beckham is itself a reflection of the deep and culturally pervasive lack of faith in meaning. To return to Calcutt's distinctions between the abstract and the concrete, David Beckham's celebrity is an embodiment of the lack of belief placed in systems of social as well as ideological and spiritual meaning that once provided the frameworks by which individuals understood the world and their relationship to it.[55]

ONE DAVID BECKHAM:
THE EXCREMENTAL OBJECT OF DESIRE

David Beckham is by no means the first athlete to be invested with particular pseudo-socioreligious significance. Passion, fanaticism, and an unwavering belief in miracles are the daily bread of global sports narratives. Nor is Beckham unique in that the significance invested in him seemingly transverses the boundaries of his sport and permeates wider social and cultural life. Athletes such as Muhammad Ali and Diego Maradona, to name but a few, have been associated with particular social movements or demands for social recognition and protest. Beckham is hardly unique in that he has been appropriated as a symbol of social and cultural change. However, what is unique about the way in which Beckham has been appropriated is that his significance as a symbol of cultural change is predicated entirely upon the personal—the clothes he wears, the music he listens to, his cultural tastes, and his familial relationships. This stands in sharp contrast to the social significance of sporting icons such as the aforementioned Ali and, to a lesser extent, Maradona, whose significance is embedded within a framework that at least on some level holds the principles of universalism and collectivism as the foundational tenets of political and social change. Beckham's cultural significance is beholden to little more than his everyday personal consumption habits and physical appearance, which are then imbued with transcendental significance.

Herein lies the traumatic quality of David Beckham's celebrity. For Calcutt, the purchase of celebrity culture and its hold on the social imagination is conditional upon a retreat from collective political action as the purposive realm of mediation and contestation of concrete social contradiction.[56] Celebrity itself is contentless and insubstantial, and yet it adopts the characteristics of an independent, substantive cultural thing, which is then invested with the ability to overcome concrete social contradictions. All of which is consistent with Lacan's notion of the *objet petit a* (see below).

It is often suggested that celebrity culture is typical of the function of desire within consumer society, a telling exemplification of what Whannel calls an "indulgence in the consumer market."[57] The association between desire, celebrity, and consumer society revolves around an understanding of desire as a function of market imperatives. These imperatives establish the coordinates between want, fulfillment, and need. The work of Chris Rojek, and Cashmore and Parker, suggests that celebrity operates as "an essential tool of commodification since it embodies desire"; additionally, "[c]onsumerism encourages and nurtures desire, which is protean, or 'abstract' in the sense that it changes in response to brand innovation and the introduction of new commodities."[58] In this sense, we might understand the desire for Beckham as the consumer's desire for a commodity produced in an economic system dominated by the production of sign values, which "permeate every thread of the social fabric."[59]

Beckham's celebrity satiates a longing in that it fulfills a need. It is perhaps not surprising, then, that at one level Beckham should be referred to as a "Christ of consumption."[60] However, care should be exercised in simply confining the analysis of Beckham's celebrity to the consumptive sphere alone. Desire is a much more dynamic cultural force, particularly in how it coordinates our understanding of self. The psychoanalytic conceptualization of desire reverses the simple need-fulfillment, market-oriented function alluded to above. Rather than a simple fulfillment of a need or demand, desire underscores a complexity born of the presence of the *Other*, or, perhaps more pertinently, what we think the *Other* wants from us. Desire is then mapped by the coordinates of lack insomuch as that which we think the *Other* lacks, the uncertainty that we cannot be sure what constitutes this lack, and, subsequently, how we might satiate this apparent lack. Desire, as Lacan suggests, is distinct from the fulfillment of need. As such, Žižek argues, the demand of desire is desire itself.[61]

Far from fulfilling our needs or wants, desire provides insufficient satisfaction. Given the impossibility of knowing what it is that the *Other* wants from us, the essential component that sustains our desire produces a need that is as much predicated upon dissatisfaction as it is upon attraction. Dissatisfaction is a principle dynamic that shapes attraction to the *Other*. Desire, then, has the paradoxical potential to repulse us. In this regard, one could argue that desire has an excremental nature.

Beckham's career has been dogged by religious and spiritual associations. It has also been associated with, if you will pardon the expression, shit! Beckham's fame and subsequent celebrity were initially established while playing for Manchester United, a club long ago dubbed by many football fans as "ManUre" or simply "the Shit." Furthermore, the tensions and fluidity exemplified in the many versions of Beckham's celebrity with its apparently seamless flow between praise and condemnation speaks to the conflict-laden but necessary attraction/revulsion function associated with desire. In his harnessing of Lacan, for instance, Žižek draws parallels with the small child who presents his or her feces to a parent as "the primordial form of gift," an externalized symbolization of one's most intimate and innermost self.[62] On the occasion of Beckham's thirtieth birthday in May 2005, for example, journalist Simon Hattenstone contrasted the twenty-one-year-old footballer who had stood "Christ-like" after scoring a "miracle goal" against Wimbledon in 1996 with the "soiled," commercialized celebrity he had since become.[63] Beckham is both the *shit* and the *Shinola*[64] in that he is situated here as a site of simultaneous attraction and revulsion, a relationship that Žižek characterizes through Lacan's concept of the *objet petit a*.[65]

> Let us take a direct "vulgar" example: when a (heterosexual male) lover
> is fascinated with his partner's vagina, "never getting enough of it,"

prone not only to penetrate it, but to explore it and caress it in all possible ways, the point is NOT that, in a kind of deceptive short-circuit, he mistakes the piece of skin, hair and flesh for the Thing itself—his lover's vagina is, in all its bodily materiality, "the thing itself," not the spectral appearing of another dimension; what makes it an "infinitely" desirable object whose "mystery" cannot ever be fully penetrated, is its non-identity to itself, i.e., the way it is never directly "itself." The gap which "externalizes" drive, turning it into the endlessly repetitive circular movement around the object, is not the gap that separates the void of the Thing from its contingent embodiments, but the gap that separates the very "pathological" object FROM ITSELF, in the same way that ... Christ is not the contingent material ("pathological") embodiment of the suprasensible God; his "divine" dimension is reduced to the aura of a pure *Schein*.[66]

This evocatively vulgar comparison of a man's desire for his lover's sexual organs with the Christians' desire for Christ encapsulates exactly the relationship that characterizes the meaning of David Beckham's celebrity. He is here the *objet petit a*, the mysterious allusive object that causes desire but is itself created by desire. Moreover, identifying Beckham as the *objet petit a* provides the basis whereby alternative readings of Beckham can be generated. If it is at all possible to characterize the postmodern condition, one might characterize it by its seemingly contradictory desire to seek and confer meaning on action, objects, and subjects while also refuting and undermining the very meaning that may be ascribed. I suggest that this is precisely the process at play in the cycles of attraction/revulsion and hope/disappointment that weave themselves around Beckham as a cultural icon. The defining character of desire is that it can never be satisfied. Rather, it is always doomed to failure, yet at the same time this disappointment underlines our desire in the first place. Beckham assumes the status of the *objet petit a* by virtue of the desire to know him, to ascribe his status, personality, and behavior with meaning and significance, and then the palpable dissatisfaction that these meanings are continually disabused. In this sense, Beckham attains the position of the mysterious object tantalizingly within reach but always far enough away to always frustrate our grasp. The reaction to Beckham's adulterous indiscretion provides a telling example of the symbolic interplay between attraction and revulsion, hope and disillusionment, that characterizes the Lacanian/ Žižekian conceptualization of desire.

ONLY ONE DAVID BECKHAM: THE FLAWED FANTASY

Assuming the mantle as 2005's universal woman, *Times* journalist Suzi Godson decried Beckham for his fall from grace following revelations of the Loos
affair. For Godson, the accusations of adultery undermine not only Beckham
but faith in men. As Godson reminds us, Beckham had become as much an
icon of male goodness as he was of sporting ability, representing an inspi-
rational hope of what men could be capable of in terms of loving, sharing,
and caring. According to Godson, however, Beckham's alleged indiscretion
"shattered [our] already fragile faith in the opposite sex." She continues:

> I admired him because he seemed to be a rare example of all that could
> be good in the opposite sex. He was hard-working, strong, disciplined
> and he was open and unembarrassed about his love for his children
> and his wife, to whom he appeared to be completely faithful. Bar the
> tattoos and the skirts, this made him an unbeatable role model for
> young men. And an aspiration fantasy for all women, he embodied all
> we had hoped for in the opposite sex, and he allowed us, for a time, to
> believe in the fantasy of love and fidelity.[67]

The pattern of revulsion/attraction is evident in the need invested in Beckham as a sexual albeit gendered role model and his subsequent failure to satiate this need. Godson's use of the term "fantasy" is telling in that it underlines
Beckham's significance as the *objet petit a*. In his work in the field of psychoanalysis in 1897, Sigmund Freud identified fantasy (written as "phantasy") as a
central facet of desire, concluding that "memories of seduction are sometimes
the product of fantasy."[68] Freud's analysis suggests that fantasy is in some
way opposed to reality, an illusory or unconscious desire that functions as
a barrier to actual perception or understanding. However, Lacan suggests a
far more radical understanding of the function of fantasy. Lacan emphasizes
the protective function of fantasy as opposed to Freud's understanding of
fantasy as a barrier to reality. Lacan uses the analogy of the cinematic image,
suggesting that fantasy is akin to a film image being frozen at a particular
point in order to protect the audience from an especially traumatic event or
scene. The importance of this protective function is that fantasy functions as
a means of veiling or masking the lack in the *Other*. In this sense, fantasy is a
compromise that both "enables the subject to sustain desire" and "by which
the subject sustains *himself* at the level of his vanishing desire."[69]

From this particular reading, we are able to surmise that Beckham embodies the particular characteristics of the *objet petit a*—that lost, mysterious, and

lacking object that assumes what Žižek deems is "a positive substantial identity independently of its being lost."[70] This insight has particular relevance to
Beckham's function as a particular floating signifier. By approaching fantasy
not as an opposition to reality but, in Lacanian terms, as the structure of
reality, it is possible to suggest that the meanings ascribed to Beckham are
not intrinsic to the image itself but, rather, "to the place which it occupies
in a symbolic structure."[71] Here, the image functions as a means to protect
one from trauma, which in this case is the realization that Beckham cannot
resolve the reality of social division. As we shall see in the following sections,
Beckham is inscribed in a system whereby he assumes value by virtue of his
difference from other elements within the system, the example in his case
being his place in traditional masculine culture derived from the normative practices of traditional football. The differential nature of the signifier
means that it can never have fixed, unequivocal meaning. Its meaning varies
according to the position it occupies in the structure. It is not that Beckham's
identity or his many representations constitute the fluid, flux-like nature of
postmodern society, but rather that the meanings invested in Beckham are
themselves fragmentary and inconclusive.

And herein lies the root of the trauma of David Beckham. Beckham's
celebrity functions as a form of fantastical protection against the realization that meanings ascribed to Beckham's celebrity are evidence not of a
progressive social inclusiveness but of regressive fragmentation. The shifting
terrains of meaning ascribed to Beckham reflect a deep insecurity on the
part of society in general to appraise and navigate its current condition in a
purposive, collectivized manner. Instead, individuals, events, and lifestyle are
invested with the characteristics and features that confirm and/or transcend
(often at the same time) this rudderless social condition. Beckham, thus,
transcends traditional masculine football culture and embodies a refutation
of commodified sport while also confirming both. He offers, as Cashmore
and Parker indicate,

> a version of masculinity that contradicts, confuses, and conflates all
> in one. He is "new-man" (nurturer, romantic, compassionate partner)
> and "new-lad"/"dad-lad" (soccer hero, fashionable father, conspicuous
> consumer—some would argue, all-round, cosmetically conscientious
> "metrosexual") while still demonstrating vestiges of "old industrial
> man" (loyal, dedicated, stoic, breadwinning).[72]

ONLY ONE DAVID BECKHAM: THE INFANTILIZED OBJECT

In February 2000, while Beckham was still a Manchester United player, reports appeared in the media that he had failed to attend a training session on the Friday before an away fixture at Leeds United that Sunday. Beckham was subsequently dropped from the game roster by manager Sir Alex Ferguson. As became apparent in the following media discussion of the event, this was not the first time the player had gone AWOL, having not turned up for training on Christmas Day ahead of the Boxing Day fixture against Burnley. Beckham was subsequently dropped for that game, also. On both occasions, Beckham cited family illness as the reason for his nonattendance, and in the latter case, that of his young son Brooklyn, who had been diagnosed with mild gastroenteritis.[73] As the story unfolded, it transpired that Beckham's wife, Victoria, at the time of their son's illness had gone on a shopping trip, literally "leaving David at home with the baby."[74] Later that evening, it was alleged that she had attended the finale of London Fashion Week.[75]

Interpretations of these events have been varied. At the time, there was within the popular sporting press a consensus that Ferguson was right to drop and castigate his star midfielder, reflecting the traditional view that loyalty and commitment to one's club must override all other ties. No player no matter how famous or talented could be seen to be flouting these important principles, especially at Manchester United, a perennial power built upon single-minded professional dedication and discipline. Among some sports columnists, there was a keen sense of a troubling gender dynamic in the Beckham household in that it was Victoria who called the shots and ruled the roost rather than her husband, and they chided him accordingly. The *Sun's* John Sadler crowed with glee at what he called Ferguson's "admirable example" of dropping "Posh Spouse."[76] Former Republic of Ireland manager and England World Cup winner Jack Charlton confirmed what most already thought—that Beckham was a cuckold, dominated by his fame-greedy wife, claiming (with an implied dig at Ferguson), "If I was a manger, I wouldn't want a woman to have that sort of influence over one of my players. It would never happen in my day."[77]

Writing in the *Guardian*, Jim White and Emma Brockes further scrutinize Beckham's circumstances from the increasingly broad lens of traditional masculinity clashing with the new. They observe that Beckham's misdemeanor, as footballing misdemeanors go, was unique in that it was not a "petulant star throwing a tantrum." As they see it, Beckham was acting as "a father being responsible, loving his sick son.[78] For them, this event dramatizes the apparently changing nature of traditional roles within the family unit, suggesting that the backlash against Beckham is reminiscent of a football culture lagging behind the rest of society. They contend:

> In football, a strong wife [own career, financially independent] has traditionally been regarded as the first indication of serial deviance. Football wives should quietly provide a stable home life and nothing more.[79]

The theme of the cuckolded, dominated husband has been a notable feature of the construction of Beckham's celebrity. Garry Whannel recalls popular comic impersonator Alistair McGowan's series on BBC1 during the late 1990s that featured a long-running sketch chronicling the opulent but increasingly dim-witted married life of Posh (played by Ronni Ancona) and Becks (played by McGowan).[80] Becks is portrayed as infantile, stupid, and gauchely nouveau riche while Posh is shown to be refined and intelligent, a worldly, wise, yet domineering wife. However, as the series continued to develop over a number of years, so, too, the dynamics between Posh and Becks. In later episodes of the series, notably following Beckham's transfer to Real Madrid in the summer of 2002, their positions were almost reversed. It is Becks who now assumes a more culturally refined but often wary counterpoint to his wife's increasingly immature, childlike utterances and misconceptions. But the roles are not totally reversed. Becks is never totally dominant, nor is Posh totally submissive. Nor should one restrict readings of their relationship and its transformation through the prism of gender. The McGowan and Ancona parody also speaks to the problematized blurring of adult/child relations.[81] Indeed, despite any obvious transitioning, Victoria Beckham remains the constant overbearing adult *Other* to her husband's "beatific" childlike innocence.

Beckham's infantilization is a prescient facet of his postmodern allure. Journalist Julie Burchill has noted with relish Beckham's childish innocence. Beckham has stated that when away from football, his favorite pastime is to trace drawings of cartoon characters, especially the Lion King, a likeness of which he sent to Victoria Adams when she was still his fiancée. As Burchill declares, Beckham has never been one to hide his predilection for children's toys. When asked by the veteran television chat show host and interviewer Michael Parkinson how Victoria and he first came to be an item, Beckham revealed that he knew she fancied him after "she bought me a big bunny."[82] As Burchill tellingly jokes: "[W]e weren't really [as] shocked as we would have been if we'd learned this about Stanley Matthews."[83]

The world of professional football is redolent with the narrative of the child. Argentinean football culture actively celebrates it through the concept of *il pibe de oro* or the golden child, a name given to players of outstanding talent, vision, and purity of genius, such as Maradona. British football culture, too, has had its fair share of children, but this is usually a reference to their boorish behavior.[84] But Beckham's childlike status is of a very different nature. It is both a source of celebration, the essence of beatific innocence, and a source of absolution. In an article entitled "Female Fans Style Pubic Hair Like Beckham's Mohican," journalist Shane Green indirectly draws attention to the nonthreatening, almost asexual nature of Beckham's image, which is particularly interesting given that Beckham is co-consciously constructed as a highly desirable body for both heterosexual women and homosexual men. Accordingly, at least in the Far East, Beckham's looks are "quite acceptable to Japanese people." As Yuji Kiminami, editor of the Japanese edition of Beckham's autobiography, *David Beckham: My Side*, contends: "It is much easier for Japanese women to accept his moderately sexy appearance than Italian soccer player Francesco Totti, who is too sexy for Japanese women."[85]

This theme is also evident in media discourses surrounding the Rebecca Loos affair. Indeed, it was utilized as a narrative device by which Beckham was practically absolved from responsibility for his adulterous indiscretion. It is Victoria Beckham serving in the role of *Other* who is often perceived to be at fault for his indiscretion, as she failed to offer proper support by not moving to Madrid and for being so outwardly entitled. As one journalist couched it, Mrs. Beckham's fatal flaw was not perceiving her internationally renowned husband as a victim of his own attractiveness:

> What I find hard to understand is his wife, Victoria, leaving Beckham on his own in Madrid. The world is full of predatory females ready and willing to seduce sweet, charming men like Beckham.[86]

Surprisingly, Beckham's irresponsibility is presented as a justifiable reaction to the indifference and selfishness of others, notably his wife. Beckham as infantile subject had also been a predominant feature of his career at Manchester United.

On joining Manchester United when not even a teenager, Beckham became an integral member of the club's "Golden Generation," a group of young, talented players including Ryan Giggs, Paul Scholes, Nicky Butt, and brothers Gary and Phil Neville. This group of players were to be key to United's unparalleled success during the 1990s. Infamously, BBC football pundit and ex-Liverpool and Scotland defender Alan Hansen claimed with glee that United would "win nothing with kids" following an opening-day 3–1 defeat at Aston Villa in 1995 when Ferguson fielded a team that included many of

United's burgeoning youth squad. But United would go on to win their third Premiership trophy in four years, winning pretty much everything with kids. Apart from the fact that this was perhaps an unprecedented collection of homegrown young talent gathered on one club, the most prescient aspect about this generation of players was the relationship they have enjoyed with Ferguson, typically portrayed as a domineering father figure, an image consciously fostered by Ferguson himself. Ferguson has known this group of players since they were young boys, and he has known Beckham since the age of eleven, when the latter began training at the club. Ferguson's much-vaunted bedside manner (e.g., he had a knack for remembering parents' and family members' names and frequently visited them at their homes) was often cited as his most endearing quality as he sought to secure the signatures of some of the country's most exciting young talent. For Ferguson, United, and these young charges, this was a relationship that was to bear fruit upon fruit. But it was not without its tensions, as one might expect, betwixt father and son.

Similarly, former Manchester United captain Roy Keane was often referred to as the on-field embodiment of the United manager: hard, uncompromising, unforgiving, unrepentant, and driven by a relentless desire to win. However, the group of players who won the FA Youth Cup in 1993–1994 and were to force their collective way onto the all-conquering United teams of the mid- to late 1990s had largely been shaped by Ferguson, but not in his own image. Rather, he molded them in the image of model professionals in that they remained subservient, turned up on time, went home when dismissed, and, above all, did as they were told. And this vaunted Golden Generation remained forever children—at least, that is, until they left the club—voluntarily or otherwise.

In his autobiography *My Side*,[87] the publication of which suitably coincided with his 2003 departure from Old Trafford, Beckham claimed that Ferguson had taken exception to his outgrowing the familial parameters that had so far defined the relationship between player and manager. Beckham explains: "I'd grown up as a person, and [Ferguson] didn't seem to like what I'd become."[88] Later, writing on Beckham's transfer to Real Madrid, the *Times*' William Langley noted that, given the nature of the mystical narrative that surrounded the Beckham-Ferguson mentor and protégé/father and son relationship, any "severing of the bond" was both inevitable and natural.[89] "Protégés," Langley explains, "as do sons, outgrow their mentor/father. They grow up and move on," although it is perhaps noteworthy that Beckham was twenty-eight years old when he finally moved on, so to speak.

As Andrew Calcutt suggests, this self-image of the child has a strong presence in contemporary culture. He asserts that its predominance is in and of itself a reflection of deep social distrust of rationality as well as purposive, reflective authority, characteristics typically associated with adulthood that turn to effusive and emotionally spontaneous forms of expression associated with a child. The emotional reorientation of the cultural perception of self, Calcutt argues, resides not in the child but rather in a childlike vulnerability of the victim. Notable elements of Beckham's allure lie in part to this (re) turn to the vulnerable, childlike victim.[90]

(THERE IS) ONLY ONE DAVID BECKHAM . . .

Social, economic, and scientific development have historically been accompanied by a rejection of former forms of authority and a questioning of the norms and moral codes by which society is governed. For example, the claims and once unquestioned demands of religious morality have been undermined by the material rationality of science. New forms of authority, new ways of understanding society and our relationship with it, have usurped the old and consigned them to the dustbin of history. But, increasingly, contemporary social and cultural theory suggests that the erosion of traditional forms of solidarity, of communal and religious norms, has produced increasingly fragmented and privatized life experiences. What was once certain is now questioned. Where there was trust and certainty, there is now mistrust and fear. It is within this context of detraditionalization and moral skepticism that the therapeutic nature of David Beckham's celebrity finds its expression.

Frank Furedi suggests that the therapeutic ethos that continues to inform contemporary life fills this moral and autorotative vacuum. It promises to provide answers to the individual's quest for meaning, which would have otherwise been conferred by traditional forms of authority. Increasingly, pseudoreligious and relativized spiritual impulses promise to redraw subjective experiences, endowing the private emotional sphere with special significance.[91] In this regard, David Beckham's seemingly transformative social qualities are representative of this type of therapeutic investment whereby meaning is sought in the personal characteristics, behavior, and emotional foibles of otherwise unconnected and temporal individuals. It is in this respect, then, that the symbolic institution of celebrity is predicated wholly upon the very fragmentation of the communal and collective impulse itself.

And yet, the therapeutic ethos invested in David Beckham's celebrity fails to offer an alternative to the ideological collectivity, as the very ideologies that underpinned institutional commitment have fractured and fallen into disarray.[92] Still, it is in this sense that the therapeutic investment in David

Beckham's celebrity represents not a moment of transcendence but, as Furedi observes, a fundamental accommodation to the weakening of moral and social collectivities, and the elevation of the contemporary condition of the self as an end in and of itself that reveals, among other matters, that despite all the transcendental promise and hope invested in him, there is indeed . . . only one David Beckham![93]

NOTES

1. "Beckham Tops Football's Rich List," *Guardian*, May 3, 2005, https://www.theguardian .com/football/2005/may/03/newsstory.sport4, accessed May 12, 2005.

2. Ellis Cashmore and Andrew Parker, "One David Beckham? Celebrity, Masculinity, and the Soccerati," *Sociology of Sport Journal* 20, no. 3 (September 2003): 214.

3. Jean Baudrillard, *For a Critique of the Political Economy of the Sign*, trans. Charles Levin (St. Louis: Telos Press, 1981).

4. Fredric Jameson, *Postmodernism; or, The Cultural Logic of Late Capitalism* (London: Verso, 1991).

5. Slavoj Žižek, *The Plague of Fantasies* (London: Verso, 1997).

6. Mohmin Rahman, "Is Straight the New Queer? David Beckham and the Dialectics of Celebrity," *M/C Journal* 7, no. 5 (2004), http://journal.media-culture.org.au/0411/15-rahman .php, accessed February 16, 2017.

7. Garry Whannel, "David Beckham, Identity and Masculinity," *Sociology Review* 11, no. 3 (2002): 2.

8. Andrew Parker, quoted in Denis Campbell, "Beckham Is the Most Influential Man in the UK—Even with That Sarong," *Observer*, February 2, 2003, https://www.theguardian.com/ uk/2003/feb/02/football.deniscampbell, accessed August 2, 2005.

9. Sarah Gee, "Bending the Codes of Masculinity: David Beckham and Flexible Masculinity in the New Millennium," *Sport in Society* 17, no. 7 (2014): 917–36.

10. Gee, "Bending the Codes of Masculinity," 921.

11. Gee, "Bending the Codes of Masculinity," 920.

12. Gee, "Bending the Codes of Masculinity," 932.

13. Gee, "Bending the Codes of Masculinity," 918.

14. Barbara Ellen, "Black Like Beckham," *Observer*, March 23, 2003, https://www.theguard ian.com/theobserver/2003/mar/23/features.magazine7, accessed April 30, 2003.

15. Carol Midgley, "Young, Gifted and . . . Black?," *Times* (UK), March 27, 2003, https:// www.thetimes.co.uk/article/young-gifted-and-black-d8sfpnog9fd, accessed April 30, 2003.

16. Michael Eboda, cited in Midgley, "Young, Gifted and . . . Black?"

17. Sarfraz Manzoor, "The Fall of the Last Good Man," *Guardian*, April 14, 2004, https:// www.theguardian.com/football/2004/apr/14/sport.comment, accessed May 3, 2005.

18. Donald MacLeod, "Has Beckham's Pulling Power Pushed Off?," *Guardian*, April 19, 2005, https://www.theguardian.com/uk/2005/apr/19/highereducation.education, accessed May 12, 2005.

19. Jacques Lacan, *Ecrits: A Selection*, trans. Alan Sheridan (London: Tavistock, 1977).

20. Cashmore and Parker, "One David Beckham?," 214.

21. Garry Whannel, *Media Sports Stars: Masculinities and Moralities* (London: Routledge, 2002).

22. Don Slater and Fran Tonkiss, *Market Society: Markets and Modern Social Theory* (Cambridge: Polity Press, 2001), 181–82.

23. Lacan, *Ecrits: A Selection*, 272.

24. Cashmore and Parker, "One David Beckham?"

25. Frank Furedi, *Therapy Culture: Cultivating Vulnerability in an Uncertain Age* (London: Routledge, 2004).

26. Andrew Calcutt, "Celebrity Turns and the Return of Politics," paper presented at Celebrity Culture: An Interdisciplinary Conference (University of Paisley, Scotland, September 12–14, 2005), 2.

27. Calcutt, "Celebrity Turns and the Return of Politics," 2.

28. Calcutt, "Celebrity Turns and the Return of Politics," 2.

29. Christopher Lasch, *The Minimal Self: Psychic Survival in Troubled Times* (New York: W. W. Norton, 1984), 67.

30. Frank Furedi, *Culture of Fear: Risk-Taking and the Morality of Low Expectation* (London: Continuum, 2002); and Furedi, *Therapy Culture*.

31. Furedi, *Therapy Culture*.

32. See James Heartfield, *The "Death of the Subject" Explained* (Leicester, England: Perpetuity Press, 2002).

33. James L. Nolan, *The Therapeutic State: Justifying Government at Century's End* (New York: New York University Press, 1998), cited in Furedi, *Therapy Culture*, 10.

34. Furedi, *Therapy Culture*, 18–19.

35. Calcutt, "Celebrity Turns and the Return of Politics"; Furedi, *Therapy Culture*; and Frank Furedi, "Celebrity Culture," *Society* 47, no. 6 (November 2010): 493–97.

36. Furedi, "Celebrity Culture."

37. Furedi, *Therapy Culture*.

38. Calcutt, "Celebrity Turns and the Return of Politics"; and Andreas Schedler, "Introduction: Antipolitics—Closing and Colonizing the Public Sphere," in *The End of Politics: Explorations into Modern Antipolitics*, ed. Andreas Schedler (London: Macmillan, 1997), 1–20.

39. William Rees-Mogg, "England's Young Hamlet Must Not Quit the Stage," *Times* (UK), April 28, 2003, https://www.thetimes.co.uk/article/englands-young-hamlet-must-not-quit-the-stage-8x3ppfwgsv8, accessed May 23, 2005.

40. Manzoor, "The Fall of the Last Good Man."

41. Manzoor, "The Fall of the Last Good Man."

42. Garry Whannel, "Punishment, Redemption and Celebration in the Popular Press: The Case of David Beckham," in *Sports Stars: The Cultural Politics of Sporting Celebrity*, ed. David L. Andrews and Steven J. Jackson (London: Routledge, 2001), 138–63.

43. *Time Out*, Easter 1999, cited in Whannel, "Punishment, Redemption and Celebration."

44. Whannel, "Punishment, Redemption and Celebration."

45. Chris Vallance, "His Left Foot," *Chicago Tribune*, May 21, 2002, http://articles.chicagotribune.com/20020521/features/0205210016_1_beckingham-palace-mr-posh-spice-mrs-beckham/2, accessed February 16, 2018. The World Cup was to begin on May 31 with a match between Senegal and France.

46. Vallance, "His Left Foot."

47. Johan Huizinga, *Homo Ludens: A Study of the Play-Element in Culture* (Boston: Beacon Press, 1992); and Rudolph Brasch, *How Did Sports Begin? A Look at the Origins of Man at Play* (Harlow, Essex, England: Longman, 1972).

48. Jay Coakley, *Sports in Society: Issues and Controversies* (St. Louis: C. V. Mosby, 1994); and Shirl J. Hoffman, ed., *Sport and Religion* (Champaign, IL: Human Kinetics, 1992).

49. John Nauright and Tara Magdalinski, "Religion, Race and Rugby in 'Coloured' Cape Town," in *With God on Their Side: Sport in the Service of Religion*, ed. Tara Magdalinski and Timothy J. L. Chandler (London: Routledge, 2002), 135.

50. Michael Novak, *The Joy of Sport* (New York: Basic Books, 1976), cited in Ruphine S. Obare, "Can Sports Exist without Religion?," Sheffield University, February 2000, https://www.sheffield.ac.uk/polopoly_fs/1.71451!/file/obare.pdf, 6.

51. Tara Magdalinski and Timothy J. L. Chandler, epilogue to *With God on Their Side: Sport in the Service of Religion*, ed. Tara Magdalinski and Timothy J. L. Chandler (London: Routledge, 2002), 198.

52. Michael Mann, *Macmillan Student Encyclopedia of Sociology* (London: Macmillan, 1983).

53. Obare, "Can Sports Exist without Religion?"

54. Calcutt, "Celebrity Turns and the Return of Politics."

55. Calcutt, "Celebrity Turns and the Return of Politics."

56. Calcutt, "Celebrity Turns and the Return of Politics."

57. Whannel, *Media Sports Stars*, 202.

58. Chris Rojek, *Celebrity* (London: Reaktion Books, 2001); quotation from Cashmore and Parker, "One David Beckham?," 218.

59. Cashmore and Parker, "One David Beckham?," 218.

60. Whannel, "David Beckham, Identity and Masculinity," 3.

61. Žižek, *The Plague of Fantasies*, 39.

62. Slavoj Žižek, *On Belief* (London: Routledge, 2001), 59.

63. Simon Hattenstone, "Reality Bites for Madrid's Beckham," *Irish Times*, May 4, 2005, https://www.irishtimes.com/sport/reality-bites-for-madrid-s-beckham-1.437526, accessed February 16, 2007.

64. Shinola is a reference to an American shoe polish product that dates back to the early to mid-twentieth century. When combined with "shit," the word forms a colloquial expression that connotes the extremes of excellence and incompetence.

65. *Objet (petit) a* is the object that we continually desire. In Lacan's work, the term remains untranslated (akin to an algebraic sign) and always lowercase. The *objet petit a* is the object of anxiety. The lowercase *a* denotes an object that can never be obtained, which is itself the cause of desire; it is the object that sets desire in motion. The *objet petit a* is, thus, different from the *A* of the *Big Other*. According to Lacan, the *Big Other* represents a radical and irreducible alterity (the state of being other or different) that coordinates the structure of symbolic authority. The *objet (petit) a* introduces anxiety to this structure. See Dylan Evans, *An Introductory Dictionary of Lacanian Psychoanalysis* (London: Routledge, 1996), 124–26.

66. Žižek, *On Belief*, 94–95, original emphasis.

67. Suzi Godson, "Hero Who Fell to Earth," *Times* (UK), June 29, 2004, https://www.thetimes.co.uk/article/hero-who-fell-to-earth-qr5zkrwt860, accessed May 23, 2005.

68. Evans, *An Introductory Dictionary*, 59.

69. Lacan, *Ecrits: A Selection*, cited in Evans, *An Introductory Dictionary*, 60, emphasis added.

70. Žižek, *On Belief*, 68.

71. Lacan, *Ecrits: A Selection*, 272, cited in Evans, *An Introductory Dictionary*, 61.

72. Cashmore and Parker, "One David Beckham?," 225.

73. Steve Curry, "Stand-Off," *Sunday Times* (UK), February 21, 2000, 9.

74. Curry, "Stand-Off."

75. Jim White and Emma Brockes, "The Player, the Baby, His Wife and the Manager," *Guardian*, February 22, 2000, https://www.theguardian.com/football/2000/feb/22/newsstory.sport, accessed May 23, 2005.

76. John Sadler, "Fergie Was Right to Axe Posh Spouse," *Sun* (UK), February 23, 2000, 41.

77. Jack Charlton, quoted in Sadler, "Fergie Was Right to Axe Posh Spouse," 41.

78. White and Brockes, "The Player, the Baby, His Wife and the Manager."

79. White and Brockes, "The Player, the Baby, His Wife and the Manager."

80. Whannel, "Punishment, Redemption and Celebration."

81. See Andrew Calcutt, *Arrested Development: Pop Culture and the Erosion of Adulthood* (London: Cassell, 1998); and Furedi, *Therapy Culture*.

82. Julie Burchill, *Burchill on Beckham* (London: Yellow Jersey Press, 2001), xii.

83. Burchill, *Burchill on Beckham*. Stanley Matthews (February 1, 1915–February 23, 2000) was an English professional footballer. Considered one of the greatest players of the British game, Matthews played until he was fifty years old, the oldest player ever to play in England's top football division and the oldest player ever to represent the country on its national team. In narratives on the contemporary game, Matthews is often evoked as a historical counterpoint to the modern game's overt commercialization.

84. See, for example, Richard Giulianotti and Michael Gerrard, "Evil Genie or Pure Genius? The (Im)moral Football and Public Career of Paul 'Gazza' Gascoigne," in *Sports Stars: The Cultural Politics of Sporting Celebrity*, ed. David L. Andrews and Steven J. Jackson (London: Routledge, 2001), 124–37, for a discussion of Paul Gascoigne's publicness.

85. Shane Green, "Female Fans Style Pubic Hair Like Beckham's Mohican," *Sydney Morning Herald*, June 18, 2003, https://www.smh.com.au/articles/2003/06/17/1055828330865.html, accessed June 19, 2003.

86. Heather Nicholson, "A Man Let Down by His Wife and Club," *Times* (UK), June 29, 2004, https://www.thetimes.co.uk/article/a-man-let-down-by-his-wife-and-club-6mgjkg6sm57, accessed May 23, 2005.

87. David Beckham, *David Beckham: My Side* (London: Collins Willow, 2003).

88. Cited in David Bond, "Beckham's Autobiography: My Bust Up with Fergie," *Sunday Times* (UK), August 31, 2003, sec. 2, 7.

89. William Langley, "The End of the Affair," *Times* (UK), September 1, 2003, sec. 2, 7.

90. Calcutt, *Arrested Development*.

91. Furedi, *Therapy Culture*, 90.

92. Furedi, *Therapy Culture*, 92.

93. Furedi, *Therapy Culture*, 91.

THE APOTHEOSIS OF TIGER WOODS

Monetizing Racial Transcendence and Sexual
Transgression for a Quarter of a Century

HENRY YU

INTRODUCTION

As a historian, I often find it useful to remember that my own life has at times been embedded in the same flux of historical time that I study. My research, focused on ideas about race, culture, and immigration in the United States and Canada, has been shaped by a personal and academic interest in sports and popular culture. Inescapably, however, over the past two decades (since around the year 2000), this has involved a growing interest in Tiger Woods.

While Woods's quarter century of celebrity as a golfer has provided a revealing window into American popular culture, his career has also unfolded along the same time line of history as my own, providing a near-constant mirror as I continue to grapple with the complexities of cultural discourses about race and gender and sex. For half of my life, and coincidental with the whole period that I have been a professional historian, Tiger Woods has been a professional golfer. Indeed, 1995, my first year as an assistant professor of history at UCLA, was the same year that Woods entered his first Professional Golfers' Association major tournament, reinforcing in my own mind that our histories are somehow entwined.

Even my desultory hobby as a hacker—I would hesitate to use the term "golfing" to describe what happens when I walk around a golf course carrying clubs and the excessive supply of golf balls I am continually losing—paralleled the period between 1996 and 2009 during which Woods won a prodigious number of tournaments. To be honest, my time swinging the sticks was spent much less profitably, a decade of fairly consistent failure intermittently interrupted by a ball actually landing where it was intended to go. However, I did spend many hours under the same southern California sun where Woods learned to play golf as a child, discussing his latest accomplishments with colleagues in the early mornings before work while squeezing in a weekly half round on a nine-hole public course in Santa Monica.

This chapter is not offered as a biography of Eldrick "Tiger" Woods nor as a treatise on my own athletic foibles. Rather, it is intended to serve as a retrospective to a series of Tiger Woods's most public of moments when narratives and representations of him escaped the sports pages and landed on the front pages of media coverage. In that, I will examine three moments in his storied and controversial career:

(1) The wake of stories between 1995 and 1997 after Woods turned professional.
(2) The sex scandal and dissolution of his marriage in 2009–2010 that marked the beginning of a period of physical and popular decline.
(3) The return to competitive triumph with his win at the Masters Tournament in 2019 followed by a celebration of his apotheosis as an athlete overcoming disgrace and failure.

In choosing these three watersheds, my goal is in part to mark how observers have used them to complete a narrative arc of individual redemption while tracing how interpretations of Tiger Woods reflect the changing intersections of representations of race, sex, and sports over those twenty-five years. It is thus my contention that broad shifts in media consumption have blurred and reformatted conventions in the production and distribution of narratives about race, masculinity, and sex, and that each of these three chapters in his story refract larger changes.

These changing contours in the Tiger Woods story highlight several interesting developments in popular discourses about race, sex, and sports:

(1) The quickening and then the passing of fascination with race mixing as a utopian solution to racial division.
(2) The triumphant mundanity of interracial black-white sex, transformed from vicious and violent taboo to titillating fetish in popular cultural discourse.
(3) The ways in which narratives and terminology suggesting the transcendence of racial divisions have become intertwined with those fixated on the sexual transgression of racial differences.

And the monetizing of these narratives through commercial branding, whether by narrating desires for racial transcendence or sexual transgression, has been a prominent feature of how representations of Tiger Woods have shaped and been shaped by discourses of racial and sexual difference.

THE CHOSEN ONE?

The newsprint metaphor of media coverage being divided into sections ("sports pages" folded deep inside a newspaper, separate from "front-page" headline news) still held dominance in 1995 as a tangible way of understanding the genres of storytelling that diverted everyday life into events worthy of news coverage. Daily television news refracted a similar division of headline news at the beginning of newscasts, with sportscasts generally appearing after several commercial breaks, delivered not by the news anchors but by a separate talking head sportscaster. The genre of narrative representation also differed during sportscasts, almost invariably reflecting the simple winner-and-loser summation of sports results. Front-page headlines focused on the significance, impact, and potential consequences of local and global events. In contrast, sportscasts focused on the human drama of competition; the challenges associated with expectations, unanticipated losses, dips in the standings, and returns from injury dominated story lines, which were continually shaped and reworked to fit a preconceived narrative.

Such a physically tangible differentiation between front-page and sports-page stories remained relatively stable for so long, from daily newspapers in the early twentieth century through the rise of radio and television in the mid- to late twentieth century, that it bears mentioning how exceptional it was for sports stories to erupt from their confines into front-page news. The primary manner of this limited genre crossing was in the form of annual championships of national or international importance along with the occasional scandal. Tiger Woods's migrations into headline news over the past quarter century were subsequently shaped into a narrative framework for telling stories about his uniquely transcendent golfing genius while also offering a glimpse of the massive shift in media industries created by the rise of the internet and the immediacy of digital distribution systems.

Some observers saw Woods as a "black" golfer, anticipating his breaking racial barriers in a way that UCLA alumnus Jackie Robinson had done for baseball. That golf had been historically associated in the United States with racially exclusive country clubs augured the possibility that Woods, in breaking racial barriers, would also smash class barriers and disturb the bastions of wealth and privilege that private country clubs represented, at a time when Venus and Serena Williams were setting similar precedents in tennis.[1] Early Nike advertisements featuring Woods pointed out that there were country clubs in the United States where he would still not be allowed as a member. There had been a small handful of African American golfers before, but nobody with the athletic potential of Woods, who was able to intimidate his opponents while inspiring a generation of nonwhite children to pick up golf. A decade before the 2008 election of Barack Obama to the US presidency, Tiger was already a symbol of racial hope embodied in a single individual. As Hazel Carby notes in her 2000 work *Race Men*, there is a long history of representing African American men as transcendent leaders of their "race," from W. E. B. Du Bois to Paul Robeson to C. L. R. James. But Carby goes on to point out that, at the same time, the leadership of African American women has been too easily erased through the embodiment of the "black race" in these "race men."[2] Her examination of racialized masculinity explains how narrative representations of these men as leaders and potential saviors projects the hopes of others onto their bodies. The media hype over Tiger Woods seemed the latest moment in the serial desire for a savior to wash away the sins of racism and the legacies of slavery.

Confusing the categorization of Tiger Woods as a "black" golfer, however, was his actual family story. In December 1996, four months after Woods announced that he was turning professional, I wrote an op-ed in the *Los Angeles Times* entitled "How Tiger Woods Lost His Stripes,"[3] a first foray for me into understanding the transcendent hope that media narratives were projecting onto Woods, a phenomenon that extended well beyond his anticipated impact as a golfer. I noted that Woods had a complex family ancestry born of migration that was provoking fascination in the media, even if many could not quite fathom his complicated racial "stripes." The term "Cablinasian," coined by Woods himself as a child, was now being widely explicated and repeated as his own unique racial admixture of white, black, American Indian, Thai, and Chinese (CAucasian + BLack + INdian + ASIAN).

On his father Earl's side were westward migrations of formerly enslaved African Americans to Kansas, who had formed families with descendants of indigenous Cherokee and Chinese migrants riding the railroads they had helped build from the Pacific coast. On his mother Kultida's side were descendants of Chinese who had migrated to Thailand centuries before and had intermarried with Thai women to create the Chinese-Thai families who formed the kingdom's educated and economic elite. Earl and Kultida had met during the Vietnam War when Earl, serving as a Green Beret, was stationed in Bangkok. In this regard, Woods was the product of global migrations, including wartime movements.[4]

The complexity of Woods's personal family history mirrors the complicated global migrations that have shaped all people through a history of crossing paths and intermingling, and it is difficult to determine when static categories of racial belonging were applied to Woods. Newspaper articles tried to explain his complicated history as a series of fractions adding up to a whole person. A *Los Angeles Times* article of August 27, 1996, the day after Woods turned pro, declared that he had a "rich ethnic background," calculating that his father was "a quarter Native American, a quarter Chinese and half African American" and that his mother was "half Thai, a quarter Chinese and a quarter white." The political work of race as a category was to flatten such calculations, bludgeoning such arithmetic complexity out of existence with formulas such as the "one-drop rule" used in the antebellum South: the idea that even one drop of "black" blood made a person "black," leaving the category of "white" pure and untainted. But, as I argued in December 1996, beyond his default blackness:

> Tiger Woods's eagerly anticipated professional debut was hailed in August 1996 as a multicultural godsend to the sport of golf. As a child of multiracial heritage, Woods added color to a sport that was traditionally preserved for those who were white and rich. For its very significance as a bastion of hierarchy, golf had also become a marker of the opposition to racial and class exclusion. Similar to how Jackie Robinson's entry into baseball symbolized for Americans more than just the eventual desegregation of baseball but also that of American society, Woods's entry into golf was heralded as the entry of multiculturalism into the highest reaches of country club America. A multi-colored Tiger in hues of black and yellow would forever change the complexion of golf, attracting American inner-city children to the game in the same way in which Michael Jordan had done for basketball.[5]

Several weeks after my op-ed, a *Sports Illustrated* story by Gary Smith announced Woods as "Sportsman of the Year." Beyond even the anticipation of greatness referred to in my *Los Angeles Times* piece, Smith quoted hyperbolic pronouncements by Woods's father hailing Tiger as the "Chosen One." Elaborating on his messianic choice of words, Earl Woods prophesized that his son would have the impact of a Gandhi:

He's the bridge between the East and the West. There is no limit because he has the guidance. I don't know yet exactly what form this will take. But he is the Chosen One. He'll have the power to impact nations. Not people. *Nations*. The world is just getting a taste of his power.[6]

Looking back a quarter of a century on, the hubris of that quotation, the sports dad megalomania of Earl Woods, seems almost quaint. And yet as ludicrous and ridiculed as that quotation was at the time it was published, we should remember that many people took very seriously the idea that Tiger Woods would transcend the world of sport. Nike and American Express among a number of other companies signed endorsement deals with Woods almost immediately—Nike for an unprecedented $40 million—even before Tiger had won a single professional tournament. Others predicted an impact on the racially and economically exclusive country club world of golf in ways beyond what Jackie Robinson had done in breaking the color barrier in baseball half a century before. The fact that Robinson had accomplished this feat almost exactly fifty years earlier seemed to suffuse the coming year of 1997 with mystical numerological meaning.

The destiny suggested by Earl Woods, even if over the top, became eerily prescient when only months later—nearly as predicted—Tiger Woods would go on to smash records and racial barriers at the 1997 Masters. He not only won at the course in Augusta, Georgia, by a ridiculous margin of twelve strokes, but his success forced the private, restricted club into the center of a media frenzy, made all the more agitated once fellow tour member Fuzzy Zoeller commented on Woods's victory by making an off-color joke about serving "fried chicken" for the traditional Masters Champions Dinner. Zoeller's resulting loss of endorsements from companies such as Kmart demonstrated the powerful alchemy that Tiger Woods's rise had wrought, a brew of commercial endorsements and the monetization of hope for racial salvation that afforded no space for story lines such as Zoeller's racist joking.[7] Racism and racial exclusion in country club America were being highlighted by Tiger's rising greatness, and the resulting racial branding would firmly, it seemed, be on the side of antiracism. The awesome power of American corporate branding now seemed aligned with the overcoming of racial exclusion. The idea that Tiger Woods was predestined to have an impact beyond athletics no longer seemed ridiculous.

In his 1996 *Sports Illustrated* story, Gary Smith distilled Earl Woods's prophetic predictions of Tiger's greatness into a promised future unfolding through time. Smith warned, however, of the effects of the "machine" of celebrity and commercialism that threatened to consume Tiger Woods. His metaphor of the all-consuming machinery of desire that fueled mass consumption and the branding of products captured how the story of Tiger Woods as a brand intertwined the hype of potential greatness with the monetization of that hype. Smith projected how such a combination would inevitably eat Tiger alive:

> The boy will marry one day, and the happiness of two people will lie in his hands. Children will follow, and it will become his job to protect three or four or five people from the molars of the machine. Imagine the din of the grinding in five, 10, 15 years, when the boy reaches his golfing prime.[8]

Smith predicted with prophetic certainty that "the machine will win" and that whatever moral leadership the young Tiger Woods might possess at that moment could not be safeguarded or maintained for long. Smith dismissed the prophecies of Earl Woods and the absurdity of their presumption. How was a single individual, no matter how gifted a golfer, going to change the course of humanity while at the same time profiting from the crass commercial marketing of his greatness?

> The machine will win because the whole notion is so ludicrous to begin with, a kid clutching an eight-iron changing the course of humanity. No, of course not, there won't be thousands of people sitting in front of tanks because of Tiger Woods. He won't bring about the overthrow of a tyranny or spawn a religion that one day will number 300 million devotees.[9]

And yet, Smith allowed that he might be wrong, and that there really was something to the words of Earl Woods:

> But maybe Pop is onto something without quite seeing what it is. Maybe it has to do with timing: the appearance of his son when America is turning the corner to a century in which the country's faces of color will nearly equal those that are white. Maybe, every now and then, a man gets swallowed by the machine, but the machine is changed more than he is.[10]

The demographics of the United States had changed, and the potential gains to be made by appealing to these new consumers were great. Tiger Woods's endorsement deals seemed to put a new, high price tag on this potential, and that alone marked a significant change in the marketing industry. The rise of Tiger Woods had indeed changed the machinery. But Smith's insight into the moral debilitation that such successful market branding would bring also echoed prophetically in the years to come:

> Let's be honest. The machine will win because you can't work both sides of this street. The machine will win because you can't transcend wearing 16 Nike swooshes, you can't move human hearts while you're busy pushing sneakers. Gandhi didn't hawk golf balls, did he? Jackie Robinson was spared that fate because he came and went while Madison Avenue was still teething. Ali became a symbol instead of a logo because of boxing's disrepute and because of the attrition of cells in the basal ganglia of his brain. Who or what will save Tiger Woods?[11]

By 2009, just over a decade later, it seemed that Gary Smith's prophetic predictions, rather than those of Earl Woods, had come to pass.

A TIGER LOSES HIS STRIPES

For a decade, Tiger Woods fulfilled all of the promise that initial investments of hope—both in terms of athletic potential and in returns on advertising dollars—had charted for his future. Woods smashed scoring records, obliterating golf courses and overwhelmed competitors alike with an awe-inspiring, grinding efficiency. "Tiger-proofing" golf courses by lengthening individual holes or installing new defenses such as sand traps and trees took on a frantic urgency as Woods relentlessly took apart the PGA tour. By 2009, he had established a pace that could one day make him the greatest golfer in history, and he seemed well on his way to breaking the record total of career major golf tournament wins of his childhood hero, Jack Nicklaus.

When Woods played at a tournament, the number of spectators attending and watching on television soared. When he was in contention for victory on the final round of a tournament on Sunday, viewers tuned in just to watch him finish off the course and the competition. Woods was a global marketing phenomenon, more successful than any athlete who had ever lived, including basketball star Michael Jordan, who had set the previous high bar.[12] Woods also carefully guarded his privacy, protecting his Swedish wife Elin and their two children from curiosity and speculation. Gary Smith's earlier prediction of the marriage and children to come seemed prescient, while his ominous and disturbing descriptions of the maw of marketing machinery eating alive Tiger and his young seemed, in hindsight, alarmist and overblown.

In November 2009, however, just as Americans were enjoying family gatherings for Thanksgiving, Tiger Woods's family and private life began to unravel before the all-consuming eyes of the world. A year later, after constant speculation on the front pages of tabloid newspapers, the fame and fortune of Tiger Woods had been transformed beyond comprehension. From being seen as the most transcendent sports sensation in history and the harbinger of a better humanity, a Tiger Woods burning bright had lost his stripes to a series of exposés about salacious sex scandals. The revelations of tawdry texts and racy romps with porn stars, strippers, and waitresses had irrevocably tarnished Woods's previously perfect branding. That some of the women were involved in sex work created a corrosive contrast to the clean image that the marketing of Tiger Woods as racial savior had crafted.

At first limited to one woman, Rachel Uchitel, the list of Tiger's paramours grew in number inexorably day by day and week by week to fifteen women. A November 2010 retrospective in the *Daily Mail* summarized the year:

> It was almost a year ago that the previously discreet Tiger fled his Florida home in the middle of the night after his furious wife Elin discovered Rachel's texts. He crashed his car into a fire hydrant and a neighbour's tree and was transported, dazed and bloody, to hospital. The superstar golfer's highly paid image-makers went into overdrive to try to contain the PR fallout amid swirling rumours of an extramarital affair. But the scandal ballooned out of all control as a colourful procession of 15 women, including porn stars, strippers, waitresses and prostitutes, came forward to say that they had slept with Tiger. The sordid revelations led to the implosion of the sports star's marriage, destroyed his career and forever wrecked his image as a calm, caring family man. The global icon at the centre of a multi-billion-dollar commercial empire was exposed as a deeply flawed man with feet of clay.[13]

Indeed, the fall of Tiger Woods was swift and devastating. Endorsement deals and marketing campaigns were quietly withdrawn or suspended. The regal respect accorded to him by competitors and commentators alike seemed to vaporize as the scale of his cheating on his wife emerged in tabloid headline after headline.

Of course, tabloid newspapers in the United Kingdom like the *Daily Mail* had long trafficked in gossip and scandal. In the United States, dominant supermarket checkout tabloids such the *National Enquirer* and dailies such as the *New York Post* fed the same consumer desire for revelations about celebrities' private lives and their secrets. A newer phenomenon, however, were online websites that competed with printed news in breaking scandalous stories, and the speed by which these could be published quickened the news cycle. Weekly publication cycles became obsolete, and even daily news risked being scooped by online outlets such as TMZ and Radar Online, which could be instantaneously updated. The twenty-four-hour cable news cycle that had been introduced by CNN was now reinforced by online news outlets that could break a story with the same real-time immediacy.

Although I lived through those changes, I recognize as well that it is difficult to comprehend in hindsight the transformative effects of such rapid media shifts, especially in one's own lifetime. Media studies scholars and sociologists have analyzed the impact of changes in media industries in the late twentieth and early twenty-first centuries, but it is not my purpose here to examine these changes in themselves. I am interested in how narrative representations of race and racial difference have been affected and reshaped by these changes, and in this context the quickening of knowledge distribution as a process and the sense of immediacy of discovery and revelation are crucial. The novelty has been the ability of consumers to find almost immediate gratification without having to wait for the morning newspaper or the evening newscast. Consuming a story is only a quick online search away, and new salacious details refreshing current stories break continuously in real time.

The sexual escapades of Tiger Woods and the revelations of his extra-marital relationships with fifteen women are a perfect vehicle for illustrating this. Selling information to the tabloid marketplace for stories about Woods's relationships was not new. Indeed, many of the early headlines in December 2009 were printed in daily tabloids. For example, Brian Kimbrough, the ex-boyfriend of one of the women involved, Julie Postle, sold his story to the *New York Post* with the headline "Tiger Pounced on My Hot Girlfriend."[14] Kimbrough told the *Post* that Postle was a waitress when she met Woods in 2004 and supplied a pair of details custom designed for scandal mongering. The first juicy detail was that Postle had once called him from Woods's house in the middle of the night:

> "She was in his closet at 5 a.m. calling me, and he was in the background telling her to get off the phone. He knew she had a boyfriend and was like, 'Don't call him,'" Kimbrough said.[15]

The uncertain moral and emotional compass of a man who did not mind his girlfriend calling him at dawn from the bedroom closet of a rich and famous celebrity was perfect narrative fodder for the *New York Post* and its readers. Kimbrough offered the explanation that because it was "still early" in their own relationship, he "wasn't pissed." He added as way of further explanation for both his and Woods's simultaneous mutual attraction to Postle: "She was hot."[16]

The credibility of Kimbrough's testimony seemed to be strengthened rather than undermined by his own questionable good faith. Neither he nor Postle came across as morally upstanding citizens or as role models for America's youth. Indeed, the point of the article was the clear contrast between the pair's dubious morality and Tiger Woods's carefully crafted role model image as a devoted family man and racial savior. The *Post* article reveled in the lure of money and wealth in its portrait of Kimbrough and Postle. When the couple broke up in 2005, Postle confessed to Kimbrough that at one point the golfer had "invited her to Vegas, offered her money and said, 'If you want to break up with your boyfriend, I can give you some money to get you on your feet.'"[17] Tiger's generosity, and Postle and Kimbrough's dubious intentions, provided a fascinating pairing.

The conspicuous trappings of wealth popped up again, for example when Kimbrough added a gratuitously catty touch to his scandalous story of the 5:00 a.m. phone call from Tiger Woods's closet: "Kimbrough said Postle told him, 'I'm not too impressed with the house.'"[18] The recurring theme of money in the *Post* story was not so subtly designed to insinuate that at least one of Woods's female companions, Julie Postle, had entertained the possibility of the relationship with Woods being financially lucrative. The *Post* story teased readers with this potential story line—a morality tale about a series of ethically suspect women who were after Woods's money.

The possible skepticism of readers about the dubious credibility of witnesses such as Kimbrough and Postle was addressed explicitly. Several of Kimbrough's claims, the *Post* reporter stated, were verified by Nola Coles, the mother of Postle's former Orlando roommate, Morgan Coles. Nola Coles also relayed that she had shared with Postle her own sage advice about the opportunity she had been granted: "She was 20, and I said, 'You've got to get a condo out of this.'" According to Coles, Postle had replied: "Oh, no, I can't do that to Tiger."[19] Whether readers were convinced by Postle's apparent virtue is an open question.

The second salacious detail highlighted by the *New York Post* story concerned Tiger Woods's marriage:

> Kimbrough said that when Postle finally 'fessed up to the affair, she insisted Woods hadn't married his Swedish wife, Elin Nordegren, for

love.... "She said Tiger told her that his marriage was for publicity. She said it was for his image, and the tabloids and wasn't real," [Kimbrough said].[20]

This was a clever piece of tabloid metanarration, outlining for readers that Woods's marriage to the beautiful Swedish blonde model "wasn't real" because it was an "image" crafted for the "tabloids." As a self-referential wink at how tabloids work symbiotically with public relations spinmeisters and image makers to create believable yet manufactured realities, this detail perfectly captures how the Tiger Woods story lines about exposing secret scandals were themselves the crafted products of the media industry. The enmeshing of commercial branding and image making within the operations of the tabloid media was nothing new, of course, a process perhaps most cleverly captured by television talk show host Stephen Colbert's use of the term "truthiness" in 2005 to describe alternative realities that were believed or felt to be true despite being factually incorrect.[21]

What is particularly interesting about the ways in which the Tiger Woods scandal played out in tabloid headlines and story lines is how inversion worked narratively to achieve a truth beyond confirmation. Tabloids commonly deploy this version of what Roland Barthes calls a "reality effect." Barthes describes how fictional genres such as realist novels employ narrative effects—for example, long, detailed descriptions of mundane objects in a room—that give readers a sense of reality and truth.[22]

Tabloid stories often achieve a corollary reality effect and the sensation of truth by deploying narrative inversions. In this instance, the revelation of "fakeness" in the manufactured images of Woods's loving marriage contrasts with the "truthy" and more believable "reality" of his sexual affairs and secretly loveless marriage. By constantly exposing the secret and sordid humanity that lies beneath all the carefully crafted imagery of celebrity representations, tabloid stories reveal the secret truth of hidden reality. And to be sure, the inauthenticity of Tiger Woods and Elin Nordegren's marriage felt true even without confirmation because of the reality effect of inverting suspicious versions of reality that had clearly been manufactured by image makers and marketers. As proof, the ugly authenticity and sordid sincerity of Woods's sexual relations with other women were more than sufficient.

As with conspiracy theories, stories of the "real" truth underlying the "fake" surface reality are most effective when confirming suspicions about the motives of those who are powerful and rich. Tiger Woods's image was clearly crafted in order to sell millions of dollars' worth of golf equipment and sportswear. Therefore, the self-serving image was likely false, and secret details that confirmed the falseness of that image were persuasive precisely because people wanted and felt them to be true. The appeal of such tabloid exposés lies in how they invert claims to truth about the wealthy and powerful. By exposing the insincerity of carefully crafted truths that serve the interests of the rich and famous, even suspect claims from "powerless nobodies" such as Brian Kimbrough are persuasive. By effecting a reality that feels more real in its inversion of accepted but manufactured truths, their appeal lies not in the confirmation of the empirical reality of a story's details but in the "reality effect" of their inversion of suspect claims, such as Tiger Woods's to moral purity.

On December 7, 2009, a week before Brian Kimbrough's story broke, the *New York Post* had already reported a version of the same "truthy" details, under the headline "Tiger Woods' Marriage Is a Sham":

> One of Tiger Woods' latest mistresses, an unnamed former Florida cocktail waitress, says the world's best golfer's marriage is a sham. "It's only for publicity," Michael O'Quinn, attorney for the unidentified Florida cocktail waitress, told TMZ.com she said of Woods' marriage to Elin Nordegren.[23]

The *New York Post* was limited here to describing its source as an "unidentified Florida cocktail waitress" because they had been scooped by the online gossip website TMZ, which kept the identity of the waitress unknown to others in order to publish it themselves exclusively. This did not stop the *Post* from tracking down the waitress's ex-boyfriend and her former roommate's brother in order to produce its own exclusive version of the story one week later.

Observer Tim Dahlberg, writing for the Associated Press, notes that the loss of control suffered by Tiger Woods's image handlers demonstrates both twentieth and twenty-first century realities:

> The silent strategy had always worked well for Woods whenever he didn't want to discuss other issues, whether it was women at Augusta National or his responsibilities to be a role model for young African-Americans. He had always controlled the message and, if he really wanted to make a point, it would be done in a clever Nike ad or from the safe confines of his Web site. But this was different. This didn't just appeal to golf writers or the mainstream media. The other tabloids geared up to find whatever dirt the *National Enquirer* didn't. Celebrity

Web sites were suddenly filled with pictures of other women and tales which had never been told.[24]

The digital evidence of sordid *sexting* between Woods and a string of women was a perfect match for the new digital media, where quick links to the newest revelation could be posted online and spread with viral intensity. Pictures of the women repurposed from existing websites became the primary means of visualizing their growing number in an ever-expanding photo lineup. An online story from TMZ on November 28, 2009, illustrates the crucial role that web searches and screengrabs of images already online played in the unfolding scandal:

A Facebook search for "Julie Postle" yields a listing for a "Jewelie Purple," who claims to be an account manager in Houston and is related to a David Postle. The profile says "I miss Orlando." A Myspace search leads to a similar profile, for Downtown Jewelie Purrple, a 26-year-old from Houston whose mood is currently identified as "amused." While it is not clear whether these profiles belong to the woman allegedly linked to Woods, they appear to share the same age, as the *Post* says Postle turned 21 in 2004, which would make her 26 today. Furthermore, the Facebook and Myspace profile pictures bear some resemblance to the woman photographed in the *Post* article.

A Twitter profile also links the two names: the Twitter ID is @jeweliepurple, but the listed name is Julie Postle. The profile has posted just three tweets, all from March and April. One says, "Jewelie has no freaking clue what twitter is and needs to know how people have time for this?" In another, the person says she is "order clothes from china." As with the Facebook and Myspace profiles, it is not clear whether the Twitter page belongs to the woman alleged to have had an affair with Woods.[25]

Tiger Woods's sex scandals unfolded in the media within an existing economic model of how tabloid newspapers market salacious stories. However, the distribution of images of the women and the revelations about his private text conversations with them were accelerated and intensified by access to existing online material and the ease of republication. The business model of tabloid newspapers—selling print advertising by maximizing circulation via teaser headlines that tempt women waiting in supermarket checkout lines—was at first augmented rather than displaced by digital advertising online. But the tabloid frenzy in 2009–2010 over Tiger Woods's affairs with other women presaged the eventual eclipse of print advertising by digital models based on click-throughs and clickbait.

This is not to argue that Tiger Woods's troubles were a cause or harbinger of these media trends, but that the revelations of 2009–2010 provide an ideal moment for understanding how the rapid online distribution of information serves as a new vehicle for storytelling and the sharing of narratives, in particular about sex. Social media in 2009 was not yet ubiquitous as it would be a decade later—Facebook had 350 million users in 2009, compared to 2.45 billion in 2019. Website search algorithms and bookmarked links rather than individually tailored social media links were still the dominant means of disseminating information. There is no doubt, however, that by 2010 the kinds of stories being told about Tiger Woods had expanded from sports pages to gossip pages, both print and virtual, and neither he nor his image handlers had any hope of controlling narratives about him.

SEX, SCANDALS, AND THE SANCTIFICATION OF SUCCESS

In order to understand how the revelations about Tiger Woods's sordid sexual secrets became objects of fascination, it is useful to place them in the context of a series of sex scandals involving famous men in the 1980s and 1990s. In the early 1980s, Jim and Tammy Faye Bakker were among the most famous and certainly among the wealthiest televangelists in the United States, until their Praise the Lord (PTL) empire fell apart after revelations about Jim Bakker's solicitation of a sex worker in 1987 exposed an adulterous and luxurious lifestyle paid for by donations from followers. After condemning Bakker for his sins and hypocrisy, fellow televangelist Jimmy Swaggart suffered a similar fate a year later in 1998 when his own payments to prostitutes surfaced. And when basketball star Magic Johnson announced an HIV-positive diagnosis in 1991, the story was accompanied by revelations about a mind-boggling number of sexual encounters with women, alongside confirmations that Wilt Chamberlain had had even more. By the time of President Bill Clinton's impeachment trial in 1998 following his dalliance with a White House intern, the trope of scandalous stories about the secret sexual encounters of famous and powerful men had become commonplace, all some twenty years before the whispers of Hollywood's most powerful crescendoed into the full-throated response labeled #MeToo.

On the surface, these salacious stories served as a way of undermining the lofty and high-minded claims to greatness of famous men. Whether charismatic evangelical ministers or athletic stars, images of the Platonic ideal of the Hero did not include a priapic penis. And yet in the cases of Swaggart and Clinton, emotional confessions with displays of contrition and regret seemed effective in salving the sin of sexual scandal. Admitting weakness and asking (in the case of Swaggart, begging) for forgiveness fit a narrative of sin and salvation, fallen men asserting their mortality and deferring ultimate judgment to a higher power. Many Americans seem ready to forgive the sexual weaknesses of men, especially if the morality and motives of the women who accuse them are suspect.

Interestingly, despite initial shock and prurience, the potential for redemption for evangelical Christian white men in positions of power seemed to extend to black male sports stars in the 1980s and 1990s. That the scandalous secret sex lives of great men are not more marked by racial difference is actually quite surprising, given the long history of racial fearmongering that targets the alleged sexual threat of black men as "rapists" and "beasts." The violent stricture against black men having sex with white women, a vicious justification for extrajudicial murder and lynching throughout the late nineteenth and well into the late twentieth centuries, is a dominant feature of how the sexualization of racial threat operates in the violent political discourse of white supremacy. Throughout more than a century of vigilante lynching used to terrorize African American communities from Reconstruction through Jim Crow segregation, horrifically exemplified by the kidnapping, torture, and mutilation of fourteen-year-old Emmett Till in Mississippi in 1955, the invocation of the figure of the "black beast rapist" as a threat to white women has been endemic to American racial violence.[26]

The revelation that all of Tiger Woods's women were white—from his tall, blonde Swedish model wife through the cocktail waitresses, erotic movie actresses, and exotic dancers with whom he had adulterous sexual relations—framed the scandals within both a moral language, judging immoral women who were referred to as "prostitutes" and "porn stars," and the long history of sexual transgression across racial lines:

The *New York Daily News* reports that porn star Holly Sampson is the seventh woman connected to Tiger Woods' expanding sex scandal. The *Daily Mail* also referenced Sampson over the weekend.

Who is Holly Sampson? According to her IMDb page, she is a 36-year-old actress whose film appearances include racy titles such as *Descent into Bondage* and *Diary of a Horny Housewife.* Her filmography contains 85 titles, most of which appear to be pornographic or erotic films.[27]

What these women found so attractive about Tiger Woods was noted in the *Huffington Post*, an online aggregator of current news:

> Sampson recorded a video in May at the porn site Naughty America in which she says she slept with Tiger Woods at "a bachelor party for" him. Woods was allegedly "amazing," and Sampson used some bizarre language to describe the golfer: "He's like the whitest black boy you've ever met. His teeth are perfect and he's the perfect gentleman. He's beautiful."[28]

What Sampson meant by the phrase the "whitest black boy" and why he was "beautiful"—generally a feminine term of evaluation—was not fully explicated. Part of the explanation of what made Tiger Woods seem different from other "black" men in the eyes of Sampson, as well as of several of the other women coming forward, was how gentle they found him. Rather than wanting them only for sex, Woods seemed to yearn for genuine human contact and intimacy. He was a "perfect gentleman," genuinely interested in sharing details of his life and listening to them during conversations in person and through text messaging.

Jaimee Grubbs, a twenty-one-year-old cocktail waitress who had a thirty-one-month-long relationship with Woods after they met in Las Vegas in 2007, shared with celebrity gossip magazine *Us Weekly* more than three hundred text messages from Tiger, many of which combined "racy texts" with affectionate banter.[29] Following one late-night tryst, after Tiger had slipped out when Grubbs fell asleep, she texted, "[W]ell I appreciate you not wanting to wake me up but if u couldn't sleep I would have rather sat up and talked to u more . . . find out why I keep falling more and more for u ;)." Tiger responded as to why she was falling for him with a reference to his mixed black/Asian race: "Because I'm blasian :)."

Humorously playing with race and sex was a recurring theme between Grubbs and Woods. In one text exchange, Grubbs remarked that she did not follow golf, stating, "I only watch football." Tiger replied with an allusion to black men and phallic size: "Figured you would say that. Big black guys." Grubbs asserted, "[U] are my first, last and only black guy! U should feel special." Tiger responded, "[W]hy do I not believe that?"[30] Woods's suspicion that he was not the first nor last black man Grubbs would be with points to a broader context of discourses on race and sex in which their sexting and word play took place.

MANDINGO MARKETING AND RACIAL TRANSGRESSION: FROM "BLACK BEAST RAPIST" TO "BIG BLACK GUY"

The image of a threatening "black beast rapist" was an invention of the cause of "Redemption" that served to justify the violent and vicious white supremacy that ended post–Civil War Reconstruction in the American South in the 1870s and 1880s. The representation of black men as sexual threats continued via the terrorist vigilante tactics of so-called White Power groups such as the Ku Klux Klan from the aftermath of the Civil War through the civil rights movement of the mid-twentieth century.

Black athletes in the twentieth century served to both embody and repudiate these representations of the sexual threat of black men. African American boxer Jack Johnson, for example, who arose from the Jim Crow South to fame and notoriety as the first black heavyweight champion in 1908, was arrested in 1912 for taking his white girlfriend (eventually his wife), Lucille Cameron, across state lines and thus violating the Mann Act, a law passed in 1910 forbidding the transport of women for "immoral purposes." Convicted in 1913 by an all-white jury for what prosecutors argued was a "crime against nature," Johnson's lucrative career as a boxer was ruined, and he was eventually imprisoned.[31]

Johnson and other athletes of color, including heavyweight boxing champions Muhammad Ali and Mike Tyson, symbolize through their athletic prowess and subsequent notoriety the societal and sexualized threat of black male bodies. The sexual threat is mythic and malevolent, the bodies aesthetically "beautiful" as transgressive figures of desire and revulsion all at once. As Gregory Smithers argues powerfully in *Slave Breeding: Sex, Violence, and Memory in African American History*, the narrative trope of black male bodies as both sexually desirable and a threat to white supremacy is inextricably tied to the sexualized political violence that dominates popular cultural representations of black masculinity.[32]

One of Smithers's best examples is the mythic Mandingo character who first appeared in a 1957 novel of that name. At the height of the civil rights struggles, author Kyle Onstott invented a fictional 1832 plantation called Falconhurst, creating an erotic sexual fantasy that sold more than five million copies and inspired a long series of sequels and imitators. The Falconhurst novels used titillating themes of interracial sex and described the selective breeding of enslaved men and women in a process akin to dog breeding. A 1975 movie version, *Mandingo*, visually satisfied the popular demand for such narratives, a demand that increased into the 1980s with thirteen sequels to the original Falconhurst novel selling more than sixteen million copies in total.

Andrew DeVos, in his aptly titled critique of the film, "'Expect the Truth': Exploiting History with *Mandingo*," writes:

> *Mandingo* opens with a long shot of Falconhurst, a decaying antebellum plantation ruled by the Maxwells, an aging widower and his adult son. Falconhurst is a breeding plantation, and the Maxwells have become renowned for selling slaves of a particularly exceptional pedigree. Male slaves are inspected for blemishes and sold to other slavers like chattel, while female slaves are given the "honor" of being deflowered by the young Hammond Maxwell (played by Perry King). After the "wench" is broken in by the Master, and if their encounter has not already impregnated her, she will be paired up with a suitable "buck" in the hopes of breeding more human chattel. The elder Maxwell (played by James Mason), whose aging body is racked with rheumatism, is troubled that his son has not fathered any children with "human blood" (children of "pure" white parentage), thus placing the future of the family business in jeopardy. He compels his son to find a wife to bear them a male child, and Hammond dutifully enters into a marriage of convenience with his cousin, the aptly named Blanche (played by Susan George). Hammond is horrified to discover on their wedding night that his delicate Southern belle has been previously "pleasured" by another man. Her impurity disgusts him, and he angrily withholds sex from her, opting instead to cohabitate with Ellen (played by Brenda Sykes), a beautiful slave for whom he has grown "tender." . . . The emotionally and sexually spurned Blanche responds to this affront by demanding sex from Mede . . . , her husband's prize-fighting "Mandingo buck," blackmailing the slave with accusations of rape if he refuses. Blanche becomes pregnant by Mede the slave. . . . Eventually the baby is born black, triggering a flurry of violence. Hammond mercilessly poisons his wife and murders Mede the Mandingo. . . . Hammond's violence incites a slave revolt that results in his father's murder. The film closes with the lives of the denizens of Falconhurst in complete devastation, wrenched apart by the horrid institution of slavery.[33]

The film, like the original novel, turned Southern fantasies about the purity of white womanhood and the moral superiority of white men on their head, inverting the antebellum plantation delusion of Margaret Mitchell's *Gone with the Wind* by revealing the sordid sexual secrets that underpinned chattel slavery as a form of sexual and social reproduction.[34] As DeVos declared:

Mandingo was the first Hollywood film to affirm the constituent nature of sexual exploitation in American slavery, and these tangled issues of race, sex, and violent exploitation in American history were invoked and debated through criticism of the film. This point is particularly interesting for, although I would never make such an absurd claim that the film accurately represents history, it absolutely tells "the truth" (although in a mediated manner) about America's racial and sexual history.[35]

It is no coincidence that heavyweight champion boxer Ken Norton played Mede, the "Mandingo buck" who becomes an iconic visualization of the athletic, muscular black body as an object of lurid sexual fantasy. For the purposes of this chapter, however, the main point I would like to make about the 1975 movie and the four decades of Mandingo novels connected to it is how much money could be made by narrating and representing the sexual transgression of racial boundaries.

Tracing the ways in which the publishing and movie industries monetized popular fascination with this transgression in the latter half of the twentieth century, it is no surprise that there was a tabloid media frenzy in 2009–2010 to break stories about Tiger Woods's adulterous sexual encounters with a series of white women. The black male body, imagined as a desirable object in the Onstott novels and aesthetically visualized through the muscular athleticism of Ken Norton in the 1975 movie, discursively endures as the "big black guy" Tiger Woods joked about while sexting with Jaimee Grubbs. The large, muscular "football player" imagined by Woods to be attractive for Grubbs as a white woman is perhaps intended as no more than a trite, "racy" throwaway line. But the most visible and ubiquitous manifestation of the narrative fascination in the United States with transgressive interracial sex is online pornography. Pornhub, which claims to be the largest and most visited website in the world for pornographic video clips, published an analysis of its search data patterns for 2018. According to their review:

2018 was an impressively big year for Pornhub and its users. Visits to Pornhub totaled 33.5 billion over the course of 2018, an increase of 5 billion visits over 2017. That equates to a daily average of 92 million visitors and at the time of this writing, Pornhub's daily visits now exceed 100 million. To put that into perspective, that's as if the combined populations of Canada, Poland and Australia all visited Pornhub every day![36]

Although the data analysis should be viewed with some skepticism, it is nevertheless revealing in areas where the patterns described are the most mundane.[37] In particular, comparisons of search category statistics by the national locations of IP addresses reveal a striking predominance of categories involving racialized fetishes in US searches, compared to those of other countries. Although, in 2018, "lesbian" remained the most searched for and viewed category on Pornhub in the United States, searches for the "category 'black' grew in popularity," and "interest in 'Latina' porn was evident, as the term gained 14 spots to become the 6th most popular search in the country overall." The statistical analysis went on to report that, compared to "other parts of the world, Americans are 62% more likely to view 'Latina' videos, 60% more into 'Ebony' and 36% more into 'Interracial.'"[38]

A look at the videos that were returned in dynamic search results using tags such as #Interracial show the predominance of pornographic video clips showing black men and white women, with only a small proportion of the clips showing white men and black women. In contrast, adding the tag #Asian in a Boolean search with #Interracial returned a predominance of videos of white men and Asian women. The same pattern recurred for other racialized terms such as #Latino, #Muslim, #Arab, and #Oriental, which all predominantly showed white men with nonwhite women. Although it is highly likely that the self-reported identities of searchers—whether by gender or ethnicity or race—reflect purported or imagined identities, the subject categories of searches and the clear differences in search results do reflect some aggregate patterns of both supply and demand in Pornhub searches. In particular, for searches originating in the United States, there are clear patterns in the representations of what "interracial sex" means.

In this sense, "interracial sex" is dominated by images of black men with white women. If we consider the long, sordid history of racialized and sexualized popular representations of black men, the long-term historical arc is truly remarkable. From vicious images of lynched and mutilated bodies meant to terrorize, to images of aesthetic beauty and desirable black bodies described through narratives of sexual breeding that invert mythologies of the purity of white womanhood, there has undoubtedly been a shift. While the fetishizing and monetizing of black/white sexual transgression is preferable to its historical use to foment political and physical terror, it may be a Pyrrhic victory. The commercial success of portraying interracial sex as a transgressive, fetishized act is clear. It makes great clickbait.

WHO IS TO BLAME FOR TIGER'S TRANSGRESSIONS?

The prurient interest in the secret sex life of Tiger Woods was clearly fueled by a significant element of envy and delight in his fall from greatness. In a forum discussion in March 2010 on Blue Gartr about the more than three hundred text messages between Jaimee Grubbs and Tiger Woods, one poster, for instance, commented with a modicum of self-awareness about why readers in the forum thread, and people in general, were so fascinated with what was being revealed about Woods:

> I can't help but wonder all this shame and embarrassment is just here to make us (unsuccessful and poor) feel like we have an upper hand on Tiger Woods, who is basically superhuman when it comes to the game of Golf and outrageously successful.[39]

The sheer volume of media attention, and the ugly righteousness of some of the moral indignation, garnered some judgment of its own. As occurred in the 1980s with the revelations about Jim Bakker and Jimmy Swaggart, a number of Woods's defenders and apologists derided the moral character of the women. The latter were seen as temptresses, fallen women, dangerous because they were willing to morally compromise themselves and the married men they consorted with for money and material gain. Although the men should have resisted their temptations, for many who sympathized with the weakness of men who commit adultery, blame was rightly placed on loose women, who should have left married men alone.

A year after Woods rammed his SUV into a fire hydrant outside his Florida home, in a long feature article in the *Daily Mail* entitled "I Only Wanted to Be Loved," Rachel Uchitel broke "her silence on her affair with Tiger Woods." Uchitel's willingness to talk to the press was clearly aimed at setting the record straight and rehabilitating her reputation, especially in comparison to the other fourteen women. As she lamented, "People have called me all sorts of names, but they don't know me. I am not the same as the other girls and I never ever imagined in my wildest dreams that I would be caught up in a scandal like this."[40] Clearly, what she had in mind were narratives that blamed the women who had broken up the Woods family:

> I'm only telling my story now so that people can discover what sort of girl I am and learn the truth about me. If they still choose to hate me, then so be it. But I never set out to hurt anyone.

[A dress she bought for a photoshoot] is not something I would
normally be caught dead in. But I want to show a different side of
me. I've been branded as a scarlet woman but I am much, much more
than that.[41]

Caroline Graham, the interviewer and author of the *Daily Mail* article, not so
subtly juxtaposed throughout the article the "fake authenticity" that Uchitel
does not seem self-reflective enough to realize she is trying to fake. Like the
"pretty floral dress" bought only for the photoshoot that she would not "normally be caught dead in," Graham consistently allows Uchitel to undermine
her own portrayal of a better version of herself, the "much, much more" than
a scarlet woman that she wants people to know:

In person, Rachel is tiny. Like so many women in Los Angeles, she
has generously proportioned artificial breasts, plumped-up lips and
a body kept whippet-thin with daily two-hour sessions in the gym
(she's clearly obsessed by her weight and constantly asks me if she
looks fat).[42]

Uchitel shares that she lost her fiancé Andy in the attack on New York's
World Trade Center on 9/11, and that from that point forward "she has been
trying to fill the void left in her life with a series of affairs with unsuitable
men—of which her doomed love affair with Tiger Woods is just one."[43] De-
prived of the chance to have a happy married life by the trauma of her loss,
Uchitel reflects on what might have been:

If things had been different and 9/11 had never happened, my life would
have taken a different course. I'd be fat and happy, living in a big house
in Long Island with a load of kids.[44]

Instead, she moved to Las Vegas and became the head of VIP operations at
the Tao Nightclub in the Venetian Casino, eventually moving on to similar
jobs at other Vegas clubs including the opulent Bellagio. Her jobs brought
her "into contact with the world's richest men: 'I still have my little black
book and it has 5,000 men in there who are pretty much the men who run
the world,' she says grandly." Uchitel was at pains to counter any insinuation
that she'd dated Tiger Woods for his money, declaring: "I am not a whore,
nor am I a girl impressed by money or fame. . . . I have a brain and I came
from money. I never needed any man's money."[45] And yet her assertion that
she did not care about money and was not impressed by it was undermined
by her description of her Las Vegas life:

My life became one of private jets. My job was to get the high-rollers, or whales—as we called them—into the club and give them anything and everything they wanted to have the best night of their lives—guys who would order 100 bottles of Cristal champagne in a night or even blow $500,000 . . . on one night of partying.[46]

As Uchitel insisted she was "not a whore," she provided as evidence the fact that she procured girls for the men rather than being paid for sex herself. She also admitted that she was paid a fee for lining up sex workers for male clients. The fact that many readers might not make the same fine moral distinction in sex work did not seem to occur to her:

"And if they wanted girls, I'd get them girls, though you have to understand I never got involved in that side of things. Of course, some of the girls were hookers. And others would sleep with men for gifts. But I didn't force anyone to do anything. These were consenting adults. I was there to work and make money. It was strictly business." She claims she earned £300,000 a year: "I was paid well and got huge tips. I deserved it. I was good at my job."[47]

Still, it was while working as a nightclub hostess that she met Tiger Woods, and they "embarked" on their affair. As Graham tried to clarify:

According to friends, the golfer bombarded her with texts and emails promising to leave his wife and calling her his "soul mate."
    One source told me: "They were both emotionally immature. Tiger was trapped in an unhappy marriage and Rachel worshipped him. They both thought they had found the love of their lives and got caught up in the drama."
    Rachel refuses point blank to discuss her affair with Tiger. It is widely rumoured that a £6 million commercial settlement was reached a year ago. When I ask Rachel directly about the pay-off, she smiles sweetly and says: "Naughty you. You know I can't say anything."[48]

Graham goes on to point out that despite Uchitel's insistence that money did not impress her, "the signs all point to the fact that Tiger 'invested' in her silence." Uchitel had recently bought an apartment on Park Avenue in New York for more than £2 million and owned multiple apartments in Las Vegas, Beverly Hills, and Malibu, "where a £10,000 tan Hermes bag sits casually on a side table." Graham also mentions that Uchitel had "bizarrely" applied for a professional "private eye's license," saying with a "wry smile":

[Y]es, that means I will be hunting down cheating husbands. It is all part of me moving on with my life and I figured I may as well do something career-wise that I have a flair for.[49]

When Graham tells her that "she is much prettier than most of Woods's other women," Uchitel giggles:

"It's hard not to be," . . . calling Tiger's lover Mindy Lawton "poor Mindy" (referring to her looks) and adding about cocktail waitress Jaimee Grubbs: "The poor girl had a tooth missing. Honestly! She was toothless!"[50]

To be sure, Uchitel portrayed herself as different from and much better than Tiger Woods's other women. That most readers might find these less-than-subtle attempts unpersuasive led her to explain why her defiance should engender sympathy:

Women don't like me because they see me as a threat. But I just want to be loved and that got me into trouble because I made some bad choices in men. What woman doesn't understand that?[51]

THE 2019 MASTERS

If moral redemption seemed out of reach for many of the women caught up in the media stories about Tiger Woods, by 2017, on the twentieth anniversary of his stunning 1997 victory at the Masters, sportswriters seemed to have softened their portrayals of him. His fall from grace had now stretched on for years; plagued by physical injuries, Tiger was but a shadow of the towering player he had been before 2009.

Wright Thompson wrote a long feature article for ESPN in 2016 entitled "The Secret History of Tiger Woods" that attempts to humanize him, providing an interpretation of what went wrong with his career and why it seemed to all fall apart in the wake of Earl Woods's death in 2006.[52] A thoughtful, even empathetic portrayal, Thompson's piece centers on the damage wrought by the legacies of his father's dreams for him and the pressures of celebrity those dreams brought. He notes that Woods's mind had begun to stray from those things he valued most, and he became fixated on women as well as the military, both reflections of Earl Woods, before it all came to a boil in the late fall of 2009. As Thompson explains, that was when the erstwhile phenom watched his life and reputation "split open in the most public and embarrassing" fashion:

> In an odd way, it was the end. Everything he's endured these past seven years, including admitting that his golf career might be finished, is a consequence of decisions he made in the three years after he lost Earl. He'd been hurtling toward that fire hydrant for a long time.[53]

Rather than crafting a story with a beginning, middle, and end that begins with the revelations of Woods's more secretive life, Thompson restructures the narrative into one underscored by a father's death, which sparked an obsession in the son to vicariously understand that lost father, by embracing Earl Woods's Special Forces training and fraternizing with the elite units in which he'd served, and, as Thompson suggests, indulging in his father's penchant for extramarital affairs. To Thompson, the price that fame and celebrity had wrought was isolation and loneliness, a void that Tiger Woods ultimately filled with desperate attempts to connect with women like Rachel Uchitel, who had also suffered personal loss.[54]

Thompson's invocation of Woods's fate as an inevitable karmic chain of causal links, spilling into the future from the moment of Earl Woods's death, is a valiant attempt to rehabilitate a figure who had fallen so far from grace that he seemed close to the bottom. It seemed unlikely that Woods would ever return to his former greatness, and so Thompson turned toward a sympathetic postmortem that attempted to diagnose what had gone wrong. From hindsight, this assessment continued to resonate in subsequent retrospectives, such as Chris Korman's 2017 article written in the wake of a recent arrest of Woods for driving under the influence that happened to correspond with the twentieth anniversary of his 1997 Masters victory:

> By now you may see Tiger Woods' arrest as merely another tumble, the inevitable and only forward motion for a man in ruins. You may forget—or may have never realized—how the world once felt about Tiger Woods. He has plummeted from the sort of grace few athletes have ever known.[55]

Korman's article, entitled "Before the Scandals: Remembering What Tiger Woods Once Meant," is an attempt to excavate the profound sense that what was happening with Tiger Woods in 1997 was a world historical event, the kind that Hegel might have described in terms similar to the impact of Napoleon Bonaparte on world history. Korman points to a particularly devastating article published in *GQ* in April 1997, a journalistic exposé so critical and mocking of the celebration of Woods as a messiah that it led to Woods withdrawing into a protective shell, distrustful of reporters for years to come from what Korman insightfully proclaims to be a deliberate hit job:

> Consider this: *GQ* printed Charlie Pierce's classic profile of Woods 20 years ago [in 1997]. Woods had just turned 21 and would win his first major, the Masters, a month later. And Pierce was not introducing us to him. Quite the opposite: he was deconstructing the existing narrative around Woods that cast him as a savior. For mankind, not just golf.[56]

In looking more closely at Pierce's 1997 piece, Korman reflects on a range of direct and indirect assaults on the growing Woods legacy. For instance, Pierce opens with a cheeky rejoinder to Earl Woods's announcement of Tiger as the coming of the messiah by taking a shot at both the father and the company that would each have a hand in Tiger Woods's success in the same line:

> In the Book of Saint Earl of the Woods, let us now turn to the next chapter, verse 1997, in which the presumed messiah—halo, swoosh and all—is revealed to be, gasp! a 21-year-old kid.[57]

Mocking the "swoosh" branding of Tiger's Nike endorsement and noting the immature, off-color jokes that Tiger had shared during their interview, Pierce sarcastically entitled his piece "Tiger Woods, the Man. Amen." Taking the twenty-something Tiger down a notch—from the Second Coming to barely postadolescent, unproven wunderkind—was a carefully aimed shot across the bow of the supertanker of "Tiger hype" blindly plowing ahead. Pierce captured the skepticism of many observers who wondered if Nike was selling an elaborate con by misrepresenting return on investment for racial reconciliation.

In this regard, Tiger Woods was not striped in black and yellow or red—he was a solid green. For a twenty-one-year-old who had not won anything of consequence yet, Tiger seemed to be making a lot of money for accomplishing very little. Pierce had meant to poke a human hole of frailty into golf's savior, introducing an immature naïf cracking off-color sex jokes that were eerily similar to the jokes he made while sexting with Jaimee Grubbs. Throughout, he attempts to capture this Tiger in the cage of the same inverting narrative of a secret hidden underbelly exposed for all to see that would dominate tabloid sensationalism in 2009–2010:

In the limo, fresh from a terribly wearisome photo shoot that may only help get him laid about 296 times in the next calendar year, if he so chooses, the Redeemer is pondering one of the many mysteries of professional sports.

"What I can't figure out," Tiger Woods asks Vincent, the limo driver, "is why so many good-looking women hang around baseball and basketball. Is it because, you know, people always say that, like, black guys have big dicks?"[58]

By revealing the "real" Tiger, obscured and hidden by the camouflaged, fake image spray-painted by the ruthless image makers of the capitalist jungle that now owned his soul, Pierce assumes the role of large animal veterinarian, rendering a proper gelding to the undeserving beast adorned with both a "halo" and a "swoosh." It was indeed a masterful piece of cynical, sardonic writing that buzzed in fashionable circles, mocking Earl Woods's use of prophetic messianic terminology and the suggestion that somehow this silly child was transcendent.

But then, as Korman quite rightly observes following two decades of hindsight, Pierce's petulant piece was forgotten just a month later, overwhelmed by Woods's astounding victory at the 1997 Masters, where "[d]oubters and non-believers were silenced by the global impact of Tiger's triumph, just as father Earl had prophesized."[59] Tiger *was* transcendent.

Korman's article, it should be pointed out, was written before Tiger Woods's improbable 2019 Masters victory. Korman's echoing of the prophetic biblical terminology that had dominated early stories about Woods, and which Pierce had sarcastically mocked, was in the service of an eschatological narrative, a somber weighing of one's soul at the end of days. Korman's retrospective in 2017 invoked the reckoning and final judgment on the sum total of a life.

But in many ways, Korman's story also drew from a template for celebrity story making at the time, perhaps best exemplified by the popular formula of cable channel VH1's *Behind the Music*, a forty-four-minute broadcast series that started in 1997. Featuring nostalgic storytelling about once-popular bands or singers that had faded from celebrity, the recurring formula would trace the rise to fame of a band or a singer, with the inevitable climax a fall from grace roughly two-thirds of the way through each episode. The celebrity needed to hit rock bottom from an admixture of drugs, a sex scandal, or a band breakup due to petty jealousies, only to reemerge in a comeback in the episode's last fifteen minutes. Some recountings of redemptive return seemed weaker than others, but the affective power lay in the simplistic narrative arc of rise to celebrity, cut short by a tragic fall, followed by an emotional rerising from the ashes. The last act of redemption was crucial for the story to end on the right emotional tone of closure: a nostalgic reunion tour, or drug rehab and therapy, or a new marriage and hope, a little older and wiser and perhaps even a little heavier in the paunch. The core message to be revealed week to week, rinse and repeat, was this same redemptive tale of fallibility and return to grace.

Korman's 2017 portrait painted a picture of a fallible Tiger broken by the machine in 2009, just as Gary Smith had predicted on Christmas Eve, 1996. Chastened and now appreciative of the mutability of life and the transient nature of success and victory, Tiger in the 2017 portrayal was a much more sympathetic, human-scale figure. Rather than a messiah come to save the world, he was a fallen angel struggling to alight one last time. Written as he undertook yet another comeback attempt after chronic injuries and physical setbacks, the story clearly was meant to leave the reader cheering Tiger Woods's resilience amid his struggle to return to prominence. And this is where Korman's story reads like just another episode of *Behind the Music*, a "whatever happened to . . . ?" revisiting a past just slipping out of memory. Clearly, after Woods's victory at the 2019 Masters, Korman's story would prove prophetic.

CONCLUSION (OR THE PRICE OF TRANSCENDENCE AND TRANSGRESSION)

Tiger Woods's triumph at the 2019 Masters was quickly recognized as not just a return to the top of the golfing world. Even more, after years of trial and tribulation, the win marked the apotheosis of Tiger Woods.

For some writers, such as Curt Sampson in his 2019 career biography *Roaring Back: The Fall and Rise of Tiger Woods*, the Masters victory of that year was the perfect ending to a process that involved narratively reframing the beginning, middle, and end of the Tiger Woods story.[60] Unlike Wright Thompson's 2016 piece, which had made Earl Woods's death the beginning of the story and Tiger Woods's fire hydrant crash the inexorable end, Sampson's book marked the scandal as the beginning point of a "return to greatness" narrative.

Understood within this narrative arc of personal triumph after years of struggle, the Masters win was a feel-good story. The sheer depth of Woods's fall amplified the height of his rerise as the traverse of a distance even greater than his original climb to the top in 1997. At his age, after his injuries, and after his foibles, this was Tiger Woods truly coming full circle, back up from the depths of his own personal hell. But was there a greater meaning to his comeback?

For generations, great black athletes had been symbols of transcendence. They were seen as representatives of their race, for better or worse, while having the mantle of leadership thrust upon them whether or not they were deserving or even willing to bear that burden. A long line of black male star athletes, from Jack Johnson to baseball's Jackie Robinson to Muhammad Ali to National Football League legend Jim Brown to basketball's Kareem Abdul-Jabbar, had borne the brunt of representing their race. Tiger Woods's original rise to prominence had inspired a similar anticipation of his incipient stardom as a catalyst of social transformation, especially in the traditional country club environment of golf. But was this latest triumph also seen as representative of something bigger? Was it a harbinger moment of racial transcendence to come? Would it even inspire sexualized racial transgression in the way the novel *Mandingo* had done in 1957? The answer was clearly "no." The exotic smorgasbord available in the world of online porn hardly needed any new inspiration. Indeed, the top new search for 2018 on Pornhub turned out to be "Stormy Daniels," the porn star linked to President Donald Trump, rather than anything Tiger Woods was doing. Woods's Masters victory in 2019, unlike his first win there in 1997, was not the spark that would inspire a generation.

Woods's triumph remained his alone, making this a story of individual redemption insomuch as it was neither an act of racial transcendence with rippling effects for others nor an act of erotic transgression of bounded mores and social taboos. Nor was Woods's stirring victory a palliative offered on behalf of those suffering injustice. It was unclear in 2017 whether he would ever taste victory again; in fact, he had become an exemplar of the irredeemable and fallible nature of man, struggling to escape the muck of his own making. Unlike narratives about long-suffering victims of injustice whose resilience and eventual triumph are a victory for the oppressed and victimized everywhere, Tiger Woods's suffering had been by his own hand.

Biblical language had been used to communicate the meaning of Woods's story throughout the first half of his career. Well-educated sportswriters indulged in narratives of transcendence—messianic, prophetic, Christian redemption. Tabloid writers exploited narratives of sexual transgression—sordid, secret, forbidden, shameful. The language of humiliation and exposure had been used to challenge the power of norms to control and uphold morality, flipping mores and hierarchies of right and wrong. As with the differences in English between the use of Germanic terms versus Greek and

Latin terms for sex, the terminology invoked to understand Tiger Woods has bifurcated into two categories. The one focused on transgression has been guttural, redolent of the lust of the body and its strengths and weaknesses. The other focused on transcendence has been spiritual, yearning with hope, with the soul's salvation and its moral failings.

Ultimately, Tiger Woods's long career exemplifies how both kinds of narratives, in making sense of his life and giving it a moral order, also produced powerful stories of desire and aspiration. The two are not incompatible; indeed, the three moments I have highlighted from Tiger Woods's twenty-five-year career illustrate how compatible and entwined they became as narrative representations that could be mass distributed.

Perhaps most strikingly, both became highly marketable narrations of desire, helping to market items such as sports apparel that embodied hope, triumph, and the desire for recognition. Other items like pornography visualized the pleasure of transgressing norms and the beauty of black male bodies as sexual objects. Whether fantasizing about black males as slaves or saviors, the apotheosis of Tiger Woods has been a Pyrrhic victory, a triumph of mass consumption clothed in saints' robes. The machine that produced Tiger Woods led millions to consume his image. As Gary Smith prophesized in 1997, the machine ultimately consumed him, although in retrospect, it seems to have consumed us as well.

POSTSCRIPT

On the morning of February 23, 2021, Tiger Woods was involved in a single-car accident near the border of Rolling Hills Estates and Rancho Palos Verdes in southern California.[61] Preliminary investigation shows that while Woods was unimpaired at the time of the accident, he was also driving at seventy-five miles per hour in a forty-five-miles-per-hour zone at the time of impact on what locals consider to be a notorious stretch of road.[62]

Once he was freed from the wreckage of his 2021 Genesis GV80 SUV, a vehicle renowned for its safety record,[63] Woods was transported to the Harbor-UCLA Medical Center, where he underwent a lengthy surgical procedure to repair multiple compound fractures to his lower right leg and ankle. As Dr. Anish Mahajan, chief medical officer and interim CEO at the center, explained, "Mr. Woods suffered significant orthopedic injuries to his right lower extremity that were treated during emergency surgery by [o]rthopedic trauma specialists at Harbor-UCLA Medical Center, a level one trauma center."[64]

Although the long-term prognosis for Woods's health and the possible impact on his career are yet to be determined, adding a surgically repaired back leg stabilized by a rod through the tibia with an ankle and foot held together by an assortment of screws and pins to his precollision litany of ailments suggests that his future on the tour is in jeopardy. Still, as of April 2021, surrounded by well-wishes from friends, fans, and tour rivals amid yet another tumultuous round of celebrity tabloid reportage, Woods was already easing his way back into the public eye, tweeting and sharing pictures of himself and his dog Bugs, whom he refers to as his "faithful rehab partner."[65]

NOTES

1. Earl Smith and Angela J. Hattery, "Venus and Serena Williams: Traversing the Barriers of the Country Club World," in *A Locker Room of Her Own: Celebrity, Sexuality, and Female Athletes*, ed. David C. Ogden and Joel Nathan Rosen (Jackson: University Press of Mississippi, 2013), 72–91.

2. Hazel V. Carby, *Race Men* (Cambridge, MA: Harvard University Press, 2000).

3. Henry Yu, "How Tiger Woods Lost His Stripes," *Los Angeles Times*, December 2, 1996.

4. The nickname "Tiger" had been given to Woods in honor of a colleague in the South Vietnamese military alongside whom his father had fought.

5. Henry Yu, "Tiger Woods at the Center of History: Looking Back at the Twentieth Century through the Lenses of Race, Sports, and Mass Consumption," in *Sports Matters: Race, Recreation, and Culture*, ed. John Bloom and Michael Nevin Willard (New York: New York University Press, 2002), 320–53. For a collection of interesting documents about Jackie Robinson's career, see Jules Tygiel, ed., *The Jackie Robinson Reader: Perspectives on an American Hero* (New York: Dutton, 1997).

6. Gary Smith, "The Chosen One," *Sports Illustrated*, December 23, 1996.

7. Richard Sandomir, "Zoeller Learns Race Remarks Carry a Price," *New York Times*, April 24, 1997.

8. Smith, "The Chosen One."

9. Smith, "The Chosen One."

10. Smith, "The Chosen One."

11. Smith, "The Chosen One."

12. See Mark Kreidler, "Jordan Was Then; Tiger Is Now," ESPN, September 25, 2020, http://www.espn.com/columns/kreidler/1254420.html. According to Kreidler, who writes for the *Sacramento Bee*, Woods's elite status is best viewed through the reactions to when he doesn't win. He writes: "When you reach the point at which your perceived failures actually generate more ink and international consternation than your routinely comprehensive successes, you have achieved some sort of bizarre standing in your field."

13. Caroline Graham, "I Only Wanted to Be Loved: Rachel Uchitel Breaks Her Silence on Her Affair with Tiger Woods," *Daily Mail* (UK), November 13, 2010.

14. Rebecca Rosenberg, "Tiger Pounced on My Hot Girlfriend," *New York Post*, December 14, 2009.

15. Rosenberg, "Tiger Pounced on My Hot Girlfriend."

16. Rosenberg, "Tiger Pounced on My Hot Girlfriend."

17. Rosenberg, "Tiger Pounced on My Hot Girlfriend."

18. Rosenberg, "Tiger Pounced on My Hot Girlfriend."

19. Rosenberg, "Tiger Pounced on My Hot Girlfriend."

20. Rosenberg, "Tiger Pounced on My Hot Girlfriend."

21. Stephen Colbert, *The Colbert Report*, October 17, 2005. See also Ben Zimmer, "Truthiness," *New York Times Magazine*, October 13, 2010, https://www.nytimes.com/2010/10/17/magazine/17FOB-onlanguage-t.html.

22. Roland Barthes, *The Rustle of Language*, trans. Richard Howard (New York: Hill and Wang, 1986), 141–48.

23. Rebecca Rosenberg, "Tiger Woods' Marriage Is a Sham: 'Mistress,'" *New York Post*, December 7, 2009.

24. Tim Dahlberg, "Two Weeks That Shattered the Legend of Tiger Woods," Fox News, December 12, 2009, https://www.foxnews.com/wires/2009Dec12/0,4670,GLFTigerapossTerribleTime,00.html.

25. "Tiger Woods Injuries: Caused by Wife, Not SUV," TMZ, November 28, 2009, https://www.tmz.com/2009/11/28/tiger-woods-elin-nordegren-fight-accident-suv-lacerations/. The Facebook, Myspace, and Twitter posts have been removed from the TMZ article.

26. Martha Hodes, ed., *Sex, Love, Race: Crossing Boundaries in North American History* (New York: New York University Press, 1999).

27. "Holly Sampson Pictures: Photos of Porn Star, Tiger Woods' Alleged Mistress," *Huffington Post*, March 18, 2010, https://www.huffpost.com/entry/holly-sampson-pictures-ph_n_382242.

28. "Holly Sampson Pictures: Photos of Porn Star," *Huffington Post*.

29. "Tiger Woods: New Woman Surfaces," TMZ, December 1, 2009, https://www.tmz.com/2009/12/01/tiger-woods-us-weekly-jaimee-grubbs-affair-elin-nordegren-voicemail/; and "Text Messages between Tiger Woods and Jaimee Grubbs," *New York Post*, December 12, 2009, https://nypost.com/2009/12/09/text-messages-between-tiger-woods-and-jaimee-grubbs/.

30. "Text Messages between Tiger Woods and Jaimee Grubbs," *New York Post*.

31. Geoffrey C. Ward, *Unforgivable Blackness: The Rise and Fall of Jack Johnson* (New York: Vintage, 2006).

32. Gregory D. Smithers, *Slave Breeding: Sex, Violence, and Memory in African American History* (Gainesville: University Press of Florida, 2012).

33. Andrew DeVos, "'Expect the Truth': Exploiting History with *Mandingo*," *American Studies* 52, no. 2 (2013): 5–21.

34. Margaret Mitchell, *Gone with the Wind* (New York: Macmillan, 1936). See also Susan Courtney, *Hollywood Fantasies of Miscegenation: Spectacular Narratives of Gender and Race, 1903–1967* (Princeton, NJ: Princeton University Press, 2005); and Tim A. Ryan, *Calls and Responses: The American Novel of Slavery since "Gone with the Wind"* (Baton Rouge: Louisiana State University Press, 2008). For the monetizing of black bodies in the domestic slave trade, see Walter Johnson, *Soul by Soul: Life inside the Antebellum Slave Market* (Cambridge, MA: Harvard University Press, 1999).

35. DeVos, "Expect the Truth," 18. Reviews of *Mandingo* include Vincent Canby, "Vapid 'Mandingo': Sex and Humiliation of Slave-Breeding," *New York Times*, May 8, 1975; and

Rudy Maxa, "The Master of Mandingo: A Washington Publisher Helps Shatter the Myth of Moonlight and Magnolias," *Washington Post*, July 13, 1975, 193–94.

36. For details of these search data results, see https://www.pornhub.com/insights/ 2018-year-in-review#us.

37. The financial model for online video aggregator websites such as YouTube, as well as for pornography websites such as Pornhub, involves accumulating small amounts of per-unit advertising revenue while generating large aggregate numbers of views and click-throughs, in addition to some limited subscription revenue generated for a small number of content producers.

38. See https://www.pornhub.com/insights/2018-year-in-review#us.

39. BRP, post #63, "I can't help but wonder all this shame and embarrassment," BG Forum, thread "Joslyn James Makes Sexting Sessions with Tiger Woods Public!," March 19, 2010, 1:31 a.m., https://www.bluegartr.com/threads/90430-Joslyn-James-makes-sexting -sessions-with-Tiger-Woods-public!/page.

40. Graham, "I Only Wanted to Be Loved."

41. Graham, "I Only Wanted to Be Loved."

42. Graham, "I Only Wanted to Be Loved."

43. Graham, "I Only Wanted to Be Loved."

44. Graham, "I Only Wanted to Be Loved."

45. Graham, "I Only Wanted to Be Loved."

46. Graham, "I Only Wanted to Be Loved."

47. Graham, "I Only Wanted to Be Loved."

48. Graham, "I Only Wanted to Be Loved."

49. Graham, "I Only Wanted to Be Loved."

50. Graham, "I Only Wanted to Be Loved."

51. Graham, "I Only Wanted to Be Loved."

52. Wright Thompson, "The Secret History of Tiger Woods," *ESPN Magazine*, May 9, 2016, http://www.espn.com/espn/feature/story/_/id/15278522/how-tiger-woods-life -unraveled-years-father-earl-woods-death.

53. Thompson, "The Secret History of Tiger Woods."

54. Thompson, "The Secret History of Tiger Woods."

55. Chris Korman, "Before the Scandals: Remembering What Tiger Woods Once Meant," *USA Today*, May 30, 2017, https://ftw.usatoday.com/2017/05/tiger-woods-before -scandals-gq-sports-illustrated-new-yorker.

56. Korman, "Before the Scandals." For the *GQ* article, see Charles P. Pierce, "Tiger Woods, the Man. Amen," *GQ*, April 1997, https://www.gq.com/story/tiger-woods-profile.

57. Pierce, "Tiger Woods, the Man."

58. Pierce, "Tiger Woods, the Man."

59. Korman, "Before the Scandals."

60. Curt Sampson, *Roaring Back: The Fall and Rise of Tiger Woods* (New York: Diversion Books, 2019).

61. "Updates: Tiger Woods Posts First Photo since Car Crash," PGATour, April 23, 2021, https://www.pgatour.com/news/2021/02/23/tiger-woods-injured-single-car-crash-leg -injuries-california.html.

62. Faith E. Pinho, Christina Schoellkopf, and Hayley Smith, "Road Where Tiger Woods Crashed Known for High Speeds, Sharp Turns and Danger, Residents Say," *Los Angeles Times*, February 23, 2021; and Dan Mangan, "Tiger Woods Was Speeding as Fast as 87 mph before Car Crash, LA Sheriff Says," CNBC, April 7, 2021, https://www.cnbc.com/2021/04/07/golf-star-tiger-woods-was-speeding-before-car-crash-cops-say.html.

63. Nathan Bomey, "Genesis GV80 SUV, Which Tiger Woods Crashed In, Is Named Top Safety Pick+ by Auto Safety Organization," *USA Today*, March 18, 2021, https://www.usatoday.com/story/money/cars/2021/03/18/tiger-woods-accident-genesis-gv-80-iihs-top-safety-pick/4734226001/.

64. "Updates: Tiger Woods Posts First Photo," PGATour.

65. "Updates: Tiger Woods Posts First Photo," PGATour.

"SHE'S A PRINCESS, AND I'M A PILE OF CRAP"

Retroactive Apologia and the Tonya Harding Olympic Debacle

KEVIN A. STEIN, MATTHEW H. BARTON, AND ARTHUR T. CHALLIS

INTRODUCTION

The particulars of the 1994 Nancy Kerrigan–Tonya Harding scandal remain somehow present in the minds of those who watched it all unfold. On January 6, 1994, a man later identified as Shane Stant struck Kerrigan on her right leg following a practice at Cobo Hall in Detroit. Obviously in a great deal of pain, Kerrigan was shown in raw video footage screaming through tears, "Why? Why? Why me?"[1]

The FBI soon after launched an investigation on Harding's supposed bodyguard, Shawn Eckhardt, and her ex-husband, Jeff Gillooly. Based on evidence uncovered during the investigation, Eckhardt confessed to being involved in the plot and implicated Gillooly, Stant, and Derrick Smith, the getaway driver. Eckhardt claimed that he had asked Stant to slice Kerrigan's Achilles tendon, but Stant refused, and they settled on injuring her just enough to prevent her from skating.[2]

Fortunately for Kerrigan, the blow to her leg was just above the kneecap and below the muscle, allowing her to recover quickly and resume practicing within ten days. Two weeks after the attack, Gillooly turned himself in to the FBI and later testified against Harding, who would continually deny any involvement in the assault despite the recovery of some handwritten notes verified by an expert to be written by Harding and containing information about Kerrigan's practice arena in Massachusetts.[3] Without enough evidence to formally charge Harding for a crime or to remove her from the

US skating team, Kerrigan and Harding would compete against each other for the gold medal at the Lillehammer games in Norway the following month. Kerrigan would eventually win the silver Olympic medal, while Harding did not medal.[4]

Although more than twenty-five years old, this scandal still occupies an important space in the public consciousness. Newspaper columnist Greg Cote has labeled it "a dormant canker sore" and argues that there should be no "statute of limitations on her [Harding's] shame"[5] because she brought the scorn of the masses on herself. Harding remains a highly recognizable figure not only in the sporting world but in the broader pop cultural landscape because of her role in the conspiracy to physically disable her chief rival.

The incident is worth revisiting for several reasons. First, it is one of the most noteworthy sport-related scandals of all time. Sportswriter Bell Malley calls it "one of the more unethical, unsportsmanlike, and disgusting moments in sports history."[6] Similarly, a recent newspaper editorial argues: "There has never been an incident in sport like it. Twenty-five years ago, to the day, ice skater Nancy Kerrigan was turned into one of sport's most famous victims and her compatriot Tonya Harding among the most infamous villains."[7] Terry Hall, founder of the *Portlandian* and very active member of the Tonya Harding Fan Club, explains why the story continues to resonate with people:

> Her life has all the ingredients of a gripping story. It's got sex, violence, glamour, revenge, greed, mystery, tragedy, and comedy. There's comic relief in the form of the bumbling antics of what Christine Brennan called "the Gang That Couldn't Whack Straight." There's mystery—we still don't know how much Tonya REALLY knew, and probably never will. Then there's the whole commentary on the tabloidization of our media, not to mention a strangeness factor that sends the weird-o-meter right up to 11.[8]

In short, no sports journalist ever discusses the most prominent sports scandals of all time without having the Harding-Kerrigan assault either at the top or near the top of the list.

Second, publicity surrounding the award-winning 2018 film *I, Tonya* has spurred the public to reengage the scandal and reconcile new portrayals of the event with a collective memory that has evolved over decades.[9] As writer Caitlyn Fitzpatrick describes this renewed interest in the Tonya Harding case: "The scandal occurred over 20 years ago, yet the movie offers a new reason to revisit the case. In a time when some women choose to tear each other down for the sake of their own careers and relationships, the movie will surely open a fresh perspective."[10] Cote offers a similar thought: "The Harding-Kerrigan scandal, though, is back in our faces . . . a month from the start of the next Winter Olympics, thanks to the new movie *I, Tonya*, and an accompanying promotional tour that has sought to rehab Harding's well-earned reputation as despicable by rebranding her as somehow the victim in all this."[11] Cote goes on to suggest that the movie not only attempts to rebrand Harding's image but afforded her an opportunity to engage in a promotional tour for the film. In reality, however, the promoted message was less about generating revenue for the film and more of a reiteration of her lack of culpability and a reframing of herself as a victim.[12]

Third, Tonya Harding has recently changed important details from her original account, affording us an opportunity to examine a new type of apologia—a retroactive one. In her initial statements, she claimed that she knew nothing about Gillooly and Eckhardt's plans to attack Kerrigan, and that she only found out after the fact that they were involved. In her 2018 interview with ABC's *Truth and Lies*, she admitted that she had an inkling that "something was up" and mentioned comments specifically made by her husband and bodyguard: "I did, however, overhear them talking about stuff, where, 'Well, maybe we should take somebody out so we can make sure she gets on the team.'"[13] Her comment seemed to be a complete reversal of previous statements indicating that it was well after the incident that she knew Gillooly and Eckhardt had been involved in the attack.

Harding also seemed to lash out against public derision in much more dramatic ways during her recent interviews. For example, in a 2018 interview with the *New York Times*, Harding blasted her critics: "I've had rats thrown into my mailboxes, shit left on my door, left in my mailbox, all over my trucks. You name it, it's been done to me."[14] She also called the entire state of Oregon—her home state—a bunch of "buttheads" for turning their backs on her after the scandal. These types of statements are a change from her 1994 verbal attacks, which were directed primarily at those people involved in the assault who had named her as a coconspirator. Even when Harding's apologia strategies may have remained consistent, it is important to examine the nuances of her language choices today versus twenty-five years ago, to track not only changes in the verbal strategies but also shifts in the rhetorical exigencies over time.

This chapter will first provide a discussion of theoretical developments in academic studies of apologia, in particular the area of image repair in sports. Second, we will provide a summary of William Benoit's framework, which functions as the foundation for our analysis. Third, we will offer specific illustrations of Tonya Harding's recent retroactive apologia and contrast those strategies with those explicated by Benoit and Robert Hanczor in 1994.[15] Last, we will draw some conclusions about why retroactive apologia ought to be explored as a new (or potential) theoretical development in this genre of discourse and how the Tonya Harding case in particular provides insights into how we could reasonably view apologia that occurs years after an initial attempt at image repair.

RELEVANT LITERATURE

As the editors of this series can attest, research on image repair in sports is fairly sparse, given that this developing genre is in its earliest stages. Most scholars in the field have directed their attention to image repair in political and corporate contexts, although they have occasionally examined religious leaders, media organizations, nation-states, and Hollywood celebrities.

The first real foray into sports apologia occurred when Noreen Kruse examined the apologies of team sports figures in order to assess the circumstances that trigger a self-defense and to describe the strategies used by players to account for negative behavior. Kruse identifies negative behaviors in the sports world as those actions that violate the team ethic and that are perpetrated by those who place their own interests above team interests. Kruse argues that when confronted with situations requiring self-defense, "sports figures use the same strategies other apologists employ."[16] However, they also include statements asserting their positive attitude toward the game, and the discourse is generally more brief than other types of apologies.

While Kruse's study is primarily theoretical, Jeffrey Nelson offers the first real case study analysis in sports image repair by examining tennis star Billie Jean King's apology after it was publicly revealed that she had had an affair with her former secretary, Marilyn Barnett. Nelson argues that King's defense consisted of three rhetorical phases. In the first phase, King utilized the strategy of bolstering by illustrating her close relationship with her husband and emphasizing her personal honesty and forthrightness. She also shifted blame to Barnett for leaking the information to the press. In the second phase, King was defended by her peers, who argued that she had contributed a great deal to the tennis world. In the third phase, the media defended King by showing strong support for her in its coverage and by providing her with ample opportunities to articulate her defense. Nelson concludes that King's defense was relatively successful, allowing her to continue her career with little difficulty beyond the loss of a few endorsement deals.[17]

It was nearly a decade later before Benoit and Hanczor examined the apologia offered by Tonya Harding following her involvement in the attack on Nancy Kerrigan.[18] The authors note that Harding utilized strategies of bolstering, denial, attacking the accuser, and defeasibility in her February 10, 1994, interview on CBS's *Eye to Eye with Connie Chung*.[19] They conclude that Harding's chosen strategies were sound but largely ineffective because the image she portrayed in her interview was inconsistent with the audience's prior knowledge of her persona, and because she offered no evidence to support the statements she made in her defense.[20] Stephanie Foote examines *New York Times* coverage of Harding's journey, specifically how the newspaper focused incessantly on how Harding "was unable to transcend her class" and how she failed to embody the traditional script for working-class behavior. Foote offers a scathing indictment of the superficiality of the media coverage, arguing that it presented a very "hackneyed" interpretation of class as being merely economic mobility as opposed to something more in line with lifestyle or heritage. Offering such a limited interpretation of class functioned to discount Harding's real self by dismissing ways in which she might be uniquely experiencing the challenges she faced.[21]

It has only been more recently—since around 2010—that there has been an expanded focus on examining cases of sports apologia, and these studies have centered on a wide variety of athletes, sports, and the types of offenses. For example, many studies have explored the image repair of athletes accused of using performance-enhancing drugs (PEDs), such as major league pitcher Roger Clemens,[22] major league hitters Mark McGwire[23] and Barry Bonds,[24] Olympic track star Marion Jones,[25] and professional cyclists Floyd Landis[26] and Lance Armstrong.[27] Some studies have examined issues of sexual assault or infidelity, such as Kobe Bryant's alleged rape of a woman in his hotel room in Colorado,[28] the false accusations of rape against three Duke University lacrosse players,[29] and Tiger Woods's numerous extramarital affairs.[30] Other studies have dealt with violent or overly aggressive actions on the field, such as French World Cup player Zinedine Zidane's head butt to the chest of his Italian rival Marco Materazzi,[31] University of New Mexico soccer player Elizabeth Lambert's intentional yanking of a Brigham Young University player's hair during a match,[32] and Serena Williams questioning a crucial call at the 2009 US Open tennis championship by yelling at the line judge, "I swear to God I'm going to take this ball and shove it in your f***ing throat."[33] Other deviant behaviors by athletes are considered both unique and unexpected, such as New York Giants wide receiver Plaxico Burress shooting himself in the thigh while visiting a nightclub,[34] Texas Tech football coach Mike Leach locking a player in a shed,[35] NFL quarterback Tom Brady knowing that team attendants were illegally deflating footballs for better grip,[36] pictures of Olympic gold medalist Michael Phelps smoking marijuana from a bong,[37] Michael Vick's involvement in a dogfighting ring,[38] and Gilbert Arenas bringing guns into the Washington Wizards' NBA locker room.[39]

Perhaps the reason a scholarly focus on sports apologia has exploded in recent years is because athletes are more celebrated now than they ever were before. In addition to praise for athletic accomplishments on or off the field, athletes are now viewed as a brand. For example, sportswriter Kurt Helin maintained that the 2019 NBA no. 1 overall draft pick, Zion Williamson, would undoubtedly sign a shoe contract as a rookie that would surpass LeBron James's $87 million deal with Nike, likely making his endorsement contract even more lucrative than his player contract with the team that drafted him (the New Orleans Pelicans, as it turned out).[40] This fascination with sports attests to the marketing power of athletes today, and the amount they risk in engaging in deviant behaviors that function to depress their overall brand value. The public interest and drama surrounding athletes' misdeeds is seemingly also of interest to numerous scholars in our field.

We believe that this study expands on the existing body of literature in important ways. First, most sports apologia studies take a case study approach, which tends to focus on a specific context at a particular moment in time. Scholars do not generally revisit instances of apologia even when the discourse surrounding a particular crisis is ongoing. This approach makes sense in light of the fact that researchers likely do not want their analyses to take too much time to complete. Even when some events resurface after a substantial amount of time, there may be a fear that the context is no longer important or has become stale in some way.

Our approach in this study recognizes that recent attacks have created additional exigencies in the Tonya Harding–Nancy Kerrigan case. Halford Ross Ryan argues that persuasive attack and defense create a speech set, and that both need to be examined together in order to understand the interplay between the two.[41] While we do not critically evaluate the newest attacks against Harding, we do recognize that those attacks have generated a renewed need for additional image repair on the part of Harding.

Second, the cultural appropriateness of some offenses can shift over time. Some actions that were deemed offensive might not be as offensive today as they once were, or, conversely, some actions that were deemed inoffensive before might now be viewed as inappropriate. The same is true with the appropriateness of certain rhetorical strategies. Tactics that worked well before might not work as well anymore. Examining Tonya Harding's strategies in both 1994 and more recently will not necessarily allow us to see how the cultural appropriateness of her behaviors and apologia have demonstrably shifted, but rather how Harding now perceives the new exigencies based on the strategies she chooses. Third, we believe that there is room in this field to push the theoretical boundaries beyond simply applying Benoit's framework to a new context.[42]

To be sure, there have been some very important theoretical offshoots in apologia research, such as Joseph Blaney's quantitative testing of image repair strategies,[43] Jordan Compton's analysis of apologies for apologies (regretted apologies),[44] Jason Edwards's examination of community-focused apologia,[45] and Emil Towner's work on reconciliation as a unique form of apologia.[46] We individually and collectively believe that we have made our own important contributions to this body of work, such as Stein's development of *antapologia* (discursive responses to apologia)[47] and Stein and Barton's mortification-specific framework of substrategies.[48] Our hope is that an examination of Harding's retroactive apologia will yield another important theoretical development in this ever-evolving genre of discourse. Therefore, we pose the following research questions:

RQ 1: What are the retroactive apologia strategies used by Tonya Harding?

RQ 2: How do the retroactive apologia strategies differ from the initial apologia strategies?

METHODOLOGY

In order to answer these questions, we have utilized Benoit's image repair framework.[49] Although there are inherent limitations in using any preconceived framework, such as not allowing important new strategies to emerge inductively, we feel that it is an appropriate starting point since our intent is to compare Tonya Harding's new strategies with what Benoit and Hanczor discovered in their initial analysis.[50]

As a means of brief review, we remind here that Benoit's framework consists of fourteen primary strategies. They are denial (I didn't do it), shifting responsibility (He did it), provocation (I was pushed into doing it), defeasibility (Things were out of my control), accident (I didn't mean to do it), good intentions (I meant well), bolstering (I have positive attributes), minimization (It wasn't that bad), differentiation (I did something bad, but not what they say I did), transcendence (I did the deed for a higher purpose), attacking the accuser (The person attacking me has negative qualities), compensation (I'll give you a payoff to make up for it), corrective action (I'll fix the damage), and mortification (I'm sorry).[51] In addition to Benoit's typology of strategies, we have also utilized Stein and Barton's mortification framework for any statements in which Harding takes responsibility for any of her actions.[52] Although the use of this framework makes direct comparison impossible between any mortification in 1994 and in more recent years, we still feel that the application of the improved theory is helpful for illuminating our understanding of the mortification in Tonya Harding's latest statements.

Texts used in the analysis include Harding's interview with the *New York Times* printed on January 10, 2018; her interview on *The Ellen DeGeneres Show* on February 26, 2018; her statements on ESPN's *30 for 30* film, *The Price of Gold*, which aired on January 16, 2014; her statements on an episode of ABC's *Truth and Lies*, "The Tonya Harding Story," on June 16, 2018; and her interview on *The Oprah Winfrey Show* from April 23, 2009. We attempted to use primary sources whenever possible. Nevertheless, while ABC, ESPN, and the *New York Times* all provided fragments of their interviews with Harding, they did not make full transcripts available even for purchase.

In applying the framework, each of this chapter's three authors examined the texts looking for specific instances of Benoit's strategies as well as substrategies present in Stein and Barton's mortification framework.[53] We were also open to the presence of unique strategies that might be operating independent of these two frameworks.

TONYA HARDING'S IMMEDIATE AND RETROACTIVE APOLOGIA

Tonya Harding's immediate apologia during her 1994 interview with CBS anchor Connie Chung included strategies of bolstering, denial, attacking the accuser, and defeasibility.[54] In her retroactive apologia, Harding again used these same strategies, but also strategies of shifting blame and mortification that were not present in her earlier statements. Additionally, her use of bolstering and attacking the accuser were much more extensive in recent interviews, as she utilized the strategies in ways that were quite different from her immediate apologia.

Below are comparisons of the strategies used in both the immediate and retroactive apologia followed by a review of those strategies only present in the retroactive apologia:

1. Bolstering

In both her immediate and retroactive apologia, Harding used bolstering statements in an effort to offset negative scrutiny of her perceived involvement in the attack on Nancy Kerrigan. In 1994, Harding told Connie Chung that her "life was not easy growing up" and that she had very few friends: "I never got to sleep the night at anybody's house. You know, go to slumber parties or dances or anything."[55] In more recent interviews, Harding continued this pattern of emphasizing the difficulty of her childhood, particularly with regard to persistent verbal and physical abuse from her mother. For instance, she told Ellen DeGeneres in their interview: "When someone tells you that you're fat, you're ugly, you're never going to amount to anything, it makes you want to overcome that and be the best that you can be."[56] And in her interview with Oprah Winfrey, Harding emphasized the physical abuse: "Probably when I was about six, seven is when it started. She became very abusive, drinking all day long. Beating me, dragging me off the rink. Hitting me with a hairbrush, a hanger, right in front of everyone. And finally, my coach at one point said that if you [Harding's mother] touch her [Harding] anymore, we're turning you in to social services."[57] These statements about Harding's difficult childhood all functioned to garner sympathy from her audience for the challenges she overcame.

Harding also bolstered her image in 1994 by telling Chung that she had tried hard to contact Kerrigan in order to apologize for the incident: "I feel really sorry. I really do. I even wrote her a small letter, and I don't know if she received it or not. But I tried to say I'm sorry that this all happened."[58] This statement emphasized Harding's compassion in reaching out to Kerrigan even though her attempt to apologize was not successful. But Harding continued to emphasize her positive feelings toward Kerrigan in her recent interviews. She told Winfrey that she would "love to give her [Kerrigan] a hug" and tell her how proud she was of her for "being able to go forward with her life and everything." She also praised Kerrigan for her silver medal at the 1994 Olympics: "She deserved it. She worked her whole life to get where she was."[59] Harding's statements created a perception of her as a caring person who could feel authentic joy for even the bitterest of rivals.

Harding also stressed in her immediate apologia how tirelessly she worked toward her goals. She told Chung in 1994: "I've worked twenty years for it. I mean, it's my dream and I think I deserve it."[60] She would also emphasize in her retroactive apologia her love of skating, her innate talent, and her accomplishments.

During her interview on ABC's *Truth and Lies*, for example, Harding explained why she loved skating: "It was so dainty, but yet it was so powerful. I always thought it was so beautiful, you know, being out there and just doing your thing. I caught on very fast and then it just became something that you know turned out to be a gift from God."[61] One of her favorite topics was her feat of being the very first American woman to land a triple axel in competition: "I was like yes! It was awesome, there's no way of explaining how it really truly feels, except knowing, just knowing you just nailed it. The crowd just stood up and everything. Everybody was clapping for me, and I was just like oh my God. I did it."[62] During one important moment in the 1994 interview, Connie Chung asked Harding if she thought that people were talking incessantly about her because of the scandal or because of her skating. Harding defiantly responded that it was all about the skating.[63] Although that statement was made twenty-five years ago, her retroactive apologia, which continued to tout her on-ice accomplishments, was clearly meant to overshadow the infamy of the attack by emphasizing her skating over the assault on Kerrigan.

In addition to statements about her childhood, her relationship with Kerrigan, and her skating prowess, Harding also used bolstering in a couple of ways not present in her immediate apologia in 1994.[64] For example, her retroactive apologia highlighted the loyalty exhibited by many of her fans in the aftermath of the scandal, particularly those who showed up at the arenas holding placards or signs of support: "The people that were there all the time almost felt like part of me, so that was pretty neat."[65] In her recent interviews, Harding also spoke of her current state of happiness as Tonya *Price* rather than Tonya Harding and her relationship with her new family, which eliminated any contact with her mother, LaVona Golden. As Harding revealed on ABC's *Truth and Lies*: "I've been with my husband for seven years. With my husband and my son, I get my second chance at life to be loved and happy. I don't look back anymore unless I'm forced to. I am very blessed because my whole life, I would not change anything."[66] Overall, bolstering remained a preferred strategy for Harding throughout both her immediate and retroactive apologia.

2. Denial

Another common strategy used by Tonya Harding in both 1994 and in recent interviews is that of denial. In her immediate apologia, Harding was asked by Chung if she had any previous knowledge of the plan to attack

Kerrigan, to which she replied: "No, I did not . . . Absolutely not." During the interview, Chung also played an earlier Harding sound bite in which she denied knowledge of the attack: "I didn't do anything wrong, and neither did anybody else. I don't know anything. I don't know for sure anything about what's going on, at all."[67]

She did concede that she had failed to report some things she'd learned about the attack after she returned home from the nationals, but she always maintained her innocence in what she knew prior to the assault. She also called statements from Gillooly and Eckhardt implicating her in the conspiracy to be lies, saying, "What Jeff and Shawn say is not true. Anybody who knows me knows it's not true."[68] In her retroactive apologia, Harding continued to deny any knowledge of the plan to attack Kerrigan. Specifically, during her interview on ESPN's *30 for 30*, she said: "Of course not, everybody out there that truly knows me knows that I was not involved in any of the planning or anything."[69]

She also offered several denials that were slightly different from those presented in her immediate apologia. First, she denied involvement by claiming that she was surprised when she found out about the attack and was even scared that she might be the next victim. For example, after receiving a phone call from Portland, Oregon, area sports broadcaster Ann Schatz telling her about the attack: "She said what? Are you kidding? Really? How could something like this happen? And then when we went to the rink, I couldn't focus. I mean, they never caught anybody, so how do we know that this person isn't here trying to take out anybody else?"[70]

Harding also denied that she had felt any relief that Kerrigan would not be able to skate during the US National Figure Skating Championships, the tournament to decide the two skaters who would represent the United States in the Olympics. To this accusation, she responded curtly, "Absolutely not."[71] Harding also offered a new denial regarding the presence of her handwriting on a note the FBI uncovered with information about the address of Kerrigan's practice facility in Massachusetts. Although forensic evidence at the time verified that the handwriting was Tonya Harding's, she dismissed that she had written the notes: "My handwriting was on a piece of paper, I did not write that." When asked again, she said: "Correct, I did not write that. Nobody wanted to believe me."[72] Harding used these denials to extend earlier denials regarding her knowledge about the planned attack and implications of her involvement with her alleged coconspirators to more specific denials regarding the evidence collected by the FBI, as well as her own state of mind after learning of the attack.

3. Shifting Blame

Surprisingly, Harding did not engage in strategies of shifting blame during her 1994 interview, but she used the strategy frequently in her retroactive apologia. However, in her 2018 interview for ABC's *Truth and Lies*, she said that she knew that Gillooly and Eckhardt were involved in the attack, but only after the assault took place: "Yes, I knew Shawn was involved, I knew that Jeff had done something wrong, but I didn't know how far at that point."[73] When asked if Gillooly had acted differently after the attack, she said, "Not at that time, it was like within the next five days or something, he started acting funny." She also recounted how Gillooly had physically beaten her after she asked him about his involvement: "I point blank asked him what's going on, have you . . . what did you do? He freakin' just went bam and just nailed me. You know, and that's when I started wondering, and you know trying to piece things together and stuff."[74]

Harding also claimed that Gillooly threatened to kill her if she spoke to the authorities: "I was scared to death, Jeff told me he's going to kill me if I ever open my mouth about anything. But I told them what I knew, and what I had heard, what had happened, and was said in phone calls, and things like that since I had gotten back."[75] Although Harding's immediate apologia included denials of her involvement and attacks against Gillooly and Eckhardt as liars, she did not specifically blame them for the assault on Kerrigan. However, she does this explicitly in her retroactive apologia.

4. Attacking the Accuser

Another strategy present in both the immediate and retroactive apologia was attacking the accuser. In 1994, most of Harding's attacks were directed at Jeff Gillooly, the ex-husband who along with bodyguard Shawn Eckhardt had told the FBI that Harding was involved in the plot against Kerrigan. Harding returned fire at her accusers during her interview with Connie Chung. She argued that Gillooly was doing this to hurt her: "I just want to know why. I never did anything to hurt him. If I ever did anything it was to stick up for him and protect him. And he does this to me."[76]

Additionally, she painted Gillooly as an abuser who made her fear for her safety. Because Harding also accused her own mother of being an abuser, we believe that a clarification here is in order: Harding's portrayals of Gillooly as a violent man functioned to attack a person who directly implicated her in the conspiracy. When he accused Harding of helping to plan and execute the scheme, her hostile statements in response functioned as attacks against the accuser. Harding's mother, on the other hand, created harsh conditions during Harding's childhood that she, in turn, used to generate sympathy from her audience. Harding's mother was not in any direct way a player in the scandal to attack Kerrigan, making those statements instances of bolstering.

In the retroactive apologia, Harding continued to attack Gillooly. She called him an abuser, a controlling person, and an idiot. For example, in her interview on ABC's *Truth and Lies*, she recounted the following: "One that sticks out in my head, we were at the 7-Eleven, and I got nachos, and he said that they would make me fat. And he hit them out of my hand, and then he grabs me and says, let's go and just bam."[77] She also described how her real-life relationship with Gillooly was even worse than the one portrayed in the film *I, Tonya*: "People don't understand that what you guys see in the movie is nothing. That was the smallest little bits and pieces. I mean, my face was bruised. My face was put through a mirror, not just broken onto it. *Through* it. I was shot. That was true."[78] She also mocked Gillooly and Eckhardt as "idiots," claiming that Eckhardt in particular was "dumb as a post,"[79] and that her biggest regret was "being married for the first time to an idiot."[80]

What separates the instances of attacking the accuser in the immediate and retroactive apologia is the level of disdain emanating from Harding toward the public, the media, the US Figure Skating Association, and particularly Nancy Kerrigan. These attacks were not present in the initial apologia in 1994. For example, Harding lashed out at the public during her interview with the *New York Times*: "You all disrespected me, and it hurt. I'm a human being, and it hurt my heart. I was a liar to everybody but still, 23 years later, finally everybody can just eat crow. That's what I have to say."[81]

She also felt that the ridicule directed toward her had reached unjustifiable levels: "I moved from Oregon to Washington because Oregon was buttheads. I *disappointed* them. It's like, how can I disappoint a whole state? Wait a second, how can I disappoint a whole *country*?"[82] She claimed that the public wanted to hit her "with sticks and baseball bats or whatever."[83] Harding also aimed a fair amount of vitriol toward the media for its coverage of the incident. In her *New York Times* interview, she maintained that the media had "abused" her,[84] and during her *Truth and Lies* interview, she argued: "The press threw me to the wolves, pretty much everybody treated me like I was nothing."[85] Harding also attacked the US Figure Skating Association for barring her from skating competitively for the rest of her life:

I lost everything, I mean everything. I never get to skate again, ever in competition, I'm kicked out of the association, but yet we'll let her skate in the Olympics. That's fine, let her skate. It's ok, she won't win.

> She won't get the marks that she deserves, she won't get anything in her life to do with skating ever again. Ever, ever, again. . . . I mean that was pretty much the worst thing that could ever happen to me, because I didn't have any other source of where I could go, what I could do, I mean what am I going to do with my life now?[86]

Understandably, Harding expressed hostility toward the people who either ridiculed her or had a role in her being barred from competitive skating. However, the most surprising target of Harding's attack during her retroactive apologia was Nancy Kerrigan herself.

Harding attacked Kerrigan from all directions—even in spite of having complimented Kerrigan's skating as part of her bolstering strategies. One such attack against Kerrigan was over her endearing public image as opposed to Harding's "rough around the edges" persona. Harding expressed this frustration in her interview with ESPN's *30 for 30*: "Nancy is a princess, you know, that's how everybody has seen her. She's a princess, and I'm a pile of crap. So, you know, I stayed at the dorms, I had security with me 24/7, and she got to do whatever she wanted to do. But that's okay . . . [extended pause]. You know, it's not okay, it's not okay—how I was treated by everybody out there was not okay."[87]

Apart from the contrast in their public images, Harding was also upset at Kerrigan's behavior at the Olympic medal ceremony following her loss to Ukrainian skater Oksana Baiul: "She was the crybaby who didn't win the gold, you know. I'm sorry, I've never said this before, just shut up, nobody wants to hear your whining, OK, you got a silver medal at the Olympics and all you can do is poo poo it away? I just don't think it's right."[88] Harding's verbal attacks against Kerrigan reflect a level of resentment over public adoration for Kerrigan and her Olympic achievements. Harding was also upset at Kerrigan for a perceived slight after she tried to apologize for the attack:

> I went up right to her when I first saw her and told her how sorry I was for being around the people that had done this to her. For being involved with people that were there, you know, because I mean that used to be my husband, you know. But, she just blew it off like it was nothing, I thought we were friends, all of us had been on tour for years and for her to treat me like that, like I was nothing, like she was above me, I mean that was . . . that's rude.[89]

These statements demonstrate unique attacks against the accuser. Harding criticized Kerrigan for her image as a princess, for her poor sportsmanship after winning the silver medal, and for being unresponsive to Harding's attempts to reconcile with her after the assault.

5. Defeasibility

Defeasibility was not frequently used either in 1994 or in Harding's more recent interviews. Benoit and Hanczor argue that Harding used defeasibility in her interview with Connie Chung when she said that she did not go to the authorities right away because "everything just happened so fast."[90] She also claimed that she was afraid of being hurt.

Similarly, in her *30 for 30* interview, Harding reiterates the same strategy to explain why she was not more helpful in the investigation: "I mean everything just, you know, you get hit by everything all at once and you just want to crawl in the closet and say 'Oh hey, leave me alone,' because you just don't know what's happening."[91] These strategies function to explain why a rational choice for most people, such as cooperating with the authorities, may have eluded Harding during the chaos that followed the attack on Kerrigan.

6. Mortification

Although Harding denied any role in the attack in her 1994 immediate apologia, she retroactively took some responsibility for parts of the incident in her recent interviews. For example, she described her deal with prosecutors in which she pled guilty to hindering prosecution. In her *30 for 30* interview, she said: "I pleaded guilty to hindering prosecution. My attorney said that either I would take that, or I would have to go to jail for a year, or something like that. I admitted to knowing after the fact, but because I did not report it, that's hindering prosecution."[92]

Obviously, this statement does not function as a very powerful example of mortification, since Harding only admitted that she did not immediately report what she knew rather than concede involvement in the attack itself. Additionally, she admitted to pleading guilty to something, which is far different from saying she believed that she actually did impede prosecution.

Harding also used mortification to express that she had already apologized to Kerrigan. Even though she did not explicitly apologize in her recent interviews, she did imply that at one point she felt remorse simply by identifying earlier instances in which she had apologized. For example, when asked about her earlier apologies to Kerrigan during her *Truth and Lies* interview, Harding said: "Enough apologizing. She's got her life. I've got my life. We both have wonderful lives. And that should be all that matters."[93]

In her interview with Oprah Winfrey, Harding was again asked if she had apologized enough to Kerrigan: "I believe I have. I believe I have."[94] These statements fall within Stein and Barton's mortification framework as examples of asking forgiveness and seeking acceptance. Harding did not ask for forgiveness here, but she pushed her audience to accept previous apologies as sufficient to satisfy her rhetorical constraints and thereby avoid having to apologize any more in the future.[95]

Harding's most surprising mortification in her retroactive apologia came as she admitted to overhearing Jeff Gillooly and Shawn Eckhardt discuss the attack months before Kerrigan was assaulted. During her interview on ABC's *Truth and Lies*, Harding stated: "I did, however, overhear them talking about stuff where, well, maybe we should take somebody out so we can make sure she gets on the team. And I remember telling them, I go 'what the hell are you talking about? I can skate.'"[96] When asked if this conversation took place before the attack, she answered: "This was like a month or two months before. But they were talking about skating and saying 'well, maybe somebody should be taken out then so then, you know, she can make it.'" The interviewer then asked if this conversation came back to her recollection after the attack, and Harding said, "It popped into my head two, three days after we got back."[97] Here, Harding admitted that she did know something was being planned months before the assault on Kerrigan, even though she had denied any knowledge of the plan in all of her previous instances of apologia and persistently claimed that she only found out about the plot days after the attack occurred.

DISCUSSION

Several interesting insights can be gleaned from this analysis as we work from the particular case out toward the implications of a broader conceptualization of image repair. Let's first consider the strategies employed by Harding in her immediate and retroactive apologia and whether they were effective.

Harding utilized six different strategies, namely bolstering, denial, attacking the accuser, defeasibility, shifting blame, and mortification. Of these, two were exclusive instruments in the retroactive apologia (i.e., shifting blame and mortification). Our discussion here is primarily focused on those strategies that provide new insights into how apologies can be understood over time.

Harding used bolstering as a constant strategy throughout her discourse. We are not as concerned with the frequency of the strategy as much as about the way this strategy functions. Harding's use of bolstering is unique because it insulated her from attacks that attempted to pigeonhole her image as nothing more than that of a common villain to be held in disdain, despite her athletic prowess. The rhetorical friction occurred because Harding was trying to define her legacy in precisely the opposite manner. Harding's approach was a way of mediating the context while trying to ensure that the knocks against her image did not outweigh her accomplishments. The attempt was designed to generate feelings of guilt in the audience for cynical, jaded, and unfair judgments against her. Despite what bolstering can or should do, in this case we suggest that the strategy was insufficient notwithstanding her consistent use of it. Simply stated, her accomplishments, like landing a triple axel in competition, never outweighed her self-perpetuated negative image, like referencing her friendless childhood and lack of dating opportunities, and referring to herself as "trailer trash."[98] Once the scandal took an additional toll on her image, the imbalance was even more pronounced.

Another ineffective strategy came in Harding's use of denial. Perhaps not surprisingly, Harding, like many people would, continued to deny allegations of her involvement in the conspiracy and also to deny accusations that had not surfaced the first time (such as the handwritten note). The trouble is not that she denied these claims but that she changed her story. Further, she chose to pair her denial closely with her bolstering statements, which appears to be a subtle attempt to keep the public from examining the inconsistencies in the denial too carefully. However, this decision was not as masked as perhaps she had hoped. For instance, note that in the first apologia, she more directly denied knowing about the plan to attack Kerrigan. In later denials, she used a more implied premise (e.g., being surprised and scared), leading the audience to conclude that she had nothing to do with it because a person who was actually involved in a crime would likely not express genuine shock at the offense or fear for her personal safety. We should also note that Harding's shifting blame strategies functioned as a bridge, making it seem logical for the audience to accept her denials and view her attacks on her accusers as a natural next step in her image repair effort. This bridge happens because no one can shift blame without also denying personal involvement, nor can a person shift blame for a grievous act without simultaneously attacking the offender's character, which is exactly what Harding did.

Oddly enough, Harding's attacks, which clearly berated Kerrigan, were mitigated by her bolstering strategies, which praised Kerrigan's accomplishments. The inconsistency here suggests that Harding felt Kerrigan had character deficiencies in spite of her silver medal Olympic performance. Such characterization was precisely how Harding wanted the general public to view her own identity and her legacy. The implication is that Harding is not a perfect person, but we should ignore that and focus on her skating prominence. Moreover, the fact that she unleashed such a litany of attacks in the retroactive apologia attests to a human need to be heard. Harding's frustrations, likely mounting for as long as twenty-five years, were bound to erupt when the opportunity presented itself. Perhaps the simplest explanation for the plethora of attacks is that Harding was incapable of improving her own public image and, therefore, had no other choice than to diminish Kerrigan's stature.

Our analysis leans heavily toward Harding's inability to demonstrate appropriate emotional responsibility, though she did attempt to show some remorse in her retroactive apologia. However, in the process, Harding essentially unraveled her entire denial. She could not claim to find out about an attack after it occurred and then claim she knew beforehand of the attack. Even though her efforts could be viewed as a traditional form of mortification because she attempted to take some responsibility, it is an extremely weak form of mortification because she never claimed to have directly hindered prosecution or to have misled the public. Harding also never admitted to having written the note found in the dumpster containing the address of Kerrigan's practice facility. Even in saying she heard Eckhardt and Gillooly talking, she did not admit to being a part of the plot. Harding was also clearly frustrated that she was repeatedly asked about her apology to Kerrigan, responding that she had apologized enough.

Stein and Barton, in an earlier article, argued that it is the offended individual who gets to determine the timeline for when forgiveness is granted, and not the offender. In the case of Kerrigan, it seems natural that she would be unwilling to forgive Harding if she genuinely believed that Harding had an instrumental role in planning the attack. An apology from Harding for being married to a man who attacked her and an admission of misleading investigators would certainly not be enough to reconcile her relationship with Kerrigan.[99]

CONCLUSION

This analysis demonstrates the importance of examining apologia responses over time to better understand how and why they are created. Retroactive apologia is an important theoretical development in image repair studies for three reasons.

First, certain behaviors are so inexplicable that they offer an ever-present fissure in the cultural zeitgeist. Even in a situation like the Harding-Kerrigan controversy, which has been marginally resolved or has somewhat escaped the news cycle, there remains an unanswered question about the nature of sports and how far one is willing to go to succeed. It might be easy to conclude that one "would never do something so heinous," but the haunting reality is that we cannot be totally sure what we might do in our own desperate moments. When we look at Harding's retroactive apologia, we remember that an important role of sports figures is to provide an entertaining diversion from the stress and responsibility of everyday life. Such satisfaction can only occur when athletes execute their primary responsibility, which is to perform well while following the rules, thereby satisfying the public's need for competition, involvement, and winning. Harding did not do this because she had turned herself into, according to one blogger, "the First Lady of American Garbage, the mother of our trailer-park monarchy"—someone completely unworthy of public adoration.[100]

Second, as Herb Simons suggests, a deeper understanding of the rhetorical situation is necessary to move apologia scholarship beyond simple classifications of rhetorical strategies.[101] Although our retroactive analysis does classify strategies, its primary purpose is to examine the evolution of those strategies over time as well as how they interact with each other. This approach allows for more complete conclusions about why the strategies are effective or why they resonate uniquely with different audiences.

Finally, retroactive apologia investigations allow critics to view Halford Ross Ryan's speech set (attack and defense) in a noncompartmentalized way by recognizing that more attacks can follow a seemingly completed case of apologia and necessitate a further need for more image repair. Ryan argues that there is an interplay between the parts of the speech set, which implies that those parts are dynamic and in constant flux. When seeking a definitive accuracy with their interpretations, critics need to consider as much of the rhetorical situation as possible at the time of analysis. If critics hope to derive answers to the larger question of "What does this all mean?,"[102] they need to consider the totality of available textual evidence, which often includes discourse beyond the boundaries of the original case.

As we conclude this analysis, we are reminded of the fact that extraordinary cases like the Kerrigan attack create a natural impulse to conclude that the perfect blend of strategies can "make everything all better." However, this case makes clear that sometimes even the best apologies might not ever settle the wake. The Harding-Kerrigan scandal has already lasted more than twenty-five years, and the fallout may continue for years to come. Even Harding herself is resigned to this realization that this shadow will "be with me for the rest of my life."[103]

NOTES

1. Peggy Truong, "A Definitive Timeline of the Tonya Harding and Nancy Kerrigan Figure Skating Controversy," *Cosmopolitan*, January 16, 2018, https://www.cosmopolitan .com/entertainment/celebs/a15172746/tonya-harding-nancy-kerrigan-timeline-scandal-hit/.

2. Matt Crossman, "Harding-Kerrigan 20 Years Later: Remembering the Stunning, Life-Changing Attack," *Bleacher Report*, December 19, 2013, https://bleacherreport.com/ articles/1887592-harding-kerrigan-20-years-later-remembering-the-stunning-life-changing -attack.

3. Truong, "A Definitive Timeline."

4. Harvey Araton, "Winter Olympics; Baiul Wins as Kerrigan Smiles Away Her Tears," *New York Times*, February 26, 1994, https://www.nytimes.com/1994/02/26/sports/winter -olympics-baiul-wins-as-kerrigan-smiles-away-her-tears.html.

5. Greg Cote, "Pathetic, Hopeless Effort to Unburden One Athlete from Her Shame 24 Years Later," *Miami Herald*, January 10, 2018, https://www.wnewsj.com/sports/local-sports-1/60598/ column-the-pathetic-hopeless-effort-to-unburden-one-athlete-from-her-shame-24-years -later.

6. Bell Malley, "The 20 Biggest Scandals in Sports History," *Bleacher Report*, September 28, 2011, https://bleacherreport.com/articles/854416-the-20-biggest-scandals-in-sports-history.

7. "Remembering the Nancy Kerrigan–Tonya Harding Scandal, 25 Years Later," *New Zealand Herald*, January 7, 2019, https://www.nzherald.co.nz/sport/news/article.cfm?c_id=4& objectid=12186635.

8. Viviana Olen and Matt Harkins, "The Cult of Tonya Harding," *Vulture*, December 6, 2017, https://www.vulture.com/2017/12/the-cult-of-tonya-harding.html.

9. Craig Gillespie, dir., *I, Tonya*, 30West Films, 2017.

10. Caitlyn Fitzpatrick, "The Tonya Harding and Nancy Kerrigan Scandal Is Still Completely Unsettling, Even 2 Decades Later," *Popsugar*, April 22, 2018, https://www.popsugar .com/celebrity/Tonya-Harding-Nancy-Kerrigan-True-Story-44103595.

11. Cote, "Pathetic, Hopeless Effort to Unburden One Athlete."

12. Cote, "Pathetic, Hopeless Effort to Unburden One Athlete."

13. David Sloan, prod., "Truth and Lies: The Tonya Harding Story," ABC, June 16, 2018. See also Lauren Effron and Alexa Valiente, "Tonya Harding Says She 'Knew Something Was Up' before Infamous 1994 Baton Attack on Nancy Kerrigan," ABC News, January 2, 2018, https://abcnews.go.com/US/tonya-harding-knew-infamous-1994-baton-attack-nancy/ story?id=52048510.

14. Taffy Brodesser-Akner, "Tonya Harding Would Like Her Apology Now," *New York Times*, January 10, 2018, https://www.nytimes.com/2018/01/10/movies/tonya-harding-i-tonya -nancy-kerrigan-scandal.html?_r=0.

15. William Benoit and Robert Hanczor, "The Tonya Harding Controversy: An Analysis of Image Restoration Strategies," *Communication Quarterly* 42, no. 4 (1994): 416–33.

16. Noreen W. Kruse, "Apologia in Team Sport," *Quarterly Journal of Speech* 67, no. 3 (1981): 283.

17. Jeffrey Nelson, "The Defense of Billie Jean King," *Western Journal of Communication* 48, no. 1 (1984): 92–102.

18. Benoit and Hanczor, "The Tonya Harding Controversy."

19. Connie Chung, *Eye to Eye with Connie Chung*, CBS, February 10, 1994.

20. Benoit and Hanczor, "The Tonya Harding Controversy."

21. Stephanie Foote, "Making Sport of Tonya: Class Performance and Social Punishment," *Journal of Sport and Social Issues* 27, no. 1 (2003): 6.

22. J. Scott Smith, "From the Mitchell Report to Brian McNamee: Roger Clemens's Image Repair Discourse," in *Repairing the Athlete's Image: Studies in Sports Image Restoration*, ed. Joseph R. Blaney, Lance R. Lippert, and J. Scott Smith (Lanham, MD: Rowman and Littlefield, 2013), 9–26.

23. John McGuire, Lori Melton McKinnon, and Wayne Wanta, "'Big Mac' with a Side of Steroids: The Image Repair Strategies of Mark McGwire," in *Repairing the Athlete's Image: Studies in Sports Image Restoration*, ed. Joseph R. Blaney, Lance R. Lippert, and J. Scott Smith (Lanham, MD: Rowman and Littlefield, 2013), 203–22.

24. J. Scott Smith, "Defense of an Anti-Hero: Barry Bonds's 'State of the Great Address,'" in *Repairing the Athlete's Image: Studies in Sports Image Restoration*, ed. Joseph R. Blaney, Lance R. Lippert, and J. Scott Smith (Lanham, MD: Rowman and Littlefield, 2013), 41–58.

25. Michael R. Kramer, "Image Repair Media Interview as *Apologia* and *Antapologia*: Marion Jones on *The Oprah Winfrey Show*," in *Repairing the Athlete's Image: Studies in Sports Image Restoration*, ed. Joseph R. Blaney, Lance R. Lippert, and J. Scott Smith (Lanham, MD: Rowman and Littlefield, 2013), 59–70. See also David C. Ogden and Joel Nathan Rosen, eds., *A Locker Room of Her Own: Celebrity, Sexuality, and Female Athletes* (Jackson: University Press of Mississippi, 2013).

26. Mark Glantz, "The Floyd Landis Doping Scandal: Implications for Image Repair Discourse," *Public Relations Review* 36, no. 2 (2010): 157–63.

27. Jimmy Sanderson and Marion E. Hambrick, "Riding Along with Lance Armstrong: Exploring Antapologia in Response to Athlete Adversity," *Journal of Sports Media* 11, no. 1 (Spring 2016), 1–24.

28. Rachel A. Griffith, "Power, Privilege, and the Surprising Absence of Repair: Kobe Bryant and Interest Convergence," in *Repairing the Athlete's Image: Studies in Sports Image Restoration*, ed. Joseph R. Blaney, Lance R. Lippert, and J. Scott Smith (Lanham, MD: Rowman and Littlefield, 2013), 97–122.

29. María E. Len-Ríos, "Image Repair Strategies, Local News Portrayals and Crisis Stage: A Case Study of Duke University's Lacrosse Team Crisis," *International Journal of Strategic Communication* 4, no. 4 (2010): 267–87.

30. William L. Benoit, "Tiger Woods's Image Repair: Could He Hit One Out of the Rough?," in *Repairing the Athlete's Image: Studies in Sports Image Restoration*, ed. Joseph R. Blaney, Lance R. Lippert, and J. Scott Smith (Lanham, MD: Rowman and Littlefield, 2013),

89–96. See also L. Paul Husselbee and Kevin A. Stein, "In the Rough: Tiger Woods' Apology and Journalistic *Antapologia*," *Journal of Sports Media* 7, no. 1 (2012): 235–52.

31. Kevin A. Stein, Paul D. Turman, and Matthew H. Barton, "Understanding the Voice of the Fan: *Apologia, Antapologia*, and the 2006 World Cup Controversy," in *Sports Mania: Essays on Fandom and the Media in the 21st Century*, ed. Lawrence W. Hugenberg, Paul M. Haridakis, and Adam C. Earnheardt (Jefferson, NC: McFarland, 2008), 86–102.

32. Jordan L. Compton, "Unsports(wo)manlike Conduct: An Image Repair Analysis of Elizabeth Lambert, the University of New Mexico, and the NCAA," in *Repairing the Athlete's Image: Studies in Sports Image Restoration*, ed. Joseph R. Blaney, Lance R. Lippert, and J. Scott Smith (Lanham, MD: Rowman and Littlefield, 2013), 253–66.

33. LeAnn M. Brazeal, "Belated Remorse: Serena Williams's Image Repair Rhetoric at the 2009 U.S. Open," in *Repairing the Athlete's Image: Studies in Sports Image Restoration*, ed. Joseph R. Blaney, Lance R. Lippert, and J. Scott Smith (Lanham, MD: Rowman and Littlefield, 2013), 239–52.

34. Mark Glantz, "Plaxico Burress Takes His Best Shot," in *Repairing the Athlete's Image: Studies in Sports Image Restoration*, ed. Joseph R. Blaney, Lance R. Lippert, and J. Scott Smith (Lanham, MD: Rowman and Littlefield, 2013), 187–202.

35. Kevin A. Stein, Paul D. Turman, and Matthew H. Barton, "In the Dark at Texas Tech: News Coverage Involving the Image Repair Discourse of Mike Leach and Adam James," in *Repairing the Athlete's Image: Studies in Sports Image Restoration*, ed. Joseph R. Blaney, Lance R. Lippert, and J. Scott Smith (Lanham, MD: Rowman and Littlefield, 2013), 203–22.

36. Mary Lou Sheffer, Brad Schultz, and Willie Tubbs, "#deflategate: Sports Journalism and the Use of Image Repair Strategy on Twitter," *Newspaper Research Journal* 39, no. 1 (2018): 69–82.

37. Rod L. Troester and Lindsay Johns, "The Michael Phelps Saga: From Successful Olympian, to Pot Smoker Caught on Camera, to Renewed Role Model and Brand," in *Repairing the Athlete's Image: Studies in Sports Image Restoration*, ed. Joseph R. Blaney, Lance R. Lippert, and J. Scott Smith (Lanham, MD: Rowman and Littlefield, 2013), 71–88. See also Joseph Walsh and Sheila M. McAllister-Spooner, "Analysis of the Image Repair Discourse in the Michael Phelps Controversy," *Public Relations Review* 37, no. 2 (June 2011): 157–62.

38. J. Scott Smith, "Bad Newz Kennels: Michael Vick and Dogfighting," in *Repairing the Athlete's Image: Studies in Sports Image Restoration*, ed. Joseph R. Blaney, Lance R. Lippert, and J. Scott Smith (Lanham, MD: Rowman and Littlefield, 2013), 151–68. See also Mark Holdener and James Kauffman, "Getting Out of the Doghouse: The Image Repair Strategies of Michael Vick," *Public Relations Review* 40, no. 1 (March 2014): 92–99.

39. Theodore F. Sheckels, "The Failed Comedy of the NBA's Gilbert Arenas: Image Restoration in Context," in *Repairing the Athlete's Image: Studies in Sports Image Restoration*, ed. Joseph R. Blaney, Lance R. Lippert, and J. Scott Smith (Lanham, MD: Rowman and Littlefield, 2013), 169–86.

40. Kurt Helin, "Zion Williamson May Sign Record Rookie Shoe Contract before NBA Draft Lottery," Yahoo! Sports, April 2, 2019, https://sports.yahoo.com/zion-wil liamson-may-sign-record-160222108.html. *Axios* reports that the actual number was $75 million; see Michael Sykes, "Zion Williamson Signs Sneaker Deal with Nike's Jordan Brand," *Axios*, July 24, 2019, https://www.axios.com/zion-williamson-nike-jordan-brand -sneaker-deal-e58941b4-eb27-47e7-a073-e22ca9a87adc.html.

41. Halford Ross Ryan, "*Kategoria* and *Apologia*: On Their Rhetorical Criticism as a Speech Set," *Quarterly Journal of Speech* 68, no. 3 (1982): 256–61.

42. William L. Benoit, *Accounts, Excuses, and Apologies: A Theory of Image Restoration Strategies*, 2nd ed. (Albany: State University of New York Press, 2015).

43. Joseph R. Blaney, ed., *Putting Image Repair to the Test: Quantitative Applications of Image Restoration Theory* (Lanham, MD: Lexington Books, 2015).

44. Jordan L. Compton, "Sorry Sorries: Image Repair after Regretted Apologies," *Public Relations Review* 42, no. 2 (January 2016): 353–58.

45. Jason A. Edwards, "Community-Focused Apologia in International Affairs: Japanese Prime Minister Tomiichi Murayama's Apology," *Howard Journal of Communication* 16, no. 4 (October 2005): 317–36.

46. Emil B. Towner, "Apologia, Image Repair, and Reconciliation: The Application, Limitations, and Future Directions of Apologetic Rhetoric," *Communication Yearbook* 33, no. 1 (2009): 430–68.

47. Kevin A. Stein, "Apologia, Antapologia, and the 1960 Soviet U-2 Incident," *Communication Studies* 59, no. 1 (February 2008): 19–34.

48. Kevin A. Stein and Matthew H. Barton, "'I'm Sorry You Interpreted My Behavior the Way You Did': Toward a New Understanding of the Nuances of Mortification," *Western Journal of Communication* 83, no. 2 (2019): 252–64.

49. Benoit, *Accounts, Excuses, and Apologies.*

50. Benoit and Hanczor, "The Tonya Harding Controversy."

51. Benoit, *Accounts, Excuses, and Apologies.*

52. Stein and Barton, "I'm Sorry You Interpreted My Behavior the Way You Did."

53. Stein and Barton, "I'm Sorry You Interpreted My Behavior the Way You Did."

54. Benoit and Hanczor, "The Tonya Harding Controversy."

55. Benoit and Hanczor, "The Tonya Harding Controversy," 423.

56. Andy Lassner, prod., "Heidi Klum/Tonya Harding/The Tonga Sisters," *The Ellen DeGeneres Show*, February 26, 2018.

57. Oprah Winfrey, "Interview with Tonya Harding," *The Oprah Winfrey Show*, April 23, 2009.

58. Benoit and Hanczor, "The Tonya Harding Controversy," 423.

59. Winfrey, "Interview with Tonya Harding."

60. Benoit and Hanczor, "The Tonya Harding Controversy," 423.

61. Sloan, "Truth and Lies: The Tonya Harding Story."

62. Sloan, "Truth and Lies: The Tonya Harding Story."

63. Chung, *Eye to Eye with Connie Chung.*

64. Chung, *Eye to Eye with Connie Chung.*

65. Sloan, "Truth and Lies: The Tonya Harding Story."

66. Sloan, "Truth and Lies: The Tonya Harding Story."

67. Benoit and Hanczor, "The Tonya Harding Controversy," 423.

68. Benoit and Hanczor, "The Tonya Harding Controversy," 423.

69. Nanette Burstein, dir., *The Price of Gold*, ESPN Films, January 16, 2014.

70. Sloan, "Truth and Lies: The Tonya Harding Story."

71. Sloan, "Truth and Lies: The Tonya Harding Story."

72. Sloan, "Truth and Lies: The Tonya Harding Story."

73. Sloan, "Truth and Lies: The Tonya Harding Story."

74. Sloan, "Truth and Lies: The Tonya Harding Story."

75. Burstein, *The Price of Gold.*

76. Benoit and Hanczor, "The Tonya Harding Controversy," 424.

77. Sloan, "Truth and Lies: The Tonya Harding Story."

78. Brodesser-Akner, "Tonya Harding Would Like Her Apology Now."

79. Sloan, "Truth and Lies: The Tonya Harding Story."

80. Winfrey, "Interview with Tonya Harding."

81. Brodesser-Akner, "Tonya Harding Would Like Her Apology Now."

82. Brodesser-Akner, "Tonya Harding Would Like Her Apology Now."

83. Burstein, *The Price of Gold.*

84. Brodesser-Akner, "Tonya Harding Would Like Her Apology Now."

85. Sloan, "Truth and Lies: The Tonya Harding Story."

86. Burstein, *The Price of Gold.*

87. Burstein, *The Price of Gold.*

88. Burstein, *The Price of Gold.*

89. Burstein, *The Price of Gold.*

90. Benoit and Hanczor, "The Tonya Harding Controversy," 425.

91. Burstein, *The Price of Gold.*

92. Burstein, *The Price of Gold.*

93. Sloan, "Truth and Lies: The Tonya Harding Story."

94. Winfrey, "Interview with Tonya Harding."

95. Stein and Barton, "I'm Sorry You Interpreted My Behavior the Way You Did."

96. Sloan, "Truth and Lies: The Tonya Harding Story."

97. Sloan, "Truth and Lies: The Tonya Harding Story."

98. Cat Rakowski and Lauren Effron, "Tonya Harding's Mother Says Steak Knife Incident Never Happened, Denies Former Olympic Skater's Abuse Allegations," ABC News, January 11, 2018, https://abcnews.go.com/US/tonya-hardings-mother-steak-knife-incident-happened-denies/story?id=52261073.

99. Stein and Barton, "I'm Sorry You Interpreted My Behavior the Way You Did."

100. "First Lady of American Garbage: 'I, Tonya' Is One Long Impression of White Trash," *Encore*, February 6, 2018, http://www.encorepub.com/first-lady-of-american-garbage-i-tonya-is-one-long-impression-of-white-trash/.

101. Herbert W. Simons, "A Dilemma-Centered Analysis of Clinton's August 17th Apologia: Implications for Rhetorical Theory and Method," *Quarterly Journal of Speech* 86, no. 4 (2000): 438–53.

102. Ryan, "*Kategoria* and *Apologia*."

103. Brodesser-Akner, "Tonya Harding Would Like Her Apology Now."

SYMBOLIC RUPTURE

"Take a Knee" and the NFL as Commodified Spectacle

BRIAN CARROLL

Something is seen not because it's visible; it's visible because it is seen.
DANIEL WALLACE, *MR. SEBASTIAN AND THE NEGRO MAGICIAN*

INTRODUCTION

It is no small irony that in attempting to draw attention to racial inequality and police brutality, Colin Kaepernick, a professional football player of color, found his "Take a Knee" protest maligned, misunderstood, marginalized, and otherwise muted by, among others, white millionaires and billionaires, many of them pro football team owners and one of them the leader of the free world. When US president Donald J. Trump in September 2017 called on National Football League owners to fire "son of a bitch" players who refuse to stand for the national anthem and, therefore, participate in a pregame ritual in which they have been publicly included only since 2009, he shifted the debate away from anything related to policing and profiling in America and instead to the decorum expected of highly paid professional athletes during the quasi-sacral playing or singing of the national "hymn."[1]

Such symbolic, quasi-religious displays, which rely on players as jingoistic props, support a highly militaristic brand of patriotism through expressions perhaps more accurately termed nationalistic. As such, they can be read or seen as an articulation of the politics of war, defying the naïve calls by many sports fans to keep the politics out of their spectacle. Rites and rituals like standing for the national anthem at a football or baseball game also seem to demonstrate Daniel Boorstin's idea that often we "invent our standards and then respect them as if they had been revealed or discovered."[2]

The professional sports leagues invited the "national anthem" communication crisis by so thoroughly integrating into their brands and marketing to
fans what appears to valorize only hypermilitaristic forms of national fealty,
a program that depends upon and receives the cooperation of the networks
and media outlets that "cover" these leagues and broadcast their games. At
the same time, by relying on the players as symbols and on the pageant of
their games as celebrations of at least the appearance of national unity, the
leagues furnish their players with symbolic power to wield in disharmonious
protest, as well. The fusing of professional and otherwise high-profile sporting events with displays of military power and knee-jerk patriotism idealizes
militarism, contributes to fervent, even hegemonic nationalism cloaked in
hypermasculinity, and commercially exploits these activities through the
commoditization of every aspect of the spectacle: "Get your official camo
gear at NFL.com/shop." It is likely no coincidence that such rhetorical strategies and communicative acts dominate national politics, as well.

This chapter explores the rhetorical strategies of symbolic patriotism
as enacted by professional sports leagues, especially the National Football
League and Major League Baseball, with the full participation and sponsorship of their media "partners." The media-sport-military troika is interrogated
here using the "Take a Knee" campaign as a case study and Jean Baudrillard's
and Guy Debord's approaches to, respectively, simulacra and the spectacle
as theoretical lenses. Also helpful in this analysis are Gaye Tuchman's ideas
about symbolic annihilation as a rhetorical strategy of erasure.[3]

BACKGROUND

Although its lyrics date back to 1814, "The Star-Spangled Banner" became
the nation's official anthem in 1931. And although it has been played before
baseball games sporadically since World War I, the anthem did not become
a part of regular-season games throughout big-league baseball until, not
coincidentally, another war, in 1942. The anthem was first played to begin
a Major League Baseball game in 1918, when a brass band at a Cubs–Red
Sox World Series game in Chicago struck up the tune. The fans, who were
already standing prior to the spontaneous anthem performance, quickly
joined in.[4]

In 1972, twenty-five years after shattering Major League Baseball's color
barrier, Jackie Robinson published these words in his third and final revi-
sionary autobiography:

There I was, the black grandson of a slave, the son of a black share-cropper, part of a historic occasion, a symbolic hero to my people. The air was sparkling. The sunlight was warm. The band struck up the national anthem. The flag billowed in the wind. It should have been a glorious moment for me as the stirring words of the national anthem poured from the stands. Perhaps, it was, but then again, perhaps, the anthem could be called the theme song for a drama called The Noble Experiment. Today, as I look back on that opening game of my first World Series, I must tell you that it was Mr. [Branch] Rickey's drama, and that I was only a principal actor. As I write this twenty years later, I cannot stand and sing the anthem. I cannot salute the flag; I know that I am a black man in a white world.[5]

Robinson published these words the same year that Black US Olympians Vince Matthews and Wayne Collett were tossed from the 1972 Munich Games for, in the estimation of the International Olympics Committee, failing to show proper respect on the medal stand. After taking gold and silver in the 400-meter sprint, Collett stood casually on the stand barefoot, hands on hips, chatting with Matthews as if the two were waiting for the next bus, all while the anthem played. The sprinters' dismissals recalled a similar action by the US Olympic Committee in the Mexico City Olympics just four years prior. Tommie Smith and John Carlos, also Black sprinters, each raised a black-gloved fist on the medal stand at the 1968 Games, also as the US national anthem was played, and wearing no shoes. They were subsequently thrown out of the Olympics by the IOC's president, Avery Brundage. Importantly, as Urla Hill notes, Smith and Carlos "have [since] ascended their place as villainous traitors to become a sort of brand for gallantry and pluck in the face of inestimable odds," celebrated with a twenty-foot-high monument of the raised fist moment that was unveiled on the campus of San José State University in 2005 as well as a statue located in the National Museum of African American History and Culture in Washington, DC, in 2016.[6]

Just months later, in February 1969, Black students at the University of New Mexico marched onto the gym floor during the national anthem preceding the Lobos' basketball game with Brigham Young, each student with one fist raised, the same Black Power salute employed by Smith and Carlos.[7] Fast forward to 1991, when Chicago Bulls guard Craig Hodges was blackballed by the National Basketball Association for his protest of the Gulf War during the team's visit to the White House, or 1996 when the NBA suspended Denver Nuggets guard Mahmoud Abdul-Rauf, formerly Chris

Jackson, for failing to participate in the national anthem, or 2003 when college basketball vilified Manhattanville College's Toni Smith for turning her back on the American flag to protest the George W. Bush administration's plans to go to war in Iraq.[8] "I did it for my own self-respect and conscience," Smith told the *New York Times*. "A lot of people blindly stand up and salute the flag, but I feel that blindly facing the flag hurts more people. There are a lot of inequities in this country, and these are issues that needed to be acknowledged. The rich are getting richer and the poor are getting poorer, and our priorities are elsewhere."[9] Also that year, Toronto Blue Jays first baseman Carlos Delgado, at the peak of his career, explained to the *Toronto Star* why he could not stand on the dugout steps for "God Bless America," telling that newspaper's readers, "I don't (stand) because I don't believe it's right. I don't believe in war."[10]

The "Take a Knee" movement, if a movement it was or is, began quietly on August 14, 2016, when then San Francisco 49ers quarterback Colin Kaepernick sat on the bench during the playing of the national anthem rather than stand with his teammates in order to protest systemic oppression of and police brutality toward people of color.[11] "I am not going to stand up to show pride in a flag for a country that oppresses black people," Kaepernick told the NFL Network. "When there's significant change, and I feel that flag represents what it's supposed to represent, and this country is representing people the way that it's supposed to, I'll stand."[12] Following correspondence and a conversation with Nate Boyer, then a Seattle Seahawks long snapper and a former Green Beret, Kaepernick altered his nascent protest to instead take a knee alongside his (mostly) standing teammates. Boyer had explained that US soldiers take a knee in front of a fallen brother's gravesite to show respect, seemingly offering the 49ers quarterback symbolic cover.[13] It took three games for anyone to even notice what Kaepernick was, or was not, doing.

A former Super Bowl quarterback frequently described as an ideal teammate, Kaepernick was soon joined on one knee by a teammate, star safety Eric Reid, who explained his decision in an opinion piece in the *New York Times* a year later. Reid wrote that they chose to kneel "because it's a respectful gesture. I remember thinking our posture was like a flag flown at half-mast, to mark a tragedy."[14] This aspect of the protest was quickly forgotten, if it had ever been apprehended in the first place, much as Tommie Smith's holding of an olive branch with his non-fist-clenched hand in 1968 was overlooked and cropped out.[15]

Sideline postures enacted in protest grew to include raising fists, locking arms, laying hands on shoulders, and simply remaining in the stadium's tunnel until the anthem finished. As the expressions became variegated, it became increasingly difficult to track exactly what the gestures were protesting. What began as solidarity in joining Kaepernick to draw attention to social injustice, after Trump's outburst became a protest of the president's hypocrisy and bullying. Kaepernick's motivating purposes were annihilated, in other words, by Trump's provocations and later by Houston Texans owner Bob McNair, who criticized the players' social justice agenda by saying, "We can't have the inmates running the prison."[16] Protests grew further as a response to McNair and, more generally, to what was seen as equivocation by NFL owners in general.

In displacing and, therefore, symbolically annihilating Kaepernick's symbolic gesture, the debate about proper decorum during the national anthem also further obscured larger questions about the politics of war. Patriotism became, again, dependent upon behavior at stadia that reflexively, unthinkingly endorses, embraces, and uncritically applauds the central role and prominence of the military in US foreign policy, reminiscent of similarly delimiting notions of patriotism in the commemorations and tributes staged on and around 9/11 each year. *San Francisco Chronicle* sportswriter Gwen Knapp, for example, once dared to assert that the ritual of jet flyovers before games is "fundamentally disrespectful to military operations. The presence of those planes at a sporting event trivializes their real purpose."[17] Filip Bondy wondered in the pages of the *New York Daily News* what an eagle trained to fly nowhere or merely to his handler on the mound has to do with freedom. But, if during any of these nationalistic expressions, a fan "dares to feel uncomfortable, if you think this is not the place or time for such introspection, you're un-American," Bondy wrote, calling these expressions, collectively, "creeping nationalism."[18]

After being told by the 49ers after the 2016 season that he was going to be released, Kaepernick opted out of his contract on March 3, 2017, and became a free agent.[19] By the end of the 2017 season, the number of protesting players had shrunk to fewer than twenty, according to media outlets such as the Associated Press and the *New York Times*, or about 1 percent of the league's players.[20] The games' broadcasters had stopped showing them on air, rendering them invisible to the spectacle's viewers. The president's famously short attention span had led him elsewhere for controversy and attention. And Kaepernick had been largely silenced, the result of what he asserted in a 2017 lawsuit to be collusion on the part of NFL teams to keep him out of professional football.[21] Once one of the best football players in the world, Kaepernick watched the 2017 season from home as forty other quarterbacks were taken off the unemployment rolls.[22]

PATRIOTISM AS *GOOD HOUSEKEEPING* SEAL

Viewership of NFL games not coincidentally declined nearly 10 percent in 2017, a drop attributed at least in part to counterprotests by viewers disaffected with the Kaepernick-inspired protests.[23] The double-digit drop followed a roughly 8 percent decline the year prior, a falloff that inspired efforts by the NFL to shorten games and seek alternative distribution for its telecasts, such as streaming and Facebook Live. To the extent that 2017's erosion in viewership can be assigned to fans' disaffection with the politics of player protests, a dissatisfaction fanned by Trump's ultimatum, the NFL can blame only itself. In endorsing such a narrow band of what may or may not be patriotism, one for which the defaults are war and war preparedness, pro sports' image makers are capitalizing on, in the case of football, the sport as a metaphor for war and, for both football and baseball, a post-9/11 fervor for flag and country expressed in conspicuously pro-military ways. In so doing, these image makers have foreclosed other conceptions of patriotism, including those espousing pacifism or protest, and they did so in such a way that players and fans seeking to express these alternative conceptions have found themselves resisted, even vilified and retaliated against.[24] Kaepernick's employment status is perhaps evidence. David J. Leonard has called such treatment by the NFL and its more "patriotic" fans a form of "symbolic lynching."[25] In deploying players as props for its pageant of patriotism, the NFL risks those same players wielding their own symbolic meaning in some other communicative act for other rhetorical goals.

Since 9/11, professional sports have doubled down on their bet on nationalistic expressions in support of the military, drinking with both hands from the goblet of pro-military spectacle, much of it Pentagon funded.[26] In staging events and packaging games, the leagues since 9/11 have expanded the visual and symbolic vocabulary for this fusion of pro sports and nationalism to include fighter jet flyovers, field-sized US flags, color guards, police and fire first responders, majestic eagles and birds of prey, Lee Greenwood and Ronan Tynan, "Proud to Be an American" and "God Bless America," highly choreographed American veteran family "reunions," players and coaches in camouflage-styled uniforms on, for example, Flag Day and Veterans Day, basketball games played on aircraft carriers, and Major League Baseball played in the middle of Fort Bragg, North Carolina, on a field constructed just for the occasion.[27] As ESPN writer Howard Bryant puts it, patriotism in professional sports has devolved into what could be described as "a lucrative *Good Housekeeping* seal for marketers."[28] As spectacle, these displays and rhetorical strategies have turned ballparks and football stadia into sites of ritualistic memorializing that articulate and endorse the politics of war, communicative acts amplified by the leagues' media partners and by the configuration of the stadia themselves, which can be considered billion-dollar television studios as much as playing fields and sporting arenas.[29]

In exchange for subleasing its playing venues to displays of pro-military spectacle, such as the many tearful family reunions of veterans home from Afghanistan or Iraq with those they had left behind, sports teams have traditionally received payments from the Department of Defense. In duping fans into believing that pro teams and leagues are genuinely, voluntarily grateful for the sacrifices of members of the armed forces, to the tune of $53 million in only a few years according to Arizona senators John McCain and Jeff Flake, the leagues are articulating a political ideology. Of the five major sports leagues in the United States (including Major League Soccer), the DoD spent the most on marketing contracts with NFL teams. McCain and Flake's report disclosed contracts with nineteen NFL teams from 2012 to 2015 that totaled $6.1 million in taxpayer money.[30] The Wisconsin National Guard paid the Milwaukee Brewers $49,000 to play "God Bless America" during the seventh-inning stretch of games in 2014, while the Atlanta Falcons, owned by the billionaire founder of Home Depot, Arthur Blank, collected $879,000 to produce and stage homecoming reunions at midfield before home games. The two Arizona senators proposed a bill to oppose this spending, saying that they believed such "paid patriotism" to be "morally fraudulent," trivializing military service by profiting off veterans and turning participating soldiers into mere marketing gimmicks.[31] The bill died in committee.

Beyond direct payments from the Pentagon, however, the leagues have energetically, creatively, and systematically sought to present their games as panegyrics to "nation," employing religious-like rituals and tributes that are in a way sacralized by the opening "hymn" that is or has become the national anthem. It is common at Pittsburgh Pirates games for Air Force Reserves to perform the anthem.[32] At Cardinals games in St. Louis, firefighters unfurl a huge American flag in center field with a video tribute played on the scoreboard to the soundtrack of Lee Greenwood singing "Proud to Be an American."[33] For the anthem in Denver, on one occasion the Colorado Rockies executed a plan proposed by their owner, Jerry McMorris, to have Rockies and Arizona Diamondbacks players hold up a field-wide flag while fans waved their own personal US flags distributed at the turnstiles.[34] Public address announcers and TV and radio broadcasters serve as the ritual's unofficial clergy, reminding viewers and listeners to appreciate the sacrifices of those serving the country in the armed forces.[35] In approximating religious rite and ritualistic practice, these displays as symbols provide spectators and participants with a ready-made accessibility and clarity, and, therefore, symbolic power.

IRRESISTIBLE STAGING

For the media-sport complex, such gimmicks are perhaps irresistible. As spectacle, they rely on a panoply of symbols that further fuse the leagues as brands with something that looks and feels and smells like patriotism but that in the aggregate, ironically, serves to delimit freedom, democratic participation, and individualism, presumably three cornerstone cultural values for which "America" as concept has come to represent or comprise. Seeing the New York Mets take on the San Diego Padres in "alternate" camouflage uniforms, which are available for purchase at MLBshop.com, can be stirring, particularly when TV images of the players are interposed with scene-setting shots of the aircraft carriers docked just a mile or so away from Petco Field in San Diego. Switch to the football season for images of overweight NFL coaches in military-style jackets, replete with name tags and matching camo-themed headsets, images juxtaposed with those of "real" soldiers and national guards standing ready to consecrate the next NFL-coproduced militaristic rite or ritual.

The slide in ratings clearly got the owners' attention, especially because the NFL has been able to assume TV ratings dominance since around the year 2000. Of the twenty most-watched TV shows in American history, nineteen are Super Bowls (the other is the final episode of *M*A*S*H*).[36] This rupture of the real-but-unreal image of the NFL, one meant to project harmony and, therefore, to disappear disharmony, political diversity, dissatisfaction, and unrest, is a rupture also of what is a commodification of nearly every aspect of the NFL as spectacle. As Guy Debord described the spectacle's dependence on commodification and commodification's dependence on the spectacle as spectacle, "waves of enthusiasm for particular products [are] fueled and boosted by the communication media. . . . The sheer fad item perfectly expresses the fact that, as the mass of commodities become more and more absurd, absurdity becomes a commodity in its own right . . . the commodity's *indulgences*—glorious tokens of the commodity's immanent presence among the faithful."[37]

Among the more absurd of these indulgences or glorious tokens during the 2017 NFL season was the jersey of Pittsburgh Steeler offensive lineman Alejandro Villanueva, which trended if for only a few days at NFL.com and other online retailers. A former captain in the US Army, Villanueva found himself standing for the anthem in Chicago's Soldier Field while the rest of his team remained in the locker room before a game with the Bears. Villanueva said that he had walked down the tunnel and, because he had walked too far and therefore could be seen by the stadium and television audiences, felt he had to remain standing during the playing of the anthem. This awkward moment was enough to put jersey makers into overdrive producing Villanueva's number 78 jersey, a reaction to his name trending on Twitter in the aftermath of his reluctant "patriotic" moment. The sports apparel manufacturer Fanatics even has a name for this sort of ephemeral, commodifying marketing opportunity: a "micro-moment."[38] Villanueva jersey sales skyrocketed, making number 78 the best-selling jersey in America, if for only part of one week, even though the micro-moment was only a pregame ritual mistake, one for which the player apologized to his coach and team. Villanueva's stumble with the NFL's symbols had been commoditized, and with great commercial success, punctuating the protest-plagued season with another image of "blissful unification of society through consumption."[39]

SPORT AS SPECTACLE

The leagues have embarked on what Debord might call "an immense accumulation of spectacles" and, therefore, as preferred by the former president, mere representation of or tribute to patriotism rather than real, actual, or lived patriotism, which would more likely include or authorize the risk of approbation by drawing attention to the treatment of those vulnerable in and to society, an activity and expression specifically protected by the First Amendment to the US Constitution.[40] In commenting on the Supreme Court case that rendered compelled participation in national flag salutes unconstitutional, historian G. Edward White writes that "freedom of speech became closely associated with the intertwined ideals of creative self-fulfillment (freedom to express oneself) and equality (freedom from discrimination or oppression). Free democratic speech . . . signified the power of the human actor, liberated from the dominance of external forces, free to determine his or her individual destiny, required only to respect the freedoms of others."[41] In the NFL's pregame rituals, some are more equal than others, at least as symbols.

Importantly, for Debord the accumulated or aggregate spectacle that, in this case, is a professional football game is not a collection of images but rather a social relationship between people that is mediated by images. As such, this spectacle, one epitomized and taken to its own illogical extremes by the annual Super Bowl, is simultaneously the outcome and the goal of the mediators, the major sports networks such as ESPN and Fox that pay so much to be able to carry the games and, therefore, to weld and recast with their own brands those of the big pro leagues, all of them, not coincidentally, red, white, and blue. As Debord describes it: "[T]he language of the spectacle is composed of *signs* of the dominant organization of production—signs which are at the same time the ultimate end-products of that organization."[42]

Although Americans do not stand for the playing or singing of the national anthem at, say, concerts or operas or plays, to do so at a sporting event is accepted as natural, even God-ordained as part and parcel of the quasi-religious event or pro game–cum–political rally that the games might be considered to simulate. As communicative act, this appearance of unity is presumably meant to disappear disharmony and disagreement over, among many other things, what it means to be American and the role (and levels of funding) that should be considered proper for the country's armed forces. This is pro (spectator) sport's power as culturally specific spectacle, one long recognized in the literature. David Rowe has argued that national governments and their militaries get involved in sports, especially televised sports, because of the "highly effective way in which sport can contribute to nation building."[43]

The irony of celebrating democratic values, which must begin with or otherwise prominently feature freedom of expression and freedom of association, by so conforming to an accepted orthodoxy of rites and rituals is confabulated or otherwise turned on its head such that participation is a precondition to being allowed to self-identify as patriotic or as American. Colin Kaepernick and those who joined him were frequently called un-American, further uniting them with sporting history's protest heroes: Tommie Smith, John Carlos, Muhammad Ali, Curt Flood, Jackie Robinson, and others. Thus, the spectacle, specifically those aspects that tacitly demand lockstep fealty to flag and country, is "both the outcome and the goal of the dominant mode of production," as Debord describes it,[44] and not something merely added to the experience of witnessing professional sporting events in the United States.

Standing for the national anthem isn't simply decorative, a sign of something else, but rather it has become an essential aspect of the hyperreal unreality that is the obsessively choreographed, executive-produced, rigidly timed, and relentlessly commercialized "event" in American society that is a pro football or baseball game. As such, the spectacle of "patriotism," narrowly defined, should not be considered in opposition to "concrete social activity" but in important ways as the social activity of being patriotic, one that is supportive of those serving in the armed forces and expressive of what it essentially is or has come to mean to be American. This is the challenge the

NFL's protests face not only to succeed, however that might be measured or determined, but even to be understood, because the spectacle's mechanisms of contemplation, by so incorporating the symbolic and spectacular, now constitute their own reality. This spectacle is real, in other words, even hyperreal.

The French semiotician Jean Baudrillard likely would qualify these descriptions. Such displays, demonstrations, and, perhaps the better word here, *enactments* of patriotism (or something like patriotism) as spectacle are both less real, even unreal, and at the same time more than real, or hyperreal.[45] As simulacra, these ritualistic enactments are copies of an original that never existed, just as the "heroes" on the field are simulations (and dissimulations) of the true or real warriors (even soldiers) whom they are meant to resemble, at least in terms of risk and achievement. Consider Curt Schilling's bloody sock in pitching his Red Sox to improbable victory, or Michael Jordan's "flu game" in 1997 in which he willed himself beyond illness to score thirty-eight points. As simulations of patriotism, rites such as standing for the national anthem follow their own logic, one that has little or nothing to do with facts or reason: symbolic Gordian knots or Möbius strips of symbols and symbolic expression that seemingly cannot be untied or undone or else the entire spectacular firmament might unravel and become, again, just another game. Closer to a conjoining of desire and values, the rite of standing for the national anthem has acquired a semisacred status as professional sports and college football have displaced organized religion in American life as the places and spaces where ritualized, tribal affiliation and behavior are sanctioned, even demanded and rewarded. As sacred ritual, it has both contributed to and benefited from pro sports' quasi-religious status.

In Baudrillard's framework, such behaviors, or structures as he would more likely call them, are in their way utopian, which should suggest something of their power to exclude, in this case, any disharmony such as that caused or introduced by taking a knee or raising a fist. They are utopian in their paradoxical, even absurd conjoining of the real and something other than the real in a context or of an aesthetics of the hyperreal, the spectacle, "a frisson of vertiginous and phony exactitude, a frisson of simultaneous distancing and magnification," in Baudrillard's description.[46] To pick up the metaphorical snow globe that the anthem tableau presents as a microcosm of the sports-media-military troika, notice the prototypical "fan" standing at allegiance, perhaps hand over heart wearing the same jersey the players are wearing, eyes on the pageant of "patriotism" being enacted on the field of play. He is distanced from the principal actors of that pageant, but at the same time, through camera close-ups displayed on a six-story "halo" video board, he is so close to those same actors and to the players standing on the sideline that the tears of inspiration (or sweat of having just warmed up) are seemingly shared, offering the appearance or seeming of intimacy that is of course simply an image. Less real and hyperreal, this distortion of scale that the uninitiated might find bewildering, perhaps even disturbing, presents an excess of transparency that might or might not be real in terms of authenticity, because the same tear-stained athlete is both a product and a prop of the very same production unfolding on the field, emotionally manipulated by the same produced, choreographed pageantry in service to nation and, perhaps more than anything else, brand building. Because patriotism sells.

Such displays offer "the pleasure of an excess of meaning," in Baudrillard's analysis, but only because the bar of meaning has fallen below the usual waterline by being made up of mostly if not exclusively signs and symbols.[47] The nonsignifier, for example an eagle (or other bird) trained to fly from some high perch and then to land on cue on the gloved hand of its trainer, is exalted by that most modern of meaning-makers and signifiers, the camera.

TWO EXAMPLES, ONE OLDER AND ONE NEWER

For the one-year anniversary of 9/11, Major League Baseball centered its tributes on the New York Yankees, the team to which President George W. Bush turned for support in the run-up to the invasion of Iraq by practicing for hours his "first pitch" for the first game after the attacks a year prior, a game that featured the spontaneous chanting of "U-S-A, U-S-A" by fans of both teams throughout that emotional restart of the season. In the 2002 tribute:

> There was an uncomfortable pause in the Sept. 11 pregame ceremony, just after Ronan Tynan finished a stirring version of "God Bless America." Nothing happened for a moment, and the fans seemed unsure if they were supposed to remain standing.
>
> So they did what came naturally. Unscripted and uninhibited, they filled the silence with a chant. "U-S-A! U-S-A!" they cheered, and a few minutes later they applauded and waved flags as the Yankees dedicated a memorial in Monument Park to the rescue workers and the victims of the terrorist attacks last Sept. 11. . . . There were flags all over, including one from the World Trade Center that was presented by the Marines, and a giant one unfurled in center field as the Harlem Boys Choir sang the national anthem. The flags above the facade flew at half-staff. Representatives from the Army, the Navy, the Air Force and

the Marines stood in the outfield, and the Yankees and Orioles stood on the baselines, arranged at random, during the ceremony. Challenger, the bald eagle featured prominently last October, took his place on the mound, though he did not swoop in from center field as usual. When four Navy F-18 Hornets flew over the stadium after the anthem, the applause reached its peak. The planes [had] recently returned from combat operations in Afghanistan off the U.S.S. *John F. Kennedy*. . . . The fans who came were passionate, and they cheered "U-S-A!" again during a video tribute from Major League Baseball that followed a moment of silence in the bottom of the fifth inning. The clock turned to 9:11. . . . The Orioles, the umpires, the base coaches and [the batter, Yankees second baseman Alfonso] Soriano stood at their positions and faced the center-field flag for a moment of silence, the organist Eddie Layton playing a slow, poignant version of "Ave Maria."[48]

As sports communication scholar Michael Butterworth reasoned, after describing another, similar MLB-produced tribute: "It is not unreasonable to read this sequence as tacit support for Bush and his vision of America," and as support for war against a country that had nothing whatsoever to do with the 9/11 attacks.[49]

A fresher example comes from Super Bowl LII in February 2018, when halftime act Justin Timberlake "interrupted" his singing in order to take "a Super Bowl selfie" with someone presented to viewers as an ordinary fan, while approximately 110 million American households looked on to witness the celebration of an otherwise mundane "event," a microscopic simulation that paradoxically enables the real to pass into the hyperreal while at the same time being so much less than what otherwise would be less than real—the making of an image of the making of an image of nothing happening. As a juxtaposition of the ordinary with the *celebrified*, it enabled and even relied upon the voyeuristic appetites of its viewers, a moment strikingly similar in its transparency and distancing to pornography.

That such an "intimate" moment with Justin Timberlake and a presumed fan in what was otherwise the halftime lull in the middle of a football game proved, paradoxically, so alienating, just as viewing pornography does, shows the blending and blurring of the real with the hyperreal and, in that blending and blurring, the simulation and dissimulation that is occurring as a result of the illusory power of having televised or broadcast it *as if* viewers weren't there, or as if Timberlake were authentically seeking to connect with a fan while on the job of being an *über*celebrity during what is de facto a national holiday.

This is the allure of reality television, to use one of the more oxymoronic terms ever coined to mask a genre's own shortcomings, a genre not unlike pornography in its same trick of seeming voyeuristic transparency and simultaneous distancing that comes with being able only to watch. But this is to say that such a "moment" of being there without being there is neither true nor false, and thus it might be called utopian. Baudrillard would use this description. As such, it fascinates in its perversity, just as the moment of, say, seeing on a sixty-foot video board the expressions of Cam Newton or Alex Rodriguez during a performance of the national anthem via a close-up that seemingly takes the viewer inside the head or heart of the athlete does, a perverse pleasure of violating someone's personal privacy for the *faux verité* or even something like communion that that moment promises.[50] The video board–projected moment of a fan asking his fiancée to marry him at the big game is a similar "moment," one in which the image replaces actual, lived experience in terms of its meaning and memory, both unreal and simultaneously transcendently "real," choreographed and coproduced to become spectacle, or part of the larger spectacle saying plainly:

People's lives are *changed* and even made here! Now, back to the game!

Thus, the spectacle cannot be set in opposition to the lived "real," because in this spectacular snow-globe world, reality, whatever it might be, and the representation and projection of that reality cannot be parsed or distinguished. Considering here Atlanta's Mercedes-Benz "wonderplex," which opened in 2017 and proudly boasts on its website two thousand screens,[51] in Debord's description, both reality and image "will survive on either side" of any such distinction that we might attempt to make between them.[52] The spectacle, therefore, turns reality on its head by being a product of "real activity," or of "real" people standing, singing, kneeling, and emoting. This ritualized activity, so normalized by repetition and even sacralized, has therefore become a referendum on one's patriotism, especially since 9/11, reified to the point that assaults on its hegemony, like those of Kaepernick, Malcolm Jenkins, and Baton Rouge–born Eric Reid, among others, are seen as inappropriate, even dangerous, especially if they come from athletes of color: the Black Man Rises.[53]

The spectacle is tautological; therefore, its means and ends are the same. Knitted into the fabric of professional sport as it is enacted in America, such a rite contributes to "an empire of modern passivity," to borrow Debord's exquisite description, an empire on which the symbolic sun never sets, basking as it does in the perpetual warmth of its own glory. "The real consumer thus becomes a consumer of illusion. The commodity is this illusion, which is in fact real, and the spectacle is its most general form," as Debord describes it.[54] It is in this context that Kaepernick's symbolic rupture should be recognized as a threat, a recognition that might help us understand, but not excuse, the reactions it elicited from owners, presidents, and the "patriots" who turned off their televisions to the tune of 9.7 percent.

For the Pentagon, such spectacles are superior to propaganda in the way they subsume the means in being the ends. Propaganda is typically a narrative argument. Good narratives and strong arguments, then, are persuasive, meaning they have successfully engaged the audience or relevant publics. The spectacle "forgoes persuasion in favor of fostering disengagement," according to Roger Stahl. "Whereas propaganda addresses an audience that matters, the spectacle presumes an audience that does not," one that has been distanced even as it has been invited into what is an illusion of democracy, community, and unity; "propaganda seeks to answer the question of *why we fight*, the spectacle loses itself in the fact *that we fight*," Stahl wrote in his book, *Militainment, Inc.*[55] Consider the aforementioned Carrier Classic basketball gamed played on the deck of the USS *Carl Vinson*; the July Fourth weekend baseball game in 2016 played in the middle of Fort Bragg, North Carolina; college football's Bell Helicopter Armed Forces Bowl sponsored by a military hardware manufacturer and, since 2013, owned by ESPN; and ESPN's flagship program, *Sports Center*, broadcasting from what resembled a machine gunner's nest on location at Camp Arifjan in Kuwait in 2004, the set designed by the US military replete with camouflage netting and an anchor's desk made of sandbags. ESPN is of course owned by Disney, which hired Rush Limbaugh to do color commentary for *Monday Night Football* but would not distribute or air Michael Moore's documentary film *Fahrenheit 9/11* because it was "too political."[56]

Media-sport's production of military-themed spectacles has worked to normalize a culture of war and, perhaps more corrosively, to delimit democratic deliberation and expression, especially dissent. This perhaps explains why the nation that is still trying to figure out how best to serve the people of Puerto Rico following the devastation wrought when Hurricane Maria slammed into the island in September 2017, or the nation with the highest infant mortality rate in the developed world, can still manage to spend more on defense—$750 billion in 2020—than the next eight countries combined.[57]

CONCLUSION

More than one hundred NFL players took a knee in week three of the 2017 campaign. In the last week of the regular season, that number had dwindled to seven: Duane Brown, Marquise Goodwin, Eli Harold, Louis Murphy, Eric Reid, Kenny Stills, and Olivier Vernon. In Miami, where Stills took a knee alone, the game was preceded by a fighter jet flyover, courtesy of the Homestead Air Reserve Base. A giant US flag covered the Hard Rock Stadium field as retired Air Force Sergeant Mark J. Lindquist sang the national anthem.[58] An $89 million commitment from the NFL earmarked for social justice causes and organizations over the ensuing seven seasons neutralized much of the Kaepernick-initiated protest, a donation negotiated without the participation of Kaepernick or any of the seven who remained on one knee at season's end.

For their part, Kaepernick and the kneelers vowed to press on, recognizing that effective protest is collective and contingent; success depends upon what legendary organizer Ella Baker called "spade work." They will indeed need their shovels, because the machinery of spectacle built by the media-sport-military troika has by relentless acknowledgment created a new normal for what is deemed patriotic, even American, at least in ballparks and stadia and on the telecasts that connect their events to those watching at home. As Butterworth notes, this new or reconstituted normal "absorbs the most conspicuous forms of nationalistic display" in such a way as to render the spectacle largely immune to rhetorical or symbolic challenge.[59] Kneeling, as standing, is a communicative, symbolic act, and as such, for efficacy, it must be seen and noticed. As protest, it depends on being on camera, on being broadcast as part of the coverage, along with the giant flag, jets, eagles, and requisite color guard. It must be consumed.

These ceremonies and pageants of patriotism, as staged and produced by professional sports in full partnership with the networks that broadcast them, are so immune to symbolic challenge, however, that it became possible, perhaps even expected in some quarters, for the highest elected official of a presumably free country to demand that those refusing to participate in a ritual that may or may not belong at a professional sporting event be fired from their jobs and, therefore, lose their means of livelihood for silently exercising their First Amendment rights in drawing attention to the lack of accountability of law enforcement in shooting and killing people of color in wildly disproportionate numbers. Censoring the symbolic speech of Kaepernick and the NFL's protesters, both as a prior restraint and as punishment, is a lesser evil for this elected official than is any interruption in a selectively patriotic NFL ritual inclusive of the players publicly since only 2009. This fetish for merely the symbols of democracy paired with hostility toward those who attempt, even silently and respectfully, to put democratic ideals into practice represent a civic death at the hands of the "terministic screen," the spectacle that purports to celebrate and display something that looks like democratic unity while symbolically annihilating democratic expression.[60] That the call to fire such otherwise patriotic Americans was so favored, cited by many as inspiration to turn off their TVs, demonstrates the dangers even to a society of relying so heavily on symbols and allowing the signifiers to replace that which is signified, in this instance meaningful conversation about social justice in "the land of the free."

POSTSCRIPT

Returning the national conversation to the topics of police brutality, oppression against Black Americans, and "lynching" were, in short succession, the deaths of Breonna Taylor (Louisville, Kentucky), Ahmaud Arbery (Glynn County, Georgia), and George Floyd (Minneapolis, Minnesota).[61] The country convulsed in protest and even riots. Confederate monuments symbolic of a time when white society was nearly united in its subjugation of Blacks were removed from public spaces. Sadly, nearly three years after Colin Kaepernick's pregame displays of courage addressing these very wrongs, those who seek justice through even peaceful protest continued to be demonized, attacked, and victimized by fellow Americans, including many with badges and guns, tasers and tear gas, helicopters and pepper spray. Yes, the relevance, validity, and urgency of the movement Kaepernick helped to reinvigorate have been recognized, but state violence against Black people remains largely unchecked. Clearly, however, this is much, much larger than professional sports.

The journey toward justice and, therefore, away from the cultivated ignorance of white supremacy presupposes a reasonable conversation about structural racism and prejudiced systems that treat black bodies as the enemy, including the signs and symbols of this racism. This journey is made all the more complicated by the exclusionary, nationalistic false "patriotism" produced by the big professional sports leagues and enacted as part of the pageantry of their games. America's pro sports as spectacles, like America's policing, would seem urgently to need a reimagining, including a reconsideration not only of *how*, but *why*. NASCAR made an important first move by removing the Confederate battle flag from its events, a response to the principled stand of its only Black driver, Darrell "Bubba" Wallace. Nike joined a wave of American companies making Juneteenth an official paid holiday. And NFL commissioner Roger Goodell attempted to apologize for the league's failure to support players who protested police violence, although he

"Take a Knee" by Nicholas Jay D'Acquisto

managed to cause additional furor by not specifically mentioning Kaepernick by name in his prerecorded remarks.[62]

However, as if to underline the dangers of relying so heavily on symbols rather than embarking on that reasonable conversation, American political tribalism turned the seemingly basic first step toward safeguarding public health during a pandemic of wearing a mask into a referendum on something some called "liberty." Foregoing or even banning the wearing of masks, even in the rare instance in which they might have been worn to symbolize liberalism or whatever, which, as when kneeling during an anthem, would be lawfully protected expression, instead became symbols of "freedom" and "acts" of safeguarding liberty. This symbolic annihilation occurred despite the ironic fact that masks do not protect primarily the wearers but those in the vicinity of the wearers. Society would seem to need social distancing from its symbols, if for no other reason than in backing up and away, society might just bump into the false logic that produced those symbols in the first place.

NOTES

1. Ted Johnson, "Trump Calls for NFL Boycott in Continued Criticism of Anthem Protests," *Variety*, September 24, 2017, http://variety.com/2017/politics/news/trump-nfl -boycott-1202569237/, accessed February 20, 2018. In 1943, the US Supreme Court, in *West Virginia State Board of Education v. Barnette*, held that a compulsory flag salute in a public school is unconstitutional under the First Amendment, noting that "if there is any fixed star in our constitutional constellation, it is that no official, high or petty, can prescribe what shall be orthodox in politics, nationalism, religion, or other matters of opinion or force citizens to confess by word or act their faith therein"; in Samantha Barbas, *Laws of Image: Privacy and Publicity in America* (Stanford, CA: Stanford University Press, 2015), 125–26. For 2009 as the start of players publicly participating in the playing of the anthem, see Tom E. Curran, "NFL Teams Being on the Field for Anthem Is a Relatively New Practice," NBC Sports, April 29, 2016, http://www.nbcsports.com/boston/new-england-patriots/nfl-teams-being-field -anthem-relatively-new-practice, accessed February 23, 2018.

2. Daniel Boorstin, *The Image: A Guide to Pseudo-Events in America*, rev. ed. (New York: Vintage, 1992), 5. The first edition of Boorstin's text was published in 1961.

3. Gaye Tuchman, "The Symbolic Annihilation of Women by the Mass Media," in *Hearth and Home: Images of Women in the Mass Media*, ed. Gaye Tuchman, Arlene Kaplan Daniels, and James Benet (New York: Oxford University Press, 1978).

4. Louis Jacobson, "A Short History of the National Anthem, Protests and the NFL," Politifact, September 25, 2017, http://politifact.com/truth-o-meter/article/2017/sep/25/short -history-national-anthem-and-sports, accessed February 23, 2018.

5. Jackie Robinson and Alfred Duckett, *I Never Had It Made* (New York: G. P. Putnam's Sons, 1972), 9. Robinson refers to Branch Rickey, general manager of the Dodgers, who was responsible for signing Robinson to the team.

6. Urla Hill, "Racing after Smith and Carlos: Revisiting Those Fists Some Forty Years Hence," in *Reconstructing Fame: Sport, Race, and Evolving Reputations*, ed. David C. Ogden and Joel Nathan Rosen (Jackson: University Press of Mississippi, 2008), 104.

7. Hill, "Racing after Smith and Carlos," 114.

8. Bill Pennington, "Player's Protest over the Flag Divides Fans," *New York Times*, February 26, 2003, http://www.nytimes.com/2003/02/26/sports/college-basketball-player-s-protest -over-the-flag-divides-fans.html, accessed February 23, 2018.

9. Pennington, "Player's Protest over the Flag Divides Fans."

10. In Dave Zirin, *What's My Name Fool? Sports and Resistance in the United States* (Chicago: Haymarket Books, 2005), 139.

11. Julia Craven, "More Than 250 Black People Were Killed by Police in 2016," *Huffington Post*, January 1, 2017, https://www.huffingtonpost.com/entry/black-people-killed-by-police -america_us_577da633e4b0c590f7e7fb17, accessed February 6, 2018.

12. In Cindy Boren, "Colin Kaepernick Reportedly Will Now Stand during the National Anthem," *Washington Post*, March 2, 2017, https://www.washingtonpost.com/news/early -lead/wp/2017/03/02/colin-kaepernick-reportedly-will-now-stand-during-the-national -anthem/?utm_term=.04e5d3b955c4, accessed February 5, 2018.

13. Will Brinson, "Here's How Nate Boyer Got Colin Kaepernick to Go from Sitting to Kneeling," CBS Sports, September 27, 2016, https://www.cbssports.com/nfl/news/heres-how -nate-boyer-got-colin-kaepernick-to-go-from-sitting-to-kneeling/, accessed February 20, 2018.

14. Eric Reid, "Why Colin Kaepernick and I Decided to Take a Knee," *New York Times*, September 25, 2017, https://www.nytimes.com/2017/09/25/opinion/colin-kaepernick-football -protests.html, accessed February 5, 2018.

15. Hill, "Racing after Smith and Carlos," 102.

16. Ken Belson, "Texans Owner Bob McNair Apologizes for 'Inmates' Remark," *New York Times*, October 27, 2017, https://www.nytimes.com/2017/10/27/sports/football/bob-mcnair -texans.html, accessed February 20, 2018.

17. Gwen Knapp, "Bullheaded Decision by Hall President," *San Francisco Chronicle*, April 13, 2003, B2.

18. In Michael L. Butterworth, "Ritual in the 'Church of Baseball': Suppressing the Discourse of Democracy after 9/11," *Communication and Critical/Cultural Studies* 2, no. 2 (June 2005): 121.

19. Will Brinson, "The 49ers Would've Cut Colin Kaepernick if He Hadn't Opted Out of His Contract," CBS Sports, May 31, 2017, https://www.cbssports.com/nfl/news/ the-49ers-wouldve-cut-colin-kaepernick-if-he-hadnt-opted-out-of-his-contract/.

20. John Branch, "The Year's Biggest Sports Story, All but Forgotten," *New York Times*, January 2, 2018, B5.

21. Mark Maske, "Colin Kaepernick Files Grievance Accusing NFL Teams of Colluding against Him," *Washington Post*, October 15, 2017, https://www.washingtonpost.com/news/ sports/wp/2017/10/15/colin-kaepernick-makes-plans-to-pursue-collusion-case-against-nfl -owners/?utm_term=.7c5126567713, accessed February 20, 2018.

22. For a comparison of Kaepernick's statistics with those of other, employed quarterbacks, see Reuben Fischer-Baum, Neil Greenberg, and Mike Hume, "The Colin Kaepernick Tracker,"

Washington Post, September 7, 2017, https://www.washingtonpost.com/graphics/2017/sports/kaepernick-tracker/?utm_term=.7b964f1ab0b9, accessed January 15, 2018.

23. Darren Rovell, "NFL Television Ratings Down 9.7 Percent during 2017 Regular Season," ESPN, January 4, 2018, http://www.espn.com/nfl/story/_/id/21960086/nfl-television-ratings-97-percent-2017-regular-season, accessed February 20, 2018.

24. Such reactions recall the intense criticism Minnesota Twins manager Ron Gardenhire faced when he complained in 2003 about the long interruption of play and, as a result, negative effects on his pitcher associated with the seventh inning–stretch performance of "God Bless America" by Ronan Tynan at Yankee Stadium, another American "hymn" woven into the pageant of games by the Yankees since the 2001 season after the 9/11 attacks. Following Tynan's lengthy performance, the Twins pitcher, Brad Radke, hit a batsman. See Associated Press, "Gardenhire Not a Fan of This Kind of Music," *Los Angeles Times*, October 3, 2003, http://articles.latimes.com/2003/oct/03/sports/sp-twinsyankeesnotes3, accessed February 23, 2018.

25. David J. Leonard, "Curt Flood: 'Death Is a Slave's Freedom,'" in *Reconstructing Fame: Sport, Race, and Evoking Reputations*, ed. David C. Ogden and Joel Nathan Rosen (Jackson: University Press of Mississippi, 2008), 39.

26. Rebecca Kheel, "McCain, Flake Slam 'Paid Patriotism' at Sporting Events," *The Hill*, November 4, 2015, http://thehill.com/policy/defense/259120-mccain-flake-slam-so-called-paid-patriotism-at-sporting-events, accessed February 21, 2018.

27. In 2011, ESPN and Morale Entertainment, a sports promotions company, joined to stage the Carrier Classic, opening the men's college basketball season on Veterans Day by pitting North Carolina against Michigan State on the deck of the USS *Carl Vinson*, the aircraft carrier charged with burying Osama bin Laden at sea ("Carrier Classic: UNC–Michigan State," *Sports Illustrated*, November 21, 2011, https://www.si.com/college-basketball/photos/2011/11/14carrier-classic-unc-michigan-state#1, accessed February 24, 2018). On July 3, 2016, Major League Baseball, the Pentagon, and ESPN partnered to produce the first regular-season game of a major professional sport to be played on an active military installation, bringing the Miami Marlins and the Atlanta Braves to Fort Bragg, North Carolina, in a temporary $5 million facility built just for the occasion (Jay Jaffe, "Fort Bragg Game a Success as Marlins Top Braves on Historic Night," *Sports Illustrated*, July 3, 2016, https://www.si.com/mlb/2016/07/03/miami-marlins-atlanta-braves-fort-bragg-game, accessed February 24, 2018).

28. Howard Bryant, "When Leagues Pay for Patriotic Acts, Sports Fans Cover the Costs," ABC News, November 27, 2015, http://abcnews.go.com/Sports/leagues-pay-patriotic-acts-sports-fans-cover-cost/story?id=35447340, accessed February 6, 2018.

29. The Mercedes-Benz Stadium in Atlanta, for example, which *Forbes* describes as a $1.5 billion "wonderplex," requires a footprint of two million square feet and features an eight-panel translucent, retractable roof, a nearly six-story-high, 360-degree video board, the world's largest standalone video scoreboard, and two "skycams" alongside space for more than one hundred TV cameras. See Keith Flamer, "A Bird's-Eye View of Mercedes-Benz Stadium, Atlanta's Epic Wonderplex," *Forbes*, August 30, 2017, https://www.forbes.com/sites/keithflamer/2017/08/30/a-birds-eye-view-of-mercedes-benz-stadium-atlantas-epic-nfl-wonderplex/#1312b5d2659d, accessed February 24, 2018.

30. Darren Rovell, "Roger Goodell Offers to Return Money if Tributes Specifically Paid for by DOD," ESPN, November 4, 2015, http://www.espn.com/nfl/story/_/id/14051326/nfl-audit-teams-marketing-contracts-patriotism-tributes, accessed February 6, 2018.

31. Bryant, "When Leagues Pay for Patriotic Acts."

32. Erik Brady, "Patriotism Boosts Pastime," *USA Today*, September 18, 2001, C1.

33. Michael Obernauer, "Ballparks Full of Fans, Flags and Patriotism," *New York Daily News*, September 19, 2001, 114.

34. Tom Haudricourt, "Patriots Come Out for Baseball," *Milwaukee Journal Sentinel*, September 18, 2001, C5.

35. For the notion of broadcasters as clergy, and for many other remarkable parallels linking professional sport spectatorship to religion, see Butterworth, "Ritual in the 'Church of Baseball,'" 107–29.

36. Derek Thompson, "Why NFL Ratings Are Plummeting: A Two-Part Theory," *Atlantic*, February 1, 2018, https://www.theatlantic.com/business/archive/2018/02/super-bowl-nfl -ratings-decline/551861/, accessed February 23, 2018.

37. Guy Debord, *The Society of the Spectacle*, trans. Donald Nicholson-Smith (New York: Zone Books, 1995), 44; from the original *La société du spectacle* (Paris: Buchet-Chastel, 1967).

38. Zach Schonbrun, "Fanatics, Maker of Sports Apparel, Thrives by Seizing the Moment," *New York Times*, November 20, 2017, https://www.nytimes.com/2017/11/20/business/fanatics -apparel.html, accessed February 23, 2018.

39. Debord, *The Society of the Spectacle*, 45.

40. Debord, *The Society of the Spectacle*, 12.

41. G. Edward White, "The First Amendment Comes of Age: The Emergence of Free Speech in Twentieth-Century America," *Michigan Law Review* 95, no. 2 (1996): 331. The case is *West Virginia State Board of Education v. Barnette* (1943).

42. Debord, *The Society of the Spectacle*, 13, original emphasis.

43. David Rowe, *Sport, Culture, and the Media: The Unruly Trinity* (Buckingham, Bucks., England: Open University Press, 1999), 22.

44. Debord, *The Society of the Spectacle*, 13.

45. See Jean Baudrillard, *Simulacra and Simulation*, trans. Sheila Faria Glaser (Ann Arbor: University of Michigan Press, 1994).

46. Baudrillard, *Simulacra and Simulation*, 28.

47. Baudrillard, *Simulacra and Simulation*, 28.

48. Tyler Kepner, "At Yankee Stadium, Tributes and a Monument to Heroism," *New York Times*, September 12, 2002, D1, http://www.nytimes.com/2002/09/12/sports/baseball-at -yankee-stadium-tributes-and-a-monument-to-heroism.html, accessed February 20, 2018.

49. Butterworth, "Ritual in the 'Church of Baseball,'" 117.

50. Filmmaker Chris Marker smartly, wonderfully explores this paradox in his 1962 short film *La Jetée*.

51. "Technology and Video Displays: A World-Class Experience," Mercedes-Benz Stadium, http://mercedesbenzstadium.com/technology-video-displays/, accessed February 24, 2018.

52. Debord, *The Society of the Spectacle*, 14.

53. This element of perceived danger is another echo of the 1968 Olympics. John Carlos said in a 2001 article that it was the fist that scared people. "White folks would have forgiven the black socks, the silk scarf, the bowed head," he wrote. "But they saw that raised black fist and were afraid." In Hill, "Racing after Smith and Carlos," 104.

54. Debord, *The Society of the Spectacle*, 32.

55. Roger Stahl, *Militainment, Inc.: War, Media, and Popular Culture* (New York: Routledge, 2009), 31.

56. Zirin, *What's My Name Fool?*, 135.

57. "DOD Releases Fiscal Year 2020 Budget Proposal," US Department of Defense, March 12, 2019, https://www.defense.gov/Newsroom/Releases/Release/Article/1782623/dod-releases-fiscal-year-2020-budget-proposal/.

58. Natalie Weiner, "The NFL's Last Men Kneeling," *Bleacher Report*, January 3, 2018, http://bleacherreport.com/articles/2752195-the-nfls-last-men-kneeling.

59. Michael L. Butterworth, "Public Memorializing in the Stadium: Mediated Sport, the 10th Anniversary of 9/11, and the Illusion of Democracy," *Communication and Sport* 2, no. 3 (2014): 11.

60. The term "terministic screen" is from Butterworth, "Public Memorializing in the Stadium," 6.

61. Prior to this work going to press, while the Breonna Taylor and Ahmaud Arbery cases are still working their way through the courts, the man accused in the George Floyd murder, patrolman Derek Chauvin, was found guilty of one count each of second-degree unintentional murder, third-degree murder, and second-degree manslaughter. Chauvin's sentencing is still to follow. See Eric Levenson, "What's Next for the 3 Other Ex-Officers Charged in George Floyd's Death?," CNN, April 26, 2021, https://www.cnn.com/2021/04/26/us/tou-thao-thomas-lane-alexander-kueng/index.html.

62. Vincent Frank, "Why Didn't Roger Goodell Mention Colin Kaepernick in NFL's Black Lives Matter Statement?," *Forbes*, June 6, 2020, https://www.forbes.com/sites/vincentfrank/2020/06/06/why-didnt-roger-goodell-mention-colin-kaepernick-in-nfls-black-lives-matter-statement/?sh=4b13632c55f4.

"RUSSIAN SENSATION" OR "MEAN GIRL"?

Maria Sharapova, Drug Bans, and Schadenfreude

RORY MAGRATH

INTRODUCTION

This chapter focuses on one of women's tennis's most discernible athletes—Russian player Maria Sharapova. Having fled the fallout of the Chernobyl disaster in 1986, Sharapova's parents moved to Nyagan, a small town in northwestern Russia. Athletically talented from a young age, Sharapova began developing her game at a time when the Soviet Union was emerging from a period of athletic wilderness.[1] Best evidencing this, many Western nations, including the United States and West Germany, boycotted the 1980 Olympic Games in Moscow, an action reciprocated by the Soviets at the 1984 Games in Los Angeles.[2] These factors combined make Sharapova a fascinating case study.

Her prominence in global tennis also means that since around 2010 she has become one of the most *marketable* tennis players—and even athletes in general—in the world.[3] More problematically, however, Sharapova has also gained considerable notoriety because of her fifteen-month drug ban that stretched from the 2016 to the 2017 season.

This chapter is structured thus: first, it contextualizes some of the important gendered dynamics of tennis's structure. Second, I provide a biography of Sharapova's career: her early years developing as a tennis player, her move to the United States, her transition to professionalism, and her success on the global tennis tour. Third, I provide a media analysis of Sharapova's drug ban, outlining media responses, player responses, and the impact of her ban on professional tennis. Finally, I conclude with some short observations about the importance of Sharapova's prominence in tennis and the impact of her doping on the professional game.

TENNIS, GENDER, AND MEDIA

Tennis is generally considered to be the most popular individual competitive sport in the world.[4] Evidencing this popularity, the professional game's coveted Grand Slam tournaments—the Australian Open, the French Open, Wimbledon, and the US Open—play host to millions of spectators each year. In 2017, more people attended these events than ever before.[5] These events also continue to command significant levels of global media attention.[6]

One of the factors that separates tennis from other popular sports—and likely facilitates its global popularity—is the dynamic under which the sport operates. Physically demanding for all its athletes, it is unlike popular and traditional team sports in that it can be both gender segregated—that is, men versus men or women versus women—and unsegregated, albeit only in its doubles format. At the sport's elite level, the unusual dynamics of tennis also mean that there are various different versions of the sport, such as singles, doubles, and mixed doubles. There are various adaptations for disabled participants, too.

One of the biggest controversies in tennis, however, concerns the length of matches. Men's matches, for example, are typically longer, comprising the best of five sets. By contrast, women's tennis comprises only the best of three sets. The reasons and traditions for this are unclear, but it is widely accepted that it is due to perceptions regarding the comparable weakness of women's bodies.[7] Amanda Roth and Susan Basow, for example, note that "sports often value male strengths . . . over female strengths."[8]

These gendered dynamics have been the source of consistent controversy over the past few decades. Even as far back as 1973, the infamous Battle of the Sexes match in which Billie Jean King defeated Bobby Riggs represented a clash of traditional gender ideology with the growing feminist politics of the era.[9] A similar event was staged twenty years later, when Jimmy Connors defeated Martina Navratilova. Highlighting the public interest in mixed-gender tennis, each of these events drew significant viewing figures, with thousands watching inside the arena and millions more watching at home on television.[10]

While these debates have not altogether disappeared,[11] contemporary gendered debates are largely situated around prize money, specifically over whether male and female players should receive equal pay given the disparity in match length. Indeed, it has only been since around 2010 that all Grand Slam tournaments have offered equal pay for both male and female champions.[12] Discussions concerning equal pay have been particularly evident in sport media's coverage of tennis.[13] The topic has been frequently discussed by both current and former high-profile players. For instance, Sergiy Stakhovsky, Serena Williams, and Martina Navratilova have all acknowledged the issue in recent years. Former top-ranked Australian player Pat Cash even has a page on his personal website dedicated to the topic, in which he proposes two solutions to the question of equal pay.[14] The game's current crop of players also weigh in; Serbian star Novak Djokovic and leading Spanish player Rafael Nadal recently claimed that because men bring greater levels of media attention to the sport, they should earn more in prize money.[15] Both were widely condemned in the sports world for their comments.[16]

This line of reasoning has fostered significant interest in the academic world. Indeed, a plethora of research has documented how sport media's representation of women's tennis has been complicated by a range of factors, including underrepresentation, misrepresentation, sexualization, eroticization, racism, sexuality, and trivialization, as I will discuss in the context of Maria Sharapova later in this chapter.[17]

On the surface, then, Djokovic's and Nadal's comments are problematic. As the research above implies, women's tennis continues to receive far less scrutiny than the men's game, although this conclusion is clouded by a number of issues. Nevertheless, some of the most successful tennis players—both male and female—are among sport's most prominent athletes. Swiss champion Roger Federer, the most successful male tennis player of all time, even has his own fashion label, as does female player Serena Williams. These athletes, along with several other high-profile tennis players, represent what Matthew Thomson calls the "human brand."[18] Accordingly, claims that male players are the primary drivers in tennis's popularity is shortsighted and thus worthy of greater academic attention.[19] However, while these calls for greater academic scrutiny are of course legitimate, they are beyond the scope of analysis for this chapter. Instead, I focus on the sporting life of Maria Sharapova, starting first with her early years and the development of her tennis game.

THE EARLY DAYS

Maria Sharapova was born on April 19, 1987, in Nyagan, a small town in northwestern Russia, then still the Soviet Union. Her parents, Yuri and Yelena, hailed from the now-Belarusian town of Gomel, around two hundred kilometers northeast of Chernobyl. In 1986, shortly before Yelena became pregnant with Maria, the family learned of the catastrophic disaster at the Chernobyl Nuclear Power Plant. Despite being initially reassured by local officials, the family fled the deadly radiation by heading north, an escape that Yuri Sharapova described as a "crazy, crazy time,"[20] recalling their long and crowded trip first to Siberia, then to Yekaterinburg, before finally settling in Nyagan. Interestingly, Sharapova credits the Chernobyl disaster as the event that ultimately made her a tennis player, as it resulted in her family's relocation to a more developed part of the Soviet Union.

In her autobiography, *Unstoppable: My Life So Far*, Sharapova fondly describes her parents' early years, recalling how they had met at school and quickly became enamored of one another. While her mother was educated, her father had left school at an early age to pursue a career in maintenance. An athletic man, he had a particular interest in ice hockey and mountain climbing. Interestingly, however, it was not until he was an adult that he played tennis for the first time, which was likely due to the fact that in the Soviet Union, tennis was a sport typically reserved for any remaining aristocracy and was rarely played by the working class.[21] This, as Sharapova writes, was a seminal moment. She recalls: "He fell in love with the game. . . . He was preparing himself, though he did not know it. He was in training to become that strange and exotic thing, a tennis parent."[22]

Her family would move to Sochi in 1989, and two years later Sharapova was presented with her first tennis racket while being assigned to her first tennis club and coach, Yuri Yudkin. Having been involved in tennis for several years, Yudkin was a well-known figure in Sochi insomuch as parents in the area would wait for his assessment of their children's tennis ability. Shortly after her arrival in the club, Sharapova was soon receiving private training from Yudkin, whom she credits for helping her build stamina, toughness, and speed, which make up the bulk of her enviable skill set.

But after training Sharapova for less than a year, Yudkin advised Sharapova's father that in order to progress her career, she would need to seek better training elsewhere. Thus, in a matter of weeks, Yuri Sharapova resigned from his job and dedicated himself to supporting the development of his daughter's career. In 1993, they began attending a Moscow tennis clinic run by Martina Navratilova, one the most successful players of all time, who soon recommended that the talented Sharapova seek training at the IMG Tennis Academy in Miami, Florida, which was known for developing future champions, including Andre Agassi and Monica Seles. When they returned to Sochi, Yuri immediately began planning the family's move to the United

States. However, the political climate of the time complicated matters for the family.

Indeed, despite the breakup of the Soviet Union two years earlier, travel to countries like the United States, which remained for many the "capitalist enemy," was still heavily restricted.[23] In her autobiography, Sharapova recalls her father pleading with officials at the Russian Ministry of Foreign Affairs to allow the family to travel. Eventually, they were granted a three-year visa to travel to the United States, an outcome that she described as a "golden ticket ... [a] miracle."[24] There were, however, two major complications. First of all, Sharapova's mother had not been permitted to travel with them, and she only joined Maria and Yuri some two years later, in 1995. And second, Yuri was forced to spend all of his life's savings and borrow around US$700 on top of that to make the trip. Indeed, upon arrival in the United States, Yuri worked a series of low-paying jobs to support his daughter's tennis lessons.

Having initially trained at the Rick Macci Tennis Academy in Boca Raton, Maria was then signed by IMG in 1996, who funded her $35,000 tuition fee. Joining IMG was a significant moment for Sharapova and her father, for it eliminated their financial concerns. They now had guaranteed rent, food, travel, and medical support. In addition, joining IMG led to the now eleven-year-old Sharapova signing with Nike, becoming one of their youngest athletes. Her first Nike contract was worth $50,000 plus opportunities for performance bonuses.

But despite Sharapova's improved economic situation and obvious tennis talent, she describes her life at the tennis academy as having been "miserable." In her autobiography, for example, she recalls:

> I want to call it a prison, but I guess it was really just a tennis prison. All the academies are like that—laid out like prisons, with the stout buildings and the neat paths, the curfews and yards, the food lines, the bragging and the arguing, with the women over there and the men are over here. . . . I was lonely. I barely saw my father. . . . Life in the dorm was no fun.[25]

Given that previous research has documented the likeness between sports academies and prisons,[26] Sharapova's comparison here is perhaps unsurprising. Erving Goffman formulates the concept of the "total institution" to conceptualize a person living within strict confines—usually referring to prisoners or patients in a mental asylum.[27] In sports academies, as with Sharapova's example above, athletes also operate in an isolated, enclosed, and controlling environment, which Eric Anderson describes as a "near-total institution."[28] Anderson argues that while athletes hold more power than prisoners given that athletes have the ability to quit sport should they desire, there nevertheless remain similarities between these two circumstances. This is especially the case in professional sport. In Sharapova's case, there was an added weight of expectation—from sponsors, for example—for her to be a successful athlete. Accordingly, she had a particularly grueling training schedule in the academy:

5:30 a.m. Wake up

5:45 a.m. Breakfast

6:15 a.m. Practice on Nick's court

7:30 a.m. Clinics and drills

12:30 p.m. Lunch

1:30 p.m. Practice

4:00 p.m. Fitness

5:00 p.m. Dinner

7:00 p.m. "Schoolwork"

9:00 p.m. Bed[29]

This schedule, Sharapova recalls, remained the same throughout her time at the academy. Moreover, as corroborated by research on professional sports friendships,[30] she describes her dorm mates as "competitors, not friends," suggesting that she enjoyed few close friendships during her time at the academy.[31] This facet of her experience at IMG would later prove an integral part of Sharapova's life in professional tennis.

Nevertheless, despite her unhappy time at the academy, Sharapova continued to develop into a talented tennis player. By 2000, she began to compete in notable, but still amateur, tournaments. This, she maintains, was an extremely competitive time in her transition from amateur to professional tennis player, and she recalls: "Only the best youth players in the world make it into these tournaments. Only the best of the best make it out. It's like the eye of a needle.

Just a handful get through to the next stage."[32] At first, her wildcard entry into many of these tournaments resulted in defeats.[33] However, through the perseverance of her coaches in developing her into a professional tennis player, she competed in her first pro event at age fourteen.

She consistently ranked highly in the junior world singles rankings and reached the final of eight junior singles tournaments, including two junior Grand Slam events, Wimbledon and the Australian Open in 2002, winning three. Her grounding in these events, coupled with her training and development in the United States, had prepared her for participation in professional tennis.

TURNING PROFESSIONAL

In 2003, at just sixteen, Sharapova joined the professional tennis circuit. Despite her excitement at turning professional, Sharapova describes how she initially "struggled to find a rhythm on the tour."[34] Thus, it is perhaps unsurprising that in each of the first two Grand Slam tournaments of the year, the Australian Open and French Open, she was defeated in the first round. As previous research has documented with respect to professional athletes' migration and travel across the world,[35] Sharapova struggled to adapt; she recalls the long trips to Melbourne and Paris for Grand Slam tournaments, only to lose in the early stages of each, thus marring her enjoyment of her location. What was perhaps also problematic here, however, was the fact that she had begun to develop a reputation for being a "cold" person and had few friends on the tennis circuit,[36] a theme to which I will return later in the chapter.

In 2003, the same year as her breakthrough in the professional game, Sharapova also participated at Wimbledon for the first time, beating Ashley Harkleroad in the first round, Elena Bovina in the second, and Jelena Dokic in the third before losing to Svetlana Kuznetsova in the fourth round. But her progression to the fourth round was a "rebirth,"[37] and her success led to her being described as a "Russian sensation."[38] A small caveat to her success, however, were critics who described as being "noisy" on the court. For instance, one reporter described her as having "the scream of a small jet engine," rendering her as the "Queen of Scream."[39] She responded to such criticism by admitting: "I don't even know I'm doing it."[40]

Nevertheless, in September 2003, Sharapova finally secured her first professional victory at the Japan Open. She followed that success by winning the Challenge Bell in Quebec City that December; as a result, she was named the Women's Tennis Association's Newcomer of the Year. By the following year, having reached the third round of the Australian Open and the quarterfinals of the French Open, Sharapova had begun to pave the way for her Wimbledon success later in the year.

Having settled in London prior to the start of the tournament, Sharapova recalls being in a relaxed mood, ready to compete. Having made it through matches against the likes of lesser-known talents including Amy Frazier, Daniela Hantuchová, Anne Keothavong, Yuliya Beygelzimer, and Ai Sugiyama, Sharapova met the fifth seed, the more heralded Lindsay Davenport, in the semifinals. This matchup, she recalls, made her nervous, and she began to question her own ability and experience in the professional game. Sharapova was also in awe of the Wimbledon traditions, such as the quality of the court and the fan base's knowledge of the game. Moreover, she had never played against Davenport, who was much more experienced in that she had been playing professionally since the early 1990s. Such anxieties contributed to Sharapova's poor start to the match, which she herself acknowledged: "I was overpowered, overmatched. She was a woman. I was a girl. She was big. I was small. She hit the corners. I hit the net."[41] And yet, following what turned out to be a welcomed rain delay, Sharapova recovered to beat Davenport in three sets, thus setting up the final against Serena Williams.

Williams, the top seed at Wimbledon in 2004, had won the previous two tournaments as well as the Australian Open the previous year. She would later, of course, become one of the most successful female tennis players of all time. But Sharapova, despite her complaints of a mild illness before the final, shockingly defeated Williams in straight sets. Although Sharapova was ranked thirteenth in the world prior to this tournament, she was not expected to be this successful, leaving a *Washington Post* sportswriter to describe her victory as "the most stunning upset in memory."[42] In doing so, she also became the third-youngest winner of the women's singles event and the second-youngest in the Grand Slam era.

Given Sharapova's stunning achievement in winning Wimbledon in this fashion, one might expect the earlier "Russian sensation" narrative to dominate the proceedings. But, despite her success, her achievements were largely trivialized in favor of sexualization. Indeed, in their analysis of sports media's coverage of tennis Grand Slams, Michael Messner, Margaret Carlisle Duncan, and Nicole Willms write: "Commentators rarely seemed to report on Sharapova without also commenting (often jokingly) on her appearance."[43] Such remarks were sometimes subtle, but often not. In a 2002 article, John Harris and Ben Clayton outline how sport media's representation of female athletes, perhaps unsurprisingly, centers on sensuality,[44] heterosexuality, and sexualization, a point that is taken up in more recent research as well.[45] John Vincent and Jane Crossman's analysis of sport media further shows how Sharapova was "replete with ambivalent and seemingly contradictory references to her fellow Russian, Anna Kournikova."[46]

In the late 1990s and early 2000s, Kournikova's prominence in professional tennis facilitated sport media's coverage of women's sports to "individual athletes presented as icons of white, heterosexual, feminine attractiveness."[47] While Kournikova had some nominal success—she won Australian Open doubles events in 1999 and again in 2002—it is generally accepted that she was an inferior player to Sharapova. She never won a singles Grand Slam tournament, and her peak achievement had been to reach the Wimbledon semifinals in 1997, losing to the eventual winner, Martina Hingis. In spite of Sharapova's greater success, however, she received the same treatment as Kournikova and was framed as "an object of desire and beauty to be gazed upon."[48]

General media attention on Sharapova increased exponentially following her initial Wimbledon success. She became increasingly marketable, receiving numerous requests to "brand" certain products after her stunning upset. Indeed, she recalls the immediate aftermath of her win in her autobiography: "The telephone rang, the agents called, the offers poured in.... How do you say no when the world is on the line?"[49] She soon began representing such prominent organizations as Motorola, Canon, Head, and ESPN. A new and attractive commercial entity, a freshly minted top-ten tennis player who was also one of the youngest Wimbledon champions of all time, Sharapova had arrived on the big stage, generating in her wake what CNN's Chris Isidore described as "Maria Mania."[50]

"MARIA MANIA" AT CENTER COURT

Although Sharapova failed to win any of the four 2005 Grand Slam events, making it to three semifinals and one quarterfinal before losing to the eventual winners of each tournament, she ended that Grand Slam season ranked number one in the world. In 2006, having reached the semifinals of the Australian Open and Wimbledon, she won the US Open by beating Justine Henin-Hardenne in the final. She was later defeated by Serena Williams in the final of the Australian Open in 2007, but won that tournament the following year without dropping a set and despite being an underdog for most of her run there.

Still, with the competitive nature of professional tennis, Sharapova's Grand Slam achievements were largely underwhelming, particularly given the early

Maria Sharapova's Grand Slam Record				
Year	Australian	French	Wimbledon	US
2004	3R	Q-F	W	3R
2005	S-F	Q-F	S-F	S-F
2006	S-F	4R	S-F	W
2007	F	S-F	4R	3R
2008	W	4R	2R	-
2009	-	Q-F	2R	3R
2010	1R	3R	4R	4R
2011	4R	S-F	F	3R
2012	F	W	4R	SF
2013	SF	F	2R	-
2014	4R	W	4R	4R
2015	F	4R	S-F	-
2016	Q-F	-	-	-
W: Winner	F: Finalist	S-F: Semifinal	Q-F: Quarterfinal	1–4R: First–Fourth Round

promise she displayed during her adolescence. More importantly, Sharapova also had numerous injuries including a recurring shoulder injury, a hamstring injury, and an ankle injury, all of which impacted her court performance. Indeed, she missed the 2008 US Open and the 2009 Australian Open due to ailments. In all, her injuries, along with the increasing dominance of Serena Williams, contributed to her lack of success in Grand Slam tournaments moving forward; it would take her another four years to win another, the French Open in 2012 (see table 2).

Sharapova's reputation for "coldness" also meant that she received little support or sympathy from her fellow competitors. Although previous research has documented that close friendships are often restricted in elite sport due to sport's competitive nature,[51] it is particularly unusual in an individual sport like tennis for a player to gain such a reputation for distance. In 2013, Sharapova herself confirmed her distance from other players: "I'm not really close to many players. . . . Just because you're in the same sport doesn't mean that you have to be friends with everyone."[52] This, of course, did little to settle any mounting controversy and led to numerous personal slights, such as when the *Telegraph* described her as a "locker-room loner"[53] while the *New York Post* asked: "Why does everyone in tennis hate Maria Sharapova?"[54]

But it is her conspicuous absence from any Grand Slam tournaments beyond the 2016 Australian Open and the public reaction to this absence that is worthy of consideration here, as it was during this tournament that she failed a routine drug test conducted at the request of the International Tennis Federation (ITF), a matter she tackles head on in the prologue of her autobiography:

> Three weeks into the season, I got an e-mail from the ITF. . . . Meldonium had been found in my urine, and in January 2016 Meldonium had been added to the World Anti-Doping Agency's list of banned substances. In other words, I was now a drug violator. I'd be suspended from competition immediately.[55]

As this statement illustrates, Sharapova took great pains to both address and examine her doping issues in her autobiography. Meldonium, she writes, is a supplement that she had been taking for a decade after it was recommended by a family doctor to reduce her fatigue. She is critical of the drug's inclusion on the banned substance list, and she has denied that it enhances performance in any way. But she also accepts responsibility for her failed drug test, which appears to have forever tarnished her reputation.

A CONTROVERSIAL FIGURE

Following Sharapova's 2016 positive drug test, she was provisionally suspended in March by the ITF, before the Court of Arbitration for Sport (CAS) announced that she would be banned for two years, ultimately reduced to fifteen months on appeal. The ban was reduced largely because she had taken Meldonium for over a decade and had not faced any doping issues during that time. The CAS also determined that she had taken the drug for medical reasons, rather than as an attempt to enhance performance.

The media response to these revelations was primarily one of shock under the guise of both condemnation and sympathy. Several newspapers were critical, pointing to the apparently ample warnings Sharapova had received prior to her drug test informing players that Meldonium was now on the World Anti-Doping Agency's banned substance list. In the *Daily Mail*, John Greechan was positively scathing in his attack on Sharapova:

> It is the unblinking arrogance that really sets the gallstones rumbling. The cheating, the sneaking, the bribery and even the lame, half-hearted

excuses? None of that would be quite so bad if only it was all accompanied by even an ounce of humility.[56]

Also in the *Daily Mail*, Oliver Holt claims that Sharapova's case is evidence of an endemic drug problem in eastern European sport more broadly, arguing that "Sharapova may or may not have had legitimate medical reasons for using meldonium, but it is unlikely the hoards of Russian sportsmen and women who have been using it were all suffering from heart problems."[57] Holt makes reference to the several large-scale doping controversies surrounding Russian athletes that have arisen since around 2010.[58]

Writing for the *Independent*, however, Paul Newman was more sympathetic. He describes Sharapova as "the ultimate sporting professional," adding that her drug ban was "one rare moment of unprofessionalism [which] had cost her the chance to carry on playing tennis."[59] And in the *Times*, Martyn Ziegler queries the use of Meldonium as a performance-enhancing drug.[60] This same line of reasoning was also adopted by Russian president Vladimir Putin, who defended Sharapova, adding that Meldonium "was never considered as doping. It doesn't influence the result. . . . It just keeps the heart muscles in good condition."[61] Accordingly, in light of Putin's comments, Sharapova was provisionally selected for the 2016 Olympic squad.[62]

PEER CONDEMNATION

Given that Sharapova has gained a reputation for being cold and aloof on the tennis circuit, it is perhaps unsurprising that her fellow players were largely disinterested in aiding her during her predicament. Indeed, there was little support or sympathy toward her whatsoever. Among female tennis players, former French Open finalist Dominika Cibulková remarked: "I don't feel sorry at all for Sharapova and I don't miss her on the tour. She's a totally unlikeable person. Arrogant, conceited and cold."[63] Similarly, French player Kiki Mladenovic added that Sharapova "has no excuse that can defend what she's done. . . . She wasn't really liked. I respected her for her career but she wasn't really nice or polite."[64] Caroline Wozniacki, Petra Kvitová, and Victoria Azarenka were also scathing in their assessment of Sharapova's plight.[65] Only Serena Williams, one of her biggest rivals, expressed any sympathy, though she was also supportive of any ban imposed on Sharapova.[66]

The lack of support afforded to Sharapova was similarly evident among former players. Retired star Jennifer Capriati, for example, wrote on social media that her own career had ended prematurely because she had "refused to cheat. . . . I had to throw in the towel and suffer."[67] Former player turned broadcaster John McEnroe was skeptical about Sharapova's claim of ignorance, proclaiming: "It would be hard to believe that no one in her camp, the 25 or 30 people that work for her, or Maria herself had no idea that this happened."[68] Acknowledging this glaring lack of support for Sharapova, former player Chris Evert attributed this to her lack of popularity on tour: "She has always isolated herself from the rest of the tennis world, from the players. . . . Her friendships are outside the tennis world."[69]

Male players were equally negative in their discussions about Sharapova. The highest-ranked players at the time, the so-called Big Four of Andy Murray, Rafael Nadal, Roger Federer, and Novak Djokovic, publicly criticized Sharapova's actions, claiming among other matters that she deserved her punishment. Nadal, who has been frequently accused of doping in the past, added that while "mistakes happen . . . she must be punished."[70] Djokovic initially expressed sympathy for Sharapova but would later proclaim that "she must be prepared for punishment."[71] And Britain's Andy Murray was especially critical of Sharapova, of whom he remarked: "It's your responsibility to know what you're taking is legal."[72]

In the aftermath of Sharapova's announcement, Murray, who had always been particularly critical about doping in tennis, told Britain's *Daily Mail* that he had been "suspicious" of certain players because "they don't seem to be getting tired."[73] However, former German champion Boris Becker, who at the time of Sharapova's announcement was coaching Novak Djokovic, was in turn quite critical of Murray's comments:

> We have random drug testing and unless it's proven, they are 100 per cent innocent. . . . To assume something because somebody has won a Grand Slam or is fitter is totally out of order. Andy is one of the fittest players on tour—he often outlasts players and nobody is questioning his ethics.[74]

Thus, for Becker, Sharapova's situation was enough to inspire confidence in the way tennis authorities were addressing issues of doping, rendering her positive test and subsequent ban as evidence that the sport was indeed taking the matter quite seriously.

DAMAGE CONTROL

Sharapova's unsympathetic peers, largely supportive of her ban, failed to notice that the ban was affecting her personally and the sport as well. For example, many of Sharapova's commercial endorsements with certain organizations were also suspended, which was a huge matter given how far women have come in terms of garnering such endorsements. Prior to her suspension, she had been listed by *Forbes* magazine as the highest-earning female athlete in the world. Following the ban, however, high-profile organizations such as the sports brand Nike, the luxury watchmaker Tag Heuer, and the car manufacturer Porsche, for whom Sharapova had become the first female ambassador, either ceased or suspended their commercial relationship with her.[75] In her autobiography, Sharapova expresses disappointment with what she calls the "coldness" her endorsers showed, particularly Nike, who had sponsored her since she was eleven.[76]

In contrast to these organizations, racket manufacturer Head continued to publicly support Sharapova and even extended their contract with her. The company released a statement that read:

> Head is proud to stand behind Maria, now and into the future. . . .
> For more than a decade, Maria Sharapova has been a role model and
> woman of integrity who has inspired millions of fans around the world
> to play and watch tennis.[77]

Head celebrated Sharapova's eventual ban reduction by the CAS on social media, promoting the hashtag #WeStoodWithMaria, although they were widely criticized for doing so.[78] The *Guardian*'s Andrew Jerell Jones described Head's support as "a defining statement, showing how the loyalty by her litany of backers can produce such stunning lack of self-awareness."[79]

The aftereffects of Sharapova's ban could also be seen through her absence at major tennis tournaments. According to Dan King in the *Sun*, "Maria Sharapova's likely absence from Wimbledon would be a major blow according to the chairman [Philip Brook] of the All-England Club."[80] Indeed, Philip Brook commented: "It would be a great shame if Maria was not here."[81] These comments were made in light of Sharapova's popularity at the tournament, and there were fears that her absence from participating in the competition would negatively impact the interest of spectators and television audiences.

Finally, and arguably the most significant way in which the Sharapova doping story affected tennis, was through the numerous calls for changes to how such incidents would be approached in the future. Such calls followed in the wake of Sharapova's announcement, but also against the backdrop of problematic findings in an ESPN survey. The survey polled thirty-one professional players, finding that almost 25 percent of them knew of a fellow professional player who had doped at some stage of his or her career.[82]

Accordingly, there were calls for greater transparency in the way that professional tennis addresses doping issues. In an interview with the *Guardian*, David Haggerty, president of the ITF, acknowledged: "We've discussed the possibility of announcing provisional suspensions. . . . We understand the importance of transparency. We're also doing that with the Integrity unit; they've begun to publish a quarterly report."[83] This was also an approach advocated by Andy Murray, who, even before Sharapova's ban, agreed about the need for transparency.[84] He later called for the ITF to release the drug testing records of all players, thus removing suspicion from "clean" players. As he concluded: "Publishing your data and your testing results . . . obviously leaves much less doubt."[85]

The publication of drug testing results was also supported by Rafael Nadal, who has suffered a multitude of injuries throughout this career and successfully sued the then French minister for health and sport Roselyne Bachelot for her comments that he had served a secret drug ban in 2012. Given that this case was ongoing when Sharapova's announcement was made, Nadal captured the moment by calling for all of his drug tests to be publicly released:

> It would be much better for the transparency of the sport in general to say, "Rafa Nadal is passing an antidoping control today and the result is going to be in two weeks." In the result, you publish the results. The anti-doping control is negative.[86]

Even Sharapova criticized the ITF for their apparent poor handling of her situation. While she initially accepted responsibility for failing her drug test, she later wrote of feeling "blindsided . . . trapped, tricked" by the ITF for their failure to keep her abreast with notifications pertaining to her drug ban.

A CHECKERED RETURN

Sharapova returned to tennis in April 2017, describing it as a "dream" to be playing competitively again.[87] She also spoke of her drug ban and claimed that it was "time to move on" from discussions of it.[88] She was handed wildcard entries to tournaments in Germany, Spain, and Italy; however, she was not granted one to the first Grand Slam event for which she was eligible: the vaunted French Open. But she seemed to have rounded into Grand Slam form quite swiftly. Despite an injury that prevented her from playing at the UK's Birmingham Classic event, she returned to Grand Slam tennis after receiving a wildcard to compete at the 2017 US Open.[89] Interestingly, in stark contrast to many athletes returning to sport after a drug ban, Sharapova was not met with a negative response from fans. As Simon Briggs of the *Times* wrote, "We heard no echo of the boos that had greeted [disgraced Olympic sprinter] Justin Gatlin at London's Olympic Park."[90]

While spectators may have been forgiving of Sharapova's doping, her fellow players were not. A host of male and female players were critical of various tournaments' decisions to grant Sharapova wildcard entry. Romanian player Simona Halep, for example, said that it was "not OK to help with a wildcard the player that was banned for doping. . . . I cannot support what the tournament director did."[91] French player Alizé Cornet described it as "shameful" that Sharapova should be granted wildcard entry, claiming that any "player who has tested positive should start from scratch like everyone else and win her place back."[92] Another French player, Jo-Wilfried Tsonga, was also uneasy: "I would not do it. . . . It's like if you give a sweet to a kid who did a bad thing, it's going to do it again. It sends the wrong message."[93] Similar opposition was vocalized by Roberta Vinci, Caroline Wozniacki, Dominika Cibulková, Agnieszka Radwańska, and Angelique Kerber.

Sharapova only received support from a handful of other players. Czech player Karolína Plíšková said that "tennis definitely needs a star like Sharapova is, so I don't have anything against it."[94] Spanish player Garbiñe Muguruza praised Sharapova for her hard work in returning to professional tennis. She countered that Sharapova was "a great fighter, great attitude, big fight, spirit on the court. . . . I guess she will improve the tournament."[95] And former player Kim Clijsters argued that since Sharapova had served a suspension, that should be deemed the end of the matter. Clijsters maintained that by having served her sentence, Sharapova had paid her debt to the sport in a way that was probably more difficult for her than many seem to have imagined.[96]

It is also important to note that the 2017 US Open itself had to overcome several high-profile players missing from the tournament. Neither Serena Williams nor Novak Djokovic competed, nor did Stan Wawrinka or Victoria Azarenka. And Andy Murray, struggling through injury, was subsequently defeated early in the tournament. Thus, in contrast to the negative commercial effects that Sharapova's drug ban had had on Grand Slam tournaments, her inclusion in the tournament brackets seemed to be welcomed by tournament organizers struggling to maintain viewership. As the *Telegraph*'s

Simon Briggs would write: "All these absentees make Sharapova . . . an even more valuable currency than usual."[97] This could be the case in terms of fan popularity or even the fact that a previously banned player could spark more interest due to the ban's controversial nature.

ANSWERING DIFFICULT QUESTIONS

Despite Sharapova's drug ban, she has always been a controversial figure in the often buttoned-down tennis world. From the challenges of being a talented young athlete in early post-Soviet Russia to the family difficulties she suffered in her early years in the United States, her life in a "prison-like" tennis academy, her matriculation into professionalism, and her professional career and its demands, Sharapova has always shown a troubling though rarely dull career arc. And yet, her reputational and personal foibles notwithstanding, it would ultimately be injuries that would prevent her from fulfilling her complete promise. Indeed, at the time of writing, Sharapova has won five Grand Slam tournaments, which would be an astonishing feat for most on the tour, though hardly the career total that many assumed would mark her place (see table 2).

In sport, of course, reputations are made quickly and nearly impossible to alter. As I noted in the previous section, the negative fan reaction to American sprinter Justin Gatlin at the 2017 World Athletics Championships in London is prime evidence of this. It is thus unsurprising that, following her return to tennis, Sharapova was asked difficult questions about her doping—as well as having to contend with the fact that numerous fellow players condemned various tournaments' decisions to grant her wildcard entry. Thus, even for a highly promising and successful athlete like Maria Sharapova, the negative stigma of doping sticks to athletes throughout their career.[98]

The example of Sharapova also raises several key questions regarding doping in tennis—and indeed in sport more broadly—a few of which might be:

1. Is greater transparency with regard to tennis and doping required?
2. Are there are ongoing issues in tennis and its doping, particularly given that so many players claim to know a fellow player who has doped?
3. Is there any benefit in banning drugs like Meldonium that have no known effect on an athlete's performance?
4. Do we even go so far as to say that performance-enhancing drugs in sport should be legalized? Would sport maintain its popularity if that were the case?

5. And could it be that certain sports would be more easily "sold" if drug use were legalized?

These are important questions, and while scholars have debated them many times over, they all remain open.

NOTES

1. Victor Peppard and James Riordan, *Playing Politics: Soviet and Sport Diplomacy to 1992* (Greenwich, CT: JAI Press, 1993).

2. Allen Guttmann, "The Cold War and the Olympics," *International Journal* 43, no. 4 (Autumn 1988): 554–68.

3. Isaac Ofori-Okyere and Emmanuel S. Asamoah, "Celebrity Endorser Selection Strategies as Effective Marketing Communications Tool in the Automobile Industry: A Review Paper on Related Literature," *International Journal of Business and Marketing Management* 3, no. 1 (January 2015): 1–15.

4. Christoph Breuer, Kirstin Hallmann, and Pamela Wicker, "Determinants of Sport Participation in Different Sports," *Managing Leisure* 16, no. 4 (2011): 269–86.

5. Luigi Gatto, "US Open Sets Sold Out Attendance for Four Days in a Row," *Tennis World*, September 2, 2017, https://www.tennisworldusa.org/tennis/news/Tennis_Stories/46924/us-open-sets-sold-out-attendance-for-four-days-in-a-row/.

6. Nicky Lewis and Andrew J. Weaver, "More Than a Game: Sports Media Framing Effects on Attitudes, Intentions, and Enjoyment," *Communication and Sport* 3, no. 2 (June 2015): 219–42.

7. Nancy Theberge, "Reflections on the Body in the Sociology of Sport," *Quest* 43, no. 2 (1991): 123–34.

8. Amanda Roth and Susan A. Basow, "Femininity, Sports, and Feminism: Developing a Theory of Physical Liberation," *Journal of Sport and Social Issues* 28, no. 3 (2004): 245–65.

9. Nancy E. Spencer, "Reading between the Lines: A Discursive Analysis of the Billie Jean King vs. Bobby Riggs 'Battle of the Sexes,'" *Sociology of Sport Journal* 17, no. 4 (2000): 386–402.

10. Christy Halbert and Melissa Latimer, "'Battling' Gendered Language: An Analysis of the Language Used by Sports Commentators in a Televised Coed Tennis Competition," *Sociology of Sport Journal* 11, no. 3 (1994): 298–308.

11. For example, British player Andy Murray has spoken about his willingness to participate in "mixed singles."

12. Although Grand Slam prize money is now equal, this is not the case in other tournaments in the tennis calendar.

13. Collin R. Flake, Mikaela J. Dufur, and Erin L. Moore, "Advantage Men: The Sex Pay Gap in Professional Tennis," *International Review for the Sociology of Sport* 48, no. 3 (2013): 366–76.

14. Cash proposes that both men's and women's singles tennis should play the best of five sets, or that men continue to play five and women play three—with men being paid more. See "Equal Prize Money at the Grand Slams? It's Not Equal. Simple As," Pat Cash, May 28, 2016, https://www.patcash.co.uk/2016/05/equal-prize-money-at-the-grand-slams-its-not-equal-simple-as-that/.

160Rory Magrath

15. Jack de Menezes, "Novak Djokovic Questions Equal Prize Money after Official Sparks Sexism Row with 'Go Down on Your Knees' Remark," *Independent* (UK), March 21, 2016, https://www.independent.co.uk/sport/tennis/novak-djokovic-questions-prize-money-after-tennis-official-accused-of-sexism-with-go-down-on-your-a6943696.html.

16. James Dator, "Nobody Needs Rafael Nadal's Bad Take on Women's Pay in Tennis," *SB Nation*, June 13, 2018, https://www.sbnation.com/tennis/2018/6/13/17459962/rafael-nadal-equal-pay-tennis-male-models.

17. John Vincent and Jane Crossman, "Champions, a Celebrity Crossover, and a Capitulator: The Construction of Gender in Broadsheet Newspapers' Narratives about Selected Competitors at Wimbledon," *International Journal of Sport Communication* 1, no. 1 (March 2008): 78–102; and John Vincent, Paul M. Pedersen, Warren A. Whisenant, and Dwayne Massey, "Analysing the Print Media Coverage of Professional Tennis Players: British Newspaper Narratives about Female Competitors in the Wimbledon Championships," *International Journal of Sport Management and Marketing* 2, no. 3 (2007): 281–300.

18. Matthew Thomson, "Human Brands: Investigating Antecedents to Consumers' Strong Attachments to Celebrities," *Journal of Marketing* 70, no. 3 (2006): 104–19.

19. Flake, Dufur, and Moore, "Advantage Men."

20. Maria Sharapova, *Unstoppable: My Life So Far* (New York: Sarah Crichton Books, 2017), 14.

21. James Riordan, *Sport in Soviet Society: Development of Sport and Physical Education in Russia and the USSR* (Cambridge: Cambridge University Press, 1980).

22. Sharapova, *Unstoppable*, 13.

23. Russell King, ed., *The New Geography of European Migrations* (London: Belhaven Press, 1993).

24. Sharapova, *Unstoppable*, 26.

25. Sharapova, *Unstoppable*, 85.

26. In sport academies, athletes spend large amounts of time together in a controlled environment, training, attending college, socializing, and even living together. Andrew Parker's research in soccer academies documents this very closely. See Andrew Parker, "Professional Football Club Culture: Goffman, Asylums and Occupational Socialization," Scottish Centre Research Papers in Sport, Leisure and Society, 1996, 123–30.

27. Erving Goffman, *Asylums: Essays on the Social Situation of Mental Patients and Other Inmates* (Garden City, NY: Anchor Books, 1961).

28. Eric Anderson, *In the Game: Gay Athletes and the Cult of Masculinity* (Albany: State University of New York Press, 2005).

29. Sharapova, *Unstoppable*, 87.

30. Steven Roberts, Eric Anderson, and Rory Magrath, "Continuity, Change and Complexity in the Performance of Masculinity among Elite Young Footballers in England," *British Journal of Sociology* 68, no. 2 (2017): 336–57.

31. Sharapova, *Unstoppable*, 88.

32. Sharapova, *Unstoppable*, 88.

33. Sharapova's IMG sponsorship enabled her to receive wildcard entries to certain tournaments on a regular basis.

34. Sharapova, *Unstoppable*, 88.

35. Joseph Maguire and David Stead, "Border Crossings: Soccer Labour Migration and the European Union," *International Review for the Sociology of Sport* 33, no. 1 (1998): 59–73.

36. Jim White, "Maria Sharapova Says She Does Not Get On with Other Players as She Moves into the Second Round," *Telegraph* (UK), June 24, 2013, https://www.telegraph.co.uk/sport/tennis/mariasharapova/10140044/Wimbledon-2013-Maria-Sharapova-says-she-does-not-get-on-well-with-other-players-as-she-moves-into-the-second-round.html.

37. Sharapova, *Unstoppable*, 137.

38. Georgina Turner, "Stunning Sharapova Takes Title," *Guardian*, July 3, 2004, https://www.theguardian.com/sport/2004/jul/03/wimbledon2004.wimbledon11.

39. Maurice Chittenden, cited in Vincent and Crossman, "Champions, a Celebrity Crossover, and a Capitulator."

40. Sharapova, *Unstoppable*, 138.

41. Sharapova, *Unstoppable*, 138.

42. Liz Clarke, "Sharapova Wins after Improbable Journey," *Washington Post*, July 4, 2004, http://www.washingtonpost.com/wp-dyn/articles/A25495-2004Jul3.html??noredirect=on.

43. Michael A. Messner, Margaret Carlisle Duncan, and Nicole Willms, "This Revolution Is Not Being Televised," *Contexts* 5, no. 3 (2006): 34–38.

44. John Harris and Ben Clayton, "Femininity, Masculinity, Physicality and the English Tabloid Press: The Case of Anna Kournikova," *International Review for the Sociology of Sport* 37, nos. 3–4 (2002): 397–413.

45. Janet S. Fink, "Female Athletes, Women's Sport, and the Sport Media Commercial Complex: Have We Really 'Come a Long Way, Baby'?," *Sport Management Review* 18, no. 3 (August 2015): 331–42.

46. Vincent and Crossman, "Champions, a Celebrity Crossover, and a Capitulator."

47. Messner, Duncan, and Willms, "This Revolution Is Not Being Televised."

48. Vincent and Crossman, "Champions, a Celebrity Crossover, and a Capitulator."

49. Sharapova, *Unstoppable*, 197.

50. Chris Isidore, "Maria Mania: No Stopping Her Now," CNN Money, August 30, 2004, https://money.cnn.com/2004/08/27/commentary/column_sportsbiz/sportsbiz/index.htm.

51. Roberts, Anderson, and Magrath, "Continuity, Change and Complexity."

52. White, "Maria Sharapova Says She Does Not Get On with Other Players."

53. White, "Maria Sharapova Says She Does Not Get On with Other Players."

54. Kirsten Fleming, "Why Everyone in Tennis Hates Maria Sharapova," *New York Post*, March 29, 2016, https://nypost.com/2016/03/29/why-everyone-in-tennis-hates-maria-sharapova/.

55. Sharapova, *Unstoppable*, 5.

56. John Greechan, "Short Shrift from Maria and Athletes," *Daily Mail* (UK), April 20, 2016.

57. Oliver Holt, "Sharapova Drugs Case Gets to Heart of Problem," *Daily Mail* (UK), April 16, 2016.

58. Antoine Duval, "The Russian Doping Scandal at the Court of Arbitration for Sport: Lessons for the World Anti-Doping System," *International Sports Law Journal* 16, nos. 3–4 (March 2017): 177–97.

59. Paul Newman, "Maria Sharapova Drug Ban: Tennis Star Facing One-Year Suspension after Accepting Positive Test for Meldonium," *Independent* (UK), March 7, 2016, https://www.independent.co.uk/sport/tennis/maria-sharapova-ban-tennis-star-facing-two-year-suspension-after-accepting-positive-test-for-a6918066.html.

60. Martyn Ziegler, "Sharapova Could Be Helped by Banned Drug Confusion," *Times* (UK), April 14, 2016, https://www.thetimes.co.uk/article/sharapova-could-be-helped-by-confusion-over-banned-drug-7hlrr9c52.

61. "Vladimir Putin Defends Maria Sharapova over Positive Meldonium Test," *Telegraph* (UK), April 14, 2016, https://www.telegraph.co.uk/tennis/2016/04/14/vladimir-putin-defends-maria-sharapova-over-positive-meldonium-t/.

62. Sharapova was later deselected, because the hearing regarding her drug ban was suspended until after the event.

63. Will Slattery, "'Arrogant, Cold and Totally Unlikeable': Banned Maria Sharapova Certainly Isn't Missed in Tennis," *Independent* (UK), June 30, 2016, https://www.independent.ie/sport/other-sports/tennis/arrogant-cold-and-totally-unlikeable-banned-maria-sharapova-certainly-isnt-missed-in-tennis-34846545.html.

64. Slattery, "Arrogant, Cold and Totally Unlikeable."

65. Fleming, "Why Everyone in Tennis Hates Maria Sharapova."

66. Filip Bondy, "Serena Williams Says Sharapova's Announcement Surprised Her," *New York Times*, March 8, 2016, https://www.nytimes.com/2016/03/09/sports/tennis/serena-williams-says-sharapovas-announcement-surprised-her.html.

67. "Maria Sharapova: Jennifer Capriati Launches Twitter Attack on Russian Tennis Player after Drug Test Announcement," Australian Broadcasting Corporation News, March 8, 2016, https://www.abc.net.au/news/2016-03-08/maria-sharapova-jennifer-capriati-twitter-drug-test/7229972.

68. Fleming, "Why Everyone in Tennis Hates Maria Sharapova."

69. "Muted Response from Rivals Is Because Maria Has No Friends On Tour: Evert," Fox Sports, March 10, 2016, https://www.foxsports.com.au/tennis/muted-response-from-rivals-is-because-maria-sharapova-has-no-friends-on-tour-evert/news-story/25942ce807c2b28b0038b11f981bba5d?nk=a8796246f71e978e85db5918f69e5394-1540303073.

70. Joe Strange, "Maria Sharapova Must Pay for Meldonium Mistake, Insists 'Clean Guy' Rafael Nadal," *Daily Mail* (UK), March 10, 2016, https://www.dailymail.co.uk/sport/sportsnews/article-3485479/Maria-Sharapova-pay-meldonium-mistake-insists-clean-guy-Rafael-Nadal.html.

71. Tom Perrotta, "In Tennis, No Tears Are Shed for Maria Sharapova," *Wall Street Journal*, March 11, 2016, https://www.wsj.com/articles/in-tennis-no-tears-are-shed-for-maria-sharapova-1457739940.

72. Simon Briggs and Ben Rumsby, "Andy Murray: Maria Sharapova Deserves Ban— And Head Should Not Have Extended Sponsorship Deal," *Telegraph* (UK), March 10, 2016, https://www.telegraph.co.uk/tennis/2016/03/10/andy-murray-dismayed-at-head-supporting-maria-sharapova/.

73. Martha Kelner, "Boris Becker Slams 'Totally Out of Order' Andy Murray," *Daily Mail* (UK), April 17, 2016, https://www.dailymail.co.uk/sport/tennis/article-3544745/Boris-Becker-slams-totally-order-Andy-Murray-British-No-1-admits-doping-suspicions.html.

74. Kelner, "Boris Becker Slams 'Totally Out of Order' Andy Murray."

75. Owen Gibson and Simon Cambers, "Maria Sharapova under Pressure over Meldonium Use as Sponsors Flee," *Guardian*, March 8, 2016, https://www.theguardian.com/sport/2016/mar/08/maria-sharapova-meldonium-drug-test-sponsors.

76. Sharapova, *Unstoppable*, 270.

77. Ben Rumsby, "Maria Sharapova Has Earned 'Benefit of Doubt,' Says Racquet Sponsors Head," *Telegraph* (UK), March 10, 2016, https://www.telegraph.co.uk/tennis/2016/03/10/maria-sharapova-has-earned-benefit-of-doubt-says-racket-sponsors/.

78. "Maria Sharapova's Sponsors Head Prompt Outrage by Cheering Drug Ban Reduction," *Guardian*, October 4, 2016, https://www.theguardian.com/sport/2016/oct/04/maria-sharapova-sponsors-head-outrage-cheering-drug-ban.

79. Andrew Jerell Jones, "Bizarre Celebration of Sharapova's Reduced Ban Is Profoundly Tone-Deaf," *Guardian*, October 11, 2016, https://www.theguardian.com/sport/blog/2016/oct/11/maria-sharapova-return-doping-ban-head-tone-deaf.

80. Dan King, "Fear over Maria Ban," *Sun* (UK), April 27, 2016.

81. Tony Banks, "Maria Still Club Class," *Daily Express* (UK), April 27, 2016.

82. "Pros Can Name Doping Cheats," *Daily Record* (UK), May 19, 2016.

83. Kevin Mitchell, "World Tennis Chief Calls for End of Secrecy over Players Who Fail Drug Tests," *Guardian*, May 29, 2016, https://www.theguardian.com/sport/2016/may/29/tennis-drugs-itf-president-david-haggerty-match-fixing.

84. Simon Briggs, "Andy Murray Calls for More Investment in Anti-Doping as World's Leading Players Are Quizzed on Safeguards," *Telegraph* (UK), November 13, 2015, https://www.telegraph.co.uk/sport/tennis/daviscup/11995169/Andy-Murray-calls-for-more-investment-in-anti-doping-as-worlds-leading-players-are-quizzed-on-safeguards.html.

85. Briggs, "Andy Murray Calls for More Investment."

86. Briggs, "Andy Murray Calls for More Investment."

87. Katie Kindelan, "Maria Sharapova Speaks Out about Returning to Tennis after Doping Ban: 'It's Time to Move On,'" ABC News, September 12, 2017, https://abcnews.go.com/Entertainment/maria-sharapova-speaks-returning-tennis-doping-ban-time/story?id=49787131.

88. Kindelan, "Maria Sharapova Speaks Out."

89. Sharapova did not request wildcard entry into Wimbledon.

90. Simon Briggs, "Maria Sharapova's US Open Return Sees Tears, but a Surprising Lack of Jeers," *Telegraph* (UK), August 29, 2017, https://www.telegraph.co.uk/tennis/2017/08/29/maria-sharapovas-us-open-return-sees-tears-surprising-lack-jeers/.

91. Jerome Pugmire, "Halep, Cornet Join Legion of Players Criticizing Sharapova's Wildcard," Tennis.com, April 25, 2017, http://www.tennis.com/pro-game/2017/04/halep-cornet-give-sharapova-wild-card-debate-new-impetus/65655/.

92. Pugmire, "Halep, Cornet Join Legion of Players."

93. Akshay Kohli, "Maria Sharapova Receives Mixed Reactions for Wildcard," *Tennis World*, March 11, 2017, https://www.tennisworldusa.org/tennis/news/Maria_Sharapova/41380/maria-sharapova-receives-mixed-reactions-for-wildcards/.

94. Pugmire, "Halep, Cornet Join Legion of Players."

95. "Split Opinion among Top Women Tennis Players ahead of Maria Sharapova's Return to Grand Slam Action at the US Open," *The National* (Abu Dhabi), August 27, 2017, https://www.thenational.ae/sport/tennis/split-opinion-among-top-women-tennis-players-ahead-of-maria-sharapova-s-return-to-grand-slam-action-at-the-us-open-1.623264.

96. "Players React to Sharapova's Return," Tennismash, April 26, 2017, https://tennismash.com/2017/04/26/players-react-sharapovas-return/.

97. Briggs, "Maria Sharapova's US Open Return Sees Tears."

98. Aaron C. T. Smith, Bob Stewart, Sunny Oliver-Bennetts, Sharyn McDonald, Lynley Ingerson, Alastair Anderson, Geoff Dickson, Paul Emery, and Fiona Graetz, "Contextual Influences and Athlete Attitudes to Drugs in Sport," *Sport Management Review* 13, no. 3 (August 2010): 181–97.

JASON COLLINS, MICHAEL SAM, AND THE CHALLENGE OF COMING OUT IN MEN'S TEAM SPORT

ANDREW C. BILLINGS, LEIGH M. MOSCOWITZ, AND MELVIN LEWIS

INTRODUCTION

Within the chronicles of sports history, certain athletes have found them-selves inextricably linked with another, forming a unified narrative of un-derstanding. Sometimes these pairs traverse eras, as the commonality they share relates to their athletic talents: Jack Nicklaus and Tiger Woods in golf; Michael Jordan and LeBron James in basketball. Sometimes these pairs are forged because they were of similar talents in the same era, forging elements of rivalry: Martina Navratilova and Chris Evert in tennis; Peyton Manning and Tom Brady in American football. However, there are also pairings formed not because of skill or even a common sport, instead forged under common circumstance at a unique time in history. Such was the case for Jason Collins and Michael Sam, two Black athletes with little in common other than the fact that they came out as gay in American sports within nine months of each other, each taking with him the "global norm" of the past in which male athletes stayed closeted, particularly in team sport, and replacing it with a sense of excitement and progress for the sports world and far beyond.[1] As CNN's Chris Cuomo articulated after Collins came out in 2013, "This is a big deal. We are all reporting it like major news, not just sports news."[2]

The trajectories of their stories are relatively well known to the average American sports fan. Collins ultimately played a final season for the Brooklyn Nets in 2014, coincidentally the same city that originally embraced Jackie Robinson's breaking of the color barrier, before retiring at the end of that year. Michael Sam was drafted in the last round of the 2014 NFL draft by the St. Louis Rams, played admirably in preseason games before being cut from the Rams' roster, was signed to the Dallas Cowboys' practice squad, and ultimately exited football for what he deemed "mental health" reasons. But there were many common elements within the mediated narratives of these two athletes as well. Both represented the first "out" athletes in major American men's team sport, both were Black, and both had grown up in conservative religious families. However, the differences in their stories made them a particularly odd pair to forge a consistent narrative. Even more, in the years that followed their separate announcements, the Collins narrative seems to have generated a largely positive, celebratory coda whereas the Sam narrative more ably lends itself to a refrain that lays out a cautionary tale.[3]

These points, of course, have been taken up by scholars and laypeople across the spectrum. In "Openly Gay Athletes: Contesting Hegemonic Masculinity in a Homophobic Environment," for example, Eric Anderson contends that sport is the leading definer of "orthodox masculinity and patriarchy" in a mass culture that has lost its male initiation rituals.[4] And yet, in these instances, we can see that notable progress has been forged that allowed Collins and Sam space to come out and that changed the climate for future gay athletes to come out after they did. Each forged new ground in a resistant sports culture, yet they each did so in different ways. Edward Kian and Eric Anderson argue that "the situation is bleakest for openly gay black athletes; who are extraordinarily rare in any sport, at any level of play."[5] And to be sure, the revelations offered from Jason Collins and Michael Sam counter that argument, making the diversity of such stories much more pronounced a decade later.

This chapter delves into the differences between Collins's and Sam's coming-out experiences, arguing that five related yet unique factors led to Collins's experience being relatively more positive than Sam's. We maintain that each factor worked against Michael Sam far more than in the case of Jason Collins, making the former's journey considerably more arduous. These factors each led to the media "circus" playing out differently in terms of each athlete's emergent celebrity.

FACTOR #1: PROVEN VERSUS UNPROVEN COMMODITY

This first factor serves as the basis for all others that follow, as it relates to whether there can and should be a place for each of the two athletes in their respective leagues. Neither was regarded as a star or even a starter for a team at the professional level, which could lead some to conclude that their stories are roughly equivalent in this regard. After all, while Sam had a questionable chance to make an NFL roster (58.3 percent of all seventh-round picks make an active roster in Year 1, diminishing to 16.7 percent by Year 5),[6] Collins was never regarded as a game-changing presence, relying on size, intelligence, and work ethic to "carve out a niche" in the league.[7] It is fair to question whether Sam (a Southeastern Conference Defensive Player of the Year) was unduly punished for coming out and, perhaps, represented more than seventh-round talent (as the previous seven SEC Defensive Players of the Year were all on NFL active rosters), but the juxtaposition was still clear: Collins had proven over more than a decade that he belonged on an NBA team, whereas no one knew for sure that Michael Sam could play at the next level, although most experts concurred that he was worthy of a middle-round NFL draft pick.

To argue that Collins was problematic in the locker room or athletically deficient to the point of cutting him from the team would be to contradict more than ten years of evidence. He played for six NBA teams (New Jersey/Brooklyn, Memphis, Minnesota, Atlanta, Boston, and Washington) and did so ably, "valued for his locker-room presence" if not for exceptional skills.[8] Collins possessed a veritable Rolodex of NBA colleagues who could attest to his professionalism and performance, blunting any of the standard criticisms about a gay player gawking at fellow players in the locker room. The intimate spaces in which players may feel awkwardness with a gay teammate had already been part of Collins's reality; and in one survey of professional athletes, 76 percent of respondents said that they would feel comfortable showering around a gay teammate.[9] Of course for the other, reluctant 24 percent, it was difficult for them to counter the fact that they already had showered with a gay teammate to no ill effect. Moreover, Collins's skills were still valued, particularly in the early part of his career. New Jersey/Brooklyn Nets general manager Billy King classified his career as "distinguished," adding that Collins had been "an integral part of the back-to-back Eastern Conference Championship teams" in 2002 and 2003. Upon learning of Collins's decision to come out, league commissioner David Stern said that Collins "has assumed the leadership mantle on this very important issue,"[10] but this was in no small part because Collins already was known to be a team leader and high-character presence in the locker room. In sum, Collins had earned his way onto NBA courts without anyone questioning his worthiness to be there, establishing credibility and capital that aided his coming out experience.

In relatively stark contrast, Michael Sam came out just months before the 2014 NFL draft at a time when experts were most likely to question his ability to play at the next level. Although Sam was clearly a star at the college level, most experts and fans could cite lengthy lists of players whose skills failed to translate at the professional level, a place where even Heisman Trophy winners (e.g., Eric Crouch, Jason White, Gino Torretta) sometimes fail to succeed. Michael Sam was projected as high as the second round in some early mock drafts, while others were less sanguine about his prospects before the draft. Some witnessed signs that his strengths may not match the needs of the NFL. As NPR broadcaster Phil Harrell assessed:

> Sam played defensive end in college a full three inches shorter and 20 pounds lighter than the NFL prototype, likely too small to succeed in the pros, they say. And as he showed in recent workouts, he appears too un-athletic to convert to the more fleet linebacker position. The NFL has a word for that: He's a tweener. He's a classic tweener.[11]

Labeling Sam as a "classic tweener"—because he seemed to be "in between" two playing positions—only invited more scrutiny of whether his abilities warranted inclusion, leading to media narratives about whether Sam's coming out would even "count" as a valid "first" if he failed to grace an NFL field for a regular-season game. His narrative became multipronged, requiring him to navigate being a new, openly gay presence in the locker room while also fielding questions about whether he deserved to be there in the first place. ESPN's Josina Anderson offered an awkward report about Sam's showering habits, claiming that a teammate seemed to think his habits were atypical; the combination of such stories with his performance in preseason games presented an odd juxtaposition.[12]

In the end, Sam was cut by the St. Louis Rams, with coach Jeff Fisher noting that lack of effort was not an issue: "I will tell you this: I was pulling for Mike. I really was, and I don't say that very often. Mike came in here and did everything we asked him to do."[13] Nevertheless, his story became that of a journeyman trying to prove that he belonged as a player without affording him the opportunity to lead as an openly gay man, as he was instead constantly on the defensive. Sportswriter Lindsay Gibbs reported on how Sam believed that his coming out was a determining factor in his never making an NFL active roster, quoting Sam as saying: "If I never would have came out, never would have said those words out to the public, I would still be currently in the National Football League. But because of me saying those words, I think it could have played a huge part in my current situation."[14] Such a comment invites many critics to offer contrary points of view, particularly those who believe sport to be the ultimate American meritocracy. The continual defensive crouch Michael Sam was forced into led him to make foundational claims about his ability: "I know how to play this game, I can play this game.

... I don't know what goes on in the NFL with the guys who are making the decisions, but whatever it is, hopefully it's not what I think it is."[15]

Thus, Collins—even while fighting to remain in the NBA in the twilight of his career—did not have to face the battle for legitimacy and inclusion that Michael Sam fielded continually in his brief postdraft interlude when he was trying to make an NFL team. Collins had many years of established capital to expend in his fight for inclusion, while Sam was, quite literally, starting from scratch in this regard.

FACTOR #2: SINGLE VERSUS ATTACHED ROMANTICALLY

If there is one group of people attempting to straddle two positions in the equality movement, it is likely exemplified by the oft-heard statement: "I don't care if you're gay—as long as you don't rub it in my face." This is often offered under the guise of inclusion, yet it tacitly sends the message that one can be gay as long as it is not overtly noticed, performed, or incorporated into one's behavioral identity. Here, too, the reception arcs of the Collins and Sam stories are more divergent than convergent. Collins self-reported that he was not dating anyone at the time of his coming out, while Sam had a serious boyfriend, Vito Cammisano, to whom he later became engaged before breaking it off some six months later.[16]

Perhaps most pertinently, upon hearing that he had been drafted by the Rams, Sam kissed Cammisano during live ESPN coverage. The kiss of a loved one was a regular part of draft coverage since ESPN began airing it, but the fact that it was with a same-sex partner raised concern among many who watched, and the kiss then trended on Twitter. Some wished to celebrate Sam's moment, finding it to be "groundbreaking,"[17] while others saw him "being gay" on television, and the narrative shifted to him being a perceived threat. Former NFL player Derrick Ward, for instance, tweeted: "I'm sorry but that Michael Sam is no bueno for doing that on national tv," also contending that "Man U got kids lookin at the draft. I can't believe ESPN even allowed that to happen."[18] Before the NFL draft, Sam's sexuality was regarded by some as merely an internal identity marker, yet after the televised kiss, it became an observable trait that led some to rebel against full acceptance of his outness. As Sam summarized in the Kansas *Sentinel* several years later, "When I was drafted ... I thought the headline would be 'NFL has first openly gay player,' but instead it was 'Sam kisses boyfriend.' Should I have kissed a girl? The media made it a distraction."[19]

Such televised moments were not offered up by Collins because, at the time of his coming out, they would have been impossible. As he told Andrew Billings and Leigh Moscowitz, at the time of his mediated coming out, he had never been on a date or had what he would deem a gay experience. He also was reluctant to publicly share this information for two main reasons, neither of which stemmed from any embarrassment about his gay identity. First, he worried that if he indicated he had never had a gay relationship, the inevitable question from some quarters would be: "Well, then how do you know you're gay?"[20] The second reason compounded such concerns: he had been in heterosexual relationships before, including an eight-year relationship and engagement with Carolyn Moos, a former fellow Stanford alum and WNBA player. After hearing the news of his mediated coming out, she indicated that while she could "empathize" with him and even "support" him, she remained "deeply hurt by him,"[21] as she had spent four years trying to deconstruct the relationship to determine if its dissolution had been her fault. As Moos later told *Cosmopolitan*:

> A month before I was set to marry the man I loved, he called off the wedding. I had no idea why. He and I had been together for eight years. We had planned to have children, build a family. Nearly four years later, I got my answer.[22]

Thus, Collins kept any discussion of relationships out of the early formalized discussion, partly to avoid what he would call uninformed questions about whether he was really gay and partly out of respect for his past partner. In doing so, he became a "safer" gay athlete for some Americans to support than Michael Sam, who was actively and publicly involved in a romantic relationship with a same-sex partner. Moreover, combining Sam's failure to make an NFL team with his belief that "I don't think it had to do with talent"[23] led others back to the ESPN-rendered kiss, marking it as a turning point against Michael Sam's NFL viability.

FACTOR #3: END OF CAREER VERSUS BEGINNING OF CAREER

Each coming-out experience featured a media-driven interpretation that begged the question of the duration of each story before it could reach some sort of closure, whether it be positive (actively playing on a team) or negative (failing to make an active roster). Again, this is where the stories diverged, as Collins, a twelve-year NBA journeyman, was considered by a

virtual consensus of individuals, including his agent Arn Tellem, to be enjoying the final moments of his career, while Sam was hoping to be a fixture
in the NFL for the coming decade. Ultimately, this divergence skewed the
trajectory of each man's career as reported in the media and in terms of
public perception.[24]

To wit, both Collins and Sam had very short postannouncement careers,
but Collins had by far the more positive of the two experiences, at least partly
because he came out as an established veteran rather than at the beginning
of his rookie season. Two months after coming out in May 2013, Collins
became a free agent, but he had to wait until after the NBA All-Star break in
February 2014 before he signed with the Brooklyn Nets for the remainder
of the 2013–2014 season.[25] In November 2014, Collins retired. Hunter Felt,
writing in the *Guardian*, argues that even with that limited time playing as
an openly gay athlete, Collins's story was a positive one because it was never
a media circus; Felt concludes that "our indifference is his triumph."[26]

Michael Sam ultimately was a much less positive story, even as he, too,
had very little experience actually playing as an openly gay athlete. By most
accounts, he played admirably for the St. Louis Rams in the preseason and
was a solid role player on the Dallas Cowboys' practice squad. When opportunities to make an active NFL roster failed to materialize, Sam opted
for the Canadian Football League, being inactive for the Montreal Alouettes'
first five games before playing one game on the defensive line (without making a tackle), and then retired from football, citing mental health reasons.[27]
Commentator and author Cyd Zeigler, however, saw progress even in Sam's
disappointing career, noting:

> The National Football League demonstrated that it is in fact a meri-
> tocracy. Despite the naysayers claiming that Michael would struggle to
> find a home because NFL teams didn't want the "distraction" of a gay
> player, his character, work ethic and skill shone through.[28]

Nevertheless, with Sam himself contending against the notion of meritocracy, the fact that he embarked on his journey as an NFL rookie opened
conversations of whether he was worthy of inclusion, debates Collins did
not have to generally deal with as he already had that established capital
from twelve years of experience, and individuals willing to vouch for his
athletic worthiness.

FACTOR #4: FIRST-PERSON NARRATIVE VERSUS TELEVISION INTERVIEW

Each of the three aforementioned factors could be argued as circumstances that necessarily favored Collins. Given his youth, Sam could not present himself as a proven commodity as he had not yet had the chance to build up capital within the NFL. Additionally, Collins was able to stage manage his coming out to some degree; even his ex-fiancée was part of the unveiling of the story. One could presume, though, that Sam could have followed a similar public relations rollout of his story, as Collins had done with strategically placed stories, first via a first-person article in *Sports Illustrated*[29] and then via interviews with people sympathetic to his story, such as Oprah Winfrey. Such an assumption is partly fair—and yet partly myopic, as Michael Sam was presented with a version of a ticking clock to reveal his sexuality to the press, as his coaches and teammates already knew, and, once the NFL draft vetting process commenced, the world was very likely to find out as well, leaving Sam with little control over *how* his story was told.

Sam, thus, was pressed to tell his story as best he could in a relatively short time span. As he told ESPN's Chris Connelly, "I didn't realize how many people actually knew, and I was afraid that someone would tell or leak something out about me. . . . I want to own my truth. . . . No one else should tell my story but me."[30] Thus, he came out using ESPN's *Outside the Lines*, an award-winning news program renowned for its long-running investigative angles and thoughtful interviews, as a vehicle. Nevertheless, Sam could not script every word for fear of being construed as inauthentic. He followed this appearance with a *New York Times* interview, explaining that when he'd attended the Senior Bowl two weeks earlier, it became apparent that many of the players from other teams knew. The NFL had less time to prepare for the media coverage that Sam would receive. Still, while NFL executives publicly showed support for Sam's future in the league, they also had to continue the process of assessing his fitness for the league based on scouting reports, entirely apart from his announcement. Dan Good of ABC News reported on some of the less optimistic responses from inside the NFL, ranging from unnamed coaches and executives who indicated that Sam's draft stock would plummet as a result of the announcement to a player personnel assistant who bluntly declared: "I don't think football is ready for [an openly gay player] just yet. . . . In the coming decade or two, it's going to be acceptable, but at this point in time it's still a man's-man game. To call somebody a [gay slur] is still so commonplace. It'd chemically imbalance an NFL locker room and meeting room."[31]

In contrast to the somewhat malleable narrative offered by Sam that some have characterized as haphazard, Jason Collins had earlier offered a more systematic, controlled narrative through his mediated coming-out process.[32] After initially telling a trainer who was a close friend, Collins worked with his agent Arn Tellem, his family, and his closest friends to determine the best way to proceed. In the end, the answer lay in Tellem's childhood friend, writer Franz Lidz, who remembers:

> [Tellem] asked me—hypothetically—where I'd place a story on one of his clients who wanted to publicly come out. I said, "the *New York Times* or *Sports Illustrated.*" Then, he asked whom I'd pick to write the piece. I said, "Oh, so this *isn't* hypothetical. In that case, me."[33]

The decision to make the story a first-person tell-all was made relatively quickly, before Lidz even knew the name of the athlete who would be coming out. Lidz nonetheless determined that "regardless of who the athlete was or however articulate he might be, I knew the essay would be much more powerful as a first-person account.[34]

From the opening line of Collins's *Sports Illustrated* story—"I'm a 34-year-old center. I'm black. And I'm gay"—it was clear that Collins would be weaving other notions of his personal identity into a new one for the public, that of an out professional basketball player. The opening paragraph also served to dispel any notion that his coming out would make him an instant agent of change, with Collins noting: "I'm happy to start the conversation." He also made clear that he was not planning on making his coming out the centerpiece of a quest for celebrity status, stating: "Personally, I don't like to dwell in someone else's private life, and I hope players and coaches show me the same respect."[35]

Collins also seemingly offered guideposts in the article. For instance, given his desire not to discuss his never even having gone on a date with a man, he used two short sentences to rebut any attempts to query such personal experiences: "All you need to know is that I'm single. I see no need to delve into specifics." Not only did he offer advice to the media in terms of what to ask (or not) about his announcement, he also informed fans that while he would love to avoid being booed, criticism—and outright homophobia—would not deter him. He specifically offered: "As far as the reaction of fans, I don't mind if they heckle me. I've been booed before." Meanwhile, players received a slightly less tolerant message—with a small, subtle warning of retaliation: "If I'm up against an intolerant player, I'll set a pretty hard pick on him. And then move on."[36]

The power of the first-person controlled narrative was quite simple. With Lidz's help, Collins not only advanced his thoughts but could also construct counterarguments to questions he was likely to face even before they were asked. For instance, in directly targeting homophobic reactions, he connected that possibility to his race and to his family, who lived under Jim Crow in its various guises:

> My maternal grandmother was apprehensive about my plans to come out. She grew up in rural Louisiana and witnessed the horrors of seg-regation. During the civil rights movement she saw great bravery play out amid the ugliest aspects of humanity. She worries that I am opening myself up to prejudice and hatred. I explained to her that in a way, my coming out is preemptive. I shouldn't have to live under the threat of being outed. The announcement should be mine to make, not TMZ's.[37]

Thus, it was not necessarily the case that Sam's announcements were overtly bad or ill advised in any formal manner. Rather, it was the timing of his disclosure that rendered his pair of extemporaneous interviews incapable of protecting him from future attacks in the manner that Collins's *Sports Illustrated* article was able to do.

FACTOR #5: BASKETBALL VERSUS FOOTBALL

There is a tendency to think of sports fans as monolithic. Moreover, when one runs a Google search for "sports fan," the images that first appear are those of what can best be described as avid, überdedicated Neanderthals, a far cry from the reality of most enactments of sports fandom. Nevertheless, any discussion of the modern sports fan must consider nuance and differ-ence, depending on sport, regionality, and other elements of one's identity.[38] What is abundantly clear is that the sport in which Collins excels, basketball, is demonstrably different from Michael Sam's sport, football.

One could counter back and forth with the advantages of each sport in this regard. One could say that Sam had an advantage because football teams have more players, reducing the potential distraction of any one player, as compared to the sport of basketball, with roughly one-third the number of players on a team. One could argue that Collins had the advantage because basketball is a more international and presumably more progressive sport, whereas the appeal of football is largely limited to North America, although the rest of the world is catching on thanks to some shrewd NFL marketing initiatives. One could then counter again that Sam had the advantage because his sport largely shields his body from view via helmets and protective uniforms, whereas Collins, stripped down to shorts and T-shirt, is much more immediately recognizable on a basketball court.

Regardless, both sides would concur that both the players and fan bases of each sport function differently, making coming out in one sport a unique experience that is not directly translatable to the other. Some NBA players were denounced for their homophobia years before Collins's announcement. For example, former player Tim Hardaway was roundly criticized for his 2007 comments proclaiming: "I hate gay people, so I let it be known. I don't like gay people[,] and I don't like to be around gay people. I am homophobic. I don't like it. It shouldn't be in the world or in the United States."[39] Superstar Kobe Bryant had to offer a public apology and was fined $100,000 in 2011 for calling a referee with whom he disagreed a "faggot."[40] Some prominent women basketball players had come out in earlier years, including high-profile stars such as Sheryl Swoopes and Brittney Griner. As a result of such foregrounding, Collins's announcement was met with near-universal praise, with Kobe Bryant suggesting in a tweet that even his position was evolving: "Proud of @jasoncollins34. Don't suffocate who u r because of ignorance of others."[41]

In contrast, football just seems to be lagging behind in such societal shifts. As reporter Cindy Boren recounts: "NFL players, when asked about the issue, always point to the question of how fans will react when their team is playing a team with an openly gay player, rather than how an openly gay player will be accepted in a locker room."[42] By making such comments, NFL players send the tacit message that as athletes, they are simply not ready to admit openly gay brethren to their ranks, a message they can easily project onto fans as a means of deflecting perceived conflicts or public backlash if issues arise in the locker room with an openly gay teammate. To wit, when Baltimore Raven linebacker Brendon Ayanbadejo claimed that four NFL athletes were planning to come out at the same time to share the backlash, many dubbed it a sign of the inevitable revolution.[43] When that claim failed to materialize, a counternarrative emerged: those four NFL players assessed the landscape of what it would be like to come out in the media and decided against it, assuming, among other things, that the stakes were too high and the environment just too risky. Any gay athlete in a major team sport who was contemplating coming out could read the message clearly: the time was not right for them, either. Michael Sam himself reported that other NFL players had reached out to him about coming out, but they, too, must have determined that the climate was not right for them at that given point in time, although Sam would later note: "They wished that they had the courage to come out."[44]

The popularity of football in America only tightened the crucible in which Michael Sam's story unfolded. CNN's Ralph Ellis argued that "other athletes have come out as gay, but they didn't have Sam's profile."[45] Ellis does not contend that Michael Sam was a better athlete in his given sport than the others he mentions but rather that the "profile" Sam was projecting was of an openly gay athlete in the most popular sport in America—by far. Moreover, while others in Sam's sport have come out postretirement, including Dave Kopay and Esera Tuaolo, none are as high profile an advocate as retired NBA player John Amaechi, who actively spoke about NBA culture in the hope that Collins would be fully embraced within the league. As Amaechi told Joe Sterling and Steve Almasy, he hoped that "Collins will be a catalyst for a wider acceptance of openly gay athletes" while conceding that "it may take more."[46]

IMPLICATIONS

This chapter considers the divergent nature of five factors that altered the telling and rendering of the coming-out stories of basketball's Jason Collins and football's Michael Sam. We could have explored other factors, as well as commonalities the two athletes shared that forge a joint story of a mediated moment that occurred for gay athletes in 2013 and 2014. However, it is difficult to argue that Michael Sam's path for acceptance was as wide as Jason Collins's, largely through no fault of his own. His age, place in the sport, abilities, and coming-out process all served to build resistance to a positive, winning narrative.

Eric Anderson once cautioned of a boomerang effect in sport, one in which "the declining degree of cultural homophobia that has led gay men to come out in the larger society might exacerbate the emergence of gay men from the sporting closet as well."[47] Because of this, Edward Kian argues that men's team sports are "one part of pop culture that has not contributed much to the assimilation of gays and lesbians into mainstream American society."[48] Given this implied intransigence of sport regarding progressive social issues, understanding how each athlete's story differs with respect to time, sport, circumstance, and personal standpoint becomes imperative. This chapter has attempted to provide such an understanding in the cases of Jason Collins and Michael Sam, both groundbreakers with different paths laid out before them within the sports-oriented coming-out experience.

John Pickhaver is a former college cross-country runner who came out in the aftermath of the Orlando Pulse nightclub shooting of June 12, 2016, that left forty-nine people dead in what is perceived as one of the most violent acts of homophobia in American history. Pickhaver fervently believes that professional athletes must serve a vital role in the equality movement within sport. To that end, he argues:

> [W]ith so many high school and college athletes out, it's my hope that current professional athletes can recognize the platform they have and the impact they could have on young kids struggling with who they are, if they just shared their story. It is for sure a lot to ask but there's so much more to be gained through their visibility. It's only then that I think the dam will truly break.[49]

NOTES

1. Edward M. Kian, Eric Anderson, John Vincent, and Ray Murray, "Sport Journalists' Views on Gay Men in Sport, Society, and within Sport Media," *International Review for the Sociology of Sport* 50, no. 8 (2015): 895–911.

2. Chris Cuomo, "Jason Collins, First Male Active Pro-Athlete," CNN Newsroom, April 30, 2013.

3. Andrew C. Billings and Leigh Moscowitz, *Media and the Coming Out of Gay Male Athletes in American Team Sports* (New York: Peter Lang, 2018).

4. Eric Anderson, "Openly Gay Athletes: Contesting Hegemonic Masculinity in a Homophobic Environment," *Gender and Society* 16, no. 6 (2002): 860–77.

5. Edward Kian and Eric Anderson, "John Amaechi: Changing the Way Sport Reporters Examine Gay Athletes," *Journal of Homosexuality* 56, no. 7 (2009): 799–818.

6. Topher Doll, "How Long Does the Average Draft Pick Stick Around?," *SB Nation*, May 13, 2014, https://www.milehighreport.com/2014/5/13/5713996/how-long-does-the-average -draft-pick-stick-around.

7. Howard Beck and John Branch, "With the Words 'I'm Gay,' an NBA Center Breaks a Barrier," *New York Times*, April 29, 2013, http://www.nytimes.com/2013/04/30/sports/ basketball/nba-center-jason-collins-comes-out-as-gay.html.

8. Beck and Branch, "With the Words 'I'm Gay.'"

9. Ryan Wilson, "Survey: 86 Percent of NFL Players Would Accept Gay Teammate," CBS Sports, February 17, 2014, http://www.cbssports.com/nfl/eye-on-football/24446644/ percent-of-nfl-players-have-no-problem-with-gay-teammate.

10. Joe Sterling and Steve Almasy, "NBA's Jason Collins Comes Out as Gay," CNN, April 30, 2013, http://www.cnn.com/2013/04/29/sport/collins-gay/index.html.

11. Phil Harrell, "Why Michael Sam Might Not Be Drafted," NPR, May 4, 2014, https:// www.npr.org/2014/05/04/309562135/why-michael-sam-might-not-be-drafted.

12. Richard Deitsch, "How ESPN Erred in Its Report on Michael Sam's Showering Habits," *Sports Illustrated*, September 1, 2014, https://www.si.com/nfl/2014/09/01/michael-sam-espn-josina-anderson-showering-report.

13. Tom Pelissero, "Michael Sam Keeps Attention of Rams, NFL with His Play," *USA Today Sports Wire*, August 23, 2014, http://sportswire.usatoday.com/2014/08/23/michael-sam-st-louis-rams/.

14. Lindsay Gibbs, "Michael Sam Says Coming Out as Gay Played a 'Huge Part' in NFL Teams Not Signing Him," *ThinkProgress*, May 6, 2016, https://thinkprogress.org/michael-sam-says-coming-out-as-gay-played-a-huge-part-in-nfl-teams-not-signing-him-4cf478530e5f/.

15. Gibbs, "Michael Sam Says Coming Out."

16. Steve Hopkins, "Gay NFL Player Michael Sam Kisses Boyfriend as He Wins GQ Man of the Year Award," *Daily Mail* (UK), December 5, 2014, http://www.dailymail.co.uk/news/article-2861885/Gay-footballer-Michael-Sam-kisses-boyfriend-wins-Man-Year-award.html.

17. Cyd Zeigler, "Confirmed! Michael Sam Did Get Engaged to Boyfriend Vito Cammisano," *SB Nation Outsports*, January 16, 2015, https://www.outsports.com/2015/1/16/7509139/michael-sam-engaged-vito-cammisano.

18. Holly Yan and Dave Alsup, "NFL Draft: Reactions Heat Up after Michael Sam Kisses Boyfriend on National TV," CNN, May 13, 2014, http://www.cnn.com/2014/05/12/us/michael-sam-nfl-kiss-reaction/index.html.

19. Jack Cashill, "MU's Michael Sam Blames the Media for Failed NFL Career," *Sentinel* (KS), April 14, 2017, https://sentinelksmo.org/mus-michael-sam-blames-media-failed-nfl-career/.

20. Billings and Moscowitz, *Media and the Coming Out of Gay Male Athletes*.

21. Dom Cosentino, "Ex-Fiancée Had No Idea Jason Collins Was Gay, Remains 'Deeply Hurt,'" *Deadspin*, July 8, 2013, https://deadspin.com/ex-fiancee-had-no-idea-jason-collins-was-gay-remains-708216492.

22. Abigail Pesta, "Jason Collins Is My Ex-Fiancé and I Had No Idea He Was Gay," *Cosmopolitan*, July 8, 2013, http://www.cosmopolitan.com/entertainment/celebs/news/a4547/jason-collins-is-my-ex-fiance/.

23. Hopkins, "Gay NFL Player Michael Sam Kisses Boyfriend."

24. Billings and Moscowitz, *Media and the Coming Out of Gay Male Athletes*.

25. Kelly Dwyer, "Three Months after Coming Out of the Closet, Jason Collins Is Still without an NBA Gig," Yahoo! Sports, August 2, 2013, https://sports.yahoo.com/blogs/nba-ball-dont-lie/three-months-coming-closet-jason-collins-still-without-181353522.html. The speculation is that teams were reluctant to sign him right away in part because Collins was due a veterans' minimum salary, relatively high for the bench player role he was expected to fill.

26. Hunter Felt, "Jason Collins, First Openly Gay Player, Retires: Our Indifference Is His Triumph," *Guardian*, November 20, 2014, https://www.theguardian.com/sport/2014/nov/20/jason-collins-gay-nba-player-retires.

27. "Michael Sam Tweets His Departure from Football, Citing Mental Health," ESPN, August 15, 2015, http://www.espn.com/nfl/story/_/id/13440475/michael-sam-announces-stepping-away-football.

28. Cyd Zeigler, "Michael Sam Risked Everything—And We All Won," *Time*, May 10, 2014, http://time.com/95230/michael-sam-first-gay-nfl-rams/.

29. Jason Collins with Franz Lidz, "Why NBA Center Jason Collins Is Coming Out Now," *Sports Illustrated*, May 6, 2013, https://www.si.com/more-sports/2013/04/29/jason -collins-gay-nba-player.

30. Chris Connelly, "Mizzou's Michael Sam Says He's Gay," ESPN, February 10, 2014, http://www.espn.com/espn/otl/story/_/id/10429030/michael-sam-missouri-tigers-says-gay.

31. Dan Good, "Football Reacts to Michael Sam Coming Out," ABC News, February 10, 2014, http://abcnews.go.com/Sports/football-reacts-michael-sam-coming/story?id=22437707. Bracketed phrases in the quotation inserted by Dan Good.

32. Stephen Smith, "NBA Center Jason Collins: I'm Gay," CBS News, April 29, 2013, https://www.cbsnews.com/news/nba-center-jason-collins-im-gay/.

33. In Billings and Moscowitz, *Media and the Coming Out of Gay Male Athletes.*

34. Billings and Moscowitz, *Media and the Coming Out of Gay Male Athletes.*

35. Billings and Moscowitz, *Media and the Coming Out of Gay Male Athletes.*

36. Billings and Moscowitz, *Media and the Coming Out of Gay Male Athletes.*

37. Billings and Moscowitz, *Media and the Coming Out of Gay Male Athletes.*

38. Andrew C. Billings and Kenon A. Brown, *Evolution of the Modern Sports Fan: Communicative Approaches* (Lanham, MD: Lexington Books, 2017).

39. Brett Pollakoff, "Tim Hardaway Regrets Anti-Gay Comments, but Believes Dialogue that Resulted was a Positive," NBC Sports, July 29, 2013, http://probasketballtalk.nbcsports .com/2013/07/29/tim-hardaway-regrets-anti-gay-comments-but-believes-dialogue-that -resulted-was-a-positive/.

40. Cyd Zeigler, "Moment #46: NBA Fines Kobe Bryant $100k for Using the Word 'Faggot,'" *SB Nation Outsports*, August 22, 2011, https://www.outsports.com/2011/8/22/4051704/ moment-46-nba-fines-kobe-bryant-100k-for-using-the-word-faggot.

41. Beck and Branch, "With the Words 'I'm Gay.'"

42. Cindy Boren, "Jason Collins Comes Out; NBA Player Says, 'I'm Gay,'" *Washington Post*, April 29, 2013, https://www.washingtonpost.com/news/early-lead/wp/2013/04/29/ jason-collins-comes-out-nba-player-says-im-gay/.

43. Chris Chase, "Could Four Gay NFL Players Come Out at Same Time?," *USA Today*, April 5, 2013, http://www.usatoday.com/story/gameon/2013/04/05/brendon-ayanbadejo -gay-nfl-players-four/2056205/.

44. Lisa Capretto, "Michael Sam: Other Gay Players in the NFL Reached Out to Me," *Huffington Post*, December 23, 2014, https://www.huffingtonpost.com/2014/12/23/michael -sam-gay-players-in-nfl_n_6374026.html.

45. Ralph Ellis, "Rams Release Michael Sam, the First Openly Gay Player Drafted in NFL," CNN, August 31, 2014, http://www.cnn.com/2014/08/30/us/michael-sam-nfl/index.html.

46. Sterling and Almasy, "NBA's Jason Collins Comes Out as Gay."

47. Anderson, "Openly Gay Athletes: Contesting Hegemonic Masculinity."

48. Edward M. Kian, "Sport and LGBTQ Issues," in *Defining Sport Communication*, ed. Andrew C. Billings, 121–34 (New York: Routledge, 2017).

49. Billings and Moscowitz, *Media and the Coming Out of Gay Male Athletes*, 207.

SHOOT-PASS-SLAM

Reconsidering Shaquille O'Neal

ANDREW McINTOSH

INTRODUCTION

Appropriately, the contemporaneous and still evolving career of Shaquille O'Neal receives a treatise in the final installation of a series of books exploring the intersections of fame and professional sports. A larger-than-life personality and media profile crafted a "Shaq" mythology initially dismissed as tiresome, immature, and not of championship caliber. But as with other famous NBA centers,[1] the sports media storylines delineating O'Neal's reputation among the American public eventually reevaluated their depictions of the enormously sized center. Not only was his play on the court deemed "winning" but his demeanor, personal life, business acumen, and artistic pursuits were all favorably reconsidered. How O'Neal forged, lost, and then regained a favorable reputation will form the essence of the discussion that follows.

It is without question that Shaquille O'Neal's on-court dominance from 2000 to 2002 trumps all other speculations because this is, after all, a professional sports story. This period of O'Neal's career ended forever the derision that, despite his physical presence, he was a "loser." During this three-season span as Los Angeles Laker center, coupled with the phenomenal guard play of Kobe Bryant and the already certified championship-caliber coaching of Phil Jackson, O'Neal not only won three team championships but three consecutive individual NBA Finals MVP awards. Such accolades are shared only by the likes of other basketball greats including Michael Jordan, LeBron James, Tim Duncan, and Magic Johnson. O'Neal's other accomplishments may not have been as historically singular but were no less impressive: 1993 Rookie of the Year, 1995 and 2000 Scoring Champion, fifteen-time NBA All

Star, and another 2006 NBA championship as a member of the Miami Heat, to name but a few. This is the unassailable foundation on which O'Neal's reputation as a Hall of Fame player as well as a beloved media personality and savvy brand marketer is built. Unsurprisingly, the overriding narrative of an NBA sports figure is inseparable from his athletic performance.

Nonetheless, this chapter will consider Shaquille O'Neal's ability to cement his reputational arc within the discourses of professional sports, global marketing, and hip hop culture in the 1990s. For the purposes of investigating the development and significance of O'Neal's reputation, I will focus on the period 1993–2003, which marks the first decade of his professional career as an NBA player as well as corporate sponsor, entrepreneur, movie actor, and, particularly, rap recording artist. These efforts were not only lucrative and successful for O'Neal but lay the groundwork for the initially uneasy but now essential alliance between professional basketball and the then emergent culture and music of hip hop. During his first few years in the association, his team of agents and handlers made a considerable effort through hip hop songs and creative advertising to celebrate and utilize O'Neal's immense physicality as means to dismiss his critics and enhance his brand marketing. This period is also of interest because by the end of the 1990s, O'Neal's "Man of Steel" posturing took a dent as his play on the court did not translate into championships, his recording career stalled, and his endeavors in acting were ridiculed and derided by media and fans alike. As has been uncovered throughout this book series, "the distance between fan favorite and villainy is microscopic,"[2] a matter that underscores O'Neal's narrative almost from the outset.

"CLUB SHAQ": MARKETING DOMINANCE TO ACHIEVE MARKETING DOMINANCE

O'Neal's story has been overlooked likely for reasons of bias or misconception, and arguably because he has always demonstrated self-effacing tendencies—at least publicly. However, between his sophomoric and purposely comic nature and the legacy of his recordings, movies, and media representation, there is something much more substantive about him as a cultural icon. For many, Shaquille O'Neal is simply hard to take seriously, a stance O'Neal relishes and coyly manipulates. But this aspect of his persona did not always exist. Indeed, one story has it that after his high school's victory in the Texas state basketball championship in 1989, when a reporter asked him to what the victory could be attributed, O'Neal responded, "I attribute it to me."[3] So certainly the *rube about town* persona he so deftly developed over time was at one time a work in progress.

Winning is, of course, everything. But it is not the only thing. Chronicling adversities of the famed 1960s and 1970s NBA center Wilt Chamberlain, to whom O'Neal has often been compared, Gregory J. Kaliss wondered:

> Always on a short leash from the white-dominated media, black athletes such as Chamberlain could little afford to take any missteps, as whites seemed all too eager to believe in or rely on long-held stereotypes regarding American lawlessness, sexuality and inability to lead. ... White America was not ready for a black superstar who rewrote the record books and unabashedly proclaimed his own greatness on and off the court. The question remains: Is it ready even now?[4]

Whether white America was ready is debatable, but it is evident that by the 1990s, at the dawn of his professional basketball career, Shaquille O'Neal subverted some of the same unflattering depictions and gross stereotypes that were thrown a generation prior at Chamberlain, who was often regarded as a "brutal black buck," a "petulant attention-seeker," and even a "lazy, immature, stubborn, pampered cry-baby."[5] Somewhat in parallel, when drafted number one by the Orlando Magic in 1992, O'Neal was often perceived to have little to offer beyond his seven-foot, three-hundred-pound proportions. The *Orlando Sentinel*, the daily that covered the Magic, used the following descriptors of size and silence in the summer of 1992 before O'Neal's inaugural professional season had even tipped off: "Two Giants in One Day"[6] and "Shaq Not Talking to Magic, Media."[7] Noting O'Neal's unanticipated "class," columnist Brian Schmitz admitted his surprise that O'Neal kept "swatting away misconception after misconception" of being a "$40 million prima donna." O'Neal defended himself in regard to the columnist's preoccupation with jersey numbers and veteran status: "I'm not a whiner ... I'm not a crybaby. Numbers don't define a player."[8] A 1993 *Florida Today* lead read, "Shaq's presence is so intimidating that 14 seconds into his NBA career, opponents were called [foul] for double teaming him—when he didn't even have the ball."[9] In his autobiography, O'Neal claims that endorsements initially appeared to be scarce: "[O]ne guy from Nike said: 'There's has never been in the history of basketball a center that's been an effective marketing tool.'"[10]

O'Neal's ability to transcend the initial preoccupation with his size has ironically gone unnoticed despite the howl of condemnation that once surrounded the game-altering exploits of those NBA big men who preceded him, particularly Chamberlain and Bill Russell, both of whom seemed forever pressed by public scrutiny. It would seem, rather, that we have overlooked O'Neal's triumphs in the face of such smiling bigotry for several reasons: the lucrative contracts earned by NBA players in the late twentieth century; the enduring racism made invisible when juxtaposed against blatantly oppressive Jim Crow practices that Russell and Chamberlain faced; and our own prejudices in sports analysis. Considering, for example, if anyone were able to rival Michael Jordan's "household name" stature, Todd Boyd opines: "Shaquille O'Neal was also quite good, but as a literal giant, he would have a hard time being accepted as a cultural icon ... because his size was just too enormous for people to see him as anything other than a freak of nature."[11] Or, as Kaliss explains regarding Chamberlain, the racial undertones of these descriptors are apparent—the "demeaning stereotypes of black masculinity" coloring whites' reception of ability and achievement, which would certainly and perhaps predictably follow O'Neal.[12]

Interestingly, Shaquille O'Neal's imaging and advertising embraces and deconstructs these stereotypes, celebrating his massive physical presence and penchant for breaking backboards. Recognizing the increased exposure and excitement of ESPN's *Sports Center* highlights, O'Neal champions his style of dominant play in a single from his 1993 debut rap album *Shaq Diesel*. In "Shoot Pass Slam," Shaq shouts a call-and-response chorus with his fans: "Do you want me to shoot it? (No!) / Do you want me to pass it? (No!) / Do you want me to slam? (Slam!) / Get out of my way!" The accompanying music video is equal parts O'Neal rapping about slam dunking and NBA game clips of him doing just that.[13] A 1993 Reebok commercial gathered All-Star centers of past generations, including Russell, Chamberlain, Kareem Abdul-Jabbar, and Bill Walton, to watch Shaq dunk. The advertisement sets up as a changing of the guard, but the legends play straight man as O'Neal gleefully shatters the backboard. Abdul-Jabbar scolds, "That's not enough" before handing O'Neal a broom.[14] The same year, Pepsi filmed Shaq on a ball court with young children, camera angles magnifying his enormity. After bending a rim with a dunk, Shaq reaches into a cooler for a drink while a young boy a third his size holds the last soda and refuses to share. In the last shot, O'Neal pleads "Please?" but to no avail,[15] perhaps recalling pro football's inimitable "Mean" Joe Greene and his heralded Coca-Cola spot from the 1970s.[16] Writing for *Newsweek* in 1995, Mark Starr identifies this duality, contending that "[O'Neal's] physical power is not frightening; it's curiously magnetic, even self-depreciating."[17] With O'Neal tapping into his gift for humor, these efforts sought to at once to proclaim his physicality and disarm fears of his size. And as with Yao Ming a decade later, his handlers carefully sculpted a persona emphasizing his appearance as "earthy and humble and playful."[18]

This curious, bifurcated fashion informs much of the way that O'Neal presented himself in media representations: physically intimidating but warm with humor and personality. When considering his market appeal, Shaq once quipped, "I'm part Terminator, part Bambi."[19] Such an unholy combination aside, O'Neal's joking underplays the conscious intention, innovation, and success of his management team's dualistic business strategy. O'Neal's business dealings strategically minimized his reputation solely as a gigantic basketball player and embraced a more dynamic potential and varied skill set. In 1993, O'Neal was featured in the college basketball drama *Blue Chips*,[20] starring Nick Nolte, as evidence of his acting aspirations. Beyond the usual collaborations with Reebok sneakers, Spalding basketballs, and Sports Worldwide memorabilia, O'Neal's initial endorsements were not all sports related: Pepsi, Kenner Parker Toys, Electronic Games, and Tiger Electronics were a part of the mix as well—a mix that in all grossed O'Neal over $20 million per year at the time. As O'Neal's agent, Leonard Armato, declared in 1993: "To be in Club Shaq, you need more than money to come to the bargaining table. It has to be an investment, something that both can benefit from."[21]

The pithy swagger of an enterprise dubbed "Club Shaq" (or alternately "Team Shaq") belies Armato's and O'Neal's sophisticated strategy, a plan of action well equipped to capitalize on corporate globalization and emerging trends of marketing individuation. This meant that the more O'Neal's persona could be mined and cultivated for entertainment and advertising purposes, the more consistent and coherent an image of O'Neal could emerge for the public to accept—a *brand* image, to be exact. O'Neal's rap lyrics effortlessly wove declarations of self-assurance with product placement: "Cause there's some things that I gotta do / Tape up the ankle, pump up my Shaq shoe."[22] Writing in *Forbes* in 1993, Randall Lane describes O'Neal as the "league's first prepackaged superstar," forging varied endorsement deals purposely interconnected (e.g., Shaq-adorned Pepsi "Big-Slam" bottle caps could be traded in for ten dollars off Reebok apparel), cross-marketed (e.g., Spalding gifted Shaq basketball giveaways to radio listeners requesting songs from *Shaq Diesel*), and spread across various media (e.g., Shaq's autobiography was sold in bookstores employing the same tagline as his Pepsi commercials, "Shaq Attaq," as was his Reebok line of shoes).[23]

Pepsi drinkers and book readers may not have immediately recognizable commonalities, but they become united by their interactions via O'Neal's presence on multiple mediums, creating diverse "communities of interest" highly prized by marketers. Whatever tensions about "selling out" may have existed during this era were described earlier in this book series by Jeffrey

Lane in a chapter titled "Mortgaging Michael Jordan's Reputation." Lane claims that while Jordan pioneered such a dynamic endorsement approach, O'Neal had no such issue. Rather, O'Neal's brand-generated wealth earned him a reputation initially of being more interested in sales pitches than footwork. While such criticisms were not new, when considering the laments of Jordan's body being sold as a canvas for corporate endorsements, Lane's explanation of Jordan's decisions are relevant to O'Neal as well: "Jordan understands that product endorsements offer reciprocal benefits. Brand status transfers back and forth. . . . Jordan became a product unto himself— something like . . . the American Dream embodied."[24] Lane goes on to call Jordan just as "natural" at the art of commercialism as we may describe him as being a "natural" at sport.[25] Similarly, an awestruck 1996 *Chicago Tribune* profile of O'Neal provided a familiar portrait of the icon congruent with Shaq's intentions: "The most intimidating center in the NBA is actually a very large kid with silly attitude and a penchant for games . . . [a free-spirited] multimillionaire who isn't bound by the conventional etiquette associated with such rich entrepreneurs."[26] This all may be true, but *Newsweek*'s Mark Starr recognizes something else as well when he notes that "Shaq's every public manifestation consciously presents a consistent image."[27]

Such a dichotomy coupled with clever business practices proved to be immensely profitable for O'Neal and, according to *Forbes*'s Randall Lane, made Michael Jordan's "impressive money-making skills look strictly amateur." Lane reports that while the Air Jordan logo has remained enduring and iconic, it is also still the property of Nike. As he would note: "All O'Neal-related products, from shoes to basketballs to electronic games, now boast the logo and pay royalty to O'Neal."[28] Boasting of equity interest in nearly all products endorsed Armato appeared able to deftly navigate the difference between income and capital gains taxes.[29] The wealthiest NBA players of the modern era such as O'Neal, Magic Johnson, Michael Jordan, and LeBron James shrewdly "focused on controlling the means of production in addition to being the product" themselves.[30] And yet, while O'Neal's earnings are certainly in the upper echelon among pro athletes, Shaq's commitment to hip hop culture will make his box score different from those of his NBA contemporaries and play a larger role in the negotiation of racial and hip hop discourse in America.

"THE GAME IS TO BE SOLD NOT TOLD": THE ARRIVAL OF THE HIP HOP ATHLETE

Whether in the barbershop or the classroom, Michael Jordan is the go-to reference for every professional sports discussion concerning franchising one's name, likeness, and craft.[31] In terms of O'Neal's ability to occupy that same plane, the question is, how was he able to follow Jordan's blueprint while also forging a rap career that seemed to minimize the negative associations with hip hop culture?

First, it appears that anything O'Neal chose to pursue in the liminal space of being a top draft prospect in 1991 and actually playing in the NBA in 1992 was going to be applauded. Surprisingly, descriptions of Yao Ming's arrival in the United States in 2002 are applicable to O'Neal's 1992 debut. For instance, as Dong Jinxia, Zhong Yijing, and Li Luyang write, "Yao Ming had yet to do anything substantive as a basketball player," although the media campaigns continued to cultivate interest in him as an attraction.[32] Second, both in interviews ("They used to call me Shocka Dee. When [hip hop] first came out, I started poppin', and then I started breakin'") and as directly expressed in his autobiography,[33] O'Neal shows that his interest in hip hop appeared to be a genuine product of growing up in Newark, New Jersey, rapping with peers, and hearing seminal hip hop records being broken on New York City radio stations in the 1980s.[34]

Hip hop has always had an affinity for basketball insomuch as the music itself was born in playgrounds and ball courts of the South Bronx in the 1970s. A "Basketball Throwdown" of rapping and dunking featured prominently in hip hop's first film, *Wild Style*, in 1983.[35] But that affection had never been directly reciprocated. Certainly, O'Neal is by no means the first NBA star of the loosely defined "hip hop generation."[36] While Michael Jordan and hip hop music's ascendency are parallel, it is generally acknowledged that Jordan favored the sounds of sophisticated R&B over rap.[37] And yet, Jordan's shaved head, long shorts, and Air Jordan apparel define hip hop chic. As Todd Boyd points out, "Jordan was not hip hop per se in his politics[, but] his timing on the NBA scene closely connects to the emergence of hip hop as the primary way of representing Blackness in the culture at large."[38] Unabashedly, Charles Barkley embodied a hip hop swagger both on and off the court. His allegiances then became irreversible after an appearance for the December 1992 cover story for the *Source* with Spike Lee entitled "Nineties Niggers."[39] The confrontational sarcasm of Barkley's public persona was like that of a hip hop MC or rapper with a playfulness recalling Muhammad Ali, surely the godfather of hip hop/sports braggadocio. As Larry Platt reported, "Barkley eschewed marketing for authenticity, giving rise to a whole generation of athletes—the hip-hoppers—for whom the ethic of 'keeping it real' has become a mantra."[40]

While Platt is right to highlight these changes in demeanor as significant, it is similarly important to emphasize that O'Neal's headlong foray into rap music is what separated him from 1990s contemporaries. In fact, it was his hip hop recording career beginning in 1992 that allowed him to maintain a distinct reputation among NBA stars while cultivating something far more potent: a mythology of a personal brand that references strength, perseverance, and skill. As defined by Gary Fine and echoed by Jeffrey Lane, reputations are not only made, they are used.[41] Moreover, it is in the discourse of hip hop culture and music where "Shaq Diesel" finds a way to reimagine the social order between a professional basketball player and his challengers: media critics, doubters, haters, or opponents. Clearly, such a pose aligns itself easily with his corporate sponsors Reebok and Pepsi, as rebellion in American culture has long been a favorite theme in advertising certainly not limited to hip hop.[42]

O'Neal also parlayed this stance into a globetrotting market opportunity, traveling to Japan, Australia, Spain, Italy, and France, where he amazed "crowds with rim-shattering dunks during basketball demonstrations" followed by "mini rap concerts." Randall Lane, writing in *Forbes*, suggests that "O'Neal's music helps bring a new dimension to his image and business ventures that Michael Jordan never enjoyed."[43] This begs the question: as a hip hop ambassador, how did O'Neal overcome the stigmas associated with hip hop culture without alienating the image-conscious NBA while *simultaneously* cultivating an "authentic" rap music reputation?

The misgivings by media commentors and politicians toward hip hop culture during the 1980s and 1990s were not inconsiderable. Jeffrey Lane posits that by the 1980s, racism was not as apparent as in decades past. The negative associations of race were no longer tied to the overt politics of equality forwarded in the 1960s civil rights movements or revolution in the 1970s as called for by collectives such as the Black Panthers. By the 1990s, the negative connotations of race were linked to criminality and indulgence, as particularly expressed in hip hop music and video.[44] One can assume that former NBA commissioner David Stern had not featured the advancement of the "hip hop athlete" in his business plan for the 1990s. Armato seemed aware of this. Describing in his autobiography his first live rap performance on the *Arsenio Hall Show* in 1992, O'Neal admits:

I was decked out with a bunch of gold chains, my rapping look, but before we went on, Leonard [Armato] said, "Look, Shaq, can we compromise a little here?" Leonard's got to be concerned with my corporate image and I respect that. So I took off the chains and wore more conservative jewelry, a real nice bracelet and ring. We did it, we were good, Arsenio liked us, the studio audience liked us.[45]

It is unproductive to accuse O'Neal of "selling out" at this moment. He was twenty years old at the time with a fruitful albeit fleeting financial future completely dependent on the absence of debilitating physical injury. The more clear (and still present) danger at this moment is characteristic of the way Glyn Hughes outlines his point that "black men in the public sphere are typically afforded a limited and limiting representational framework."[46] O'Neal may have created tremendous financial opportunity for himself and his family and proven that he has creative skills beyond playing basketball, but Armato was responding to the unseen limits to agency afforded African Americans. As Hughes explains further, the "NBA is marketed and managed with a specific, if not tacit, goal of making Black men safe for (White) consumers in the interest of profit."[47]

Much to the relief of the NBA, O'Neal's particular brand of rapping in 1992 did not possess a controversial edge, nor was his reputation in hip hop circles considered even remotely "gangsta." First, Shaq's hip hop debut, "What's Up Doc? (Can We Rock)," was facilitated by the Flatbush, Brooklyn, hip hop group the Fu-Schnickens, whose tongue-twisting, cartoon-referencing silly self-aggrandizement was a natural fit for O'Neal and his adopted moniker "Shaq-Fu." Shaquille O'Neal arrived as a self-professed "amateur" to hip hop, and "This Old Man" adaptations such as "I can hold my own / knick-knack Shaq-attack, give a dog a bone"[48] would attest to this. Second, as we will explore later, there is nothing in O'Neal's biography permitting the celebration of drugs, gangs, or violence. In fact, O'Neal's narrative in a song like "I'm Outstanding" acknowledges just the opposite: "Then there were a few times when Dad had to scold me / Prayed for my safety, I know how you was feeling / Didn't want me wheeling and get to drug-dealing."[49]

Many of the songs on O'Neal's *Shaq Diesel*, released in 1993, and his 1994 follow-up *Shaq-Fu* can be charitably described as "chill lectures" in that they come off as didactic, as they are vainglorious. Conscious of his limitations as a performer, a self-admitted "complementary player" among a team of musicians,[50] O'Neal, with the help of Jive Records, adroitly employed some of the era's most accomplished beat smiths and notable rappers. Particularly on the debut, *Shaq Diesel*, there is a spontaneity to the recordings, if not necessarily proficiency; a palatable excitement shared by Shaq and his featured performers. This is a moment, after all, in which some of these hip hop performers are now sharing their brightest spotlight to date by recording and performing with O'Neal. For example, in describing the photo shoot for "A Great Day in Harlem '98," hip hop's (and Gordon Park's) homage to the famous jazz photograph taken at 17 East 126th Street, S. Craig Watkins considers the moment as one reflecting hip hop's enormous influence, with O'Neal's presence signaling "hip hop's synergy with other arenas of entertainment like sports."[51] Like the cultural icons photographed, O'Neal and his "friends" on his CDs, namely rappers, producers, and DJs, are unified in their connectedness via hip hop, highlighting their "geographic and aesthetic diversity that made hip hop first a regional, then national, and finally a global phenomenon."[52]

This cultural shift and the bonding between practitioners otherwise unfamiliar with one another are manifest in O'Neal's recordings and provide a reasonable qualitative explanation as to why O'Neal's novice pursuits were generally considered authentic. There is, however, a more resonant reason for Shaq's acceptance, an intention of aesthetic that O'Neal and his producers relied on in abundance in his first two albums: borrowing. According to ethnomusicologist Justin Williams, similar to trends in blues, jazz, and reggae, the fundamental element of hip hop culture is its "overt use of preexisting materials to new ends," creating a "vast intertextual network that helps to form and inform a generic contract between audiences and hip hop groups."[53] Once again, O'Neal's binate approach to cultural production pays off. While the use of known rappers, producers, lyrics, and samples reveal familiarity with the marketplace, these inputs ultimately serve as crucial signifiers of O'Neal's credibility or "realness."

As such, when considering Williams's description of hip hop practice, one discovers that O'Neal's lyrics of self-acclaim are in reference to a variety of previously recorded lyrics performed by notable rappers of the era. This strategy creates layers of meaning largely unacknowledged or misunderstood by lay listeners. For instance, when O'Neal raps, "All you jealous punks can't stop my dunks," it is reference not only to his basketball prowess but to the 1988 rap song "Don't Believe the Hype" by Long Island's Public Enemy, from whom O'Neal borrows the line.[54] In the 1988 song, Public Enemy's rapper, Chuck D, is combating media misinformation and mischaracterization—in hip hop parlance, "hype." By alluding to the lyric, in one line O'Neal creates a vital vessel of intercontextuality necessary in the hip hop performance of the period. Initially, he starts by certifying his knowledge of hip hop history by quoting a five-year-old song. Then, he aligns himself with Chuck D and the cause of Black empowerment that Public Enemy championed. Next, he appropriates Chuck D's highly publicized scrapes with the media as his own, but because O'Neal's primary role is that of an NBA center, his lyrics have literal meaning as well. As Williams explains, "Historical authenticity is simply one strain of hip hop authenticity, albeit a particularly potent and persuasive one." The use of codes, allusions, and quotations, all of which signify place in O'Neal's work, adheres it as well to a long succession of Black American and African cultural discourse no matter how amateurishly it comes across.[55]

What is of particular importance to sports and hip hop scholarship is O'Neal's interplay between the wealth and prestige of NBA stardom and the "realness" afforded to those associated with hip hop. The very first words of Shaq's debut album on the track "Intro" are not his own but those of commissioner David Stern: "With the first pick in the 1992 NBA Draft the Orlando Magic selects Shaquille O'Neal from Louisiana State University!"[56] By beginning his CD in this fashion, he once again demonstrates a layered rationale. First, it is a nod to his employers and in particular the once omnipotent Stern, an inclusive gesture implying that the NBA and hip hop enjoy the shared purposes of providing platform and opportunity for Team Shaq. Second, O'Neal is utilizing his draft status to declare the primacy of his basketball reputation to listeners while also intimating the wealth awarded to a top pick. In 1993, such a posture was not without risk. With the exception of gangsters turned rappers like Ice-T, what noted economist, sociologist, critic of capitalism, and author of *The Theory of the Leisure Class* Thorstein Veblen once termed "conspicuous consumption"[57] could at times be regarded as "suspicious appropriation," as with the careers of early-1990s pop rap stars Vanilla Ice and MC Hammer, given that the negative connotations of "selling out" endangered a hip hop artist's credibility in this period of the culture's development.

What saves O'Neal from such a fate is the decision to include vocal snippets of hip hop lyrics by established rappers *already* proclaiming O'Neal's greatness. After Stern's draft-day pronouncement, lyrics from the 1992 song "That's How We Do It" by Grand Puba of New Rochelle, New York, are appropriated as a tagline: "First round draft pick like big Shaquille O'Neal." And then there is the cautionary lyric by Mt. Vernon, New York, rapper CL Smooth: "Niggas wanna mill' like Shaquille O'Neal" from 1992's "Death Becomes You" is converted into a celebration on O'Neal's own rap album.[58] Williams illustrates the workings of this borrowing process:

[Listeners] do not have to have the knowledge of the *exact* song being borrowed for it to communicate meaning. . . . [S]ome will know the exact song, some will recognize a genre, and some will realize that it could reference a number of elements, as hip hop is often a multivocal discourse.[59]

By using such tactics in song production, O'Neal more easily helps facilitate his acceptance as a hip hop performer. When further considering the platinum- and gold-selling status of O'Neal's first two albums, respectively, an argument can be made that O'Neal entered hip hop as its established first millionaire, thus easing the tension that immense economic success negates authenticity when practicing hip hop music. In turn, NBA executives no longer immediately blanched at the thought of O'Neal expanding his public persona into hip hop music. However, a few cleverly placed vocal samples and paraphrased lyrics could not accomplish this alone. As we saw, throughout his rapping career O'Neal has deftly utilized the reciprocity embedded in hip hop culture to mold and further his brand reputation. This initial investigation appears to reveal O'Neal challenging—if not changing—the rules of both the NBA and the hip hop game. But by digging more deeply, we discover that O'Neal's rap career is in many ways completely acquiescent to the larger (white) dominant social order, which in the end reminds us that even at seven feet and with over $100 million in earnings, Shaq or indeed no one else is bigger than the game itself.

"I'M OUTSTANDING": NEOLIBERAL ALLEGORIES OVER BOOMING BASS AND BEATS

While his first two albums fulfilled O'Neal's vision for himself as a rapper and a brand, the NBA also benefited from this fairly inoffensive exhibition. By proximity, O'Neal provided the NBA with "cool," while previous racialized anxieties about hip hop were minimized by the playful "Shaq-Fu." The league could now celebrate an innocuous diversity by its successful synergy with a new brand of *Blackness* via politically neutral hip hop targeting newly emerging "urban" demographics. Glyn Hughes illustrates this duplicity further when considering commissioner David Stern's successes in the 1990s, noting that "the NBA has rebranded itself as both an institution of racial uplift and an entrepreneur of racial flair, a move that, in practice, has involved the NBA in a somewhat conflicted double role of discipliner and promoter" of race.[60] So while the NBA and other business interests were intrigued by ways in which hip hop culture created "affective and cognitive responses in known brands,"[61] they also harbored apprehensions about its supposed lawlessness and racial overtones.

Hughes describes the NBA as a "prominent site [where] the relation between corporate and popular culture . . . articulate[s] a new variation on
the relationship between racialized representations and social structure."[62]
To be sure, the NBA is also a place where a previously stigmatized culture
could be legitimized, but only if it contributed to the bottom line and forged
a favorable reputation for the league. In this regard, initial news of O'Neal's
interest in recording rap music was not favorably received, with one Ohio
columnist opining that "Shaquille is better seen than heard."[63] Others voiced
similar concern, including pronouncements from a Philadelphia journalist
that while "[professional basketball player] Grant Hill's classical piano playing
has been widely lauded, . . . O'Neal's rap career has come under fire," indicating that it was the specifics of O'Neal's "distracting outside interest," namely
hip hop, that was the reason for the objection.[64] The Orlando Magic's early
exit from the 1994 playoffs without winning a game seemed to confirm such
skepticism.[65] O'Neal again defended himself in his autobiography, arguing
that "the reports I've heard that I want to give up basketball and concentrate
on rap are just not true. I know which side my bread is buttered on."[66] As
the controversy surrounding fellow superstar Allen Iverson's rap debut attests,[67] the NBA pro turned rapper could only be possible if the performance
aligned itself with winning championships, the NBA's vision for the league,
and, implicitly, the dominating economic and cultural social structure of
mainstream America.

One place to see the evolution in O'Neal's thinking about these matters
is his 1993 autobiography. Throughout, he celebrates basketball for offering
hope to a poor Black boy where none existed, similar to the Bill Russell narrative so favored by liberal writers of the day. While sports media coverage of
Russell was flattering in descriptions of his athleticism and sympathetic to his
former living conditions, Murry Nelson rightfully criticizes such coverage as
"tempered with a subtle racism," lionizing him as a player while marginaliz-
ing him as a man. When Russell was represented by the media, the emphasis
was on his basketball achievements with snapshots of his "early life thrown
in to emphasize his blackness," while any acknowledgment of structural
poverty and racism remained unaddressed.[68] In turn, from humble poor child
to global superstar and millionaire, O'Neal's hip hop persona unintention-
ally reinforces these same reductive media descriptions by championing a
normative American narrative in song and video.

For O'Neal, his story is grounded by the loving devotion of his mother,
Lucille O'Neal, and the strict guidelines from his stepfather, Philip Harrison,
who raised O'Neal in the absence of his biological father. Raised in a decidedly military fashion, O'Neal has repeatedly attributed his accomplishments

to his upbringing: "Look at me now successful for sure / Phil raised me well to be an entrepreneur," Shaq raps in 1994's "Biological Didn't Bother."[69] The music video accompanying the song projects indisputable family success as O'Neal and Harrison drive through urban landscapes in Shaq's convertible Mercedes-Benz.[70] Todd Boyd explains that hip hop practitioners are well positioned to champion this narrative, as "hip hop has always celebrated the triumph of the individual over unfortunate circumstances," foregrounding "their *people* as instrumental to their existence."[71] Yao Ming's familial influences were similarly celebrated in the effort to transform Yao from simply a Chinese basketball player to an international superstar.[72] Such an intimate and transparent approach was trending in the 1990s. As *Forbes*'s Randall Lane declared, the "sports business has become more focused on the players' personalities."[73]

In this light, Shaquille O'Neal's music and business dealings convey conservative and neoliberal ideals manifest as one while thrusting family togetherness, hard work, and individual achievement into the open marketplace. Because of the success of such narratives, writing for the *Sociology of Sport Journal*, Matthew Atencio and Jan Wright contend that families, community groups, and corporations such as Nike, Reebok, and Adidas continue to privilege basketball as a primary means of recuperating young Black men. The playing and winning of these sports shapes the motivations, identities, and life pathways of such individuals; by engaging in sports, they are "making something" of their lives considering their close proximity to gangs, drugs, and crime.[74] As Shaq instructs in what is likely his most famous rap song, "Biological Didn't Bother": "And if you make it big, don't be materialistic / 'Cause you'll end up another statistic."[75] "Biological Didn't Bother" should be lauded for destigmatizing "step" parenthood and dispelling notions that "broken" Black families cannot function effectively. But when considered in a larger context, O'Neal's biography, brand, and hip hop lyrics involuntarily perpetuate a racially coded dichotomy of the professional Black male basketball player as "good" versus the unprofessional, underdeveloped (and likely criminal) Black male as "bad." As sociologist Reuben A. Buford May reminds us: "This highly visible media representation of the good and bad of professional Black male basketball players gives the impression to viewers Blacks are readily sharing in the American Dream."[76]

When championing a narrative celebrating basketball as a point of entry for young Black men to create space, meaning, and value in their lives, the structural reasons why social, economic, and educational opportunities are scarce in lower-income, urban communities of color go unacknowledged. Jeffrey Lane contends that "the depoliticization of racial identity is a fundamental feature of post-civil-rights America whereby the significance of race is minimized or denied or race is denounced as destructive."[77] In a new era of subtle racism, such inequities go ignored because celebrating diversity rather than highlighting its inequities is profitable. When pressed by Florida journalists to open more to the local media rather than only through national networks, commercials, and music videos, O'Neal purportedly cracked: "Marketing, baby. Say the most with the least."[78]

The structural inequities experienced by Shaquille O'Neal and people of similar socioeconomic categorization were pushed aside as professional sports stars in the 1990s inadvertently became saviors of an apparently much bigger crisis: declining localized economies in postindustrial, late-twentieth-century America. The fate of Orlando's middle class was entirely dependent on a triumphant and affable O'Neal. In an April 1994 article titled "Shaq's Impact Has City Counting Its Blessings," *Florida Today* reported:

> O'Neal's presence already has played a part in new jobs (for instance, the Magic public relations staff has doubled) and new businesses (restaurants, bars and comedy clubs keep popping up in an area that used to offer little more than Church Street Station). And one older business, the Magic's FanAttic, has seen sales increase by nearly 40%.[79]

Although it is being pitched as such, is what is good for Shaq really good for the city? As often is the case with globalized economics, financiers and global corporations are best poised to profit from the localized trials and triumphs of O'Neal and his fans. *Florida Today* reported that the majority owners of the Orlando Magic saw ticket sales and sponsorships in such demand that they were placed on a three-year waiting list at the onset of O'Neal's first season in 1992. Ancillary products such as jerseys, hats, T-shirts, and assorted memorabilia were chiefly manufactured overseas. As University of Central Florida professor Bradley Braun noted in the *Florida Today* piece: "If it's made in Taiwan, then it's helping the Taiwanese economy." The increased sale of Reeboks and Pepsi had a minimal impact on Orlando's economy.[80] O'Neal's reputation, while favorable to the media, corporate oligarchs, and (white) middle-class values, accidentally became the nexus in which the forces of globalized economic change become normalized and acceptable. As a result, it is simply impossible to divorce sports from race, as young Black men in sports "come to negotiate prominent ideas of hope, possibility and self-empowerment,"[81] their success or failure mythologized by the media as "notions of individual responsibility, while at the same time the media fails to critically assess the structure of systemic racism, discrimination, and inequality"[82] that maintains these conditions. Hughes argues that this presentation of managing the struggle of Black men in real time and in a globalized public theater allows corporations such as the NBA to contribute "to a subtle continuation of a presumed and reassuring link between Whiteness and management while conveniently, even strategically, avoiding specific questions about race."[83] In other words, the NBA ensures our safety from Black men by presenting their triumphs in controlled spaces, selling us globally sourced products that are related to this act while permitting us to look away from the continued disempowerment of the individual and divestment of localized communities.

"DON'T CALL IT A COMEBACK": THE LOSS AND RECLAMATION OF REPUTATION

Regardless, in 1996 O'Neal's endorsement opportunities continued to grow; two new movies, *Kazaam* and *Steel*, were in the works; and his third album, *You Can't Stop the Reign*, was to be released featuring a bevy of luminary talent such as rappers Notorious B.I.G., Jay-Z, Rakim, and the multiplatinum R&B star Bobby Brown. There was only one problem: the Orlando Magic, and by extension O'Neal, had not won a championship to this point. In 1995, the Magic made it to the finals but were unceremoniously swept by the Houston Rockets, who were led by their Hall of Fame center, Hakeem Olajuwon. Then in 1996, O'Neal was sidelined for much of the season by injury. As *Newsweek*'s Mark Starr forewarned, O'Neal "remains first of all a basketball player and marketing has never won an NBA championship."[84]

David C. Ogden and Joel Nathan Rosen remind us that "it is little wonder that when an athlete's promising beginning turns sour, fans and the community take these changes quite seriously and quite personally."[85] For Orlando, the city's mores and its literal economic value hinged on a Magic winning record. Bradley Braun has studied the economic impact of the Orlando Magic franchise since its first season in 1989. According to Braun, seats were already sold before O'Neal's drafting in 1992; "winning, not Shaq, has produced more [revenue]."[86] Despite investing no less than $3 million in O'Neal, Reebok president Roberto Muller was equally direct in emphasizing winning: "First and foremost he has to become one of the greatest basketball players of all time, certainly the greatest center of all time."[87] As O'Neal's fourth season—and initial contract—with the Orlando Magic came to a close in the spring of 1996, Shaq was about to learn why being a sports goat and G.O.A.T. are homonyms.[88]

As his impressive, and at times unstoppable, professional play further developed with the Magic, O'Neal had shown a proverbial Achilles heel in his game: shooting free throws. Mastery of this most basic of basketball plays somehow eluded O'Neal, and opposing teams took advantage, fouling O'Neal particularly when the game was late and close rather than allowing him unimpeded access to the rim, a practice that has since become derisively known as "Hack-a-Shaq." Analysts and fans alike mocked O'Neal's difficulty with a shot that many believe to be a simple toss while never taking into account all that proficient shooters go through to polish this aspect of their game. As a result, critics continued to carp that O'Neal was little more than a "dunk specialist" with a "limited assortment of shots."[89] As George Diaz relayed in the *Chicago Tribune*: "O'Neal's fascination with outside fun is sometimes a point of contention with Magic fans, who want him to spend his free time on basketball activities such as free throw shooting."[90] By the time O'Neal did establish himself as a dominant, championship-caliber player, he had grown tired of criticism of his game that often lapsed into caricature: "You tell me is it more acceptable to spend four hours on the golf course or in [the] studio rappin'? What's the difference? Point is, it's four hours away from basketball. But [the media] doesn't rip guys for playing golf."[91] It would seem that no matter how much time, talent, and energy O'Neal had invested in a flexible and remunerative multimedia professional sports profile, his basketball worth would only be tallied by final scores.

By the summer of 1996, the collective distrust between O'Neal, local media, and the Magic fan base had grown to a crescendo that helped expedite O'Neal's departure as a free agent. Spurned by his decision to sign with the Los Angeles Lakers, fans expressed displeasure and jeered "good riddance" in the pages of the *Orlando Sentinel* and elsewhere. The paper conducted a poll asking if O'Neal was worth $115 million for seven seasons, his market value at the time. By a 10 to 1 margin, five thousand callers rejected the notion of the franchise investing that much in O'Neal,[92] the growing disdain for whom is captured in a letter to sports columnist Larry Guest:

> Larry: Regarding a certain immature athlete who wants more than he's worth, it is my understanding Kazaam, er, Rap Master, er. . . . Hey, wasn't he a basketball player at one time? Anyway, he wants a paltry $20 million a year to play a profession that gets about as much dedication from him as, say, a 5-year-old gives to a math assignment. —Mike Ledbetter, Orlando[93]

Similar commentary was offered up by others, including *Orlando Senti-nel* columnist Brian Schmitz, who in his column "Shaq's about Style, Not Substance" claimed that O'Neal was a "legend in his spare time" and less of basketball player than a "multipurpose entertainment center."[94] A local business posted an ill-mannered goodbye to the city's erstwhile superstar on its marquee: "SHAQ DONT LET THE DOOR POP YOU IN THE REAR WHEN YOU LEAVE."[95] A novelty song titled "Hit the Road Shaq" further inflamed the rejected masses, while local radio listeners called in to express relief that he was gone.[96] And by the end of this flurry of direct and veiled invectives, O'Neal himself had had enough and let fly that the feelings had become mutual, telling the Associated Press that the "media in Orlando kind of bashed me so much. . . . When I read something in the paper like that? Doesn't make me weak, makes me strong. I like to prove people wrong."[97]

If it were only that easy. "Ringless" after four seasons with the Magic, O'Neal's business phone began to "ring less" as well. O'Neal, according to the AP, "wasn't in the ad plans for Taco Bell, Reebok or Pepsi for the first half of '98."[98] While the soundscape of the hip hop music industry had less room for "pop" rappers by the late 1990s, Shaq was still able to collaborate with credible platinum-selling "street" artists of the day such as Jay-Z, the Notorious B.I.G., and Mobb Deep. Nonetheless, his third and fourth LPs, *You Can't Stop the Reign* and *Respect*, did not equal five hundred thousand in sales combined. O'Neal's "street cred" also faced challenges from the emergent AND1 "urban" footwear and clothing of the late 1990s, a company whose success owed no small part to "Shaq Diesel." AND1 sought a demographic *Forbes* described as "inner-city trendsetters [who] relate more closely to NBA rookies and fringe players than they do top earners like Shaquille O'Neal."[99] Perhaps most damaging, O'Neal's transparent biography and sterling moral reputation as played out in media imaging and rap video came under intense scrutiny when it was disclosed that he had fathered a child out of wedlock and was not at that time engaged in caring for the child or supporting the mother. Schmitz, again writing in the *Orlando Sentinel*, noted that "Madison Avenue image-makers can package Shaq or any other celebrity to the American public. But they can't change the drama played out in his real-life world when people are affected."[100] As the uncomfortable intimacies of O'Neal's personal life (some less accurate than others) were revealed in newsprint, talk radio, and television, lyrics such as "Biological father, left me in the cold, when a few months old / I thought a child was greater than gold but I guess not" were recast as hypocrisy.[101] By the end of the 1990s, Team Shaq needed a rebound.

FINAL SCORE: THE WINNING REPUTATION OF SHAQ DIESEL

As mentioned in the introduction to this chapter, there is no greater source for Shaquille O'Neal's reclaimed reputation than his championship play with the Los Angeles Lakers at the start of the new millennium. And to the victor go the spoils. But it is not that O'Neal would be untainted by criticism from this point forth. Questions about his conditioning and his focus persisted, as well as the belief that his stubborn streak played a role in his "feud" with Kobe Bryant that precipitated his trade from the Lakers to the Miami Heat in 2004. But the temperature of perceptions by the media had changed, and with that, O'Neal's reputation began its recuperation. Martin Fennelly, sports columnist for the *Tampa Tribune*, offered a reassessment of O'Neal's personality and professional career as O'Neal stood two wins away from his first title: "Shaq has come a long way, but that goofy *gotcha!* grin has never left. . . . Shaq was always more disciplined than people thought . . . [and] has never gotten the credit he deserved."[102] Now comfortably buffered by championships, pursuits outside basketball were considered more favorably, especially if they aligned with normative (white) middle-class values. "O'Neal Shows His Classy Side to a Great Degree" read a *Los Angeles Times* headline celebrating O'Neal earning a Master of Business from the University of Phoenix.[103]

Glyn Hughes and Reuben A. Buford May make a compelling case that not only is winning redemptive, but Black NBA athletes' acquiescence to management and coaching strategies ensures their casting as "good" in the media. Phil Jackson, O'Neal's Svengali-like coach in Los Angeles, was widely praised in equal measure for the play of his team and his role modeling behaviors that served to counterbalance what Hughes calls "threats to the inside: indecent rap music, unrestrained tempers—in Jackson's own words, 'primitive impulses'; and perhaps most of all, the team-destroying narcissism or egos of stars."[104]

By complying with such favored direction in the second half of his NBA career, and predictably upon O'Neal's retirement in 2011 and subsequent election into the Basketball Hall of Fame in 2016, the metamorphosis of O'Neal's reputation would be complete. *Forbes*'s Kurt Badenhausen lauded O'Neal as a "marketing visionary" who "broke the mold with his Reebok shoe business" when he "recognized the importance of the China market (300 million Chinese play basketball) when he took his Dunkman brand there in 2006 in a deal with apparel company Li-Ning."[105] Apparently, Shaq recognized the virtues of globalization long before the rest of America did. *Rolling Stone* even revisited what they called O'Neal's "under-appreciated, surprisingly successful hip hop career" in 2016. Noting the failures of rap forays by Kobe Bryant, Chris Webber, and Allen Iverson, writer Jake Lustick declared: "Clearly, O'Neal's musical achievements were more than just a force of personality."[106]

Even O'Neal's acting chops have been rethought. For example, as Glenn Kenny reported in his review of the 2018 basketball film *Uncle Drew*: "It's not every day that you can say, 'Shaquille O'Neal was the best actor in that movie.'" But, he continues, O'Neal "steadily builds the most complete characterization in the movie."[107]

Whether competing in mixed martial arts or taking an oath as a trained officer for the Los Angeles Port Police, the twenty-first-century iteration of Shaquille O'Neal has become largely well liked and respected as characterizations of his reputation have transformed from a once crude, impish behemoth to a savvy and beloved media personality. In this way, we recognize Jack Lule's most salient point when he claims that "the vilified sports hero does not *achieve* redemption but is *granted* redemption."[108]

In the final analysis, Shaquille O'Neal overcame lingering racially coded myths that emphasize immense Black physicality as being mutually exclusive with other creative skill sets and business acumen, assessments of his physique attempting to circumscribe his potential and humanity. Through the eye of the needle, O'Neal and his management team took advantage of his unique size and rapping ability to debunk these myths and "tap into a younger audience that extends far beyond the basketball court"[109] by availing themselves of innovative marketing strategies that exploited broader economic and cultural shifts in American popular culture during the 1990s. Here, as the "Shaq Diesel" myth emerged and offered "life-empowering visions" presented in art and magnified in song,[110] O'Neal's reputation as a rapper and entertainer serves as an indispensable vehicle for normalizing hip hop culture and urban Black male identity in the 1990s, a process that was of the utmost importance to the NBA in its attempts to shed its stigmatized racial and lawless image of the 1970s and 1980s.

As O'Neal's reputation ascended, he brought the NBA and hip hop into a new era. His music was generally embraced by hip hop recording artists and gatekeepers of the culture, winning over the begrudging respect of those who previously would consider O'Neal's initial foray into rap a gimmick and considered that his wealth would be anathema to carefully guarded ideas of authenticity within hip hop. Even his deliberate vanity projects championed hip hop culture in all its conflicting representations of young Black America, yet his music was for the most part quietly apolitical. But before we take O'Neal to task for political passivity, let us remember that his staggering wealth was realized as he was being thrust into a global spotlight before he was even twenty-one, at an age when too many aspiring star athletes have seen their hoop dreams deflate with one bad break. There were old rules to this new game of mixing and matching hip hop cool with NBA entertainment, but O'Neal was a decidedly new kind of star from a new era. O'Neal and his manager, Leonard Armato, played the game and amassed tremendous profit all the while expanding hip hop and with it NBA culture, although the normalization of subtle, new forms of racism and globalized economic disempowerment never abated.

O'Neal and his reputation paid a price for this, as young Black American entrepreneurs often do when they attempt to modify the means of production for their own gain. The inescapable truth was that O'Neal's brand was only worth what he could produce on the hardwood floor, championships notwithstanding. Upon achieving this in commanding fashion during the 2000, 2001, and 2002 NBA seasons, O'Neal, whose character often seemed as big as his body, watched as grace was finally bestowed on his now virtually unassailable reputation while the largely white media granted the big man a clear path to the basket. Considering the totality of this odyssey, the barriers and the legion of "haters" O'Neal constantly referenced in his rap lyrics no longer appear imaginary or hyperbolic.

At the start of the final verse of 1993's "Giggin' on 'Em," guest MC Phife Dawg from A Tribe Called Quest interrupts O'Neal and retorts: "You don't have to kick a third verse / Just let those people know all the fellas and peoples you gigged on." Naturally, O'Neal proceeds to list the NBA players he dominated on the court, including seven-foot, seven-inch Manute Bol, Greg Anthony, and "Grandmama" Larry Johnson, established NBA stars of the day. But tellingly, O'Neal also takes aim at a new set of adversaries that he "gigged on" who had doubted his prowess such as Flint, Michigan, rapper Me Phi Me; record executive Jeffrey Sledge, who passed on signing O'Neal; and, last, "country people" and all that phrase connotes, to which Phife responds emphatically, "Hell yeah, hell yeah, hell yeah, hell yeah . . ."[111]

POSTGAME ANALYSIS: O'NEAL STILL A STARTER IN THE 2020s

In 2010, multiplatinum Toronto rapper Drake noted, "Damn, I swear sports and music are so synonymous / 'Cause we want to be them, and they want to be us."[112] Prior to 1992, the pop music subculture of hip hop and professional athletics were still a world apart. A rapper like Public Enemy's Chuck D in 1988 may have bragged, "Simple and plain, give me the lane / I'll throw it down your throat like Barkley,"[113] but the NBA and hip hop were far from "synonymous" in 1992. As the last decade of the twentieth century unfolded, the norms of professional sports began to change as blue-chip, top-ten draft picks released rap songs and starred in "urban" motion pictures, and rap music was piped into arenas during timeouts.

Shaquille O'Neal has been at the epicenter of this seismic shift in popular culture, professional athletics, and multimillion-dollar business enterprises. As the millennium turned, the two figures often cited for accelerating this lucrative blend of hip hop beats and Wall Street boardroom acumen are recording artists Sean "Diddy" Combs and Andre "Dr. Dre" Young. Dan Charnas's exhaustive 2011 study *The Big Payback: The History of the Business of Hip-Hop*[114] somehow excludes *any* mention of O'Neal, while the expansive 2016–2020 Netflix series *Hip-Hop Evolution*[115] neglects to cover O'Neal's presence in hip hop culture. These are but two casual examples of the conspicuous omission of O'Neal's fame and reputation in the discourse of hip hop history, academic or otherwise.

But if anyone is keeping score, Shaq is still "giggin' on 'em," as he rapped in 1993, and by a large margin. The retired O'Neal has presumably long since tuned out critics, as his presence has remained utterly ubiquitous in the NBA, high-profile business ventures, and, yes, still in hip hop circles. An informal sampling of six months of news headlines from October 2019 to April 2020 reveals that Shaquille O'Neal persists as an elder statesman of the NBA from his position as analyst on TNT, an "extra, extra large" celebrity persona, and a valuable brand unto himself with a net worth of approximately $400 million dollars.

Foremost, the untimely death of Kobe and Gigi Bryant and seven others in a helicopter accident on January 26, 2020, in southern California thrust O'Neal's grief and sorrow into the international spotlight. For all the supposed acrimony between Bryant and O'Neal, the tragic circumstances revealed a far more intimate bond between them than the public previously understood. O'Neal's speech at the celebration of Bryant's life on February 24, 2020, addressed this dynamic:

> As many of you know, Kobe and I had a very complex relationship throughout the years.... But not unlike another leadership duo, John Lennon and Paul McCartney, whose creativity forever led to some of the greatest music of all time, Kobe and I pushed one another to play some of the greatest basketball of all time.

It is notable that O'Neal considers his and Bryant's accomplishments to be comparable to those of the Beatles' two principal songwriters, reinforcing the fact that his blurring of basketball, performance artistry, and commerce have been hallmarks of his career. Also consistent with his comedic persona, O'Neal had the biggest laugh of the difficult night when he revealed the rebuff of his criticism of Bryant's game. Declaring that Bryant needed to pass the ball more, he intoned, "Kobe, there's no 'I' in 'team,'" to which Bryant retorted, "I know, but there's an 'm-e' in that, motherfucker."

As O'Neal further pronounced in his speech that he and Bryant had shared a "deep respect and a love for one another,"[116] Bryant's death has forced fans, sports journalists, and historians to reconsider the duo's reputedly "combative but ultimately strong relationship."[117] Public discussion of fantasy matchups has begun to favor the "Shaq Kobe Lakers," as ESPN's Ariel Helwani offered up to O'Neal in an interview that the "three-peat" Los Angeles Lakers would have beaten the 1990s six-championship Michael Jordan Bulls; O'Neal playfully agreed with the hypothetical, even indirectly downplaying the importance of coaching guru Phil Jackson's contribution to the outcome.[118]

Even before Bryant's death, O'Neal—and notably Charles Barkley as well—have used their positions at TNT almost as a bully pulpit, regularly reframing the sporting event being broadcast on a given night as not being as physical or hard-nosed as their style of basketball in the 1990s. Occasionally calling out underachieving players by name, O'Neal will defend this type of intergenerational trash talk as mentorship, but it creates a curious dynamic between the youth playing the game on the floor currently and the old guard calling it from the studio. As O'Neal made a name for himself early in his playing career by defying the "traditions" of center play, one wonders how he would have reacted if the likes of Wilt Chamberlain or Bill Russell would have criticized his play publicly from the relative comfort, power, and reach of a cable television platform. Golden State Warriors center JaVale McGee went so far as to call O'Neal's denigrations of his play "'cooning,' playing the black minstrel for a white audience, and in doing so tearing other black men down."[119] O'Neal has continued to push the envelope in entertainment in ways not appreciated by all, his fame an impenetrable firewall detractors cannot breach.

But O'Neal's reputation has hardly been defined by the clickbait sports headlines his television banter has produced. As O'Neal obtained a doctorate in education from Miami's Barry University in 2012, his children Amirah and Shareef have been recognized as highly touted student athletes for Louisiana State University. LSU men's basketball head coach Will Wade acknowledged: "The name O'Neal is a part of LSU basketball history," a fact surely on the mind of the O'Neal family when committing to the patriarch's alma mater.[120]

On one hand, there is the pressure of living in the shadow of O'Neal's legacy and the inevitable comparisons, but on the other, these moves are the shrewd capitalizing of the O'Neal legacy and family name and all the benefits that may bring the younger family members either on or off the court. It would appear that the younger O'Neals are ready for the task; taking a page from his father's playbook, Shareef used his social media platform of choice, TikTok, to announce that his father had bought a new boat and named it *Free Throw* because then he wouldn't sink it.[121]

As a celebrity, O'Neal's presence is not limited to TNT sports broadcasts; he also appears in a TNT reality television docuseries called *Shaq Life* that bills O'Neal as the "ultimate renaissance man" as well as in the nationally syndicated "Big Podcast with Shaq" on PodcastOne. Reports on his celebrity news reputation have ranged from stories about missteps to tales of the heroic, but again, they are consistent with his brand and highly visible. O'Neal had previously endorsed the infamous Joe Exotic of the 2020 Netflix documentary *Tiger King*, an association he quickly clarified and distanced himself from in April 2020.[122] As DJ Diesel, O'Neal has toured internationally and is featured on XM Satellite Radio. Portland Trailblazers point guard Damian Lillard plans to release a hip hop mixtape featuring O'Neal, a surprise turn of events as O'Neal and Lillard exchanged "diss tracks" in 2019 criticizing each other's game.[123] To round things off, in October 2019, O'Neal donated a year's rent to an Atlanta family after their twelve-year-old son was paralyzed from a shooting at a high school football game;[124] and in January 2020, O'Neal stopped traffic in the East Village of Manhattan after a woman collapsed from a diabetic spell.[125]

As for the box score, O'Neal is one the highest-compensated professional athletes in the world. As it was in 1992, diversification appears to be a hallmark of his business strategy: O'Neal was an early investor in Google; he is a shareholder in the Authentic Brands Group, which manages the celebrity licenses of clients such as "Marilyn Monroe, Elvis Presley, Muhammad Ali and Michael Jackson"; and he reportedly owns 155 Five Guys restaurants, 150 car washes, forty 24 Hour Fitnesses, seventeen Auntie Anne's, and a Krispy Kreme.[126] Other partnerships include Carnival Cruise Line and a high-profile seat as an adviser on Papa John's executive board. Here, O'Neal has been well compensated for leveraging his fame and reputation "in order to help Papa John's improve its culture and engagement with its customers and communities" after its former owner tarnished the brand with racist comments in 2018.[127] In a Horatio Alger–like turn of fate, O'Neal has made public his interest in buying and reviving the Reebok sneaker brand, the very company that first sponsored him in 1992.[128]

Throughout the 2010s, O'Neal's use of social media has been adept, maintaining his reputation and expanding his fame. His skill in that regard has surely been honed by years of navigating the recording and movie industries and, of course, 24-7 sports coverage. O'Neal has confessed to avoiding political controversy online and has purposely created indirect content as a method of marketing: "60% [of what I post is] to make you laugh, 30% to inspire you and 10% to tell you what I'm selling."[129] As O'Neal's family danced, via their social media outlets, to their father DJ Diesel's music during the spring 2020 COVID-19 quarantine,[130] one gets the sense that Shaquille O'Neal's relevance to sports and popular culture will not be fading anytime soon, even the midst of a global pandemic. While Drake's rap, "Sports and music are so synonymous," may have been an observation about the synergy of sports and hip hop at large, such a lyric is only possible because of O'Neal's remarkable, ever-evolving hip hop athletic entrepreneurial entertainment career.

NOTES

1. Three chapters from previous volumes in this series, Murry Nelson's "Bill Russell: From Revulsion to Resurrection," in *Reconstructing Fame: Sport, Race, and Evolving Reputations*, ed. David C. Ogden and Joel Nathan Rosen (Jackson: University Press of Mississippi, 2008), 87–101; Gregory J. Kaliss's "A Precarious Perch: Wilt Chamberlain, Basketball Stardom, and Racial Politics," in *Fame to Infamy: Race, Sport, and the Fall from Grace*, ed. David C. Ogden and Joel Nathan Rosen (Jackson: University Press of Mississippi, 2010), 146–69; and Dong Jinxia, Zhong Yijing, and Li Luyang's "The Interaction of Personal, Local, and Global Forces: Yao Ming's Rise and Sustained Influence in Chinese Sport," in *More Than Cricket and Football: International Sport and the Challenge of Celebrity*, ed. Joel Nathan Rosen and Maureen M. Smith (Jackson: University Press of Mississippi, 2016), 75–98, provide rich and detailed context for the challenges and victories these three large NBA centers have experienced. As African American men, Chamberlain and Russell, against the backdrop of their trials and triumphs, provide historical background from the 1950s and 1960s that particularly informs O'Neal's arrival in the NBA in the early 1990s.

2. David C. Ogden and Joel Nathan Rosen, "Introduction: Thoughts on Fame and Infamy," in *Fame to Infamy: Race, Sport, and the Fall from Grace*, ed. David C. Ogden and Joel Nathan Rosen (Jackson: University Press of Mississippi, 2010), 3–7.

3. Vin Getz, "Shaquille O'Neal Retires: The Most Ridiculous Quotes of His Career," *Bleacher Report*, June 2, 2011, http://bleacherreport.com/articles/720434-shaquille-oneal-retires-50 -most-ridiculous-quotes-of-his-career#slide0.

4. Kaliss, "A Precarious Perch," 166.

5. Kaliss, "A Precarious Perch," 152, 162.

6. Tim Povtak, "Two Giants in One Day," *Orlando Sentinel*, August 8, 1992, http://articles .orlandosentinel.com/1992-08-08/news/9208080646_1_shaquille-oneal-magic-hakeem -olajuwon.

7. Barry Cooper, "Shaq Not Talking," *Orlando Sentinel*, May 19, 1992, http://articles.orlando
sentinel.com/1992-05-19/sports/9205190669_1_shaquille-oneal-armato-won-the-lottery.

8. Brian Schmitz, "Shaquille Shows Class in Switching to No. 32," *Orlando Sentinel*,
August 25, 1992, http://articles.orlandosentinel.com/1992-08-25/sports/9208250132_1_shaq
-catledge-oneal.

9. "Magic Man," *Florida Today* (Cocoa), February 21, 1993.

10. Shaquille O'Neal and Jack McCallum, *Shaq Attaq!* (New York: Hyperion, 1993), 41.

11. Todd Boyd, *Young, Black, Rich, and Famous: The Rise of the NBA, the Hip Hop Invasion,
and the Transformation of American Culture* (Lincoln: University of Nebraska Press, 2008), 150.

12. Kaliss, "A Precarious Perch," 147.

13. Fajuraster, "Shaquille O'Neal—Shoot Pass Slam (1993)," YouTube, September 10, 2015,
https://www.youtube.com/watch?v=Fl2zl9czOcw.

14. 1987Hawkeyes, "1993—Reebok—Shaq, Russell, Chamberlain, Kareem, Walton,"
YouTube, March 21, 2008, https://www.youtube.com/watch?v=Nwb-ighjXZ8.

15. 1987Hawkeyes, "1993—Pepsi—Shaquille O'Neal," YouTube, April 29, 2008, https://
www.youtube.com/watch?v=7JZ8iQ9P9iI.

16. Roger Mosconi, dir., "Coke and a Smile," filmed October 1979, posted at Stiggerpao,
"Coca-Cola Classic Ad: 'Mean' Joe Greene (Full Version) (1979)," YouTube, July 18, 2007,
https://www.youtube.com/watch?v=xffOCZYX6F8.

17. Mark Starr, "The $16 Million Man," *Newsweek*, April 30, 1995.

18. Dong, Zhong, and Li, "The Interaction of Personal, Local, and Global Forces," 82.

19. Randall Lane, "Prepackaged Celebrity," *Forbes*, December 20, 1993, 87.

20. William Friedkin, dir., *Blue Chips*, Paramount Pictures, 1994.

21. "Magic Man," *Florida Today*.

22. Raymond Calhoun, Erick Sermon, Alisa Yarbrough, and Shaquille O'Neal, "I'm
Outstanding," Genius, November 10, 1993, https://genius.com/Shaquille-oneal-im-out
standing-lyrics.

23. Lane, "Prepackaged Celebrity," 88–90.

24. Jeffrey Lane, "Mortgaging Michael Jordan's Reputation," in *Fame to Infamy: Race, Sport,
and the Fall from Grace*, ed. David C. Ogden and Joel Nathan Rosen (Jackson: University
Press of Mississippi, 2010), 129.

25. Lane, "Mortgaging Michael Jordan's Reputation," 129.

26. George Diaz, "The World Is Mine," *Chicago Tribune*, May 17, 1996.

27. Starr, "The $16 Million Man."

28. Lane, "Prepackaged Celebrity," 86.

29. Lane, "Prepackaged Celebrity," 90.

30. Larry Platt, *New Jack Jocks: Rebels, Race, and the American Athlete* (Philadelphia:
Temple University Press, 2002), 191.

31. See once again Jeffrey Lane's "Mortgaging Michael Jordan's Reputation" as a definitive
analysis of the celebrated and conflicted reputation constructed around Jordan's career. As
a side note, one of the underacknowledged links between the two players is that O'Neal's
star clearly rose during Jordan's 1994 NBA hiatus to purse baseball with the Chicago White
Sox. This provided O'Neal with almost a full year of nearly exclusive media attention as an
emerging commercial, entertainment, and sports figure until Jordan's abrupt return to the
NBA in the 1995 playoffs.

32. Dong, Zhong, and Li, "The Interaction of Personal, Local, and Global Forces," 81.

33. O'Neal and McCallum, *Shaq Attaq!*

34. Reginald C. Dennis, "Can He Rock? Shaquille O'Neal," *The Source*, February 1994, 31–32; and O'Neal and McCallum, *Shaq Attaq!*, 95.

35. Charlie Ahearn, dir., *Wild Style*, First Run Features, 1982.

36. Bakari Kitwana, *The Hip Hop Generation: Young Blacks and the Crisis in African American Culture* (New York: Basic Civitas Books, 2003). The "Hip Hop Generation" is defined in this text as those who were born after segregation and who actively (or passively) participate in the production and consumption of hip hop culture.

37. Platt, *New Jack Jocks*, 191.

38. Boyd, *Young, Black, Rich, and Famous*, 104.

39. Chris Wilder, "Nineties Niggers," *The Source*, December 1992. The *Source* promoted itself as the "magazine of hip hop music, culture and politics," an accurate self-description particularly in the 1990s.

40. Platt, *New Jack Jocks*, 125.

41. Lane, "Mortgaging Michael Jordan's Reputation," 124.

42. Jeffrey Lane, *Under the Boards: The Cultural Revolution in Basketball* (Lincoln: University of Nebraska Press, 2007), 49.

43. Lane, "Prepackaged Celebrity," 90.

44. Lane, "Mortgaging Michael Jordan's Reputation," 133.

45. O'Neal and McCallum, *Shaq Attaq!*, 95.

46. Glyn Hughes, "Managing Black Guys: Representation, Corporate Culture, and the NBA," *Sociology of Sport Journal* 21, no. 2 (2004): 164, doi:10.1123/ssj.21.2.163.

47. Hughes, "Managing Black Guys," 164.

48. Def Jef, Shaquille O'Neal, and Meech Wells, "(I Know I Got) Skillz," Genius, September 7, 1993, https://genius.com/Shaquille-oneal-i-know-i-got-skillz-lyrics.

49. Calhoun et al., "I'm Outstanding."

50. Diaz, "The World Is Mine," 7

51. S. Craig Watkins, *Hip Hop Matters: Politics, Pop Culture, and the Struggle for the Soul of a Movement* (Boston: Beacon Press, 2008), 60.

52. Watkins, *Hip Hop Matters.*

53. Justin A. Williams, *Rhymin' and Stealin': Musical Borrowing in Hip-Hop* (Ann Arbor: University of Michigan Press, 2014), 1, 14.

54. Def Jef, O'Neal, and Wells, "(I Know I Got) Skillz."

55. Williams, *Rhymin' and Stealin'*, 46.

56. Shaquille O'Neal, "Intro," Genius, October 26, 1993, https://genius.com/Shaquille-oneal-intro-lyrics.

57. Thorstein Veblen, *The Theory of the Leisure Class: An Economic Study of Institutions* (New York: Macmillan, 1899), 64–70.

58. O'Neal, "Intro."

59. Williams, *Rhymin' and Stealin'*, 15.

60. Hughes, "Managing Black Guys," 174.

61. Nakeisha S. Ferguson and Janée N. Burkhalter, "Yo, DJ, That's My Brand: An Examination of Consumer Response to Brand Placements in Hip-Hop Music," *Journal of Advertising* 44, no. 1 (2015): 54–55, doi:10.1080/00913367.2014.935897.

62. Hughes, "Managing Black Guys," 165.

63. Terry Pluto, "Shaquille Is Better Seen than Heard," *Akron Beacon Journal*, January 17, 1994.

64. Larry Platt, *Keepin' It Real: A Turbulent Season at the Crossroads with the NBA* (New York: Avon, 1999), 150.

65. Starr, "The $16 Million Man."

66. O'Neal and McCallum, *Shaq Attaq!*, 95.

67. Platt, *New Jack Jocks*, 43–60.

68. Nelson, "Bill Russell: From Revulsion to Resurrection," 90–91.

69. Shaquille O'Neal, "Biological Didn't Bother," Genius, November 12, 1996, https://genius.com/Shaquille-oneal-biological-didnt-bother-lyrics.

70. ShaqVEVO, "Shaquille O'Neal—Biological Didn't Bother (G-Funk Version)," YouTube, January 10, 2018, https://www.youtube.com/watch?v=y2J5xEOIoCA.

71. Boyd, *Young, Black, Rich, and Famous*, 104, 157.

72. Dong, Zhong, and Li, "The Interaction of Personal, Local, and Global Forces," 77.

73. Lane, "Prepackaged Celebrity," 87.

74. Matthew Atencio and Jan Wright, "'We Be Killin' Them': Hierarchies of Black Masculinity in Urban Basketball Spaces," *Sociology of Sport Journal* 25, no. 2 (2008): 273–78, doi:10.1123/ssj.25.2.263.

75. O'Neal, "Biological Didn't Bother."

76. Reuben A. Buford May, "The Good and Bad of It All: Professional Black Male Basketball Players as Role Models for Young Black Male Basketball Players," *Sociology of Sport Journal* 26, no. 3 (2009): 446–47, doi:10.1123/ssj.26.3.443.

77. Lane, "Mortgaging Michael Jordan's Reputation," 133.

78. Martin Fennelly, "Shaq Stays Economical with Words," *Tampa Tribune*, January 19, 1995.

79. "Shaq's Impact Has City Counting Its Blessings," *Florida Today* (Cocoa), April 17, 1994.

80. "Shaq's Impact," *Florida Today*.

81. Atencio and Wright, "We Be Killin' Them," 278.

82. May, "The Good and Bad of It All," 446.

83. Hughes, "Managing Black Guys," 181.

84. Starr, "The $16 Million Man."

85. Ogden and Rosen, "Introduction: Thoughts on Fame and Infamy."

86. Ogden and Rosen, "Introduction: Thoughts on Fame and Infamy."

87. Lane, "Prepackaged Celebrity," 90.

88. G.O.A.T. in its contemporary iteration stands for *greatest of all time*.

89. Starr, "The $16 Million Man."

90. Diaz, "The World Is Mine."

91. Richie Whitt, "Does Shaq Get a Bad Rap?," *Orlando Sentinel*, May 3, 1998.

92. Larry Guest, "O'Neal Sweepstakes Goes beyond Dollars and Sense," *Orlando Sentinel*, July 17, 1996.

93. Rex Hoggard, "Shaq Attack: Callers Just Say No," *Orlando Sentinel*, July 17, 1996.

94. Brian Schmitz, "Shaq's about Style, Not Substance," *Orlando Sentinel*, July 19, 1996.

95. Tim Turner, "Magic Fans Grapple with Shaq's Departure," *Orlando Sentinel*, July 19, 1996.

96. Associated Press, "Without Shaq, the Magic Is a Different Show," *Daily Press* (Newport News, VA), July 19, 1996.

97. Associated Press, "After Gold . . . and Purple," *Daily Press* (Newport News, VA), July 19, 1996.

98. Whitt, "Does Shaq Get a Bad Rap?"

99. Rob Wherry, "Hip, Hop, Hot," *Forbes*, December 27, 1999.

100. Brian Schmitz, "Shaq Has to Answer to Only 1 Man: Himself," *Orlando Sentinel*, January 19, 1996.

101. O'Neal, "Biological Didn't Bother."

102. Martin Fennelly, "Shaq Said He'd Win, and Now He Is," *Tampa Tribune*, June 11, 2000.

103. T. J. Simers, "O'Neal Shows His Classy Side to a Great Degree," *Los Angeles Times*, June 26, 2005.

104. Hughes, "Managing Black Guys," 177.

105. Kurt Badenhausen, "Shaquille O'Neal Was a Marketing Visionary," *Forbes*, June 1, 2011.

106. Jake Lustick, "Flashback: Shaquille O'Neal's Hall of Fame Rap Career," *Rolling Stone*, September 7, 2016, www.rollingstone.com/culture/culture-sports/flashback-shaquille-oneals-hall-of-fame-rap-career-101620/.

107. Glenn Kenny, "Review: In 'Uncle Drew,' N.B.A. Stars Keep Dunking with Age," *New York Times*, June 28, 2018, www.nytimes.com/2018/06/28/movies/uncle-drew-review-kyrie-irving.html.

108. Jack Lule, "Afterword: The Globalization of Vilification; The Localization of Redemption," in *Reconstructing Fame: Sport, Race, and Evolving Reputations*, ed. David C. Ogden and Joel Nathan Rosen (Jackson: University Press of Mississippi, 2008), 131.

109. Diaz, "The World Is Mine."

110. Joseph Campbell, "The Historical Development of Mythology," in *Myth and Mythmaking*, ed. Henry A. Murray (New York: George Braziller, 1960), 1–2.

111. Dr. Question Mark, Phife Dawg, and Shaquille O'Neal, "Giggin' on 'Em," Genius, October 26, 1993, https://genius.com/Shaquille-oneal-giggin-on-em-lyrics.

112. Drake, "Thank Me Now," Genius, June 15, 2010, https://genius.com/Drake-thank-me-now-lyrics.

113. Public Enemy, "Rebel without a Pause," Genius, June 28, 1988, https://genius.com/Public-enemy-rebel-without-a-pause-lyrics.

114. Dan Charnas, *The Big Payback: The History of the Business of Hip-Hop* (New York: New American Library, 2011).

115. Darby Wheeler and Rodrigo Bascunan, *Hip-Hop Evolution*, HBO Canada and Netflix, 2016–2020.

116. Los Angeles Lakers, "Shaquille O'Neal Speaks at a Celebration of Life for Kobe and Gianna Bryant," YouTube, February 24, 2020, https://www.youtube.com/watch?v=2fqYgNR6174.

117. Jack Baer, "Shaquille O'Neal Says He Won't Watch Kobe Bryant's Hall of Fame Ceremony, Would Make Him Too Sad," Yahoo! Sports, April 17, 2020, https://sports.yahoo.com/shaquille-o-neal-kobe-bryant-hall-of-fame-ceremony-too-sad-031021189.html.

118. "Shaquille O'Neal Says His Three-Peat Lakers Would've 'Easily' Beaten Michael Jordan's Bulls in Their Prime," NBA India, April 16, 2020, https://in.nba.com/news/

shaquille-oneal-three-peat-los-angeles-lakers-easily-beaten-michael-jordans-chicago
-bulls/184p22h2gjd6f1fdkj2ophmzlf.

119. Mike Wise, "Shaq Drops His Twitter Feud with JaVale McGee on Orders from the
Top," The Undefeated, February 27, 2017, https://theundefeated.com/features/shaq-drops
-his-twitter-feud-with-javale-mcgee-on-orders-from-the-top/.

120. Tim Daniels, "Shaquille O'Neal's Daughter Amirah Commits to LSU, Joins Brother
Shareef," Bleacher Report, April 17, 2020, https://bleacherreport.com/articles/2887101
-shaquille-oneals-daughter-amirah-commits-to-lsu-joins-brother-shareef.

121. ESPN, "Lmao (via @ssjreef)," TikTok, April 12, 2020, https://www.tiktok.com/@espn/
video/6814629872355396869.

122. "Shaquille O'Neal Addresses Appearance on Netflix's 'Tiger King,' Says He 'Had
No Idea' What Went On behind Scenes at Zoo," ESPN, March 30, 2020, https://www
.espn.com/nba/story/_/id/28972773/shaquille-oneal-addresses-appearance-netflix-tiger
-king-says-had-no-idea-went-scenes-zoo.

123. Jamie Hudson, "Damian Lillard's New Mixtape Will Have a Song Featuring
Shaquille O'Neal," NBC Sports Northwest, March 24, 2020, https://www.nbcsports.com/
northwest/portland-trail-blazers/damian-lillards-new-mixtape-will-have-song-featuring
-shaquille-oneal.

124. Associated Press, "Former LSU Player, NBA Star Shaquille O'Neal Donates Year of
Rent to a Paralyzed Atlanta Boy," Advocate (Baton Rouge, LA), October 21, 2019, https://www
.theadvocate.com/baton_rouge/sports/lsu/article_a6192f66-f3f8-11e9-9dd8-7f621aa24e7d
.html.

125. Leah Bitsky, "Shaquille O'Neal Helps Woman Who Collapsed in Street," Page
Six, January 7, 2020, https://pagesix.com/2020/01/07/shaquille-oneal-helps-woman-who
-collapsed-in-street/.

126. Cole McCauley, "Shaquille O'Neal: Gander at Shaq's Massive Business Portfolio,"
Clutch Points, November 28, 2019, https://clutchpoints.com/shaquille-oneal-gander-at-shaqs
-massive-business-portfolio/.

127. Jeff Green, "Shaquille O'Neal Gets Adviser's Nod to Stay on Papa John's Board,"
Bloomberg News, April 1, 2020, https://www.bloomberg.com/news/articles/2020-03-31/
top-adviser-now-supports-shaq-s-re-election-to-papa-john-s-board.

128. Jade Scipioni, "Shaquille O'Neal Says He Wants to Buy Reebok," CNBC Make It,
June 20, 2019, https://www.cnbc.com/2019/06/20/nba-hall-of-famer-shaquille-oneal-says
-he-wants-to-buy-reebok.html.

129. Jade Scipioni, "Why Shaquille O'Neal Won't Tell You Who He's Voting For," CNBC
Make It, January 16, 2020, https://www.cnbc.com/2020/01/16/shaquille-oneal-on-why-he
-will-never-speak-out-politically.html.

130. Samantha Previte, "Shaq's Quarantine Life Is Out of Control," New York Post,
March 31, 2020, https://nypost.com/2020/03/31/shaq-has-coronavirus-quarantine-dance
-parties-in-his-kitchen/.

THE LION QUEEN

Michelle Akers and the Pride of US Women's Soccer

ROXANE COCHE

INTRODUCTION

The FIFA Women's World Cup captivated Americans in 1999 and reinforced Mia Hamm's status as "soccer's golden girl."[1] The final between the United States and China brought 90,185 people to the Rose Bowl in Pasadena, California, including then president Bill Clinton, who said after the game that it was "the most exciting sports event I've ever seen."[2] Twenty years later, this championship game is still the highest-attended women's sporting event ever,[3] and it remained the most-watched soccer game in the United States until the US men's national team played superstar Cristiano Ronaldo's Portugal squad in a critical group-stage game of the 2014 FIFA World Cup in Brazil some fifteen years later.[4]

The most iconic moment of the tournament, and perhaps in all of women's sports, came after Brandi Chastain scored the winning penalty kick in the shootout that gave the United States a second World Cup title.[5] It is, as the *Bleacher Report*'s Timothy Rapp remembers, "a moment that will live on in sports history"[6]—an exultant Chastain flapping her jersey above her head and falling to her knees in her sports bra, biceps bulging, abs glistening, while her teammates rushed toward her to celebrate reaching the top of the world. But one player was notably absent from the jubilation: Michelle Akers.

Although Hamm became the face of the team, and Chastain's belly button garnered the focus of media coverage, Akers was by every measure the heart and soul of the US Women's National Team (USWNT) in 1999 and, really, throughout the 1990s. But to this day, the general public is less likely to know her than they are Chastain, Hamm, or many of the other 1999 champions, including Kristine Lilly, Julie Foudy, or Christie Rampone. Yet Akers, the first American women's soccer star, was central to the squad. As teammate Kate Sobrero (now Markgraf) later insisted: "Without [Akers], we definitely wouldn't have won. She laid it all on the line."[7]

And she had at that! Although suffering from a little-known yet nonetheless debilitating illness, chronic fatigue and immune dysfunction syndrome (CFIDS), which had been preventing her from playing the physical style that she had displayed since the early 1990s, Akers never seemed to slow until during the extra time of the championship game's second half following an inadvertent punch to the head by her own goalkeeper, Briana Scurry, who later recalled apologetically that she had hit "some of the ball and mostly her."[8] That was one shock too many for Akers's body, and she was subsequently ruled out by team doctor Doug Brown. And even though he could see how badly she ached to get back on the field, he also recognized that while she was successfully fighting off the Chinese attacks, she was also losing her battle against CFIDS.[9] So the American side was forced to finish the job with their leader on the sidelines.

Upon seeing this, sportswriter Kelly Whiteside admitted that she thought the team would lose when Akers was replaced. As she explained: "I just thought that she meant so much, and they needed her on the field."[10] Or, as Mia Hamm had said a few years earlier: "She is our everything."[11] Regardless of the media coverage then and the social media reminiscences today that seem to remember the story differently,[12] it was to the beat of Akers's drum that this vaunted team marched arduously through mountains and valleys to achieve success in the 1999 tournament, which her teammates continue to mark through her team nickname: Mufasa. Originally bestowed upon her because of the massive mane of hair she once sported, this homage to the award-winning and multiplatformed *Lion King* franchise seemed apt despite any perceived gender bending.

Long thought to have been inspired by Shakespeare's *Hamlet*,[13] *The Lion King* series revolves around the royal family of Pride Lands, an African savanna. The first movie, from 1994, one of Disney's biggest successes, focuses on a lion named Simba and his emergence from young and intrepid cub to accomplished king. But his path is far from traditional, as he finds himself expelled from Pride Lands after his uncle, Scar, takes the crown from the savanna's king and Simba's father, Mufasa. To do so, Scar kills Mufasa, but his attempts to kill Simba fail, leaving Simba to grow up in the jungle eating bugs with his friends, a meerkat and a warthog. Meanwhile, Pride Lands becomes a dry wasteland under Scar's reign, forcing Simba's childhood friend Nala to scour the jungle in search of food. There, Nala and Simba reconnect, and after a nudge from his wise-beyond-her-years, long-lost friend, and an appearance from his father in the stars, Simba returns to Pride Lands to confront his uncle, save his father's legacy, and ultimately claim his birthright.

The 1994 movie was so successful that it became a franchise with four additional movies, a photorealistic movie, and several television series as well as short films, video games, books, and a Broadway musical that premiered in 1997 and has been running ever since.[14] For our purposes, while the franchise's considerable success ties nicely to the narrative that informs the accomplishments of the USWNT on the soccer field, select individual characters from the film also create something of a composite of Michelle Akers, the woman whose efforts in large part helped pave the way for the two decades of success since. This team, which has won more World Cups (four of the first eight) and Olympic gold medals (four of the first five) than any other women's soccer team in the world, relied most of all on one remarkable woman whom teammates took to calling Mufasa. Thus, from her cub status to a full-on "Lioness Queen,"[15] as one journalist called her, Akers emerged from a laundry list of challenges to help lead the USWNT both on and off the field, embracing many traits that the quartet of *Lion King* main characters—Scar, Nala, Simba, and Mufasa—exhibited in the franchise's many iterations. With her personality, resilience, energy, charisma, and sagacity, Michelle Akers played perhaps the key role in bringing women's soccer out from what was once a shadowy place and into the vaunted Pride Lands where it exists today.

SCAR: A CHARISMATIC ALBEIT CHALLENGING SOUL

So prepare for a chance of a lifetime. Be prepared for sensational news, a shining new era is tiptoeing nearer. . . . Be prepared!
SCAR, *THE LION KING* (2019)

Attempting to compare Michelle Akers to Scar, *The Lion King*'s chief antagonist, seems neither the most laudable nor certainly the most flattering aim. Of course, Akers is so much more than that malevolent force who angled to take what was not his. And yet, in Akers's case, elements of Scar's persona actually work. After all, despite his many unsavory and indefensible aspects, Mufasa's ethically challenged brother also demonstrated some admirable qualities. For instance, we can see that while thoroughly unprincipled, Scar could also show poise, elegance, and resilience as he held his own against the stronger Simba against the odds, much like Akers did throughout her career. Like Scar, Akers demonstrated a relentlessness reminiscent of those who simply hate to lose. Indeed, as a child, Akers would "pout, stomp off, cry, slug the winner, or simply explode" if she lost at anything, even the occasional board game.[16] The difference here is that while Scar knew from a young age that he couldn't compete physically, his inner sense of inferiority often fueled his wickedness, but this is really where attempts to compare the two wane.

Akers was unusually strong and so dominant as a teenager that when she played for the Union Bay Flyers (based near Seattle), one of the best under-nineteen club teams on the west coast, Team Adidas, their biggest rival, dreaded playing not so much the Flyers as a team but, rather, Michelle Akers herself.[17] Akers could intimidate not only her opponents but also her teammates, including fellow future USWNT legends such as Julie Foudy, who found herself "in awe of [Akers] physically" because "she was such a presence on the field,"[18] an element that struck Kristine Lilly from the beginning as well:

> The first national team camp I came to, Michelle was just such an overwhelming force that I watched her play and thought, "Holy cow!" She could be dominant wherever she was on the field. She could take any five players, get up, and still run and finish. She never stopped. She never sold herself short. She gave her all—every game, every practice, every drill we ran. I admired that. But it was intimidating.[19]

Anson Dorrance, the vaunted coach who built the University of North Carolina women's soccer program into a powerhouse, recognized Akers's talents early on. He tried to recruit her on his team, and although she chose to go elsewhere, he still got to lead her as head coach of the national team from 1986 to 1994. "I don't think people [today] appreciate how she intimidated and dominated everyone," Dorrance said in 1999. "Teams set their entire defenses to stop her."[20]

A master at making the most of her gifts, Akers used her five-foot, ten-inch physique to her advantage. She favored a style of soccer that relied on strength and power, so while she was recruited by major soccer programs across the country, she chose to attend the University of Central Florida because of their propensity to play a "tough physical brand of soccer [she] found appealing."[21]

Her transition from college to the women's national team in 1985 was perhaps even more of a challenge, but once again, Akers was up to the task. As one of the founding members of the USWNT, Akers certainly could not have known what she was getting herself into when she first put on the "old hand-me-down men's uniforms"[22] that the then remarkably disorganized

United States Soccer Federation (USSF) provided to them. She recalled the "purple sweats"[23] that forced players and staff to call upon their often rudimentary tailoring skills that had them "trimming the legs on warm-up suits, hemming shorts, [and] sewing the front of V-neck jerseys"[24] just before flying to Italy for their first tournament ever.

When FIFA finally agreed to sponsor an international women's tournament in 1991,[25] Akers was ready. She had prepared her whole life for a chance to show the world how good she was, and that chance had now arrived. The tournament was also the shot in the arm that women's soccer needed to leap into a bright new era. And as expected, Akers delivered. She scored ten goals in six games, including a record five goals in a 7–0 victory over Taiwan, and tallied both American goals in the championship game.[26] Coach Dorrance also praised her for her defensive work from the beginning of the tournament, even stating that she "saved" the team with her headers in the USWNT's opening game, won 3–2 against Sweden.[27]

But after playing what she claimed was "the best tournament of her life"[28] in which she tasted international success for the first time, Akers continued to feel exhausted. At first, she was not alarmed, thinking that she was merely coming down from the high. The 1991 tournament in China had been extremely popular with spectators and was played at quite a hectic pace, with crowds of thousands in the stadiums.[29] And yet, as time went on, Akers failed to get better. In fact, she got worse, suggesting that this was more than the subsiding of a lengthy adrenaline rush.[30]

Upon returning to Florida, where Akers and her then husband had a business running soccer camps and clinics, she remained a big draw for kids, especially girls, who were eager to meet the world champion.[31] But Akers could rarely make it to the venue, and when she did, she didn't have enough energy to participate in the drills. As she explained to writer Jane Johnson Struck:

> At my worst, in the early '90s, I was barely able to function. It was an extreme effort even to do laundry or prepare a meal. Many times, after doing these small chores, for days I was barely able to get out of bed. At my best, I could play 15–20 minutes of a 90-minute soccer match and maintain a limited appearance schedule for my sponsor, Umbro. But I'd pay the price for doing that for weeks.[32]

Although she never could muster much energy, Akers kept playing as much as she could and had the highest number of assists on the USWNT in 1993 and 1994. She even ended up as the top scorer for the team in 1994. The same year, after about three years of uncertainty and misdiagnoses, Akers finally put a name to the monster that she had been fighting: chronic fatigue and immune dysfunction syndrome, an incapacitating illness that zaps one's energy, causes nausea, and creates cognitive problems, among other symptoms.[33] Now that the evil was finally identified, she began to search for solutions, although her doctors repeatedly told her that, other than rest, there really were none. As Akers recalls:

> [T]hat answer wasn't satisfactory. That's when we really started working as a team to keep me on the field. I mean, I snacked at halftime, you know. I had to have coffee to keep my blood pressure up, IV bags, and you know if I made it a whole game, it was a huge victory.[34]

While she had lost a good deal of her physical drive, Akers had yet to lose the stubbornness and determination that had once led her to finishing a college game against North Carolina despite having broken two teeth in a collision earlier in the game. As she explained later in her autobiography, "I could get new teeth, but I couldn't replay a Carolina game."[35]

Despite what would later prove to be a frightening and incurable diagnosis, and given what had grown to be a range of other ailments, Akers continued holding on to her dream of soccer immortality, much like Scar held on to his desire to become king of Pride Lands despite his own physical limitations. And by doing so, even though she never again reached the statistical highs with which she started her career,[36] Akers remained as crucial to the USWNT's success as anyone else, while her impressive leadership skills helped her transition to her new role as a leader off the field as her health continued to decline.[37]

NALA: THE PROVERBIAL GLUE

We could get in big trouble.
NALA, *THE LION KING* (2019)

In order to qualify for the 1991 FIFA World Championship, the USWNT traveled to Haiti in April of that year to play in the regional qualifying tournament. They dominated the competition, scoring forty-nine goals with eleven by Akers herself while keeping a clean sheet defensively. The soccer community in the United States took notice, so even as the team was still in the Caribbean, the Soccer Industry Council of America extended an invitation for Akers to speak at their upcoming meeting. Akers, who had always been shy and never felt comfortable speaking publicly, was hesitant to accept, but Coach Dorrance convinced her to go. He told her that she was the first woman to ever be invited to this meeting, and that this was a chance to get some of the sport's bigwigs to invest in women, predicting: "You might be able to help alter the history of women's soccer."[38]

Akers's speech focused on the USWNT: its history and its players' commitment to correct a resource deficiency caused, in large part, by lack of support from the USSF. Among her points was the fact that the players were then receiving a paltry $10 per diem. Unbeknown to Akers, the president of the federation, freshly elected in 1990, was actually sitting in the audience. While there is no formal proof that her words were the catalyst for any change, the federation soon announced that per diem would be raised to $30 a day and that each USWNT member would receive $1,000 a month for expenses until the next competition in November.[39] But that was only the start of Michelle Akers's career as her sport's spokesperson. What followed from that initial address would be a contract with Umbro, making her the first American female soccer player with a paid product endorsement,[40] which when added to her incredible performances at the world championship in November launched her into stardom—at least within the soccer world. She recalled:

> In a matter of one month, I was placed on a pedestal expected to be outgoing and schmooze with the soccer world. I found that difficult at times because that wasn't really my personality. I could sign autographs and smile for the camera, but standing on the stage telling thousands of people how to be great was terrifying. All of a sudden, I was a role model. I didn't ask to be a role model and I didn't know *how* to be one. I just played soccer and I was good at it. That's all.[41]

Akers quickly understood that she had a unique opportunity to help define, change, and ultimately promote women's soccer in ways that no women before her had had. It was a risky move insomuch as she could lose the little she had gained at any moment, but like Nala, who never allowed Simba to claim her ideas as his own, Akers would not stand for being overlooked any longer, especially now that she wielded some sway.

Through the roles they played in the development of their respective communities, Akers and Nala took strikingly similar paths. For her part, Nala refused to accept that her beloved Pride Lands had fallen into shambles under Scar and set out into the unknown jungle to find a solution. The solution materialized when she met up with her childhood best friend, Simba.

Throughout the rest of the saga, with Pride Lands back on track and her community thriving, Nala became a visibly less prominent character, although she continued to advise Simba as his wife. And indeed, what Nala did for Simba is similar to how Michelle Akers helped change the landscape of women's soccer by repositioning the light on younger players, including Mia Hamm, while still offering her support on the national team.

To be sure, some of Akers's efforts paid off quickly once she started speaking up. For instance, whenever USWNT members gathered in the early 1990s, players had to wear Adidas gear, which they themselves had to purchase on their own. So when Akers started wearing Umbro gear to team meetings and refused to change, mandatory Adidas gear swiftly became available at no cost to all team members, many of whom were college players who could not sign endorsement deals because of NCAA regulations.[42] This is one example of how Akers's persistence combined with her sense of responsibility and strong desire for accountability on the part of the governing instances motivated her to find solutions not only for herself but for the team and the sport as a whole despite any lingering doubts. Kristine Lilly was admittedly among the skeptics at first, though she quickly saw where Akers was taking them: "I thought, 'who does she think she is?' But I soon realized she was leveraging her position to benefit us all. The opportunity sort of fell into her hands, and to her credit, she used it well."[43]

To be sure, Akers's reach proved to extend far beyond the USWNT. Despite her wish to be a team member rather than a leader, she could not escape her fate. For her to fulfill her childhood dream of proving that she was among soccer's best, she fought hard to remove whatever remaining barriers, including rampant anonymity, continued to plague women's soccer. And her hatred of losing proved to be stronger than her hatred of public speaking, so, armed with her deep-rooted belief that soccer offered "a unique common denominator which links diverse cultures and peoples," she fought through her timidity and put herself out there "to reach millions of people around the world—one person at a time."[44] Thus, much like Nala firmly speaking sense to Simba in his quest to return to his rightful throne, Akers stood as the voice of reason in front of the USSF and many other entities around the world, including the International Olympic Committee (IOC). In her own words, she "was everywhere."[45]

In the years prior to the 1996 Atlanta summer games, USWNT players who had always been encouraged to sell their sport saw an incredible promotional opportunity and joined the movement to add women's soccer to the summer Olympics.[46] As the unofficial team spokesperson, thanks in no small part to her unprecedented contract with Umbro, which allowed her to rub elbows with very powerful people in the soccer world, Akers lobbied passionately for the addition of a women's competition. In September 1993, the movement's efforts were rewarded as women's soccer became an Olympic sport.[47] Akers's role in persuading the IOC, her overall work toward the promotion of soccer in the United States and women's soccer everywhere, and her performances on the field earned her the FIFA Order of Merit, the governing body's highest honor.[48] She was the first woman to receive the award, bestowed in Paris just before the start of the 1998 men's World Cup. Five months later, she was one of twenty people to be named to the FIFA Football Committee, whose task was to "help shape and guide the future growth of soccer worldwide."[49]

In the offing, the college athlete who had once been unhappy to be elected captain because "she wasn't comfortable talking to the team"[50] had become one of the nation's most renowned advocates for women's soccer because she knew that she could not turn away the opportunity to "inspire kids to dream and achieve.[51] Her actions were part of the basis for the extraordinary success of the 1999 women's World Cup hosted by the United States, which originally was relegated to only the East Coast and in five- to ten-thousand-seat stadiums but which expanded to include West Coast venues as well as bigger stadiums.[52]

Many journalists questioned the viability of the tournament, like Jamie Trecker of ESPN in his article "What if They Threw a World Cup and Nobody Came?"[53] But Marla Messing, president and CEO of the 1999 World Cup Organizing Committee, and her team had come up with an ambitious mission "to stage a breakthrough event for women's sports and to inspire the next generation of female athletes,"[54] and they knew that that could only be achieved by going big. In Messing's words:

> Our choices in this country are stadiums with 5,000 or 10,000 seats, or stadiums with 50,000, 60,000, or 80,000 seats. Once you decide on 5,000 or 10,000 seats, the image of what you are selling is second class. Putting it in small stadiums would have sealed the fate of the tournament. You had to sell the image of a major event. Right away, it was major because it's at Giants Stadium and the Rose Bowl.[55]

And while Akers found herself throughout much of the tournament in the shadow of younger media darlings such as Mia Hamm and Brandi Chastain, she remained the undeniable leader of the USWNT if only because of the role she played in helping to bring women's soccer under such bright lights. She was the proverbial glue that kept the US women's soccer community working together toward a common goal, and she continued to spearhead the movement with brio.

SIMBA: A DAREDEVIL JOURNEYING FROM CUB TO MONARCH

Oh I just can't wait to be king!
SIMBA, *THE LION KING* (2019)

In 2016, Akers's former teammate Julie Foudy described Akers as "not only the toughest and strongest physically, but also the best technically, the fiercest mentally, and on top of it all . . . crazy committed—to the game, to getting better, to winning."[56] Yet, over time, Akers had to learn to play more of a quiet role because of the limitations caused by various physical maladies. She stuck to leading on the field but in the background rather than in the spotlight, just like Nala steers Simba in the right directions as he learns to reign over Pride Lands. Yet, Akers's career seems to resemble Simba's journey perhaps more than that of any other character in the *Lion King* story.

From a prominent cub who believed that strength and perseverance would carry her through to a humble leader who found peace through spirituality, Akers, like Simba, matured over the years, paralleling similar developments in the USWNT. When she was first called up to the squad, she simply wanted to play soccer, but her raw assertiveness quickly put her on a trajectory similar to that of then team alpha April Heinrichs.[57] Named team captain in 1986, Heinrichs "intimidated everyone," including the young Michelle Akers, Coach Dorrance observed.[58] Yet, he later revealed that he molded the USWNT's culture based on Heinrichs's fierce approach.[59] A couple of years younger than her captain, Akers was still a key player. She scored the first USWNT goal ever recorded in 1985,[60] and her confidence on the field made her Heinrichs's natural right arm—a general to a commander in chief, a natural heir, a Simba to Heinrichs's Mufasa.

And like cub-age Simba, Akers made mistakes as a young player before hitting her adult stride. In college, for example, she almost lost her scholarship as a result of partying until the wee hours of the morning, experimenting with drugs, and letting her grades slip after a bad breakup with a boyfriend.[61] But Akers grew past it all. In essence, she couldn't wait to be queen, to be the best in the world, a goal she managed to achieve during her 1991 performance in China before the constant fatigue led to her CFIDS diagnosis. Although she continued to work as hard as ever, even going to Sweden to play professional soccer in the summer of 1992,[62] she was feeling her strength dissipate every month. These years were like "pure hell," causing her to want to die at times, she says.[63] Seemingly in denial about her health, she recklessly pushed herself beyond her limits, collapsing during a match in late 1993 in San Antonio.[64] At the time, she still ignored the cause of her symptoms. She was in the midst of a string of misdiagnoses, from mild temporary conditions like muscle glycogen depletion to more serious issues like mononucleosis before the doctors got a handle on CFIDS, which turned out to be both life- and career-saving revelations.

Perhaps predictably, Akers's determination and team-first drive led her to continue pushing herself further than recommended, which was not lost on friends and fans who began to notice changes.[65] After the 1999 World Cup final, Donna de Varona, former Olympic champion and erstwhile chairwoman of the World Cup organizing committee, noticed that Akers "looked like one convulsing muscle."[66] But Akers needed to pace herself, much like the overeager Simba needed Mufasa to tell him that "being brave doesn't mean you go looking for trouble."[67]

Feeling pushed into a corner, Akers sought refuge in her religious roots. She had come from a devoutly Christian background but had strayed under the weight of her athletic responsibilities.[68] As she was managing her 1994 divorce as well as her many infirmities, she reconnected with family and reengaged her spiritual side, returning to church and remaining a faithful, outspoken advocate since. In fact, in reconciling her faith and her sport, she founded a ministry called Soccer Outreach International.

Akers's candidness about her spiritual life followed her all the way to the Rose Bowl. As the USWNT and China were waiting to go out onto the field, she shared a moment with Chinese goalkeeper Gao Hong:

> I stood midway back in the US line (since my number is 10), looking toward Gao Hong. Suddenly, she turned and made eye contact with me. She smiled and in acknowledgment, pointed to her heart, and then lifted her hand with her index finger extending upward toward heaven.
>
> I nodded, gave her a little smile, and repeated the same gestures. To my surprise, she walked back down the tunnel, shook my hand, and then immediately returned to her place at the head of the Chinese line.[69]

Akers credits her renewed spirituality in helping her overcome, among other matters, her CFIDS demons long enough to make it to the 1995 Women's World Cup in Sweden, but she was nevertheless weaker than she had once been. Seven minutes into the USWNT's first game in Sweden, she was knocked unconscious, landing awkwardly on her knee. As a result, she missed almost the entirety of the tournament, returning quite wobbly for the semifinal. Her return gave confidence to her teammates, who were facing Norway, another favorite for the title. Reflecting upon the match later, Mia Hamm was convinced that Akers would be a game changer:

> Michelle is gonna lead us to victory. And Michelle, you know, the warrior that she is, comes in and tries to play and she couldn't do it. When she physically couldn't do it, we were scrambling.[70]

Much in the same way that Pride Lands fell into disarray while Simba was in the jungle, the USWNT couldn't survive its forward's absence. Akers had yet to find the magic elixir to tame her CFIDS, and the team had no way to fill the gap in her absence. This was a tough pill for her to swallow, but her refound faith helped her through the challenging time, much like Mufasa's spirit eventually guided Simba back to his kingdom.

Perhaps the admixture of faith and confidence in her surroundings led her to proactively take charge over her illness. Certainly uncharacteristically, she seemed no longer hesitant to ask for help, receiving treatment and returning to form.[71] So with revenge against the Norwegians in her sights, she took aim at the Atlanta Olympics.

Although the competition was a mere thirteen months later, it turned out to be all she needed. She sought the aid of two experts in CFIDS, Drs. Paul Cheney and Peter Rowe. The latter had heard about Akers's ordeal when her written testimonial about life with CFIDS was read before the US Congress in May 1996.[72] He contacted Akers and soon discovered that she was also suffering from neurally mediated hypotension, namely low blood pressure because of faulty brain signals.[73] Akers had already been working with Dr. Cheney, who had put her on a special diet of "potatoes, veggies, rice, chicken, seafood, handfuls of supplements and juice from two pounds of carrots a day."[74] This diet along with further tests and treatments allowed Akers to feel better than she had in years, and she managed to survive "the demand of the games" in Atlanta's repressive heat.[75] As Charles Bricker of the *South Florida Sun-Sentinel* concluded: "[I]f the U.S. had to go into a major game in quest of a medal without a key player, it wouldn't be Hamm they would miss most,"[76] implying that Akers would be missed most of all. And quite characteristically, Akers, as stubborn as ever but managing her condition with the aid of some clever coaching decisions as to her playing time, helped lead the US side via her leadership, passing, and knack for scoring at precisely the right time to not only avenge their loss to Norway but also to bring home the 1996 gold medal.[77]

MUFASA: LIVING UP TO A LEGACY

There's more to being king than getting your way all the time.
MUFASA, *THE LION KING* (2019)

To recuperate from the demanding Olympic tournament, Akers took a temporary break, playing in only two of the USWNT's eighteen games in 1997. She was back the next year, appearing in fifteen of the team's twenty-five games in 1998 as the team prepared for what would become the biggest women's sporting event ever, the 1999 World Cup. By then, Mia Hamm's persona had eclipsed Michelle Akers's in media circles, and Akers's new position at midfield meant that she would not have as many opportunities to find the net, making her even less likely to be featured in popular accounts. Yet, her legacy managed to continue resonating with the younger generation of US soccer players because her reputation as "the game's seminal star"[78] and her strong performances leading up to the 1999 World Cup had already created a narrative suggesting that the team's fate ultimately rested on her shoulders. As teammate Julie Foudy told ESPN, "She was still our warrior in '99, even while battling chronic fatigue and knee surgeries in the double digits. We all looked up to her. And what we loved most? Our opponents feared her."[79]

This fear Akers commanded, and the respect it entailed, are comparable to Mufasa's role in *The Lion King*. The only "great lion of the past"[80] that the movie audience is introduced to, Mufasa embodied parental instinct and the wisdom of the elders. After Mufasa died, he still played a capital role in *The Lion King* by appearing as a spirit. Similarly, Akers's spirit and hatred of losing was contagious and her presence essential, despite her uncharacteristically slow start in the 1999 tournament. In the opening game at Giants Stadium in East Rutherford, New Jersey, Akers found herself struggling through menstruation, which had caused a drop in her blood pressure as well as in her estrogen level. "Even before the game started," the *New York Times'* Jere Longman indicated, "she felt exhausted," a situation that did not pair up well with her existing medical condition.[81] She held tough, though, in part thanks to her teammates' encouragement. As fellow midfielder Julie Foudy and captain Carla Overbeck would tell her, "Stay in it, stay in it, we need you."[82] So Akers did what Akers does: she powered through and held on for the entire game, which the team won, 3–0.

It wasn't Akers's best game, but Coach Tony DiCicco found her performance strong enough to keep her on the field regardless. And as yet another testimonial to Akers's lasting impression on her teammates, Mia Hamm, who scored the first goal of the tournament on a beautiful half-volley with her nondominant left foot, said: "I'm used to watching Michelle hit balls like that, so the fact that I actually got a hold of one like that felt pretty good."[83]

The next game against Nigeria at Chicago's Soldier Field was an easier win, as the US squad posted a 7–1 victory with Akers tallying the team's fifth goal. With six goals in the first period, Coach DiCicco decided to sit Akers for the second for fear of overworking her or, worse, having her get injured. With two decisive victories, the team had ensured its place in the quarterfinals, and the large margins of victory meant that they were almost certain to finish in the coveted Number 1 spot regardless of the outcome of their third game. So DiCicco let Akers rest, and the team delivered, winning 3–1 in Foxboro Stadium, home of the NFL's New England Patriots.

In the victory lap that followed, Akers had her arm extended to high-five fans until, as she recalled, "some dude grabbed my arm and jerked me off my feet," injuring her right shoulder.[84] Akers managed to play though it during the quarterfinal game in Washington, DC, staying on the field the full game while yelling, defending, and directing traffic as she does, but the game, against a dominant German side, one of the best teams in the world, would be even harder than anticipated. And yet, despite being down 2–1 at the half, the USWNT rallied to post a 3–2 victory, earning the right to meet Brazil in the semifinal.

By then, Akers was really struggling physically. Besides the arm injury and her CFIDS, the World Cup had taken a toll on her body. As she would note:

Game after game throughout the tournament, something new had happened to me physically that just added to the burden of my health and my body not working right—whether it was one more blow to my chronically bad knees, being kicked in the face, dislocating a shoulder, or getting my head cracked good any number of times.[85]

At the time, Brazil was perceived as the team that had most improved since the previous World Cup four years earlier.[86] Their star player, Sissi, had already scored seven goals in four games, so the main objective defensively would be to stop her. Naturally, DiCicco put "the lion driving the US team forward" to the task.[87] And despite her physical challenges, which led to her being helped off the field twice during the game, Akers successfully shut down the Brazilian playmaker. In the eightieth minute, she was the one who sealed the USWNT's victory by scoring a penalty kick for the 2–0 win. That was Akers's best game yet in the 1999 tournament, and it was the type of performance that her teammates raved about, the type of performance that made Akers so instrumental to the team. As Foudy said in 2016, reminiscing about her former teammate:

> When I go to normal adjectives like "courageous," "fearless," and so on, I find them all lacking when it comes to Akers. . . . I would pick her on my team even with two broken legs and no arms. Yep. She'd find a way. That's what I loved the most about Michelle Akers.[88]

In the final, Akers's role was simply to be dominant again. This time, her assignment was the Chinese team's Sun Wen, who had scored twice against the US squad earlier in the year; she also had seven goals in the World Cup and actually ended up winning the Golden Ball as tournament MVP. But once again, Akers rose to the task despite her broken body, as evidenced by a fall she took during which she tucked her right arm into her body to protect her injured shoulder.[89] She completely shut down Wen, who, as a result, seemed nonexistent. Thanks as well to Akers's defensive prowess, the Chinese team had only two shots on goal in the first half. She also stopped the half's most dangerous play from the Chinese.

At halftime, Coach DiCicco told his players to look for Akers offensively, too, so she could do her quarterback-like magic of distributing the ball effectively.[90] And though DiCicco's strategy would not pay off on the scoreboard, the fact that the Chinese only started attacking Akers's defensive zone after Akers was forced to leave the field shows how dominant she was once again that day. As DiCicco explained to Jere Longman: "The Chinese were intimidated by Michelle in 1991; they thought she was a soccer goddess, and I think that carried over."[91]

At the end of the game, Akers, who was ultimately knocked out the contest by an accidental punch to the head, was nonetheless praised for her efforts by both teammates ("Singlehandedly, she owned the midfield," [Briana] Scurry said. "I've never seen her play defense like that. She was possessed")[92] and her fiercest opponent ("Akers was their key player," Sun said. "If not for her, we would've been more successful getting forward").[93] Even broadcast commentators JP Dellacamera and Wendy Gebauer lauded her performance.[94] Of her first-half performance, Dellacamera remarked: "What a warrior Michelle Akers is for this US team. She's had too many injuries to mention, yet she's been their best field player in this tournament." Gebauer later called her simply "the most consistent player for the US" in the tournament.[95] And even though Akers was unable to play in overtime, and even though she was not able to take the first penalty kick of the shootout, and even though she was not on the field when Brandi Chastain scored her winning penalty kick and all that came with her incomparable celebration, the team's victory belonged to Michelle Akers as much of any of the day's more heralded performers.

THE PRIDE OF US WOMEN'S SOCCER

In her most Mufasa-like fashion, Akers wanted to play in the 1999 championship game's overtime for all the reasons chronicled above, but of course she was ruled out. And while it was exceedingly painful to have to miss out on this moment, her light continued to shine. Indeed, there was a little bit of her on the pitch during Julie Foudy's address to the team at the end of regulation time: "We finish this off. We beat them to every ball. They are dead tired. Remember that!"[96] And there was more than a little of the lioness still when Kristine Lilly saved the USWNT from a Chinese golden goal, heading the ball away on her line in the ninety-ninth minute. Still again, there was just a little bit of the roar as well in the way the team rallied defensively when the Chinese took advantage of a now smaller US defense.[97] So while Akers might not have been physically present on the field for the last forty minutes of the game, she had instilled enough of her inimitable spirit into her teammates for them to bring the World Cup home. As a result, while the press filled their front pages with Brandi Chastain's now iconic sports bra, the 90,185 people in attendance that day all seemed to recognize Akers's contribution, chanting her name as soon as she showed back up on the field despite looking feeble and feeling wobbly, as she collected her medal and celebrated with her teammates and friends.[98]

At thirty-three, Akers was the oldest player on the 1999 team. She was also, as Gebauer remarked, the player "who has done more for this sport than any player in the world."[99] For DiCicco, she was "the first player that created a universal acceptance of the women's game," explaining that people, including male soccer stars Pelé and Franz Beckenbauer, who also had contracts with Umbro, "saw her play and realized that women could play the game as skillfully and tactically proficient as men could."[100]

For a decade and a half, Akers built a powerful legacy nationally and internationally, yet remained approachable, because she always valued being a team member first. "Being a part of a team's a wonderful experience," she said in 2000. "You learn discipline, unity, and teamwork. You learn about pain and perseverance. There's nothing like it."[101] She particularly valued her time with the 1999 USWNT, a group she called "special" in 2013 for being both pioneering and an "anomaly."[102] Thinking of her former teammates and all other generations of soccer players, Akers, along with Brandi Chastain, is now spearheading a new study with researchers from Boston University and the Concussion Legacy Foundation about head trauma in soccer.[103] Akers, who has been suffering from chronic migraines "for decades,"[104] became interested in chronic traumatic encephalopathy (CTE), a brain degeneration most often studied in American football players, after watching a documentary. When she noticed that very little CTE research was dedicated to soccer, she decided to do something, which led to the creation of the research project Soccer, Head Impacts, and Neurological Effects, or SHINE. Using her initiative, determination, leadership, and influence, Akers contacted twenty former teammates, half of whom signed up to participate in the study.[105]

In all, while Michelle Akers does not die (as did Mufasa in *The Lion King*), her career was undone by a body that could no longer stand the rigors of such high athletic achievement. But, like Simba's father, her spirit continues to hover over her pride. She may have had to reinvent herself to remain indispensable to the national team, but, knowing her career and influence, it should come as no surprise that when she decided to retire in August 2000 despite having been selected to play in the upcoming Olympic games in Sydney,[106] the team struggled and ultimately failed in its quest to defend its Olympic title in 2000 and its World Cup in 2003.[107] Point in fact, it would take the USWNT another fifteen years to win their third World Cup.

Just as a film needs compelling characters to be successful, the USWNT needed its leader to help the program emerge from the shadows of American sport. Michelle Akers's success, born of many qualities, continues to be reflected in the various iterations of the team since she left, but her legacy remains as vivid and important as it did during her playing days. She was their lion queen by every conceivable measure, and, judging by the team's continued success, this pride is well positioned to continue thriving.

NOTES

1. Rachel Alex, "Hamm in a New League of Her Own," *Washington Post*, April 11, 2001, https://www.washingtonpost.com/archive/politics/2001/04/11/hamm-in-a-new-league-of-her-own/258e3378-4c4e-4f08-a3d2-184fb93bc67a/.

2. Ouisie Shapiro, *Dare to Dream: The Story of the U.S. Women's Soccer Team*, documentary film, HBO, 2005, 48:00.

3. Tristan Lavalette, "Women's Cricket Aims to Break Crowd Record Set by Soccer in California," *Forbes*, January 29, 2019, https://www.forbes.com/sites/tristanlavalette/2019/01/29/womens-cricket-aims-to-break-crowd-record-set-by-soccer-in-california/.

4. Chris Chase, "USA-Portugal Was Most Watched Soccer Game in American History," *USA Today For the Win*, June 23, 2014, https://ftw.usatoday.com/2014/06/usa-portugal-was

-most-watched-soccer-game-in-american-history. The women have since set a new record during the final of the 2015 Women's World Cup between Japan and the United States in Vancouver.

5. Phoebe Clarke and Ian Ayres, "The Chastain Effect: Using Title IX to Measure the Causal Effect of Participating in High School Sports on Adult Women's Social Lives," *Journal of Socio-Economics* 48 (February 2014): 62.

6. Timothy Rapp, "1999 Women's World Cup Soccer: Remembering Importance of United States Team," *Bleacher Report*, August 20, 2013, https://bleacherreport.com/articles/1744710 -1999-womens-world-cup-soccer-remembering-importance-of-united-states-team.

7. Jere Longman, *The Girls of Summer: The U.S. Women's Soccer Team and How It Changed the World* (New York: Harper Perennial, 2001), 141–42.

8. Longman, *The Girls of Summer*, 203.

9. Longman, *The Girls of Summer*, 203.

10. Shapiro, *Dare to Dream*, 51:10.

11. Ann Killion, *Champions of Women's Soccer* (New York: Philomel Books, 2018), 34.

12. In April 2019, Akers had fewer than 15,000 Twitter followers while Chastain had more than 60,000 and Hamm 183,000. Figures are similarly unbalanced on Facebook.

13. Galen Cuthbertson, "9 Reasons Why *The Lion King* Is Basically *Hamlet* (And 1 Reason It Probably Isn't)," AdelaideX, posted by Jacqui Dean, November 23, 2017, https://blogs. adelaide.edu.au/adelaidex/2017/11/23/9-reasons-why-the-lion-king-is-hamlet-and-1-reason -it-probably-isnt/.

14. One of those four movies, *Around the World with Timon and Pumbaa*, does not feature the lions from the famous franchise.

15. Charles Bricker, "Akers Has Lion-Sized Talent, Courage," *South Florida Sun-Sentinel*, July 25, 1996, https://www.sun-sentinel.com/news/fl-xpm-1996-07-25-9607250025-story.html.

16. Michelle Akers and Gregg Lewis, *The Game and the Glory* (Grand Rapids, MI: Zondervan, 2000), 48.

17. Akers and Lewis, *The Game and the Glory*, 77.

18. Akers and Lewis, *The Game and the Glory*, 121.

19. Akers and Lewis, *The Game and the Glory*, 121.

20. Akers and Lewis, *The Game and the Glory*, 119.

21. Akers and Lewis, *The Game and the Glory*, 76.

22. Akers and Lewis, *The Game and the Glory*, 84.

23. Akers and Lewis, *The Game and the Glory*, 31.

24. Longman, *The Girls of Summer*, 63.

25. Although now referred to as the first FIFA Women's World Cup, it was retroactively called that. In 1991, it was officially the FIFA Women's World Championship for the M&M's Cup.

26. Akers remains to this day the only soccer player, male or female, to score five goals in a single World Cup game.

27. Akers and Lewis, *The Game and the Glory*, 130.

28. Akers and Lewis, *The Game and the Glory*, 206.

29. Akers and Lewis, *The Game and the Glory*, 133. Akers and Lewis report that the final against Norway was played in front of more than sixty-five thousand people, while Shapiro

(*Dare to Dream*, 12:21) states that, oddly, when the team landed at New York's JFK Airport, no one, not even their bus driver, welcomed them.

30. Michelle Akers and Judith A. Nelson, *Face to Face with Michelle Akers* (Bloomington, IN: Intergrated Resources, 1996), 35.

31. Akers and Lewis, *The Game and the Glory*, 146.

32. Jane Johnson Struck, "True Grit," *Today's Christian Woman*, September–October 2000.

33. "Symptoms of Myalgic Encephalomyelitis/Chronic Fatigue Syndrome," Centers for Disease Control and Prevention, January 18, 2019, https://www.cdc.gov/me-cfs/symptoms -diagnosis/symptoms.html.

34. Shapiro, *Dare to Dream*, 20:45.

35. Akers and Lewis, *The Game and the Glory*, 88.

36. Akers scored fifty-four goals in her first fifty games for the US team from 1985 to 1991, including thirty-nine goals in twenty-six appearances in 1991 alone.

37. Scott Hanson, "She Was America's First Women's Soccer Star; Now, Michelle Akers Has Gone from Goals to Foals," *Seattle Times*, August 23, 2018, https://www.seattletimes.com/ sports/soccer/once-best-known-as-americas-first-womens-soccer-star-michelle-akers-is -now-devoted-to-a-different-passion-saving-horses/.

38. Akers and Lewis, *The Game and the Glory*, 117.

39. Akers and Lewis, *The Game and the Glory*, 118.

40. Karen E. Duda, "Current Biography: Michelle Akers," *Current Biography* 65, no. 11 (2004): 5.

41. Akers and Nelson, *Face to Face*, 34.

42. Akers and Lewis, *The Game and the Glory*, 144.

43. Akers and Lewis, *The Game and the Glory*, 144.

44. Akers and Lewis, *The Game and the Glory*, 209.

45. Akers and Nelson, *Face to Face*, 34.

46. Longman, *The Girls of Summer*, 64.

47. Associated Press, "Women Sports Get a Boost," *New York Times*, September 20, 1993, https://www.nytimes.com/1993/09/20/sports/women-sports-get-a-boost.html.

48. Duda, "Current Biography: Michelle Akers," 3.

49. Akers and Lewis, *The Game and the Glory*, 209.

50. Akers and Lewis, *The Game and the Glory*, 92.

51. Akers and Lewis, *The Game and the Glory*, 64.

52. Erin Leyden, dir., *Nine for IX: "The 99ers,"* ESPN, 2013, 8:10.

53. Shapiro, *Dare to Dream*, 40:33.

54. Leyden, *Nine for IX*, 6:32.

55. Longman, *The Girls of Summer*, 31.

56. Graham Parker, "Crazy. Committed. Fearless," *FourFourTwo*, March 2016, 79.

57. Akers and Lewis, *The Game and the Glory*, 84.

58. Longman, *The Girls of Summer*, 65.

59. Longman, *The Girls of Summer*, 66.

60. Duda, "Current Biography: Michelle Akers," 4.

61. Akers and Nelson, *Face to Face*, 32.

62. Akers and Lewis, *The Game and the Glory*, 146.

63. Longman, *The Girls of Summer*, 154. Although Akers writes that sometimes she wanted to die, she never thought seriously about hurting herself or committing suicide.

64. Akers and Nelson, *Face to Face*, 71.

65. Akers and Nelson, *Face to Face*, 16.

66. Akers and Lewis, *The Game and the Glory*, 286.

67. Jon Favreau, dir., *The Lion King*, Walt Disney Pictures, 2019.

68. Akers and Nelson, *Face to Face*.

69. Akers and Lewis, *The Game and the Glory*, 30.

70. Shapiro, *Dare to Dream*, 24:32.

71. Struck, "True Grit."

72. Akers and Lewis, *The Game and the Glory*, 187.

73. CDC, "Symptoms of Myalgic Encephalomyelitis/Chronic Fatigue Syndrome."

74. Akers and Nelson, *Face to Face*, 52.

75. Akers and Nelson, *Face to Face*, 54.

76. Bricker, "Akers Has Lion-Sized Talent."

77. Akers and Lewis, *The Game and the Glory*, 199–203.

78. Longman, *The Girls of Summer*, 49.

79. Leyden, *Nine for IX*, 12:59.

80. The Great Lions of the Past are the deceased rulers of Pride Lands.

81. Longman, *The Girls of Summer*, 163.

82. Longman, *The Girls of Summer*, 164.

83. Leyden, *Nine for IX*, 10:25.

84. Akers and Lewis, *The Game and the Glory*, 224.

85. Akers and Lewis, *The Game and the Glory*, 23.

86. "FIFA Women's World Cup USA 1999: Records Crash as USA Rejoice," FIFA.com, March 22, 2007, https://www.fifa.com/womensworldcup/news/fifa-women-world-cup-usa-1999-502003.

87. Jaime Bartlett, "Could the 2015 USWNT Beat the 1999 USWNT?," *The 18*, July 6, 2015, https://the18.com/news/could-2015-uswnt-beat-1999-uswnt.

88. Parker, "Crazy. Committed. Fearless."

89. Akers and Lewis, *The Game and the Glory*, 32.

90. Longman, *The Girls of Summer*, 169.

91. Longman, *The Girls of Summer*, 166–67.

92. Quoted in Longman, *The Girls of Summer*, 166.

93. Quoted in Longman, *The Girls of Summer*, 150.

94. Gebauer was on the 1991 world champion USWNT.

95. Quoted in Akers and Lewis, *The Game and the Glory*, 32.

96. Shapiro, *Dare to Dream*, 51:39

97. Shapiro, *Dare to Dream*, 52:26.

98. Longman, *The Girls of Summer*, 285–86.

99. Quoted in Akers and Lewis, *The Game and the Glory*, 32.

100. Duda, "Current Biography: Michelle Akers," 3.

101. Struck, "True Grit."

102. Leyden, *Nine for IX*, 47:23.

103. Alyssa Roenigk, "Akers, Chastain to Take Part in New CTE Study," ESPN, June 28, 2019, https://www.espn.com/soccer/fifa-womens-world-cup/story/3887627/akers chastain-to-take-part-in-new-cte-study.

104. Tessa Yannone. "BU Researchers to Launch a CTE Study of Former Female Soccer Players," *Boston Magazine*, June 28, 2019, https://www.bostonmagazine.com/health/2019/06/28/boston-university-cte-soccer-study/.

105. Roenigk, "Akers, Chastain to Take Part."

106. Jere Longman, "Akers Decides to Retire from Soccer Team," *New York Times*, August 25, 2000, https://www.nytimes.com/2000/08/25/sports/olympics-akers-decides-to-retire -from-soccer-team.html.

107. The USWNT once again lost to Norway in the final of the Sydney Olympics and to future back-to-back champions Germany in the semifinal of the 2003 World Cup.

A NOTORIOUS SPECTACLE

A Critical Media Analysis of the "Money" Fight between Conor McGregor and Floyd Mayweather

TED M. BUTRYN, MATTHEW A. MASUCCI, AND JAY JOHNSON

INTRODUCTION

The events leading up to the August 2017 boxing match between Ultimate Fighting Championship (UFC) lightweight Conor McGregor and undefeated, then forty-year-old boxing champ Floyd Mayweather are a case study in sport and media spectacle in late capitalism.[1] Indeed, for their entire careers, both McGregor and Mayweather had used fiery, at times offensive, and nearly always controversial rhetoric to hype their upcoming bouts in order to situate themselves as perpetual box office draws no matter the quality of opponent or the stakes of the outcome. This bout, however, took on a whole new level of hype, rhetoric, and even branding, which in this particular sport is remarkably telling.

Initially dismissed as a publicity stunt instigated by McGregor when he first suggested the fight, the deft utilization of social media, the leveraging of his larger-than-life persona, and his status as a trash talker extraordinaire[2] helped open the door to negotiations for what would eventually be a mega-event that generated an estimated 4.3 million pay-per-view buys and brought in a reported $600 million in total revenue. In fact, the figures generated by McGregor-Mayweather rank second all-time behind another, long awaited welterweight boxing title unification bout between Mayweather and Manny Pacquiao in 2015.[3]

The purpose of this chapter is to examine a series of promotional activities that occurred following the announcement of the boxing match between McGregor and Mayweather. Specifically, we examine the *spectacularized* prefight "World Tour" events meant to hype the August 26, 2017, bout, paying particular attention to how the promotional buildup to this unlikely athletic contest was almost immediately replaced by a racialized, misogynistic, homophobic, and toxic spectacle that deployed some of the least palatable types of prefight exchanges seen in recent years. In addition, we attempt to situate the media coverage of the spectacle within contemporary research on mega-events as well as the larger sociopolitical spectacle surrounding the administration of the US president, Donald J. Trump. Finally, we offer some analysis of what it means that various media outlets eventually played a key role in promoting the spectacle, leaving them complicit in the toxic rhetoric used to hype the event rather than clearly articulating the problematic aspects related to racism, sexism, and homophobia that emerged almost immediately after the announcement of the fight.

Within the academic field of sport studies, numerous scholars have argued for critically examining media narratives surrounding combat sports including boxing and, more recently, mixed martial arts (MMA).[4] Indeed, there is a substantive body of research on boxing and spectacle, including representations of race, gender, and nationalism within the sport.[5] With respect to race in particular, numerous scholars have written about the ways that the media has represented race in boxing since the early 1900s, specifically as it related to Jack Johnson. More recently, scholars have examined how whiteness in boxing, particularly with respect to working-class notions of the "great white hope," have helped frame the narratives surrounding white fighters such as Ricky Hatton and Kelly Pavlik. However, while there has been an increasing amount of research exploring the now-established sport of MMA, relatively little attention has been paid to one of the sport's biggest stars, Conor McGregor, due in part to his relatively recent rise to fame.[6]

Drawing upon the work of Joseph Campbell, Darren Kelsey, for example, uses a discourse-mythological approach and the hero's journey in order to construct a psychological case study of sorts. As he notes: "Through the characters, personas and spectacles of the UFC, moments and spaces open up for pre-existing cultural mythologies to be recontextualized through the fighters, fans and commentators."[7] And in another paper of particular relevance to our analysis here, Martha Cheng compares the attacking rhetoric of McGregor leading up to his 2015 fight against rival Nate Diaz with two of Donald Trump's 2016 campaign press conferences during which he mercilessly attacked his political opponents.[8]

Cheng identifies three different patterns common in what she terms "persuasive attack" language. First, she claims that attacks are often accompanied by self-affirmation and an attempt to raise the status of the attacker in some way. Second, she imagines that attacking rhetoric has an epideictic quality to it. In other words, insults can be used to show that one's behaviors or character are more in line with a sense of shared values or community norms than those of the target of the attack. Finally, and of great import to this chapter, attacking rhetoric often has three methods of attack, including: a pejorative labeling of the target, evidence that the attackers' claims are true, and a belittling of the opponent via mocking comments. When we consider, for instance, President Trump's attacks on his erstwhile rival Senator Ted Cruz or McGregor's attacks on Nate Diaz, it is clear that within the culture of boxing and MMA, as well as current US political discourse, attacking rhetoric is an effective and perhaps even acceptable means of taking down an opponent in a mediated public sphere.

This chapter also draws from the body of literature on mega-events, spectacle, and what several authors have labeled "presumption."[9] Following David L. Andrews and others, it is important to remember that in late capitalism, notions of the spectacularized "Mega-Events," which are more often used to refer to global sporting phenomena such as the FIFA World Cup or the Olympics, may well be applied to more localized events such as the McGregor-Mayweather fight. According to Andrews, the "twinned processes of hyper-commercialization and hyper-televisualization have combined spectacularized events and competitions with smaller spatial reaches and resonance."[10] Moreover, and intimately related to the mass-mediated corporatization of sport, is the concomitant notion of "prosumption" that has recently been taken up by sport studies scholars.[11]

From this vantage point, the spectators themselves can be intimately linked to the consumption and production of the spectacularized mega-event. As we will argue, the McGregor vs. Mayweather fight is nothing if not an exemplar of Kerstin Rieder and G. Günter Voß's contention that "[s]port spectators are working customers" and are at least partially responsible for generating the atmospheric backdrop against which the sporting drama (or otherwise) unfolds.[12] Sport spectators, thus, add to the surplus value of a sporting event. They, of course, pay for the privilege of doing so, while their very presence also positively contributes to the enactment of the live sporting contest.

THE RISE OF CONOR MCGREGOR . . . AND DONALD TRUMP

McGregor's ascension to superstardom occurred when he, as he predicted, knocked out José Aldo in thirteen seconds to win the UFC featherweight

(145 pound) title. He subsequently won the lightweight (155 pound) title to become the first UFC fighter to hold two belts simultaneously.

Leading up to the August bout, McGregor, Mayweather, and their respective entourages participated in a four-city tour that began in Los Angeles, and then traveled to Toronto, New York, and finally London, and they were all in the premiere arenas in each market. This road show took on a life of its own as many media outlets began framing the series of events as worthy of coverage if only for the fact that they predicted the verbal sparring to be more competitive than the fight. As reporter Martin Rogers wrote:

> Given the ability of Mayweather and McGregor to generate hysteria, the verbal sparring will surely make for compulsory viewing. You might even see some punches thrown, such is the level of unpredictability McGregor brings to such occasions.
>
> There will be taunts and teasing, insults and antagonism—either real or contrived. McGregor will have prepared for Tuesday's opening media event with nearly as much diligence as his bid to turn himself into a world class boxer in the space of a few short months.[13]

The resulting framing by the media is consistent with larger media narratives that emerged amid Donald Trump's entrée into presidential politics in the sense that if there are going to be quotable, clickable, or "meme-able" comments or actions of questionable taste in front of hordes of fans, it must be worth covering seriously. While not within the scope of this chapter, it is nonetheless interesting to see how spectacle is consistently nourished by the corporate media, contributing perhaps to a socializing effect whereby it may eventually take the sorts of debased, crass comments that characterized the lead-up to the fight to elicit a response from spectators-as-citizens. Indeed, this escalation of dose-response to media and sport spectacle is similar to what happened in professional wrestling in the late 1990s and early 2000s, when it took a performer being impaled on hundreds of thumbtacks or driven through a flaming table to get the "Holy shit!" chants rolling.[14]

ON SPORTING SPECTACLES AND THE MEDIA

Before we can critically examine the mediated spectacle of the McGregor-Mayweather fight, it is important to situate the event within the larger American context that was itself characterized by the emergent political spectacle prior to and following the 2016 US presidential election that brought Donald

Trump to power. Trump has an intertwined history with the UFC, boxing, and World Wrestling Entertainment (WWE). In fact, at a time when the political and social climate toward MMA was quite frosty, he hosted two of the earliest pay-per-view cards at his Taj Mahal Hotel in Atlantic City, New Jersey, in 2001. Dana White, a part owner and current president of the UFC, returned the favor through his continual praise of Trump's business acumen, political savvy, and generosity, culminating in White's public endorsement and speech at the Republican National Convention in Cleveland in July 2016.

During the 2016 campaign and continuing into his administration, President Trump's media presence was a daily spectacle rife with controversial commentary (usually via Twitter) including racist, sexist, and wholly crass personal attacks on his opponents, whomever they happened to be on that particular day. This is important because, following the administration of President Barack Obama and the reemergence of an anti–"politically correct" rhetoric, Trump's use of dog-whistling terms such as "animals," "nasty," and "low-IQ" to describe his political enemies, many of whom were women and people of color, signifies a central characteristic of media spectacles in sport as well, as evidenced by the coverage of former San Francisco 49ers quarterback Colin Kaepernick and his "taking a knee" protests during the pregame playing of the US national anthem, in order to call attention to police brutality. In fact, during Kaepernick's 2016 protests and into the more widespread protests of the 2017 NFL season, social media became a decidedly ugly space where users at times resorted to racist attacks on participating Black players. In short, media spectacles in both sport and politics are often imbued with discourses of race, gender, sexual orientation, and other identity markers in ways that are meant to somehow indicate a "real" sentiment in an era of supposedly "fake news." Further, these discourses are today often tied to characters or protagonists in mega-events, whether a Super Bowl or a national election.

In his 2016 book *American Nightmare: Donald Trump, Media Spectacle, and Authoritarian Populism,* Douglas Kellner contends that media spectacles are mediated constructions that "present events that disrupt ordinary and habitual flows of information, and which become popular stories which capture the attention of the media and the public, and circulate through broadcasting networks, the Internet, social networking, smartphones, and other new media and communication technologies."[15] A central part of media spectacle to which Kellner points is performance, whether spontaneous and authentic or completely and carefully orchestrated. As numerous scholars and journalists have noted, the rise of Donald Trump was at least in part due to his purposeful framing as a celebrity with a unique approach to spectacle, developed over the course of decades through the branding of his casinos and reality television shows, his role in the frenzy over the so-called birther question with regard to his predecessor, Barack Obama, and most recently in his own presidency. To be sure, media spectacles are arguably more common than ever, as evidenced by the barrage of constantly commented upon stories through Twitter and other social media platforms that are almost predesigned to dominate news cycles and attract viewers, or clicks. For example, Jay Coakley has long argued that sport has increasingly become a spectacle-laden endeavor, with the entertainment value of contests becoming more important than the outcome of the event itself.[16] It is not surprising, then, that sporting events in the Trump era are increasingly characterized by such spectacle. As Cheng's previously discussed work illustrates, spectacle, especially in the form of over-the-top attacks in the media, is a constituent part of the rhetorical strategies of both Trump and McGregor.[17]

THE MAY-MAC PREFIGHT PRESS CONFERENCE TOUR

Before continuing with our analysis, we must provide a brief overview of what occurred during the four stops on the promotional tour. The three-country tour started off in Los Angeles, moved on to Toronto, and then Brooklyn, before finishing in London. Glued to each fighter's side at every public promotional event was his respective organization's promoter. For Mayweather, that was Leonard Ellerbe, CEO of Mayweather Promotions, while Dana White stood in McGregor's corner. It is interesting to note that throughout, each appeared to be visibly gleeful as the spectacle unfolded. While both men came prepared to verbally spar in an attempt to "win" each press conference, and by extension the fans, it appeared as though McGregor came especially prepared with a script designed to antagonize his opponent and obviously sell the bout. And predictably, both combatants seemed quite comfortable dipping into the well of misogynistic, homophobic, and racist tropes in a bid to one-up the other in each man's quest to dominate each press stop while hyping the fight for both live audiences and those likely to purchase the Showtime Championship Boxing Pay-Per-View (PPV). While the oral assaults often came off as fabricated, there was ample evidence suggesting that the fighters were working in tandem to create a narrative dance of sorts to stir interest that would conceivably translate to PPV numbers.

As we discuss in our analysis of the media coverage of the event later in this chapter, and as an extension of Cheng's analysis, there are many parallels between the tactics of these multiple promoters of the "mega-fight" and the troublingly similar approaches utilized by Donald Trump.[18] It is important to note, however, that fans of either fighter and ardent supporters of Trump have often been amused by, rather than repelled by, the problematic rhetoric of what Elizaveta Gaufman calls the "laughing culture of carnival." As Gaufman acknowledges with regard to Trump: "One of the most significant features of [the] carnival is its perceived intimacy and multi-directionality of the discourse where people are supposed to 'debase, renew, reveal, hide, sell and entertain.'"[19] In other words, in spectacle cultures, the seriousness of otherwise offensive language is essentially meant to be shrugged off and taken as part of the act rather than taken seriously and emphatically confronted.

ANATOMY OF A PROMOTIONAL TOUR

In many ways, the four-city promotional tour was a bigger spectacle than the actual boxing match itself. Each of the tour stops is described below in some detail in order to paint a picture of the tone and tenor deployed by the promoters in order to stoke interest in the main event. This clearly orchestrated promotional strategy provides a robust example of what Cheng has characterized as debased personal attacks in sport and popular culture,[20] which, according to Kellner, are set against a broader backdrop of Trump-fueled spectacularization of the media.[21]

Such vignettes help to provide context and illustrate the clear and purposeful story arc that coursed through the collective events. Interestingly, while Mayweather and McGregor have historically employed these trash-talking tactics with their opponents, it is rare that they have had someone at their level in "giving it back," and clearly the battle of words on display in the lead-up events was deliberate. Consequently, the end result of the promotional tour was an intricately choreographed, though seemingly unscripted, sparring match in which both fighters exhibited mastery of verbal debasement and brought the audience along for the ride. We will return to a more fulsome assessment of the media's role in normalizing these elements of the spectacle, but first let us return to an overview of the promotional tour itself.

Stop #1: Los Angeles, California, United States of America

As is the modus operandi of both fighters, this initial stop started late, most likely as a result of each man's desire to be the last to arrive to build tension among fans. McGregor paced the stage with the words "fuck you" embroidered into his pinstripe suit, while Mayweather entered the arena to a loud chorus of boos from the eleven thousand fans in attendance at Staples Center, a theme that followed him throughout the press conferences regardless of the city they were in. As soon as Mayweather entered the arena, McGregor launched a barrage of insults, including calling Mayweather a homophobic slur, disparaging his opponent's tiny body, honing in on Mayweather's issues with the IRS alongside his alleged difficulties with reading, while continuing to direct racist epithets his way. For instance, as Mayweather made his way across the stage, McGregor was heard to yell, "Dance for me, boy! Dance for me, son!"[22]

Perhaps realizing that he had gone too far, McGregor then changed his text to, "Dance for me, sir. Dance for me!" This, however, did nothing to stem the tide of backlash his exchange prompted. While speaking with a reporter about the film *Rocky III*, McGregor also referenced dancing monkeys as Rocky's training partners.[23] To be clear, McGregor has a history of racist taunts and insults stemming from his promotions for several of his UFC fights. Most notably he has called Nate Diaz, a lightweight MMA fighter he has twice fought in the octagon, a "cholo gangster from the hood,"[24] while in another instance he called Diaz and his brother Nick, also an MMA fighter, "cockroaches." He has mocked another former opponent, José Aldo, drawing on his impoverished upbringing in the favelas of Brazil, stating that he wanted to turn them into Reebok sweatshops, a pointed reference that involves an official sponsor of the UFC. Last, and most notably, prior to signing the bout agreement, McGregor took to trolling Mayweather to get him to fight in the ring by describing him as "a Malteser with eyeballs" (referring to a chocolate-covered candy).[25]

Mayweather's tactics in turn were soon revealed to be financial in nature. He started by pulling out of his knapsack a check made out for $100 million, prophetic in that this what he would reportedly gross for his role in the bout. He then aimed it at McGregor as a way of mocking the MMA fighter's lack of financial clout insomuch as McGregor had made a mere $3 million for his last MMA fight, which is clearly not close to Mayweather's league.

Shortly thereafter, after some back and forth in which each man disparaged the other's chosen sport, the promotional dance onstage finally ended. But regardless of content, the intent was always to make them both very wealthy and to sell the public on a contrived chronicle. In short, this first leg of the tour literally set the stage for a lack of decorum and civility, opening the floodgates of racist, sexist, misogynistic, and homophobic discourse that was to be unleashed over the course of the final three stops of the prefight press campaign.

Stop #2: Toronto, Ontario, Canada

While the first tour stop in LA was really somewhat of a test of each other's trash-talking abilities, Toronto was an opportunity to see what tactics each fighter would apply. There, they were introduced by no less than hometown hip-hop superstar Drake, and what followed was a show in which they each upped their game in a bid to best the other in lowering the bar while continuing to drive interest through the roof. While the consensus of who won the war of words during the first press conference generally tips in favor of Mayweather, there was no doubt that McGregor took their second verbal sparring match in Toronto. McGregor was again, by far, the fan favorite, as Floyd Mayweather endured loud choruses of boos from the partisan crowd. McGregor seemed at times unprepared for the more traditional press conference format, but he came out with his guns locked and loaded, much to the delight of the sixteen thousand fans who packed the Molson Amphitheatre.[26]

Apparently, the hype and buildup from the first stop in LA worked. Ticket scalpers were apparently selling lawn seats for $60–$90, and the crowd promptly picked up on McGregor's previous theme of Mayweather's tax troubles. On several occasions the crowd drowned out the spectacle, chanting "pay your taxes, pay your taxes," while McGregor urged them to shout in unison, "fuck the Mayweathers."[27] To counter the deafening noise, Mayweather grabbed an Irish flag from a fan in the crowd, inciting ire from them and their adopted favorite. Not to be outdone, when McGregor was at the microphone, he directed some of his vitriol toward Stephen Espinoza, the CEO of Showtime, the platform hosting the event, calling him a "fucking weasel" for having cut off his microphone at the previous press conference. This of course reinforces the long-held notion that these events were being staged, with both sides colluding in such a way to prop up the Irish MMA fighter. Nonetheless, both fighters then turned matters back toward misogyny, with McGregor calling out boxers for being "pussies"[28] and both calling each other "bitch" on several occasions. McGregor also threw a jab at Mayweather's loose morals and promiscuity, announcing: "Fifty strippers on his payroll, this man has. What the f*** is he doing with that strip club? What the f***. Fifty stripper b****es on his payroll! Shoutout to *all* the stripper b****es on his payroll!"[29]

McGregor also targeted Mayweather's age once again and intimated that Mayweather lacked fashion sense, chastising the older man for coming out for the previous press conference wearing a backpack. Mayweather's shtick, in contrast, was to stick to the financial theme, underscore his own celebrated work ethic, and highlight McGregor's lack of boxing experience, all of which served to belittle his opponent, which he did while sporting a Canadian flag in order to further whip the crowd into a frenzy. Thus, in Toronto, Mayweather seemed to have comfortably shifted into his role as the heel and ultimately was bested by the younger McGregor at his own game.

Stop #3: Brooklyn, New York, United States of America

The third stop on the press tour was at Barclays Center in Brooklyn. There was of course great anticipation as to where the scripted exchanges between the two would go, as the bar had been set high (or perhaps low?) in the previous two promotional events. What was clear was that Conor McGregor had caught on to the boxing-style promotional game and came prepared.

Following what would be a decided media backlash (see below), it seemed as though McGregor was going to use the platform to issue a public apology for the starkness of his prior insults. And he did indeed start down this redemptive road, though once he proclaimed that he "was apologizing to nobody!"[30] everything resumed as perhaps expected, particularly the contemptuous racist tropes and stereotypes, which served to up the ante:

> McGregor: A lot of media seem to be saying I'm against black people. That's absolutely f-----g ridiculous. Do they not know I'm half-black? Yeah. I'm half-black from the belly button down.[31]

McGregor also went after Mayweather's friend, rapper and actor 50 Cent, calling out: "50 Cent's a b----. You and 50 are two fake money b----es. He's bankrupt and you're about to be."[32] But Mayweather pivoted back to his scheme by bringing out the checkbook once again. He derided McGregor for not making as much money as he before bringing Dana White into the discussion by referencing the $380 million White had recently made through the sale of the UFC. He punctuated his point by making it "rain" with the stacks of money (one-dollar bills apparently) he had stashed in his knapsack. He also needled McGregor for being a quitter, citing two instances in which McGregor had to tap out of previous MMA bouts due to rear naked chokes. He also managed to fling a few barbs regarding McGregor's attire for the evening, noting: "We ain't got to dress up. He ain't sh--t but a circus clown and a b--tch. I ain't never quit. And I never will."[33]

During these exchanges, the crowd was once again showered with homophobic taunts between the fighters, with Mayweather calling McGregor a homophobic slur and ending his speech by calling him "gay." Additionally, both continued to play to misogynistic rhetoric, calling each other "bitches" on several occasions.[34]

The evening ended with Mayweather coming out with an Irish flag in an attempt to irk the partisan crowd, but to no avail. Irritated, he lobbed the flag onto the stage and walked off. It would appear that this final scene was intended to be a face-off for the crowd that ultimately brought closure to this third show with one more yet to come.

Stop #4: London, England

The final stop on the media tour, and certainly the most staged, took place inside a boxing ring. At this point in the roadshow, the storylines had been fixed, and the actors had both refined and exhausted their respective approaches to promoting the show through their trash talking and theatrical antics. Once again, McGregor had the support of the partisan crowd, feasting on the nationalism of the setting in that he was so close to his home country of Ireland. Moreover, McGregor's suit countered Mayweather's more relaxed attire. But for this go 'round, McGregor seemed to add additional physicality to the script, pretending to smack Mayweather's rear end and rubbing his head while calling him a peanut head.[35] As much as the surrounding city and venue had changed, much of their promotional attacks had not. McGregor delighted in interrupting Mayweather, telling him on several occasions to "sit down and shut the fuck up."[36] Shockingly, while Mayweather wished McGregor a happy birthday, McGregor invited the crowd to join him in shouting "f*** Floyd Mayweather!," referring to the undefeated champion as a "microwave meal" while referring to himself as "home-cooked."[37]

Doubling down even more, McGregor, who sometimes calls himself "Mystic Mac," once again guaranteed a knockout, while Mayweather countered by calling his opponent "Mr. Tapout,"[38] the MMA version of boxing's "throwing in the towel." And while Mayweather continued to be drowned out by the crowd, he offered his usual blast of invectives questioning McGregor's work ethic and devotion to his craft.

Predictably, once again both fighters littered their performances with sexist and homophobic language, though interestingly, in the postevent press conference, Mayweather managed to flip the racial script by highlighting his intelligence, which he juxtaposed to McGregor's brutality. As he reminded the press:

Guys have got the best of me in the first round before, but I make adjustments, I have the IQ. He's a warrior, that's one thing I know about Conor McGregor, he's a warrior, it's kill or be killed.[39]

And later during that same presser, Mayweather offered his own assessment of the pervasiveness of racialized thought in sport, drawing on prior comments made by McGregor while noting that he would not resort to the same racially charged tactics, although he was visibly comfortable hurling misogynistic and homophobic parries. He proclaimed:

> Racism still exists, it's all about treating people like you want to be treated—to get respect you must give respect. He totally disrespected black women, he called black people monkeys, he then spoke disrespectfully to my mother and my daughter. I'm not going to stoop that low.[40]

MEDIA COVERAGE OF THE ROAD SHOW SPECTACLE

Our analysis of the four-stop promotional tour and the larger sociopolitical mediated landscape focuses on how mainstream and industry-specific outlets framed the lead-up to the fight.[41] Methodologically, we drew from more than seventy articles from online sport websites including *Sports Illustrated*, mainstream news websites including the *New York Times* and the *Irish Times*, popular magazines such as *Rolling Stone*, and popular MMA websites including www.bloodyelbow.com, mmafighting.com, and mmaweekly.com. The time period for our analysis was delimited to the time leading up to and immediately following the tour stops, through the immediate aftermath of the fight itself.

The unconventional yet slickly produced promotional events came fast and furious. Greg Bishop of *Sports Illustrated* noted that this was far removed from a standard promotional tour and that the first two legs were, by his estimation: "Vaudevillian. Kardashian. More like a WWE prelude than anything in sports."[42] Of course, both boxing and professional wrestling have long traded in spectacle in general, specifically relying on racist, sexist, homophobic, nationalistic, and xenophobic tropes in vulgar attempts to get fans to pay for scripted and hyperdramatic events. Indeed, Bishop went on to write:

> Was it sporting? Not exactly. But that's not what this is. I found it entertaining. I found myself looking forward to a fight I have dismissed as a bad idea. Rather than weigh whether the animosity was real or whether this was a WWE performance, it was easier to just enjoy it.[43]

According to Dave Meltzer, MMA fans were particularly interested in the events, perhaps believing that McGregor actually had a shot at winning. As Meltzer discovered:

> UFC did 3.39 million views on Tuesday, 2.2 million on Wednesday, 2.85 million on Thursday and 2.42 million on Friday. Showtime did 3.00 million on Tuesday, 2.72 million on Wednesday, 870,000 on Thursday and 190,000 on Friday.[44]

This rapid fall in viewership indicates that boxing fans, perhaps due to their familiarity with Mayweather's promotional style or perhaps because they, as a fan base, were more readily able to see through the spectacle to what the fight was really about, tuned out until it was time to watch the event itself.

By the end of the final two events, those in Brooklyn and London, a media backlash ensued as numerous mainstream journalists admonished both fighters while pleading with fans to refrain from buying the event. Even in a society comforted by spectacle, it appears that there are still limits to tolerance, especially in the current sociopolitical climate in which language is often central to discourses about what is deemed acceptable or unacceptable in a supposedly civil society. After the Toronto event, for example, several high-profile media outlets that were covering the fight were justifiably critical of the nature of the often shameful rhetoric. However, many of the MMA outlets continued to cover and legitimate the event, often leaning on a narrative that McGregor actually had a chance of winning the bout. In an August 26, 2017, article posted on MMA Fighting, Marc Raimondi collated the predictions of several UFC fighters weighing in on McGregor's chances. While not all were as enthusiastic as many MMA fans might have liked, some, including women's bantamweight challenger Valentina Shevchenko, remained hopeful. Recognizing initially that there is a "thin line between being a fan and supporting a fighter," Shevchenko added:

> I support fighters. I support Conor McGregor. And the fans, it's like you don't want to see the reality, you want to keep going with your hero. It's a different story. But I'm really supporting Conor McGregor, because I believe he can do this victory, he can take it. He can do things unbelievable for all the world.[45]

Overall, while some in the press continued to decry the bigotry of the prefight malevolence, media coverage of the lead-up to the match was characterized more by a reluctance to embrace the event as a legitimate sporting contest, given McGregor's inexperience in the boxing ring. For many, the genuinely absurd theater was the prospect of a brawler learning the *sweet science* of boxing on the fly, leaving most to work around the vitriolic climate or ignore it altogether.

RACISM, SEXISM, AND HOMOPHOBIA AS MARKETING TOOLS

The four promotional events showed that it took all of minutes for McGregor to turn this affair into a racist, sexist, and misogynistic spectacle that seemed to make even Mayweather, hardly a wallflower, take pause. McGregor did issue a curious "apology" in a conversation with MMA Fighting's Ariel Helwani in which he struggled to explain his use of the racialized word "monkey" in reference to African Americans on more than one occasion. In something of a Trump-esque "fake news" retort seemingly aimed toward the Mayweather camp, McGregor explained:

> "If I was to label him after any animal, it would be the rat," McGregor said. "I wouldn't even label him after the great ape. He is a f*cking rat and a weasel, because that's [what] a rat and weasel does, tries to manipulate words and create something that's not there."[46]

Of course, boxing has a long history of race-based promotional language between fighters, even when both fighters are African American.[47] But in the current sociopolitical and cultural climate, McGregor's words resonated as not so much merely trading on race and homophobia but as something that in some media accounts and commentary was framed as little more than entertainment. However, other major media stories relegated little space to these events. In the *New York Times*, for example, the only mention was the following:

> The tour has not been without controversy. McGregor has been criticized for making racially tinged statements, and Mayweather directed a gay slur toward McGregor during the final stop Friday in London. But amid the avalanche of insults between the undefeated Mayweather and McGregor, the mixed martial arts fighter who is a UFC champion and its biggest star, there are more sincere assessments among the bluster of how the fighters are preparing.[48]

Indeed, when race was mentioned, it often related directly to McGregor's whiteness rather than his racist and misogynistic comments. That this focus on McGregor's whiteness occurred is not surprising given its historical precedence. James Rhodes, for example, notes that as boxing became increasingly tied to notions of racial difference and masculinity, "the construction of the 'Great White Hope' came to symbolize far more than simply ring prowess, and also national, racial, and masculine strength, serving as a justification for, and symbol of, enduring White male privilege."[49] Will Cooley demonstrates this as well through his work on "Irish" Micky Ward. He claims that there is just something special about these tough "throwbacks." In the case of McGregor, though, the media narratives definitely veered from coverage of "respectable" boxers like Ricky Hatton or Kelly Pavlik in terms of the focus on trash talking and swagger.[50] As Darren Kelsey notes, McGregor's whiteness is at times read through the mythology of Irish struggles and displays of resistance. While not a dominant media narrative, McGregor is certainly perceived by Irish fans in particular to be imbued with nationalistic and racial meaning. As Kelsey explains, "For many Irish fans who find themselves 'in sync' before fights or celebrating victory, the metaphor resonates and the national narration continues through those affective qualities [of winning while losing with 'dignity']."[51] Of course, not all publications shared this sentiment. Writing in the *Independent*, Ewan Mackenna observes: "It's why suggesting he's a working-class hero is an insult to the working class, as if their only goal in life ought to be to make money and flaunt it in the most vacuous and obnoxious way possible. . . . For a guy that promised not to change, it turns out he lied."[52]

While perhaps beyond the scope of this chapter, further research is warranted on the larger notion of how the public, in part through their taking up of media narratives, become "in sync" with public figures as spectacles within and outside of sport. In addition, our focus here on the racialized elements of the spectacle speaks to the degree to which the accompanying sexist and homophobic language and tone of the World Tour in particular received far less coverage.

BACKLASH

Of course, there are limits to what the mainstream will tolerate, especially in the contemporary sociopolitical climate where language is often central to discourses about what is deemed acceptable or unacceptable in a supposedly civil society. To this point, after the Toronto event, several high-profile media outlets soured on the event altogether, a number of them publishing articles pleading with readers to resist buying the fight on PPV due to the racist, misogynistic, and homophobic nature of some of the aforementioned comments. Indeed, both fighters went places that we rarely see today in mainstream sport, and the fact that some mainstream media sources continued to do business with the promoters reveals the degree to which banter-as-hate-speech is currently taken for granted. While both fighters projected an image that many observers found unlikeable, McGregor was still seem by most as simply playing a role as opposed to actually *being* a racist homophobe. But what about Mayweather? Was he viewed as legitimately projecting his genuine personality?

The *Irish Times* indeed portrayed McGregor as the "babyface," a professional wrestling term that signifies the "good" character in a match, even though throughout the World Tour he was the primary agitator willing to drop references to Mayweather's Blackness, specifically as it related to his reading ability, while also alluding to other racist stereotypes. And yet, several media outlets, including the website the Undefeated, situated the spectacle historically. For example, Khaled Beydoun called McGregor out for the "Dance for me, boy" taunts at the Staples Center event, citing the range of historical imagery it conjures.[53] But however much the coverage failed to engage with these and other comments to any meaningful degree, including Mayweather's frequent references to "bitches" and "ho's," in the end, when media commentators did urge consumers to not waste their money on the fight, it was more about the event being a sham than it was about taking any moral high ground.

POSTFIGHT (FINANCIAL) RECONCILIATION

That animosity can be readily faked and just as readily believed is a symptom of a spectacle-driven society in which we all get to participate in the moral outrage surrounding whatever person or event pushes our buttons. For sporting spectacles to work effectively, and thereby generate interest, controversy, and revenue, the athletes and management must create a story arc in which fans can strongly identify with athletes and their melodramatic antics fully and deeply so as to suspend disbelief and embrace a base and toxic framing—good vs. evil, black vs. white, stalwart vs. brash upstart—in order to sell tickets and pull the crowd into doing the promotional work alongside the athletes and their handlers. In retrospect, and in the parlance of pro wrestling, this bout was always to have been a WWE-style event. Even before the bout, the notion that the fight was motivated primarily by financial gain was seen as common knowledge across the media landscape, something that neither fighter tried to hide. As Corey Kilgannon wrote in the *New York Times*:

> Mayweather said he did not want to come out of retirement, but he did so because he saw it as the biggest payday in sport. One day, he said, "They're going to talk about this business move at Harvard."[54]

And yet, days before the fight, Terence McGinley, also of the *Times*, clearly questioned the journalistic integrity of covering the fight. As he wrote: "On Saturday night in Las Vegas, after two years of coarse courtship, Floyd Mayweather Jr. and Conor McGregor will compete in a boxing match, with the bizarre and the surreal on the undercard. The *Times* will be in on the fun—with some reservations."[55] He even noted that his paper's own deputy sports editor admitted that they "wanted to cover it as a talked-about sporting, cultural and business event," and in this, we see that even reputable news outlets struggled but ultimately relented to the apparent need to cover the event and frame it as what it ultimately was.

Beydoun writes:

> Why is racism in 2017 still an integral part of boxing's promotional playbook? Why turn to racism and bigotry to sell a fight that was projected to break a billion dollars and all revenue records before it was even announced? Particularly during the volatile moment the United States finds itself at, when hate is trumpeted and rising from every corner of society.[56]

This is an important question to ask not only of us as fans but of the media as a social institution. Matthew Masucci and Ted Butryn's work on media coverage of the UFC from the early 1990s through 2006 finds that newspapers played a crucial role in helping to curb perceptions of violence and brutality via the use of what they call the "hometown hero" narrative, in which writers juxtapose arguments against the UFC with stories of local fighters "from right here!" and later college-educated fighters.[57] This serves to create for readers a sense of: "Hey it can't be that bad if Joey from the old neighborhood is doing it!" In a similar sense, through media coverage of this so-called mega-fight, we have looked at a created narrative that centralized the spectacle over the fight itself, as if the fighters were really just two performers trading in non-PC rhetoric that motivated boisterous fans to empty their pockets. And even as the media addressed the racism, sexism, and homophobia that were given voice, they were rarely taken up as part of any larger societal problems with real consequences.

Media narratives after the fight by and large failed to follow through with any critique of the World Tour, and due to the fact that the fight went longer than expected, McGregor was framed as an almost likeable, gritty fellow who had a bright future. As Rick Maese of the *Washington Post* observed:

> The night's biggest surprise wasn't that Mayweather was the one lift-ing his hand in the end but that the fight wasn't the snoozefest many feared. McGregor was making his boxing debut but managed to take the fight to Mayweather early and absorb punches and stay on his feet late. It was a resounding loss for McGregor, the brash Irishman who predicted a second-round knockout, but not one that he likely will be very embarrassed by.[58]

Writing in the *Los Angeles Times*, Lance Pugmire was even more glowing of both McGregor, "whose star continues to rise," and the perceived impact this fight might have on a boxing renaissance. With no real discussion of the lead-up to the fight, Pugmire left readers with the impression that McGregor was in fact the "mutated version of the great white hope" that one article called him. As the night closed, Mayweather and McGregor embraced, with each extending an index finger upward. "So many obstacles, so many things to overcome," McGregor would later say of his boxing experience. "I'm just relishing in it now. Options will present themselves."[59]

SOME FINAL THOUGHTS

Despite some initial hesitancy to critique sport journalism with respect to the Mayweather-McGregor fight, our analysis of more than seventy main-stream and MMA media articles has shown that the media mostly failed to hold the fighters' feet to the fire and connect their debased rhetoric with any larger concerns, especially given the expansion of discourse over racist, sexist, and homophobic language in the Trump era. Rather, the media was at times complicit in giving airtime to the spectacle, much as it was during the 2016 US presidential election. Journalists and pundits essentially and collectively shrugged their shoulders and laughed it off—or, at best, leveled moderate critiques, apparently content that the stories they could now write on McGregor's positive showing and the financial fallout of the fight would at least get clicks. Moreover, the generally acritical framing from the press and online news sources seem to validate what Masucci and Butryn,[60] David Rowe,[61] Søren Schultz Jørgensen,[62] and others have long argued: that sport journalism often facilitates what Rowe deems the "creation, maintenance, and enhancement of a sports celebrity system."[63]

Whether the spectacle was related to an overhyped boxing match or an American presidential campaign, the mainstream media, in an era when internet clicks are increasingly important, was complicit in the growth of mediated spectacle and its consequences. Future research should continue to investigate how the media negotiates, contributes to, or confronts spectacles at the intersection of sport and politics, and what that means for fandom and larger power relations.

CODA

Following the resounding financial success of the McGregor-Mayweather event for both promoters and fighters, it was clear that despite the misgivings of the media and boxing purists, violent spectacle sells. By 2020, despite a global pandemic that had shut down most in-person mega-events, any pretense that crossover contests between boxers and MMA fighters are about authentic athletic competitions had clearly been supplanted by the realization that even contests between nonprofessional athletes and YouTube personalities will draw consumers to the spectacle. The latest example of this phenomenon was the April 17, 2021, fight between former champion MMA fighter Ben Askren and YouTube celebrity-meets-wannabe-pugilist Jake Paul. As opposed to the McGregor-Mayweather buildup, when at least some of the media coverage was fairly serious in nature, the tone has shifted to what amounts to a wink and a nod. Following Askren's clever training montage video meant to mimic (or parody) a similar sequence in the film *Rocky IV*, an online article noted: "The clip concludes with Askren roaring Paul's name, a scene that will surely be matched by the spectacle that will go down when the two eventually meet in the ring."[64]

In the current US landscape, where national politics has taken on many characteristics of spectacle, sport fans and celebrity-culture followers are clearly willing to consume boxing contests between high-profile fighters (past their prime) and YouTube influencers. From a promotional perspective, it seems clear that the opportunity to monetize spectacle is not going away in the foreseeable future—a fact that even longtime boxing and MMA insiders acknowledge. For example, while some boxing purists claim that contests involving inexperienced internet interlopers or MMA fighters make a farce of the sport, Marc Raimondi notes that boxing history is littered with contrived matches that were clearly designed to amplify the spectacular and carnivalesque, including, for instance, the infamous match between Muhammad Ali and pro wrestler Antonio Inoki in 1976.[65] Raimondi quotes an ESPN boxing analyst, who sums up this sentiment:

> "People just want to be entertained at the end of the day," former boxing champion and current ESPN boxing analyst Timothy Bradley Jr. said. "It doesn't matter if it's real or not real, they don't really care about that. Is it real boxing? Absolutely not. I'm gonna tell you that right now. But it's a fight—it's a fight."[66]

While the gamble seems to have (literally) paid off for Conor McGregor in the near term, the prospects of his rumored big-money fight with Manny Pacquiao have dimmed since he lost two out of his last three UFC fights since returning to the octagon following the money fight with Mayweather, the most recent being a TKO loss (his first ever) at the hands of underdog Dustin Poirier on January 24, 2021, whom he had KO'd in 2014.

Nonetheless, and to the point above, the combat sport industry seems to have taken notice as evidenced by a recent announcement that former Olympic gold medalist and multiple-time boxing world champion turned high-profile promoter, Oscar De La Hoya, at the age of forty-eight, would be coming out of retirement to join a new fight promotion launched by Triller, a social media app. According to the press statement, De La Hoya "is targeting a 'big' UFC name" for his return to the ring. Moreover, and possibly recognizing that sport-as-spectacle seems to be the lucrative combat sport business model de jure, the deal is said to include multiple fights and will not be a "one-off bout."[67]

In any case, what remains less clear from a sport studies and sport management perspective is precisely *why* fans seem so enamored of these kinds of bouts in the first place, particularly in the United States. Therefore, further research is needed on boxing and celebrity culture identities, fan motivations to consume these combat spectacles, and the limits of pushing the sports promotion envelope in this increasingly spectacular direction.

NOTES

1. David L. Andrews and Michael L. Silk, "Sport and Neoliberalism: An Affective-Ideological Articulation," *Journal of Popular Culture* 51, no. 2 (2018): 511–33; and David L. Andrews, "Sport, Spectacle and the Politics of Late Capitalism: Articulating the Neoliberal Order," in *Routledge Handbook of Sport and Politics*, ed. Alan Bairner, John Kelly, and Jung Woo Lee (London: Routledge, 2017), 225–37.

2. See, for example, Martha Cheng, "Bums and Bimbos: Persuasive Personal Attack in Sports and Political Discourse," *Relevant Rhetoric* 8, no. 1 (2017): 1–18; and Dan Rafael, "Floyd Mayweather–Conor McGregor Pulled In 4.3M Domestic PPV Buys, $600M," ESPN, December 17, 2017, http://www.espn.com/boxing/story/_/id/21770652/floyd-mayweather-conor-mcgregor-43-million-domestic-ppv-buys-600-million.

3. Rafael, "Floyd Mayweather–Conor McGregor Pulled In 4.3M Domestic PPV Buys."

4. Matthew Masucci and Ted M. Butryn, "Writing about Fighting: A Critical Content Analysis of Newspaper Coverage of the Ultimate Fighting Championship from 1993–2006," *Journal of Sports Media* 8, no. 1 (2013): 19–44; Carla A. Santos, Scott Tainsky, K. Alexander Schmidt, and Changsup Shim, "Framing the Octagon: An Analysis of News-Media Coverage of Mixed Martial Arts," *International Journal of Sport Communication* 6, no. 1 (2013): 66–86; Charlene Weaving, "'Chicks Fighting in a Cage': A Philosophical Critique of Gender Constructions in Ultimate Fighting Championship," in *Global Perspectives on Women in Combat Sports: Women Warriors around the World*, ed. Alex Channon and Christopher R. Matthews (London: Palgrave Macmillan, 2015), 57–72; and Tywan G. Martin, Antonio S. Williams, Warren Whisenant, and Windy Dees, "Mixed Martial Arts (MMA) and the Media: An Examination of an Emerging Sport's Coverage in *ESPN the Magazine*," *Public Organization Review* 15, no. 3 (2013): 433–52.

5. Ellexis Boyle, Brad Millington, and Patricia Vertinksy, "Representing the Female Pugilist: Narratives of Race, Gender, and Disability in *Million Dollar Baby*," *Sociology of Sport Journal* 23, no. 2 (2006): 99–116; Fernando Delgado, "Golden but Not Brown: Oscar De La Hoya and the Complications of Culture, Manhood, and Boxing," *International Journal of the History of Sport* 22, no. 2 (2005): 196–211; Robert Drake, "Joe Louis, the Southern Press, and the 'Fight of the Century,'" *Sport History Review* 43, no. 1 (2012): 1–17; Lewis A. Erenberg, "Rumble in the Jungle: Muhammad Ali vs. George Foreman in the Age of Global Spectacle," *Journal of Sport History* 39, no. 1 (2012): 81–97; Jung Woo Lee, "Red Feminism and Propaganda in Communist Media: Portrayals of Female Boxers in the North Korean Media," *International Review for the Sociology of Sport* 44, nos. 2–3 (2009): 193–211; James Rhodes, "Fighting for 'Respectability': Media Representations of the White, 'Working-Class' Male Boxing 'Hero,'" *Journal of Sport and Social Issues* 35, no. 4 (2011): 350–76; and Kath Woodward, "Embodied Identities: Boxing Masculinities," in *Rethinking Gender and Youth Sport*, ed. Ian Wellard (London: Routledge, 2007), 39–51.

6. Cheng, "Bums and Bimbos"; Darren Kelsey, "Affective Mythology and 'the Notorious' Conor McGregor: Monomyth, Mysticism and Mixed Martial Arts," *Martial Arts Studies* 5 (2017): 15–35; Lamar Reams and Stephen Shapiro, "Who's the Main Attraction? Star Power as a Determinant of Ultimate Fighting Championship Pay-per-View Demand," *European Sport*

Management Quarterly 17, no. 2 (2017): 132–51; and Mark S. Williams, *Mixed Martial Arts and the Quest for Legitimacy: The Sport vs. Spectacle Divide* (Jefferson, NC: McFarland, 2018).

7. Kelsey, "Affective Mythology and 'the Notorious' Conor McGregor," 33.

8. Cheng, "Bums and Bimbos."

9. Andrews, "Sport, Spectacle and the Politics of Late Capitalism"; Michael Silk, "Neoliberalism and Sports Mega-Events," in *Leveraging Legacies from Sports Mega-Events: Concepts of Case*, ed. Jonathan Grix (London: Palgrave Macmillan, 2014), 50–60; and Michael Real, "Reflections on Communication and Sport: On Spectacle and Mega-Events," *Communication and Sport* 1, nos. 1–2 (2013): 30–42.

10. Andrews, "Sport, Spectacle and the Politics of Late Capitalism," 226.

11. David L. Andrews and George Ritzer, "Sport and Prosumption," *Journal of Consumer Culture* 18, no. 2 (2018): 356–73.

12. Kerstin Rieder and G. Günter Voß, "The Working Customer: An Emerging New Type of Consumer," *Psychology of Everyday Activity* 3, no. 2 (2010): 2–10.

13. Martin Rogers, "This Week's Floyd Mayweather–Conor McGregor Press Tour May Be as Good as It Gets," *USA Today*, July 10, 2017, https://www.usatoday.com/story/sports/boxing/2017/07/10/mayweather-mcgregor-press-tour-week-good-gets/465546001/.

14. Mick Foley, *Have a Nice Day! A Tale of Blood and Sweatsocks* (New York: Avon, 1999).

15. Douglas Kellner, *American Nightmare: Donald Trump, Media Spectacle, and Authoritarian Populism* (Rotterdam: Sense Publishers, 2016), 3.

16. Jay J. Coakley, *Sports in Society: Issues and Controversies*, 12th ed. (New York: McGraw-Hill, 2017).

17. Cheng, "Bums and Bimbos."

18. Cheng, "Bums and Bimbos."

19. Elizaveta Gaufman, "The Trump Carnival: Popular Appeal in the Age of Misinformation," *International Relations* 32, no. 4 (2018): 12.

20. Cheng, "Bums and Bimbos."

21. Kellner, *American Nightmare*.

22. Des Bieler, "'Dance for Me Boy!': Conor McGregor Criticized for Taunt at Floyd Mayweather," *Washington Post*, July 11, 2017, https://www.washingtonpost.com/news/early-lead/wp/2017/07/11/dance-for-me-boy-conor-mcgregor-criticized-for-taunt-at-floyd-mayweather/?utm_term=.872d669dba26.

23. A. J. Perez, "Conor McGregor Faces More Criticism after His 'Dancing Monkeys' Comment," *USA Today*, July 13, 2017, https://www.usatoday.com/story/sports/boxing/2017/07/13/conor-mcgregor-under-fire-social-media-dancing-monkeys-comment/476108001/.

24. Bieler, "Dance for Me Boy!"

25. Bieler, "Dance for Me Boy!"

26. Greg Bishop, "Conor McGregor Is Flying High as He Jousts with Floyd Mayweather on Publicity Tour," *Sports Illustrated*, July 13, 2017, https://www.si.com/boxing/2017/07/13/conor-mcgregor-floyd-mayweather-press-tour.

27. Luke Brown, "Floyd Mayweather vs Conor McGregor Toronto Press Conference: Read the Hilarious Full Transcript," *Independent* (UK), July 13, 2017, https://www.independent.co.uk/sport/general/boxing/mayweather-mcgregor/floyd-mayweather-vs-conor-mcgregor-press-conference-transcript-read-toronto-quotes-jokes-flag-bag-a7838746.html.

28. Pete South, "Mayweather v McGregor Press Tour: War of Words," *Playbuzz*, July 25, 2017, https://www.playbuzz.com/petesouth10/mayweather-v-mcgregor-press-conference-tour-the-best-burns.

29. South, "Mayweather v McGregor Press Tour."

30. Niall Kelly, "'I'd Like to Apologise . . . to Absolutely Nobody': McGregor's Unforgettable Post-Fight Interview," The 42, November 13, 2016, https://www.the42.ie/conor-mcgregor-ufc-205-interview-3079465-Nov2016/.

31. Khadrice Rollins, "Mayweather, McGregor Make Fans Wait for Brooklyn Press Conference," *Sports Illustrated*, July 13, 2017, https://www.si.com/boxing/2017/07/13/floyd-mayweather-conor-mcgregor-new-york-city-press-conference-highlights.

32. Rollins, "Mayweather, McGregor Make Fans Wait."

33. Tim Burke, "Mayweather vs. McGregor NYC Press Conference Highlights: Race Issues, Money in the Air," *SB Nation Bloody Elbow*, July 13, 2017, https://www.bloodyelbow.com/2017/7/13/15969772/mayweather-vs-mcgregor-nyc-press-conference-highlights-race-issues-money-mma-boxing-ufc-news.

34. South, "Mayweather v McGregor Press Tour."

35. Gareth Davies, "Mayweather and McGregor Continue Extreme War of Words as World Press Tour Ends in London," *Telegraph* (UK), July 14, 2017, https://www.telegraph.co.uk/boxing/2017/07/14/mayweather-vs-mcgregor-london-press-conference-watch-live-fighters/.

36. Davies, "Mayweather and McGregor Continue Extreme War of Words."

37. Davies, "Mayweather and McGregor Continue Extreme War of Words."

38. Davies, "Mayweather and McGregor Continue Extreme War of Words."

39. Davies, "Mayweather and McGregor Continue Extreme War of Words."

40. Davies, "Mayweather and McGregor Continue Extreme War of Words."

41. Mary G. McDonald and Susan Birrell, "Reading Sport Critically: A Methodology for Interrogating Power," *Sociology of Sport Journal* 16, no. 4 (1999): 283–300.

42. Bishop, "Conor McGregor Is Flying High."

43. Bishop, "Conor McGregor Is Flying High."

44. Dave Meltzer, "The major kickoff for the promotion of the Conor McGregor vs. Floyd Mayweather boxing match," *Wrestling Observer Newsletter*, July 17, 2017, https://members.f4wonline.com/wrestling-observer-newsletter/july-17-2017-wrestling-observer-newsletter-mcgregormayweather-press.

45. Marc Raimondi, "UFC Fighters Weigh In on How Conor McGregor Could Beat Floyd Mayweather," MMA Fighting, August 26, 2017, https://www.mmafighting.com/2017/8/26/16208022/ufc-fighters-weigh-in-on-how-conor-mcgregor-could-beat-floyd-mayweather.

46. Marc Raimondi, "Conor McGregor Addresses Racism Accusations, Says He Never Called African-Americans 'Monkeys,'" MMA Fighting, August 14, 2017, https://www.mmafighting.com/2017/8/14/16139314/conor-mcgregor-addresses-racism-accusations-says-he-never-called-african-americans-monkeys.

47. Erenberg, "Rumble in the Jungle," 81–97.

48. Corey Kilgannon, "McGregor and Mayweather Fling Taunts, Insults and a Little Honesty," *New York Times*, July 14, 2017, https://www.nytimes.com/2017/07/14/sports/conor-mcgregor-floyd-mayweather-fight.html.

49. Rhodes, "Fighting for 'Respectability.'"

50. Will Cooley, "Vanilla Thrillas: Modern Boxing and White-Ethnic Masculinity," *Journal of Sport and Social Issues* 34, no. 4 (2010): 418–37.

51. Kelsey, "Affective Mythology and 'the Notorious' Conor McGregor," 32.

52. Ewan Mackenna, "The Rise and Fall of Conor McGregor: How a Lovable Rogue Became Everything He Promised He Wouldn't," *Independent* (UK), August 25, 2017, https://www.independent.co.uk/sport/general/boxing/mayweather-mcgregor/floyd-mayweather-conor-mcgregor-lovable-rogue-promised-las-vegas-fight-live-a7912141.html.

53. Khaled A. Beydoun, "The Racism of the Mayweather-McGregor Tour Has a Long History in Boxing," The Undefeated, July 17, 2017, https://theundefeated.com/features/the-racism-of-the-mayweather-mcgregor-tour-has-a-long-history-in-boxing/.

54. Kilgannon, "McGregor and Mayweather Fling Taunts."

55. Terence McGinley, "Parsing the Mayweather-McGregor Hype," *New York Times*, August 25, 2017, https://www.nytimes.com/2017/08/25/insider/mayweather-mcgregor-boxing-spectacle.html.

56. Beydoun, "The Racism of the Mayweather-McGregor Tour."

57. Masucci and Butryn, "Writing about Fighting."

58. Rick Maese, "Floyd Mayweather Stops Conor McGregor via 10th-Round TKO," *Washington Post*, August 27, 2017, https://www.washingtonpost.com/sports/boxing-mma-wrestling/floyd-mayweather-stops-conor-mcgregor-via-10th-round-tko/2017/08/27/e10bf212-89f5-11e7-a94f-3139abce39f5_story.html?noredirect=on&utm_term=.60e343c77c85.

59. Lance Pugmire, "As Mayweather Finishes Brilliant Career, McGregor's Star Continues to Rise," *Los Angeles Times*, August 27, 2017, https://www.latimes.com/sports/la-sp-mayweather-mcgregor-20170827-story.html.

60. Masucci and Butryn, "Writing about Fighting."

61. David Rowe, "Sport Journalism: Still the 'Toy Department' of the News Media?" *Journalism* 8, no. 4 (2007): 385–405.

62. Søren Schultz Jørgensen, "The World's Best Advertising Agency: The Sports Press," Play the Game, Danish Institute for Sports Studies, *Mandag Morgen* (Aarhus), no. 37 (October 31, 2005), https://www.playthegame.org/upload//Sport_Press_Survey_English.pdf.

63. Rowe, "Sport Journalism," 385.

64. "Ben Askren Trains Like 'Rocky' ahead of Jake Paul Boxing Match," MMA Fighting, March 29, 2021, https://www.mmafighting.com/2021/3/29/22355392/video-ben-askren-trains-like-rocky-ahead-of-jake-paul-boxing-match.

65. Marc Raimondi, "Boxer or Spectacle? Inside the Attraction of YouTuber Turned Fighter Jake Paul," ESPN, January 26, 2021, https://www.espn.com/boxing/story/_/id/30668757/boxer-spectacle-attraction-youtuber-turned-fighter-jake-paul.

66. Raimondi, "Boxer or Spectacle?"

67. Marc Raimondi, "Oscar De La Hoya to Make Return to Ring after 13 Years on July 3," ESPN, March 26, 2021, https://www.espn.com/boxing/story/_/id/31143034/oscar-de-la-hoya-make-return-ring-13-years-july-3.

READING FERNANDO VALENZUELA AND FERNANDOMANIA

Broadening Americanness One Pitch at a Time

JORGE MORAGA

INTRODUCTION: OPENING DAY, 1981

On April 9, 1981, shortly after one o'clock in the afternoon, a clean-shaven, curious-looking twenty-year-old man walked to the pitcher's mound at Los Angeles's Chávez Ravine with 50,511 pairs of eyes looking on. He was tabbed as a last-minute fill-in to be the opening day starting pitcher for the Los Angeles Dodgers, whose ace, Jerry Reuss, was unable to take the mound. By the end of the afternoon, the Dodgers had defeated their National League rivals, the Houston Astros, 2–0. Perhaps more tellingly, the awkward teenage left-handed pitcher who had taken the mound some two hours and seventeen minutes earlier would not only claim the victory but also spark a cultural renaissance in baseball. That man's name is Fernando Valenzuela.

With his 1981 season debut, Fernando Valenzuela would go on to change the face of baseball for decades. His signature windup and unhittable screwball, both seemingly blessed by the heavens themselves, hamstrung many of the best hitters of his day, while his Mexican heritage, immigrant experience, and telling bodily presence would ultimately combine to elevate him to something much more than just a pitcher. Valenzuela, in short, made baseball feel cool, accessible, and fun, which in tow brought in newer generations of baseball fans. As one historian recently noted: "He was superstar pitcher, pop cultural sensation, and symbol of ethnic pride rolled into one."[1] Moreover, his popularity stretched across marketing genius, local journalism, and the

255

national sport media of the day, leaving him throughout the course of his storied career one of America's most lucrative, yet somehow still underrecognized modern sport brands.

Paralleling Fernando Valenzuela's extraordinary rise was this thing that came to be called, simply, Fernandomania. Coined initially by local media and baseball aficionados, it described the kinetic force and excitement created among fans across the United States whenever Valenzuela came to town. But in revisiting this craze for all things Fernando, we can see significance in his appearance in the popular culture that reveals a watershed moment in the cultural history of Latino Americans, particularly the Chicano/a community, navigating mainstream North American society.

Given the racial contexts and cultural realities of the 1980s, Valenzuela's stardom in American sport was unprecedented in both scope and outreach. At a time when Latin American immigrants in general and Mexican immigrants in particular were stigmatized as "unfit," "incapable," or otherwise "unwilling" to be part of American life, Valenzuela emerged onto a social and mediated landscape informed by an anti-immigrant discourse rooted in Othering brown bodies. Importantly, then, Valenzuela's success on the field, and his engagement across the Latino community, particularly in the city of Los Angeles, illustrate what Natalia Molina describes as racial scripts, or as she couches it "the ways in which the lives of peoples of color are linked across time and space and thereby affect one another, even when they may not obviously appear to do so."[2] Formed by the historical contours of "power relations, time period, location, material conditions, and the specific issues at stake," Valenzuela and Fernandomania engaged these racial scripts and at least ephemerally suspended their discursive projections, which more often than not misinterpreted, stereotyped, and otherwise placed nonwhite bodies as perpetually "un-American"; in their place, Valenzuela showcased an alternative script for Mexican people and the Latin American diaspora, one rooted in optimism, culture, and pride in being long-standing members of and continual contributors to the social fabric of America, one pitch at a time.[3]

Valenzuela's presence captures broader shifts in the ways professional sport navigated demographic developments and cultural changes. Accordingly, this chapter seeks to acknowledge the social and cultural significance of Fernando Valenzuela as a man, an athlete, and a Latino celebrity as well as Fernandomania as a popularly driven moment in American history that reaffirmed Major League Baseball as a youth-driven, bicultural, and immigrant-friendly pastime. By contextualizing the life, professional career, and lasting influence of Valenzuela in relation to the 1980s and into the twenty-first century, a major goal of this chapter is to underline the layered elements and residual effects of when he came to town—celebrating brown pioneers in sport against the broader background of containing brown people in society writ large. Thus, it is central and appropriate to provide an overview of Valenzuela's playing career with an emphasis on his rise to stardom in Los Angeles. Equally important are his status as an immigrant to the United States, his placement across racialized spaces as presented in media, and his everlasting impact on the Chicano/a and Latinx sport community.

SONORAN *PELOTERO*

Born on November 1, 1960, to mother Emergilda and father Avelino, Fernando Valenzuela was the youngest of twelve children and raised in sparse barrio conditions in the northern Mexican town of Etchohuaquila, Sonora. As he recounts in the *30 for 30* episode "Fernando Nation":

> When I was a child, we didn't have any dreams. Like all kids, I think you just live in the moment. You play, you go to school, and that's it. We never had dreams about the future.[4]

As the baby of the family, young Fernando had the good fortune to be spared the burden of having to work very hard, recalling: "I just watched and played. My brothers did all the working."[5] Freed from timely responsibilities, Fernando would invest in play, which jump-started his passion for the game of baseball. As he remembered: "It finally happened when I was about twelve years old. That's when I began to dream about becoming a professional baseball player. My dream wasn't about getting to the Big Leagues. I just wanted to get better, step by step."[6]

And get better he did. Following in the footsteps of fellow Sonoran Baldomero Melo "Mel" Almada Quirós, an outfielder who joined the Boston Red Sox and, at the age of twenty, became the first Mexican-born player to debut in the majors in 1933; compatriot José Luis "Chile" Gómez Gonzales, who debuted as a second baseman and shortstop for the Philadelphia Phillies two years later; and American League power hitter Roberto "Beto/Bobby" Ávila of Veracruz, Mexico, who debuted for the Cleveland Indians in 1949, Fernando Valenzuela would become a part of a special lineage of Mexican *peloteros*, many of whom made the jump to the majors during the Great Depression and the Jim Crow era.[7]

Indeed, like his predecessors and those who came after him,[8] Valenzuela had a gift. His oldest brother, Raphael, remembers his baby brother being something of a baseball prodigy, telling one writer: "Give him a bat, and he'll hit the ball. Give him a glove, and he'll play first base. Give him a ball, and he'll strike somebody out."[9] It is no surprise that by age seventeen, Valenzuela had begun his professional career, first with the Mayos de Navojoa and then for the Tuzos de Guanajuato a year later. By 1979, Valenzuela had made it to the peak of Mexican baseball after the Mexican Center League merged with the Liga Mexicana de Béisbol—the Mexican Baseball League. Under these new conditions, Valenzuela began playing for the Triple A–affiliated Leones de Yucatán, going 10–12 with a low 2.49 earned run average (ERA) and 141 strikeouts.[10] That same year, Los Angeles Dodgers scout Mike Brito was in Sonora to observe a prospective shortstop, but he was dazzled by a Valenzuela pitching performance. Valenzuela's athletic abilities, now (in 1979) contracted by the Angeles de Puebla of the Mexican Baseball League, convinced the Dodgers' franchise of his potential star power. And after a bit of back and forth between Brito and then Dodgers general manager Al Campanis, Valenzuela signed with the Dodgers. As Phil Elderkin reported in 1981's *Dodgers Yearbook*: "When Los Angeles purchased his contract from Puebla for $120,000 in 1979, it was understood under Mexican League rules that Fernando would receive $20,000 of that money for himself."[11] And indeed, in classic American fashion, Fernando Valenzuela used his first paycheck to purchase a home for his parents.

Once signed, Valenzuela spent time as a relief pitcher with the Lodi Dodgers of the California League, a minor league team. He spent most of his 1980 season, however, with the San Antonio Dodgers in the Texas League, where, with the help of teammate and fellow Mexican American/Chicano Bobby Castillo, Valenzuela began to perfect his signature screwball. At nineteen years of age, Valenzuela's skill and powerful pitching arm had begun to develop a reputation in the minors; he led the Texas League in strikeouts with 162 while coming in third in ERA, accomplishments that supported his late-season debut in the majors that September.[12]

By opening day 1981, with three starting pitchers—Jerry Reuss, Burt Hooton, and Bob Welch—all out due to injury, manager Tommy Lasorda called on the rookie to take the mound. As Lasorda recalled: "No one could remember the last time a rookie had been the opening day pitcher for the Dodgers. But no one seemed very nervous about it. Especially Fernando."[13] And with that first 2–0 victory over the Astros, the "Year of Fernando" was set in motion. He would go on to a remarkable rookie season in 1981, being named both Rookie of the Year as well as the Cy Young Award winner as the National League's best pitcher. This set the stage for what would be in all a seventeen-year career in Major League Baseball, where among his many accolades he was named to six consecutive All Star teams from 1981 to 1986, won Silver Slugger Awards in 1981 and 1983, and took home a Gold Glove in 1986.[14] Additionally, and arguably more vital than his remarkable career across the years, are his social and cultural influences, which span well beyond the statistics. Indeed, no Latino athlete in the modern age of American sport is more responsible for the revival of late twentieth-century Major League Baseball than Fernando Valenzuela.

CHÁVEZ RAVINE

Writing for a targeted millennial audience, ESPN's David Schoenfield recounts the truly historic 8–0 record that started Fernando Valenzuela's rookie season:

> In 1981, a chubby, 20-year-old left-hander from Mexico who threw a screwball and looked upward into the heavens when he pitched became the biggest sensation in all of baseball. There was no *Baseball Tonight* or MLB Network back then, no Internet to catch your video highlights. ESPN was in its infancy.[15]

Across major US cities, in Mexico, and throughout various cities in Latin America, the resulting Fernandomania took over newspaper headlines, radio airwaves, and TV sport highlight packages. According to the longtime Spanish voice of the Dodgers, Hall of Fame broadcaster Jaime Jarrín, a native of Ecuador who became Valenzuela's interpreter, Fernandomania left Southern California and went national as Valenzuela went from relative obscurity to begin his career undefeated in eight straight decisions, five of which were shutouts. But regardless of when the craze for all things Valenzuela started, its effect was nothing short of unprecedented for its time. As Jarrín notes:

> No single player created more baseball fans than Fernando. People in Mexico, Central America and South America became fans of the Dodgers. Especially women. They would pray the Rosary. And this was everywhere we went. Not just at Dodger Stadium. Everyone wanted a piece of Fernando.[16]

And yet Fernandomania, as a cultural and social phenomenon, went beyond the diamond fields. Its force was strong enough to break long-standing cultural norms across US society. Historian Samuel Regalado first recounts that as the major leagues moved to the West Coast in 1958, it marked a new beginning for the Spanish-speaking population of the country.[17] He adds:

> [If] Valenzuela's success symbolized for many a period of arrival for Latins in the United States, it also marked the coming of age of Spanish-language sportscasting of [M]ajor [L]eague [B]aseball, indeed a rare commodity that had only begun to emerge in the media world by 1958, when the Dodgers arrived in Los Angeles.[18]

Indeed, part of the reason why it took so long to cultivate a Mexican fan base for the Dodgers in Los Angeles can be attributed to the conflict surrounding in their home stadium in Chávez Ravine, to which they moved following their relocation from Brooklyn to Los Angeles after the 1957 season.

Centrally located just one mile from downtown Los Angeles, the Dodgers' marquee stadium was constructed on land that was and remains home to the Gabrielino/Tongva First Peoples. With the 1910 Mexican Revolution's destruction of society and the economy came an increase of Mexican immigrants to Southern California. Most settled in an area named for Julian Chávez, a fellow settler and colonial rancher turned landowning politico who moved to Los Angeles in the early 1830s and purchased land in an area known as the Stone Quarry Hills.[19] Its coarse topography, however, prohibited rigorous real estate advances, even as the growing global LA metropolis flourished around it.

By the 1920s, the roughly three hundred acres of what was now known as Chávez Ravine became home to thousands of families, chiefly of Mexican and Mexican American descent. The area would develop its own educational and economic systems, with many residents growing their own food and raising their own pigs, goats, and chickens, among other livestock. The area's lackluster appeal kept these homes affordable and underdeveloped despite their being remarkably centrally located, as Los Angeles continued to sprawl. In fact, according to a 1949 survey, "one-third of the area's houses had no toilets and a significant percentage were without running water."[20]

Still, "the Ravine" became home to close to four thousand families by midcentury. Economic expansion in the post–World War II years, however, ensured that the "emergence of three barrios, called La Loma, Palo Verde, and Bishop, each nestled in its own ravine," would not last.[21] The lucrative possibility of Chávez Ravine's real estate value had crossed the mind of Los Angeles officials such as Mayor Fletcher Bowron, who served his term during and just after World War II. With the aid of federal agencies, namely health and housing, Bowron would have the territory classified as unfit for habitation and in need of federal intervention via the often controversial policy known as "eminent domain." In citing health reports, Bowron expressed his interest in building some ten thousand units of public housing, although this proposal ran headlong into the downtown elite's own growing interests. Seeking to make Los Angeles into a twentieth-century urban ideal, these elites had little enthusiasm for subsidizing housing for the poor as originally promised, and Bowron was voted out of office in 1953. His successor, Norris Poulson, fortified by the era's Red Scare and antisocialist agenda, scrapped Bowron's development plans, thus keeping the growing brown community at arm's length.

In 1908, the then Brooklyn Dodgers had a sole owner, Charles H. Ebbets; in the ensuing decades, team ownership was expanded to various individual and minority shareholders. In 1945, Walter O'Malley, Branch Rickey, and John Smith bought 50 percent of the team from the Ebbets heirs, with 25 percent of team control belonging to minority shareholders.[22] In 1950, O'Malley became majority owner of the Dodgers by buying out Rickey's shares—Rickey was the man who first broke baseball's restrictive color covenant when he signed Jackie Robinson in 1946.[23] O'Malley, a shrewd businessman with a keen insight into the forces that had helped transform other American cities in the years following World War II, including Brooklyn, knew very well that Chávez Ravine would attract sudden interest from ambitious entrepreneurs and morally questionable government officials. With the assistance of both the *Los Angeles Times* and Hollywood stars such as Lucille Ball and Ronald Reagan, O'Malley celebrated his franchise's relocation to sunny California with the voter-approved Proposition B on June 3, 1958. Historian Eric Avila contends that the team's transition from Ebbets Field to Southern California was primarily an example of urban renewal and the restructuring of political culture and physical space in postwar America, noting:

> The death of public housing in the Chávez Ravine cleared the path for the corporate reincarnation of downtown Los Angeles during the late '50s and throughout the '60s. . . . [With] the cancellation of plans for public housing, large-scale, private redevelopment came to the forefront of downtown's political agenda.[24]

The privatization of Chávez Ravine reveals the intersections between how state-sanctioned law and homeowner legislation systematically marginalized Chicanos/as and other *brown-looking people*. This powerfully captures a more visible episode of American history whereby claims to public space and citizenship collided against the corporatization of professional sport federations, and the effect of that collision on minoritized working-class people, in particular those of color. Following in Mayor Poulson's wake and in the spirit of the American Housing Act of 1949, O'Malley's franchise relocation served to displace the dominant Mexican American barrio that had developed at Chávez Ravine.

On May 8, 1959, members of the Los Angeles County Sheriff's Department forcibly removed Aurora Vargas and the family of Manuel and Avrana Arechiga from their homes. These forced removals illustrate the racial trauma and displacement associated with the relocation and rebranding of the Dodgers. Avila continues:

> Both sides of the battle of the Chávez Ravine invested that struggle with racial meanings, but certain city officials viewed themselves as heirs to the white conquest of California and the West and foresaw an outcome that paralleled the racialized course of Western history.[25]

And it is these memories that would continue to haunt local and regional communities—at least until Fernandomania changed many of the lingering images.

A MEXICAN SANDY KOUFAX

When asked if he had been told of the struggles born out of Chávez Ravine, Fernando Valenzuela responded, "No, never. They never spoke about what happened."[26] And yet Valenzuela's entry onto the Los Angeles sport scene seemed primed to help soothe older wounds. As Daniel Gilbert observes: "If the white press could package Valenzuela in stereotypes, formerly marginalized Chicano fans could claim the superstar as a symbol of national and ethnic pride."[27]

Following decades of searching for the "right" Spanish-speaking athlete, Los Angeles's oldest Spanish-language newspaper, La Opinión, instantly focused on Valenzuela after his arrival in the city. The paper's staff sportswriter, Rodolfo García, had been waiting a long time for a Latino baseball superstar, in particular a Mexican national of working-class roots who might "help preserve and forge Mexican identity in the U.S.," which is precisely what Fernandomania does.[28] As archival footage from Cruz Angeles's 2010 documentary Fernando Nation demonstrates, Valenzuela's on-field successes continued to multiply, so Latinos began to flock to Dodger Stadium in ever-increasing numbers. Teammate and fellow Dodger favorite Steve Garvey observed of

Valenzuela's impact on the local fan base: "LA has its nights, but in 1981 you started to see the emergence of the Hispanic fan—somebody who was engaged. They were there, they were active, they were cheering."[29] Or, as Peter Schmuck recalled in the *Orange County Register*: "The fan demographics of Dodger Stadium changed in a month.... It was stunning to pull your car into the parking lot and drive by mariachi bands. Sure, Mexican Americans came to games, but not like *that*. It was so much fun, just a wonderful, unbelievable circus."[30] While the Dodgers had maintained fairly consistent attendance records—in 1978, they drew in more than 3 million fans—Valenzuela became the "Mexican Sandy Koufax," that once-in-a-generation phenomenal talent who could tap into a particular ethnic marketplace that Al Campanis, general manager of the Dodgers at the time, openly craved.[31] Certainly, Valenzuela's boosting of live attendance was a dream come true.[32]

Additionally, Fernandomania jump-started local merchants and boosted sport consumerism. Fernando Valenzuela, the man, became an instant sport brand with mass appeal who pointed the way toward cultural pride for some and sparked a revival of the sport for others. As Ryan Reft exclaimed during a baseball and ethnicity special aired on Los Angeles's PBS affiliate KCET: "Vendors began to crop up on the streets leading to Dodger Stadium, hawking all manner of Valenzuela-related fare, from souvenir T-shirts to buttons bearing slogans like I LIVE IN THE FERNANDO VALLEY."[33] From mundane items such as shirts and bubblegum to monumental artifacts such as legendary Mexican singer Lalo Guerrero's single "¡Olé! Fernando," Fernandomania foreshadowed corporate-led incentives to monetize and profit from ethnic-gender-sexuality-based differences, a practice now rampant across Latinx American sport cultural economies.[34] As sportswriter Steve Wulf would later opine, only the Beatlemania of the mid-1960s was comparable in terms of levels of enthusiasm.[35]

Another aspect of Fernandomania, then, was the media visibility allotted to Mexican males in professional sport and the unprecedented opportunity opened in advertisement and marketing. Writing in *Playing America's Game: Baseball, Latinos, and the Color Line*, historian Adrian Burgos notes: "The player who adroitly handles the media and his public image positions himself well for endorsement deals,"[36] an enterprise that Valenzuela navigated seamlessly, reaping the benefits of landing advertising deals and thus becoming an instant Mexican celebrity in white America's mainstream understanding of brown-looking "Latins." By May of his rookie season, Valenzuela signed the first of many merchandising contracts, including a $50,000 deal with a poster company selling his likeness at three dollars apiece.[37] Valenzuela's ability to market products to the growing, yet still socially constructed US

Hispanic and Mexican immigrant fan base reveals how the emergent Fernandomania circus accommodated new visibilities in consumerism and product identification. According to cultural theorists and sociologists David Andrews and Steven Jackson, "sport celebrity [is] a product of commercial culture, imbued with symbolic values, which seek to stimulate desire and identification among the consuming populace."[38] Valenzuela's sport celebrity, in other words, reveals the opening of new Latino visibilities in late capitalist America while at the same time reflecting the co-optative nature of capitalism in the post–civil rights era, which has appropriated ethnic and cultural differences to accommodate the growing cultural economy of American sport marketing.

An early Spanish-television commercial spot for Kellogg's Corn Flakes illustrates the emergence of Hispanic marketing across professional sport. A Latino family throwing a ball around in a jovial park is joined by Fernando Valenzuela, whose presence offers a strong sense of belonging for Latinos in the form of an increasingly recognizable sport celebrity. Indeed, the circus spurred by Fernandomania proved effective, influencing generations of Latinos to not only take up baseball as their sporting pastime but to take on the Los Angeles Dodgers as their team. Along the way, fans would have the chance to buy Kellogg's branded cereal, Valenzuela's *personal* favorite. As Marilyn Halter concludes in *Shopping for Identity: The Marketing of Ethnicity*: "[W]hether we like it or not, we are all deeply immersed in a commodity-driven, consumer culture that daily shapes who we are and how we define ourselves."[39] Valenzuela, read from this particular vantage point, served an important conduit whereby Mexicans, Chicanos, and "Latins" across the Latin American diaspora could revel and find affinity. Thus, in addition to his being hailed, as Gilbert recalls, as the game's "first transnational sensation in the age of free agency,"[40] Fernando Valenzuela remains one of America's first Latino sport celebrities in a major American sport.

NARRATING A MEXICAN COMING-OF-AGE MOMENT

Valenzuela's ethnoracial, gendered, and immigrant background made visible the plight of Mexican immigrants, Chicano Americans, and Latinos in general. Burgos suggests that Valenzuela's presence in North America was a coming of age for Mexican representation; his "ascent made international headlines," suggesting that his color and heritage turned him into "a cultural hero to Mexicans and many Latinos."[41] Luis Rodríguez-Mayoral, Puerto Rican public relations representative for Latino baseball players and longtime friend of the late baseball player and humanitarian Roberto Clemente, took it a step further, suggesting that Valenzuela's presence moved the dial beyond Mexico to much of the broader Spanish-speaking landscape: "Though there are differences and different levels of patriotism, when Valenzuela won, Venezuelans, Panamanians, and all Latins were happy about it."[42] To be certain, Valenzuela's leap into the American mainstream provided an important medium to identify alongside ethnic heritage and physical features at a time when these kinds of male sporting visibilities were uncommon in American sporting mediascapes.

Economic imperatives and marketing gimmicks aside, Fernandomania helped negotiate the boundaries of white America's racialized sport and sport media. Thus, a glance at how sport media covered Fernandomania can be useful. For example, in his historic rookie year in 1981, *Sports Illustrated* mentioned Valenzuela in at least five stories. Its coverage of Valenzuela ranged from the subliminally questionable to the overtly stereotypical. Take, for example, the opening paragraph of "No Hideaway for Fernando" by Steve Wulf, one of the first exposés on Valenzuela: "The Natural is supposed to be a blue-eyed boy who teethed on a 36-ounce Louisville Slugger. He should run like the wind and throw boysenberries through brick. He should come from California."[43]

Mainstream depictions of Fernando Valenzuela such as Wulf's, as well as those found in *Sporting News* and the *Los Angeles Times* throughout the 1980s, reveal how mainstream America chose to narrate and emphasize Valenzuela's ethnic cultural identities. In the process, moreover, such depictions crafted "a mythical backdrop around the pitcher that echoed the ideals of American baseball's pastoral foundations."[44] Despite attempts to associate Valenzuela's own pastoral upbringing in Mexico with the sport's bucolic origin story,[45] ultimately, Valenzuela's celebrity image in the US media was constructed solely along the "simple" and "hardworking" tropes commonly associated with Latinos. Other 1981 *Sports Illustrated* pieces, such as "Epidemic of Fernando Fever" by Jim Kaplan (May 4) and "La Voz de los Dodgers" by Ron Fimrite (June 15), document the influence of Fernandomania across the nation, emphasizing how it pertained to the "Latin market."[46] Further documentation of this treatment can be viewed in Valenzuela's two appearances on *Sports Illustrated*'s cover: his May 18, 1981, "UNREAL!" cover, and again on July 8, 1985, with the unsurprising caption "Making His Way in the U.S.A."[47] These expressions, coupled as they are with the canonic image of Fernando Valenzuela throwing a pitch, reveal the impact Fernandomania had on American sport media, but they also reflect the binary that existed between white America and its bilingual, Spanish-speaking, ethnic

American counterpart. Whereas early accounts and public fascination about Valenzuela and the resulting craze focused on his "[Babe] Ruthian image," the use of English translators, and the mysterious world of his hometown, Etchohuaquila, Sonora, the underlying racialization of brown immigrants in general came to inform Valenzuela's early inception in the major leagues, the US nation-state, and the American sport/media complex.[48] In the words of friend and famed Dodgers broadcaster Jaime Jarrín, Fernando Valenzuela transcended linguistic borders:

> Fernando was a once-in-a-lifetime experience. He became a culture, a pole to which many happenings gravitated. With him in the spotlight, many people who did not speak the language became interested in learning Spanish—people who did not know baseball became eager to know the game.[49]

And sociologist Ben Carrington attests that the "sports/media complex serves to both confirm *and* challenge ideas concerning racial equality and the supposedly meritocratic nature of western societies."[50] Indeed, as both media institution and cultural production, the American sport/media complex creates opportunities to deny the existence of race-based inequity while at the same producing and legitimizing a race-based imaginary. In other words, two opposing yet similar readings took place within the coverage of Fernandomania as mediated by "the global white sport media complex."

To be sure, much of the early coverage accentuated Fernando Valenzuela's inability to hold press conferences in English, his need to have an interpreter at all times, and his stout, round body, which suggested a lack of seriousness when it came to his own fitness. Whereas many of the articles, most written by white American males, described Valenzuela's rise as the archetypal "rags to riches," coming-of-American-age story, what is also noteworthy is how sport and baseball fans came to interpret his baseball stardom alongside his ethnic, immigrant, and brown-shaded identities. Like baseball, sport media in the United States then also underwent a bicultural shift due to Fernandomania.

THE COST OF IMMIGRANT WARFARE

Beyond the cultural and drug wars of the 1980s, the decade also elicited immigrant wars that took place in popular discourse, through various media coverage, and in the continued efforts on the part of the US government to militarize and police the US-Mexico border. This served most of all to heighten already mounting white anxiety over migratory brown bodies from Mexico, as well as from Central American countries such as El Salvador, Guatemala, and Nicaragua, suffering from increasing political instability and economic poverty. The proximity to interpret Fernando Valenzuela and Fernandomania along this line is well taken. As Michael Real and Diana Beeson describe:

> [W]e can see in *Fernandomania* an opportunity for Mexican fans to reaffirm and celebrate their "Mexicanness" in his success within the world-class competition that is MLB. There is also a more generic "Latinness" that is validated in the huge success of Latin American baseball players in the United States, this at a time when Latinos within the United States are emerging as major players in business, politics, and culture and when Spanish-speaking countries throughout the hemisphere struggle for power, authority, and recognition.[51]

While these noted sport sociologists asserted that Fernandomania was beneficial for a majority of non-Mexican Latinos, it is fitting to remember that 1980s mainstream America was etched in an anti-immigrant, xenophobic ideology, which came to disproportionately affect the Latin/a/o/x diaspora. Therefore, Valenzuela's star power was anything but absolute insomuch as it had sharp limitations.

Indeed, contemporary interpretations must tread lightly in suggesting that Fernandomania solely represents a sign of progress. Such interpretations might be better informed by pairing Valenzuela's player agency and impact as cultural icon with what sociologist Leo Chávez terms the "Latino Threat Narrative," and what historian Natalia Molina describes as "racial scripts" and "counterscripts." In elaborating an influential political public discourse, Chávez writes that the Latino Threat Narrative tends to imply Mexicans, Mexican immigrants, and Mexican Americans born in the United States, but that this threat "is often generalized to all Latin American immigrants and at times to all Latinos in the United States."[52] Simply stated, the Latino Threat Narrative argues that, unlike "previous immigrant groups, who ultimately became part of the nation ... Latinos are unwilling or incapable of integrating, of becoming part of the national community."[53] Chávez astutely notes that this "cultural dark matter" occupies the essence of mainstream American consciousness in the form of "taken-for-granted 'truths' in debates over immigration on radio and TV talk shows, in newspaper editorials, and Internet blogs."[54] Similarly, Molina uncovers the ways that racial constructions of "one group" often affect others, "sometimes simultaneously and sometimes at a much later date."[55] Noting three elements of "racial scripts," Molina exposes how racialized communities also create and voice "their own narratives in ways that speak truth to power."[56] To be sure, both the "Latino Threat Narrative" and "racial scripts," particularly the use of "counterscripts" by ethnoracially marginalized people (in this case, Mexican and Chicano people), played out in the heyday of Fernandomania.

It was, after all, a frequent occurrence for Fernando Valenzuela to navigate both explicit and microaggressive displays of white America, particularly given the 1981 baseball strike that further invoked class resentment toward baseball players' free-agency rights. As early biographies on Valenzuela capture: "A lot of people did not believe that anyone so young could be that good. So the Dodgers gave out copies of his birth certificate."[57] Fears about Valenzuela's desire to keep his "foreignness" were evident in fan commentaries as well. As Mihir D. Parekh notes in his master's thesis titled "Media and Literary Representations of Latinos in Baseball and Baseball Fiction," fans would interpret Valenzuela from a monolinguistic and monocultural lens: "One *LA Times* reader revealed her disdain for Valenzuela's failure to learn English, stating, 'My husband and I wonder why Fernando did not take a blitz course in English during the strike. This interpret bit is beginning to pall. Before our vacation in Mexico I studied Spanish.'"[58] Sentiments as these suggest that for mainstream American viewers, Valenzuela retained characteristics that warranted fear, distrust, and anxiety.

Like so many Latino major leaguers before him, Fernando Valenzuela's narrative would be anglicized. The official 1981 baseball card by Fleer introduced him as "Fernand Valenzuela: Pitcher."[59] Like Roberto Clemente, who was frequently dubbed "Bob" or even the more childlike "Bobby" by the white sport media complex, Valenzuela would also have to negotiate the politics of invisibility and erasure through language and discourse. An example of this occurred in the aftermath of his first-year breakthrough when his agent, Antonio De Marco, requested a salary increase. As Daniel Gilbert relates:

> After earning a salary of $42,500 during his rookie campaign, Valenzuela attempted to negotiate a raise for 1982 that would reflect his considerable worth to the team. When the Dodgers countered with a $350,000 offer at the beginning of spring training, the pitcher refused to report to camp, initiating a standoff that lasted nearly until opening day. . . . The holdout inspired a significant amount of animosity toward Valenzuela from many quarters, much of which was reported and amplified by the sporting press.[60]

To be sure, the 1980s reveal the tenacity of Anglo-American racial imaginaries, rather than their demise.

Reading Fernando Valenzuela and Fernandomania during the 1980s, then, requires recognition of the policing of immigrant communities. In their 1982 portable mural *Invasión de Fernando*,[61] David Botello, Wayne Healy, and George Yepes, members of the East Los Streetscapers, reveal a counterscript that captures the meaning of Valenzuela amid the anti-immigration fervor of the 1980s, particularly across US-Mexico borderlands. In explaining how the minimural serves as a contemporary example of why nascent images appearing locally do not always translate into the assimilation narratives that ultimately reject heritage, cultural geographer Daniel Arreola notes:

> Set against a backdrop of the Los Angeles skyline and Dodger Stadium, pitcher Fernando Valenzuela, a Mexican national, is shown striding over a chain-link fence—the so-called "tortilla curtain"—that divides the United States from Mexico. Beneath the majestic figure of the Dodger pitcher, illegal Mexican immigrants are cutting through the same fence.[62]

Importantly, this mural captures how Valenzuela's celebrated presence disrupted and transformed an otherwise anti-immigrant lived reality. Despite the events that witnessed the displacement and dispossession of Chávez Ravine, the emergence of Fernando Valenzuela and Fernandomania in the 1980s transformed American society in powerful ways. In the words of La Pasionaria Chicana, activist and organizer Dolores Huerta: "[Fernando Valenzuela] touched people in their hearts really.... What he was, was also part of them."[63] To be sure, Valenzuela's success on the mound, and the social and cultural aftershocks that Fernandomania marked, opened an opportunity for Mexicans/Latinos to reimagine just who exactly they were and what were their contributions to US society,[64] illustrating the need and "hunger for [more Latino] role models" across sport and society alike.[65]

Conversely, Southern California artist Ben Sakoguchi captures another counterscript dimension of Fernandomania in his paintings. For example, in *Solamente Inglés*, Sakoguchi presents Fernando Valenzuela alongside Jaime Jarrín.[66] The 2008 painting is ostensibly set in Valenzuela's playing days and reveals microphones from various media networks recording pregame or postgame media appearances. In naming it in Spanish, translated as "Only English," Sakoguchi highlights how Valenzuela's mediated exposure disrupted monolingualism in the game and acknowledges the multiethnicity and bilingualism of America's game. The young, mysterious, Spanish-speaking pitching legend provoked English-speaking journalists to engage in practices unimaginable a generation ago in which they found themselves asking their fellow bilingual colleagues and speakers for translation help.[67] What a brave new world the young Mexican immigrant initiated for the world of American baseball!

CONCLUSION: EXPANDING AMERICANNESS ONE COUNTER-NARRATIVE AT A TIME

During the opening to Game 2 of the 2017 World Series between the Los Angeles Dodgers and the now American League Houston Astros, the revered voice of the Dodgers, Vin Scully, took the mound with microphone in hand, intending to throw out the evening's ceremonial first pitch. Officially retired in 2016 after sixty-seven years as broadcaster for the Dodgers and working in his finest all-too-jovial colloquia, Vinny joked with the crowd:

> You know what I'm thinking right now? Somewhere up in heaven, Duke Snider, Jackie Robinson, Roy Campanella, and Gil Hodges are laughing their heads off. Look who's throwing out the first ball at the World Series.[68]

But then, in what was quickly becoming an amateur sketch comedy, the then eighty-eight-year-old Scully revealed that he had suffered an arm injury and began to plead for a left-handed pitcher to come in and relieve him from embarrassing himself further. That he kept calling for a left-hander for some gave it away.

And indeed, with 54,293 screaming fans in attendance, while another 32 million pairs of eyes and ears tuned in across America's sport media system tried to figure out what was to come, a rather svelte brown man made his way to the diamond just as he had done almost forty years earlier. Only this time, rather than starting the game, Fernando Valenzuela, the famed left-handed pitcher from Sonora, Mexico, with the inimitable screwball who won both the 1981 Rookie of the Year and Cy Young Awards while launching the cultural and economic phenomenon known as Fernandomania, was appearing in relief, albeit mostly in comic relief.[69]

Valenzuela's presence surely filled generations of Dodgers fans to the brim of ecstasy—at least it did at the packed sports bar where I sat in Southern California! The occasion was far from the first time the Dodgers and Astros were competing with the stakes so high, and Fernando Valenzuela's first pitch in 2017 to his old Dodger teammate, catcher Steve Yeager, was reminiscent of his September 1980 debut. And in keeping with the spirit of the moment, prior to walking off the field, Scully, Valenzuela, and Yeager led Los Angeles fanatics everywhere with Scully's famous call to arms: "It's time for Dodger baseball."[70]

Staged and corny as it may have been, this rather vaudevillian moment was also a reminder of the extent to which Fernando Valenzuela is still embraced by the Dodger faithful. And given the large number of Latino fans of the LA Dodgers, Fernandomania is in its own way alive and well. It has certainly helped mobilize a sense of cultural pride in Latino-ness that persists to the present day. For example, in discussing the meaning of Fernando Valenzuela, José Alamillo observes the importance of his legacy in shifting attitudes toward immigration. He writes: "My father is still convinced that when President Ronald Reagan invited Valenzuela to the White House for a luncheon with him and Mexico's President José López Portillo in the middle of the 1981 season, they talked more about immigration than baseball."[71] And Steve Wulf reminds us that in 1982, we also learned that President Reagan brought up the topic of the young Mexican left-hander with manager Tommy Lasorda during a White House State Dinner given in honor of the Italian president.[72] Six years later, in 1988, there would be yet another Valenzuela moment in the White House following the Dodgers' second World Series championship of the decade as Valenzuela's brown smile shared the same lawn when President Reagan greeted the "World" champions.

Akin to Alamillo's personal reflections, famed Chicano American comedian George Lopez, too, finds affinity with the cultural impact of Fernando Valenzuela, recalling:

Fernando made us believe that no matter where we came from or what we looked like, talent was the equalizer. . . . I've gone to Dodger Stadium with regularity in the years since Fernandomania. Every time I go, I remember my grandmother and grandfather and how much fun we used to have cheering and feeling proud every time Valenzuela did something great.[73]

Lopez contends that Valenzuela's working-class, "give it all you got" attitude prompted a cultural renaissance for him. And as was the case with Alamillo, Lopez's family found that Valenzuela's marquee success generated common ground across all sorts of die-hard "Los Doyers" fans.[74] But this craze for all-matters-Valenzuela is not strictly about feeling good as much as it is about an opportunity to revisit much older debates about citizenship and legitimacy for those historically kept along the margins.

Whereas Fernando Valenzuela empowered, inspired, motivated, and identified with people across generations, genders, ages, nationalities, and spatial locations, Fernandomania created a public space for contending with a fervent anti-immigrant sentiment in the United States while simultaneously revving the engines of consumerism and sport marketing. Through his cultural subtext and appeal to the working poor of all colors, but particularly Spanish-speaking immigrants, Fernando Valenzuela became the epitome of winning with humility, losing with grace, and going out swinging as symbols of the immigrant contribution to American society. His legacy is truly one in a million who found a way to capitalize on an opportunity, a vital story in our collective American history that altogether broadens the predominantly white Horatio Alger narrative.

Fernando Valenzuela's great brown American dream offers a story rooted in everyday sporting people. In the process, he complicates the discursive practice that pens Mexicans, Latinos, and immigrants of all walks as little more than threats to the national culture and security of the United States. And while his linguistic and cultural identities were ultimately co-opted by sport media and corporate lords much more inclined to put profit over social gains, he also became a symbol of possibility and hope for immigrant and Latino communities.[75] In this regard, Fernando "El Toro" Valenzuela testifies to great brown hopes in 1980s America that continue to inform legions of fans across generations.

NOTES

The author would like to thank the editors of this volume for their vision, support, invitation, and patience. Special thanks go out to Professor José E. Limón, Jason Ruiz, Annie Coleman, the Institute for Latino Studies at the University of Notre Dame, and my fellow 2018 Young Scholars Symposium participants for providing me with the opportunity to present an early draft of this chapter. I hope that this chapter captures your collective brilliance and constructive feedback.

1. Luis Alvarez, "On Los Chorizeros, the Classic, and El Tri: Sports and Community in Mexican Los Angeles," in *LA Sports: Play, Games, and Community in the City of Angels*, ed. Wayne Wilson and David K. Wiggins (Fayetteville: University of Arkansas Press, 2018), 37; and Jorge Iber, Samuel O. Regalado, José M. Alamillo, and Arnoldo De León, *Latinos in U.S. Sport: A History of Isolation, Cultural Identity, and Acceptance* (Champaign, IL: Human Kinetics, 2011), 225–27.

2. Natalia Molina, "The Power of Racial Scripts: What the History of Mexican Immigration to the United States Teaches Us about Relational Notions of Race," *Latino Studies* 8, no. 2 (2010): 157.

3. Molina, "The Power of Racial Scripts," 157; for more on the racialization of "brown" bodies, see Otto Santa Ana, *Brown Tide Rising: Metaphors of Latinos in Contemporary American Public Discourse* (Austin: University of Texas Press, 2002); and Mary K. Bloodsworth-Lugo and Carmen R. Lugo-Lugo, *Containing (Un)American Bodies: Race, Sexuality, and Post-9/11 Constructions of Citizenship* (Amsterdam: Editions Rodopi, 2010).

4. Cruz Angeles, dir., "Fernando Nation," *30 for 30*, ESPN Films, October 26, 2010.

5. Mike Littwin, *Fernando Valenzuela: The Screwball Artist* (Chicago: Children's Press, 1983), 17.

6. Angeles, "Fernando Nation."

7. Bill Nowlin, "Mel Almada," Society for American Baseball Research, https://sabr.org/bioproj/person/1797ed2c; "Chile Gomez Stats," Baseball Almanac, last modified February 1, 2018, http://www.baseball-almanac.com/players/player.php?p=gomezcho1; and John Stahl, "Bobby Avila," Society for American Baseball Research, https://sabr.org/bioproj/person/cd9fe167.

8. According to the website Baseball Reference, 124 native Mexicans have followed Almada's sport journey since 1933, each with his own experiences of American racial and ethnic relations. By the start of the 2000 baseball season, 87 Mexican baseball players had made their debut in the US major leagues, including Fernando Valenzuela.

9. Littwin, *Fernando Valenzuela: The Screwball Artist*, 18–19.

10. The Mexican League was established in 1925, was granted double-A status in 1955, and twelve years later elevated to triple-A status. In 1979, the league expanded adding four teams: Azules de Coatzacoalcos, Bravos de León, Leones de Yucatán, and Rojos del Águila de Veracruz. For Valenzuela's record with Leones de Yucatán, see "Fernando Valenzuela," Baseball Reference, last modified May 19, 2019, https://www.baseball-reference.com/bullpen/Fernando_Valenzuela.

11. Phil Elderkin, "Fernando Valenzuela: Big League Rhythm," in *1981 Los Angeles Dodgers Yearbook*, 53; see also Steve Wulf, "No Hideaway for Fernando," *Sports Illustrated*, March 23, 1981, https://www.si.com/vault/1981/03/23/825469/no-hideaway-for-fernando-forget-low-or-slender--profiles-when-youre-discussing-fernando-valenzuela-a-rookie-to-treasure.

12. Elderkin, "Fernando Valenzuela: Big League Rhythm," 53; and Littwin, *Fernando Valenzuela: The Screwball Artist*, 24.

13. Littwin, *Fernando Valenzuela: The Screwball Artist*, 31.

14. Littwin, *Fernando Valenzuela: The Screwball Artist*, 40.

15. David Schoenfield, "#TBT: Fernandomania!," ESPN, May 15, 2015, https://www.espn.com/blog/sweetspot/post/_/id/58170/tbt-fernandomania.

16. Paul Gutierrez, "Fernandomania Flashbacks: How the Dodgers Legend's Rise to Fame Began with the Astros," ABC News, October 26, 2017, https://abcnews.go.com/Sports/fernandomania-flashbacks-dodgers-legends-rise-fame-began-astros/story?id=50724218.

17. Samuel O. Regalado, "Read All About It! The Spanish-Language Press, the Dodgers, and the Giants, 1958–1982," in *Mexican Americans and Sports: A Reader on Athletics and Barrio Life*, ed. Jorge Iber and Samuel Regalado (College Station: Texas A&M University Press, 2007), 145–59.

18. Samuel O. Regalado, "'Dodgers Béisbol Is on the Air': The Development and Impact of the Dodgers Spanish-Language Broadcasts, 1958–1994," *California History* 74, no. 3 (1995): 281.

19. Elina Shatkin, "Remembering Dodger Stadium when It Was Chavez Ravine," *Southern California Public Radio*, October 31, 2017, https://www.scpr.org/news/2017/10/31/77135/remembering-dodger-stadium-when-it-was-chavez-ravi/.

20. Jason Turbow, *They Bled Blue: Fernandomania, Strike-Season Mayhem, and the Weirdest Championship Baseball Had Ever Seen* (Boston: Houghton Mifflin Harcourt, 2019), 72.

21. Turbow, *They Bled Blue*, 71.

22. "Dodgers Owners through the Years," *Los Angeles Times*, March 27, 2012, https://timelines.latimes.com/history-dodgers-ownership/.

23. For a thorough recounting of the events leading up to O'Malley's obtaining controlling interest in the Dodgers and their move to Los Angeles, as well as the battle over the Chávez Ravine removal and relocation, see Eric Avila, *Popular Culture in the Age of White Flight: Fear and Fantasy in Suburban Los Angeles* (Berkeley: University of California Press, 2006), 155–61.

24. Avila, *Popular Culture in the Age of White Flight*, 157.

25. Avila, *Popular Culture in the Age of White Flight*, 170. By this time, fewer than twenty of the original one thousand families remained in the barrio.

26. Turbow, *They Bled Blue*, 71.

27. Daniel A. Gilbert, *Expanding the Strike Zone: Baseball in the Age of Free Agency* (Amherst: University of Massachusetts Press, 2013), 79.

28. Regalado, "Read All About It!," 155.

29. Turbow, *They Bled Blue*, 77.

30. Turbow, *They Bled Blue*, 77.

31. Turbow, *They Bled Blue*, 78; and Ryan Reft, "Greenberg to Koufax to Valenzuela: Ethnicity, Identity, and Baseball in 'Chasing Dreams,'" KCET, April 7, 2016, https://www.kcet.org/shows/lost-la/greenberg-to-koufax-to-valenzuela-ethnicity-identity-and-baseball-in-chasing-dreams.

32. For a statistical quantitative discussion regarding Fernandomania's effect on live attendance, see Andrew W. Nutting, "Customer Discrimination and Fernandomania," *Journal of Sports Economics* 13, no. 4 (2012): 406–30.

33. Reft, "Greenberg to Koufax to Valenzuela."

34. Social identities and differences of race, gender, ethnicity, and sexuality fuel the cultural economy of pro sport and sport/media. Given the contemporary moment, with key words such as "diversity" and "multiculturalism," it is unsurprising to witness a resurgence of major US sport federations (particularly the NBA, NFL, MLB, and MLS) adopt marketing and advertising strategies aimed to attract and retain the Hispanic audience/sport fan base.

35. Cruz, "Fernando Nation."

36. Adrian Burgos Jr., *Playing America's Game: Baseball, Latinos, and the Color Line* (Berkeley: University of California Press, 2007), 246.

37. Gilbert, *Expanding the Strike Zone*, 80.

38. David L. Andrews and Steven J. Jackson, "Introduction: Sport Celebrities, Public Culture, and Private Experience," in *Sports Stars: The Cultural Politics of Sporting Celebrity*, ed. David L. Andrews and Steven J. Jackson (New York: Routledge, 2001), 9.

39. Marilyn Halter, *Shopping for Identity: The Marketing of Ethnicity* (New York: Schocken Books, 2000), 198. For more on the origins, development, and problematics of Hispanic

marketing in US society, see Arlene Dávila, *Latinos Inc.: Marketing and the Making of a People* (Berkeley: University of California Press, 2001).

40. Gilbert, *Expanding the Strike Zone*, 76.

41. Burgos, *Playing America's Game*, 235.

42. Samuel O. Regalado, *Viva Baseball! Latin Major Leaguers and Their Special Hunger* (Urbana: University of Illinois Press, 1998), 180.

43. Wulf, "No Hideaway for Fernando."

44. Mihir D. Parekh, "Media and Literary Representations of Latinos in Baseball and Baseball Fiction" (master's thesis, University of Texas at Arlington, 2015), 22; and Gilbert, *Expanding the Strike Zone*, 78.

45. For a riveting comparative analysis on the reproduction and layered history of baseball's "pastoral" and "sacred" origin stories, see Charles Fruehling Springwood, *Cooperstown to Dyersville: Geographies of Baseball Nostalgia* (Boulder, CO: Westview Press, 1996).

46. Jim Kaplan, "Epidemic of Fernando Fever," *Sports Illustrated*, May 4, 1981, https://www.si.com/vault/issue/70938/24/2; and Ron Fimrite, "La Voz de los Dodgers," *Sports Illustrated*, June 15, 1981, https://www.si.com/vault/issue/70944/62/2.

47. Jim Kaplan, "Will the Bubble Ever Burst?," *Sports Illustrated*, May 18, 1981, https://www.si.com/vault/1981/05/18/825643/will-the-bubble-ever-burst-fernando-valenzuela-had-to-struggle-for-a-while-in-running-his-record-to-7-0-but-by-gum-he-got-his-fifth-shutout; and Tony Castro, "Something Screwy Going On Here," *Sports Illustrated*, July 8, 1985, https://www.si.com/vault/issue/43454/1/1.

48. The field of sport media has grown exponentially in recent years; for seminal works on sport media, see Sut Jhally, "The Spectacle of Accumulation: Material and Cultural Factors in the Evolution of the Sports/Media Complex," *Critical Sociology* 12, no. 3 (1984): 41–57; Lawrence A. Wenner, ed., *MediaSport* (London: Routledge, 1998); and Pamela J. Creedon, ed., *Women, Media, and Sport: Challenging Gender Values* (Thousand Oaks, CA: SAGE Publications, 1994). For more recent texts, see Arthur A. Raney and Jennings Bryant, eds., *Handbook of Sports and Media* (New York: Routledge, 2006); Andrew C. Billings, ed., *Sport Media: Transformation, Integration, Concentration* (New York: Routledge, 2011); and the bimonthly peer-reviewed journal *Communication and Sport*.

49. Regalado, *Viva Baseball!*, 182.

50. Ben Carrington, "'What I Said Was Racist—But I'm Not a Racist': Anti-Racism and the White Sports/Media Complex," in *Sport and Challenges to Racism*, ed. Jonathan Long and Karl Spracklen (London: Palgrave Macmillan, 2011), 85.

51. Michael Real and Diana Beeson, "Globalization and Diversity in American Sports: The Meaning behind 'Fernandomania,'" in *Bodies of Discourse: Sports Stars, Media, and the Global Public*, ed. Cornel Sandvoss, Michael Real, and Alina Bernstein (New York: Peter Lang, 2012), 155.

52. Leo Chávez, *The Latino Threat: Constructing Immigrants, Citizens, and the Nation* (Stanford, CA: Stanford University Press, 2008), 22.

53. Chávez, *The Latino Threat*, 2–3.

54. Chávez, *The Latino Threat*, 2–3.

55. Natalia Molina, *How Race Is Made in America: Immigration, Citizenship, and the Historical Power of Racial Scripts* (Berkeley: University of California Press, 2014), 20.

56. Molina, *How Race Is Made in America*, 25.

57. Littwin, *Fernando Valenzuela: The Screwball Artist*, 9.

58. Parekh, "Media and Literary Representations of Latinos," 20.

59. Rich Klein, "When 'Fernand' Valenzuela Was an Early 80's Smash Hit," *Sports Collectors Daily*, August 19, 2014, https://www.sportscollectorsdaily.com/fernand-valenzuela-early-80s-smash-hit/.

60. Gilbert, *Expanding the Strike Zone*, 80.

61. "East Los Streetscapers Painting *Invasión de Fernando*," Online Archive of California, n.d., https://oac.cdlib.org/ark:/13030/hb05800569/?docId=hb05800569&brand=oac4&layout=printable-details.

62. Daniel D. Arreola, "Mexican American Exterior Murals," *Geographical Review* 74, no. 4 (1984): 423–24.

63. Cruz, "Fernando Nation."

64. The Dodgers' back-to-back World Series appearances in 2017 and 2018 reinvigorated a surge in fan appreciation and public admiration for the Boys in Blue. One notable example was "the Dodger House," a midcity monument located at 1626 South La Brea Avenue, which as of this writing is undergoing demolition. Muralist Hector Arias honored the Dodgers by painting murals of star pitching ace Clayton Kershaw and the legendary Fernando Valenzuela. See Gwynedd Stuart, "Bye Bye, La Brea Avenue Dodger House," *Los Angeles Magazine*, July 10, 2019, https://www.lamag.com/culturefiles/bye-bye-la-brea-avenue-dodger-house/.

65. David Reyes, "Fernandomania Hints of Hunger for Role Models–Latino Heroes: The Few and Far Between," *Los Angeles Times*, August 5, 1983.

66. Ben Sakoguchi, *Solamente Inglés*, http://www.bensakoguchi.com/larger/allbaseball_group9_larger21.php.

67. Regalado, *Viva Baseball!*, 181.

68. Ryan Fagan, "World Series 2017: Vin Scully Brings Pure Joy to Dodger Stadium with First Pitch Show," *Sporting News*, October 25, 2017, http://www.sportingnews.com/mlb/news/world-series-2017-vin-scully-dodger-stadium-fernando-valenzuela-yeager-astros-dodgers-first-pitch/10y3jhg74gvky1bkgh24e6n36d.

69. FOX Sports, "Vin Scully, Fernando Valenzuela Throw Out 1st Pitch before Game 2, 2017 MLB Playoffs," YouTube, October 26, 2017, https://www.youtube.com/watch?v=ecdJuWcZuRo.

70. FOX Sports, "Vin Scully, Fernando Valenzuela Throw Out 1st Pitch."

71. José M. Alamillo, "Fernando, Los Doyers and Me: How Valenzuela Taught One Mexican Immigrant to Feel Proud and Love the Dodgers," *La Vida Baseball*, April 19, 2017, https://www.lavidabaseball.com/fernando-valenzuela-dodgers-latinos/.

72. Wulf, "No Hideaway for Fernando," 57.

73. George Lopez, "On Fernandomania and the Moment I Became a Dodgers Fan," ESPN, August 19, 2016, https://www.espn.com/mlb/story/_/id/17338864/george-lopez-fernandomania-moment-became-dodgers-fan.

74. Adam Poulisse, "How the Los Angeles Dodgers Became Known as 'Los Doyers,'" *Pasadena (CA) Star-News*, October 14, 2013, https://www.pasadenastarnews.com/2013/10/14/how-the-los-angeles-dodgers-became-known-as-los-doyers/.

75. Simply consider the deployment of the Fernando Valenzuela Bobblehead starting on July 29, 2001, which in turn helped spur and ultimately influence the Dodgers organization to

acknowledge May 8, 2019, as Mexican Heritage Night—the same fateful date that fifty years earlier witnessed the final expulsion of brown people from Chávez Ravine. See "Mexican Heritage Night," Los Angeles Dodgers, https://www.mlb.com/dodgers/tickets/specials/mexican-heritage-night.

AFTERWORD

Bread, Circuses, and Desolation Row

JACK LULE

INTRODUCTION

"The circus is in town." It seems a common statement. And yet the editors have conjured a fitting title. It embraces the dramatic, scandalous stories that make up this lively volume. Yet it also captures as well the ambitious goals of the entire series, which has plumbed the essential, trivial, tragic, and perhaps ennobling conflation of media, sports, and reputation.

On one level, the phrase evokes its roots: the traveling troupe of lion tamers, acrobats, clowns, and sundry others has arrived to entertain us for a few days before moving on. It is doubtful, though, that any reader picked up this volume expecting to read of trapeze artists and tightrope walkers. The phrase has aged into metaphor.

In one modern formulation, the circus has narrowed. It has become a *media circus*. The definition proffered by Google, from the *Collins English Dictionary*, was old enough to make me smile: "If an event is described as a media circus, a large group of people from the media are there to report on it and take photographs." No television cameras? No satellite dishes? But *Collins* also offers helpful explication: "[disapproval] The couple married in the Caribbean to avoid a media circus."[1]

Kim Goldman, the sister of Ron Goldman, murdered in 1994 alongside Nicole Brown Simpson, had her life transformed by the spectacle surrounding the subsequent O. J. Simpson trial. Her resulting book, *Media Circus: A Look at Private Tragedy in the Public Eye*, captures many of the themes we have seen in this volume.[2]

But athletes learn at an early age that privacy, even private tragedy, is one of the first sacrifices they must make to the ravenous appetite of sports media. Indeed, many of the preceding chapters show sports stars trying to manipulate and exploit the media circus. From the constructed spectacle of boxers Conor McGregor and Floyd Mayweather to the careful choreography of soccer great David Beckham's public image to the monetization of Tiger Woods's "racial transcendence" to the studied attempt by tennis star Maria Sharapova to manage the fallout from her drug use, the chapters reveal the media circus as a well-established part of modern sport, and a key to the maintenance and navigation (or usurpation) of athletic reputations.

THE VIEW FROM "DESOLATION ROW"

For fans of Bob Dylan, "the circus is in town" has other meanings, anchoring the first lines of his epic song "Desolation Row":

> They're selling postcards of the hanging,
> They're painting the passports brown.
> The beauty parlor is filled with sailors,
> The circus is in town.[3]

In a surreal and Kafkaesque tune that stretches for more than eleven minutes, Dylan tours a chaotic world peopled with displaced characters wrenched from literature, history, fiction, and the Bible, their identities irrelevant to their portrayal. These include Einstein disguised as Robin Hood, Cinderella being romanced by Romeo, Ezra Pound and T. S. Eliot fighting in the captain's tower, and Ophelia gazing at Noah's rainbow.

The song is hypnotic, and, as I read this volume, I found the tune on my mind, reflecting on the nature of displacement and identity in modern sports. How many of the sports figures depicted in these chapters have viewed their media portrayals—from worshiping to degrading—and not recognized themselves at all: Michelle Akers as the Lioness Queen; Colin Kaepernick as traitor and savior; Nancy Kerrigan as the Ice Princess; and Fernando Valenzuela as a Mexican exemplar to remake America. As journalists (and scholars) strive to wring meaning from those who make a living playing sport, the players' identities can seem like just so much raw material, a canvas on which imagists can work.

And yet the players are not at all innocent and powerless in the struggle over identity. They offer idealized images of themselves to the media and the world, seeking to shape their identity, build their brand, secure their place, and manage their reputation. We see: LeBron James attempt to carefully, even artfully compose each of his career choices, from "the Decision" to "the Promise," while Jason Collins and Michael Sam try to manage the revelation of their sexual identities. And then there is Shaquille O'Neal's endeavor to craft a brand, personality, and career outside of basketball as well as Tiger Woods's hopes to reclaim the million-dollar image he squandered with sexual transgressions.

Indeed, all of the players chronicled here have struggled to control their identity and reputation. Too often, as the volume's allusion to scandal suggests, the players fail. Displaced and no longer in control of their situation or even their lives, they find scandal and ruin and tumble unmoored into "Desolation Row."

BREAD AND CIRCUSES

Certainly another evocation of "the circus is in town" hearkens to the phrase, "bread and circuses." In its original use by the Roman poet Juvenal (*panem et circenses*, in Latin), the phrase disparages a Roman populace that can easily be pacified by free wheat and entertainment:

> [T]he People have abdicated our duties; for the People who once upon a time handed out military command, high civil office, legions—everything, now restrains itself and anxiously hopes for just two things: bread and circuses.[4]

The phrase has taken on a similar critical cast in the modern media landscape, yet with a twist of power and blame. In *Bread and Circuses: Theories of Mass Culture as Social Decay*, Patrick Brantlinger looks at models of mass culture through the eyes of Marx, Nietzsche, Freud, José Ortega y Gasset, T. S. Eliot, and others.[5] He notes that a number of theorists, such as those who once made up the Frankfurt School as well as other critical theorists of the Left, have altered Juvenal's emphasis. These theorists agree that bread and circuses distract the public from political life. However, they blame not the citizenry but a capitalist-driven media system designed to entertain and divert people from political and civic involvement.

Sports stars play a pivotal, often uneasy role in the offerings of bread and circuses. On one level, the stars are essential performers in the circus. From the huge spectacles of the Super Bowl, the World Cup, and the Olympics to the everyday lineup of games, sports are powerful entertainment machines—and wholly dependent on the performance of the players. And the players make their living, their millions, from their role in bread and circuses.

Yet what happens if/when players question or recoil from their role or perhaps even attempt to introduce civic and political questions into the circus? As this volume and others in the series have clearly shown, these players can expect the wrath of a system and populace that depend on the consumption (and provision) of bread and circuses. In this volume, Colin Kaepernick serves as the exemplar. By simply taking a knee during the national anthem, Kaepernick endured condemnation from fans, pundits, owners, some players, and the US president. Juvenal's insight resonates throughout history and empires.

EXPANDING THE INQUIRY

"The circus is in town" thus serves not only as an apt phrase for this volume but for the entire series, which has taken on the admixture of media, sports, and reputation. *Reconstructing Fame* and *Fame to Infamy* investigate the fall from grace of sports stars, especially Black athletes, and the (sometimes) redemption of athletic reputations. *A Locker Room of Her Own* expands the inquiry to celebrity, sexuality, and female athletes. *More Than Cricket and Football* brings the study to international sport. Looking back, we can see that consistent themes throughout the series are the media circus that surrounds the modern sports star and the critical, conflicted relationship of media, sports, and the athletes who find fame and infamy in their circus roles.

NOTES

1. "Media Circus," *Collins English Dictionary*, https://www.collinsdictionary.com/us/dictionary/english/media-circus.

2. Kim Goldman with Tatsha Robertson, *Media Circus: A Look at Private Tragedy in the Public Eye* (Dallas: BenBella Books, 2015).

3. Bob Dylan, "Desolation Row," *Highway 61 Revisited*, Columbia, 1965.

4. Decimus Junius Juvenal, "Satire X," in *The Satires of Juvenal, Persius, Sulpicia, and Lucilius*, trans. Lewis Evans (New York: Harper and Brothers, 1881); at Project Gutenberg, https://www.gutenberg.org/files/50657/50657-h/50657-h.htm.

5. Patrick Brantlinger, *Bread and Circuses: Theories of Mass Culture as Social Decay* (Ithaca, NY: Cornell University Press, 2016).

CONTRIBUTORS

Dr. Lisa Doris Alexander is a professor in Wayne State University's Department of African American Studies. She is the author of the books *Expanding the Black Film Canon: Race and Genre across Six Decades* (University Press of Kansas) and *When Baseball Isn't White, Straight, and Male: The Media and Difference in the National Pastime* (McFarland). Her work has appeared in *Black Ball: A Journal of the Negro Leagues*, *NINE: A Journal of Baseball History and Culture*, the *Journal of American History*, and the *Journal of Popular Film and Television*.

Dr. Matthew H. Barton is a professor in the Communication Department at Southern Utah University. He is the coauthor of the book *Introducing Communication: A Digital Learning Experience* (Kendall Hunt, 2017). He has published research in the *Western Journal of Communication*, *Communication Education*, *Relevant Rhetoric*, *Communication Teacher*, the *Basic Communication Course Annual*, and several edited book volumes. He has been honored with his institutions' highest awards in teaching, including Outstanding Educator and Faculty Fellow in Service Learning.

Dr. Andrew C. Billings is the executive director of the Alabama Program in Sports Communication and Ronald Reagan Chair of Broadcasting in the Department of Journalism and Creative Media at the University of Alabama. His research interests lie in the intersection of sport, mass media, consumption habits, and identity-laden content. His books include *Media and the Coming Out of Gay Male Athletes in American Team Sports* (with Leigh Moscowitz, Peter Lang, 2018) and *Mascot Nation: The Controversy over Native American Representations in Sports* (with Jason Edward Black, University of Illinois Press, 2018). He has written for journals including the *Journal of Communication*, *Journalism and Mass Communication Quarterly*, *Mass Communication and Society*, and the *Journal of Broadcasting and Electronic Media* and serves on many editorial boards, including as an associate editor of the journals *Communication and Sport* and the *Journal of Global Sport Communication*.

Dr. Carlton Brick is a lecturer in sociology at the University of the West of Scotland, Paisley. He has written and taught extensively on sport, culture, and celebrity.

Dr. Ted M. Butryn is a professor in the Department of Kinesiology at San José State University. His research is positioned at the nexus of critical sport sociology and sport psychology. He has published in numerous leading journals on cyborg athletes and sport technology; whiteness and race in sport; doping; and athlete activism. His current research agenda with various colleagues involves athlete mental health, and sport during Covid-19.

Dr. Brian Carroll is a professor and chair of communication at Berry College in Mount Berry, Georgia, where he has been a member of the faculty since 2003. He is author of, among other books, *When to Stop Cheering? The Black Press, the Black Community and Black Baseball* (Routledge, 2007); and *The Black Press and Black Baseball, 1915–1955: A Devil's Bargain* (Routledge, 2015). Carroll earned his PhD from the University of North Carolina at Chapel Hill, where he also earned his bachelor's. He earned a master's in political science from the University of North Carolina at Greensboro. Before joining the professorate, he was a reporter, photographer, and editor.

Dr. Arthur T. Challis is a professor in the Communication Department at Southern Utah University. He is a notable contributor to the *Historical Dictionary of American Radio*, has presented papers at local and national conferences, and has been the radio broadcast voice for the Southern Utah University Thunderbird football and basketball teams for more than forty-five years. He has received eight Utah Broadcast Association Awards—including seven gold awards for his play-by-play and his live sports shows.

Dr. Roxane Coche is a sports journalist turned university professor. Born and raised in France, she worked as a freelance sports reporter and producer in Paris, collaborating with several TV networks. She is now an assistant professor in telecommunication and the associate director of sports journalism and communication in the College of Journalism and Communications at the University of Florida. Her research interests revolve around social issues in the sports media industry and sports media content.

Curtis M. Harris is a PhD candidate in history at American University in Washington, DC. His focus is on labor rights in men's professional basketball during the mid-twentieth century.

Dr. jay johnson is a full professor in the Faculty of Kinesiology and Recreation Management at the University of Manitoba. His current interdisciplinary research explores the impact(s) of climatic change on our physical experiences and interfaces with the environment. He is investigating how Indigenous youth experience the built environment and outdoor adventure/land-based education; community-based research examining the function of the bicycle; culture and community in activ(ism); child labor issues; bullying; sport doping; and the cultural intersections of gender, race, ethnicity, sexuality, and homophobia in team hazing/initiation rituals. He has published extensively on hazing, coediting (with Margery Holman) *Making the Team: Inside the World of Sport Initiations and Hazing* (Canadian Scholars Press).

Dr. Melvin Lewis is an associate professor in the Sports Business Management Graduate Program and Fellow of the Alabama Program in Sports Communication at the University of Alabama. His current research focuses on race, sport-consumer behavior, and technology in sports.

Dr. Jack Lule is a professor of journalism and communication and founding director of the Global Studies Program at Lehigh University. His research interests include digital media, globalization and media, international communication, and cultural studies of news. He is the author of three books: *Globalization and Media: Global Village of Babel* (Rowman and Littlefield); *Daily News, Eternal Stories: The Mythological Role of Journalism* (Guilford); and *Understanding Media and Culture: An Introduction to Mass Communication* (FlatWorld). Dr. Lule is also the author of more than fifty scholarly articles and book chapters and a frequent contributor to numerous newspapers and periodicals, and he has served as a commentator about the news on National Public Radio, the BBC, and other media outlets.

Dr. Rory Magrath is an associate professor of sociology in the School of Sport, Health and Social Sciences at Solent University, Southampton. He is the author of *Inclusive Masculinities in Contemporary Football: Men in the Beautiful Game* (Routledge, 2017) and coauthor of *Out in Sport: The Experiences of Openly Gay and Lesbian Athletes in Competitive Sport* (Routledge, 2016). His research focuses on decreasing homophobia and the changing nature of contemporary masculinities, with a specific focus on elite sport.

Dr. Matthew A. Masucci is a full professor in the Department of Kinesiology and currently serves as the associate dean in the College of Health and Human Sciences at San José State University. His research is interdisciplinary and interrogates sport and physical activity through the lenses of cultural studies, philosophy, and critical sport studies. Current research projects include a critical, historical, and political analysis of mixed martial arts and the Ultimate Fighting Championship, discourse surrounding the use of marijuana and CBD by professional athletes, and a multidimensional investigation of a local social movement called the San José Bike Party.

Andrew McIntosh is an associate professor of sociology at Northampton Community College's Monroe Campus. He is a lifelong DJ who married his love for hip hop and scholarship first at Bard College, Annandale, New York, in its American Studies Program. He has taught "Pass the Peas: The Sociology of Hip Hop" for twenty years at Lehigh University, Bethlehem, Pennsylvania, a class born from his graduate work there. A presentation from that course has been published in the *Oxford Handbook of Hip Hop Music* titled "Bucktown vs. 'G' Thang: The Enduring East Coast/West Coast Dialectic in Hip Hop Music."

Dr. Jorge E. Moraga is an assistant professor at California State University, Bakersfield. His research and teaching commitments are focused on ethnic studies, Latina/o/x studies, American cultural studies, and sociology of sport. Moraga has published original research in the *Journal of Sport and Social Issues* and *Social Inclusion*, and he has reviews in *Sociology of Sport Journal*, *Aztlán: Journal of Chicano Studies*, and the *Journal of Sport History*. He is currently working on his first book, *Latinas and Latinos across American Sport Media, 1990–2020*.

Dr. Leigh M. Moscowitz is an associate professor and head of the Public Relations Sequence in the School of Journalism and Mass Communication at the University of South Carolina. She teaches courses in qualitative research, public relations writing, and media and society. Her research examines the cultural production of news and the politics of media representation. She is the author or coauthor of three books: *The Battle over Marriage: Gay Rights Activism through the Media* (University of Illinois Press, 2013); *Snatched: Child Abductions in U.S. News Media* (with Spring-Serenity Duvall, Peter Lang, 2015); and *Media and the Coming Out of Gay Male Athletes in American Team Sports* (with Andrew Billings, Peter Lang, 2018).

Dr. David C. Ogden is a professor emeritus in the School of Communication at the University of Nebraska at Omaha. Dr. Ogden's research focuses on baseball and culture, with specific emphasis on the relationship between

African American communities and baseball. He is coeditor of the books *Reconstructing Fame: Sport, Race, and Evolving Reputations, Fame to Infamy: Race, Sport, and the Fall from Grace,* and *A Locker Room of Her Own,* all published by the University Press of Mississippi. He has also coauthored the book *The Call to the Hall,* reflections by Hall of Fame inductees of their reactions to being informed of their election.

Dr. Joel Nathan Rosen is an associate professor of sociology at Moravian College in Bethlehem, Pennsylvania. His research focuses primarily on the relationship between human activity and stratification as informed by cultural idioms such as music and sport. He is the author of *The Erosion of the American Sporting Ethos: Shifting Attitudes toward Competition* (McFarland), *The Erosion of the American Sporting Ethos . . . Reconsidered* (TSI Press), and *From New Lanark to Mound Bayou: Owenism in the Mississippi Delta* (Carolina Academic Press); and coauthor of *Black Baseball, Black Business: Race Enterprise and the Fate of the Segregated Dollar.* He is also the founding coeditor of a multivolume anthology project that explores the forging and maintenance of the reputations of high-profile athletes (University Press of Mississippi).

Dr. Kevin A. Stein is a professor in the Communication Department at Southern Utah University. His primary research interests include persuasive attack (*kategoria*), persuasive defense (*apologia*), and persuasive response to image repair (*antapologia*). His other research interests include political campaign communication and popular culture. His work has been published in the *Western Journal of Communication, Communication Studies, Relevant Rhetoric, Argumentation and Advocacy,* and several edited book volumes.

Professor Henry Yu is an associate professor of history at the University of British Columbia's Vancouver campus. He is the director of the Initiative for Student Teaching and Research on Chinese Canadians (INSTRCC) and the principal of St. John's College at UBC, as well as a board member of the Chinese Canadian Museum. Professor Yu's book *Thinking Orientals: Migration, Contact, and Exoticism in Modern America* (Oxford University Press, 2001) won the Norris and Carol Hundley Prize as the Most Distinguished Book of 2001. He is currently working on a book entitled *How Tiger Woods Lost His Stripes.*

INDEX

9 781496 836557